AIR POWER IN THE FALKLANDS CONFLICT

To Helen, Euan, Ellie and Maddie

AIR POWER IN THE FALKLANDS CONFLICT

An Operational Level Insight into Air Warfare in the South Atlantic

John Shields

AIR WORLD

AIR WORLD

AIR POWER IN THE FALKLANDS CONFLICT

First published in Great Britain in 2021 by
Air World
An imprint of
Pen & Sword Books Ltd
Yorkshire – Philadelphia

ISBN 978 1 39900 752 8

A CIP catalogue record for this book is available from the British Library.

Typeset by SJmagic DESIGN SERVICES, India.

Printed and bound in the UK by CPI Group (UK) Ltd, Croydon, CR0 4YY.

Pen & Sword Books Limited incorporates the imprints of Atlas, Archaeology, Aviation, Discovery, Family History, Fiction, History, Maritime, Military, Military Classics, Politics, Select, Transport, True Crime, Air World, Frontline Publishing, Leo Cooper, Remember When, Seaforth Publishing, The Praetorian Press, Wharncliffe Local History, Wharncliffe Transport, Wharncliffe True Crime and White Owl.

For a complete list of Pen & Sword titles please contact

PEN & SWORD BOOKS LIMITED
47 Church Street, Barnsley, South Yorkshire, S70 2AS, England
E-mail: enquiries@pen-and-sword.co.uk
Website: www.pen-and-sword.co.uk

Or
PEN AND SWORD BOOKS
1950 Lawrence Rd, Havertown, PA 19083, USA
E-mail: Uspen-and-sword@casematepublishers.com
Website: www.penandswordbooks.com

FSC www.fsc.org MIX Paper from responsible sources FSC® C013604

Contents

List of Tables		vii
List of Figures		viii
Acknowledgements		ix
Foreword		xi
Chapter 1	Introduction	1
Chapter 2	Methodology	25
Chapter 3	Air Power prior to Operation Sutton – *Bautismo de Fuego!*	50
Chapter 4	Air Power during Operation Sutton: *Muerte Negra* or *Los Moscardones*?	76
Chapter 5	Air Power Post-Operation Sutton – Stanley or Bust!	100
Chapter 6	Defending the British Operational Centres of Gravity – Sea Harrier: The Decisive Factor?	126
Chapter 7	Prosecuting the Argentine Operational Centre of Gravity – The British Fascination with Stanley Airport	151
Chapter 8	The Operational Level Lessons of the Falklands Air Campaign	182
Chapter 9	Conclusion	200
Annex A	*Argentine Combat Air Sorties Flown During the Falklands Conflict*	220
Annex B	*British Combat Air Sorties Flown During the Falklands Conflict*	222
Annex C	*Argentine Attack Missions on 1 May*	224

Annex D *Argentine Control of the Air Missions on 1 May* 226

Annex E *Argentine Air Power Prior to Operation Sutton: 2–19 May* 228

Annex F *Argentine Air Power During Operation Sutton: 21 May* 230

Annex G *Argentine Air Power during Operation Sutton: 20–26 May* 232

Annex H *Argentine Air Power Post-Operation Sutton: 27 May–14 June* 236

Annex I *The Reduction in Argentine Combat Air Capability during the Falklands Conflict* 244

Annex J *Sea Harrier/AIM-9L Sidewinder Employment During Operation Corporate* 246

Annex K *Employment of British Attack Weapons during Operation Corporate* 250

Bibliography 258

Endnotes 284

Index 354

List of Tables

Table 1A	Contemporary Centre of Gravity Definitions.
Table 3A	Argentine Order of Battle as at 1 May.
Table 3B	British Task Force 317 as at 1 May.
Table 3C	British Operational Centre of Gravity prior to Operation Sutton.
Table 3D	Causal Factors for Failure to Deliver Weapons during 1–19 May.
Table 4A	*Fuerza Aérea Argentina* Combat Air Priorities.
Table 4B	British Operational Centre of Gravity during Operation Sutton.
Table 4C	British Amphibious Force Composition.
Table 4D	Causal Factors for Failure to Deliver Weapons during Operation Sutton.
Table 5A	British Land Forces Falkland Islands – Task Group 317.1.
Table 5B	British Operational Centre of Gravity Post-Operation Sutton.
Table 5C	Causal Factors for Failure to Deliver Weapons Post-Operation Sutton.
Table 6A	Sea Harrier Squadron Air-to-Air Kill Comparison.
Table 6B	Causal Factors for Failure to Deliver Weapons during Operation Corporate.
Table 7A	Argentine Operational Centre of Gravity during Operation Corporate.
Table 7B	British Combat Aircraft Losses to Argentine Air Defences.
Table 8A	The Operational Level Lessons of the Falklands Air Campaign.
Table 9A	Causal Factors for Failure to Deliver Weapons during Operation Corporate.

List of Figures

Figure 1.1 Doctrinal View on the British Centre of Gravity during the Falklands Conflict.
Figure 3.1 Combat Air Dispositions as at 1 May.
Figure 3.2 Argentine Combat Air Apportionment during Operation Corporate.
Figure 3.3 The Utility of Argentine Weapons on 1 May.
Figure 3.4 The Utility of Argentine Weapons over the period 1–19 May.
Figure 4.1 Combat Air Participants at the start of Operation Sutton.
Figure 4.2 The Utility of Argentine Weapons on 21 May.
Figure 4.3 The Utility of Argentine Weapons over the period 20–26 May.
Figure 5.1 Combat Air Participants Post-Operation Sutton.
Figure 5.2 Argentine Attack Weapon Apportionment Post-Operation Sutton.
Figure 5.3 The Utility of Argentine Weapons Post-Operation Sutton.
Figure 6.1 The Sea Harrier Equipment Triumvirate.
Figure 6.2 AIM-9L Sidewinder Employment during the Falklands Conflict.
Figure 7.1 British Attack Weapons Usage by Weapon Type.
Figure 7.2 British Attack Weapons Usage by Platform.
Figure 7.3 British Attack Weapons Usage by Target.
Figure 8.1 Contemporary United Kingdom Joint Command and Control.
Figure 8.2 Argentine Operational Command and Control.
Figure 8.3 British Operation Corporate Command and Control.
Figure 8.4 The Components of Fighting Power.
Figure 9.1 The Utility of Argentine Weapons during Operation Corporate.

Acknowledgements

As a young 12-year-old, I vividly recall watching the Falklands Conflict play out on the nightly news bulletins and daily newspapers. It was my first recollection of warfare; I found it enthralling and the Conflict galvanised my desire to join the RAF. However, little did I realise that the battles, characters, and Islands would follow me throughout my career and life. I first visited the Islands in 1993, some eleven years after the Conflict, and I found myself immersed in a set of wind-swept Islands where the terrain, place names and battlefields were strangely familiar. I would become a regular visitor to the Islands throughout my military career. Indeed, over the next two decades, I would spend two and a half years on the Islands. However, and with the exception of my poor fellow aircrew on 1435 Flight who endured my lectures on the Conflict during the many poor weather days, there was no real outlet for my now increasing interest in the 1982 Conflict.

Turning an area of interest into an academic product started in 2008 and was the result of one individual, Dr David Jordan of the King's College London's Defence Studies Department located at the Joint Services Command and Staff College (JSCSC) at Shrivenham. Through copious amounts of Americano coffee at the appositely named Fieldhouse Café in JSCSC, David guided me through both my Masters and PhD programmes, each focusing on the Falklands Conflict. Without David's support, this book would simply not have become a reality. I am indebted to David for his incredible support over the last twelve years.

The Conflict remains divisive. There are significant sensitivities that still divides the Services and nations. Throughout the research and writing phase of the book, I was acutely aware of the perceptions of any bias towards my own Service and nation. Consequently, I have endeavoured to be as agnostic as I possibly could be; you can judge for yourself how successful I have been in that endeavour. To meet that neutral goal, I needed access to Argentine material. However, as a non-Spanish speaker, I was limited to the few Argentine historians who write in English about the Argentine perspective. Nevertheless, I was fortunate that the Argentine aviation journalist and historian, Santiago Rivas, does exactly that; not only did he provide the book that sparked the genesis of my PhD thesis and this book, but he was also incredibly supportive throughout the process. Likewise, Mariano Sciaroni, an Argentine lawyer and military historian, also provided additional material to support the book.

My six-year, part-time PhD was funded by the RAF as part of the Chief of the Air Staff (CAS) Fellowship programme. The CAS Fellowship has a broad range of part-time and full-time academic programmes for all ranks, it is an excellent mechanism for individuals to expand their knowledge, understanding and utility to themselves, their Service and nation. Consequently, I would like to thank the various Directors of Defence Studies (RAF) during my period of study for their investment, support and guidance to meet the goal that we set out in 2013.

Despite the COVID travails, the team at Pen and Sword warrant recognition for their support and enthusiasm; Ken Patterson deserves particular thanks for his meticulous and skilful editing.

I first met Peter Harris in 2000 when, as Air Officer Commanding 1 Group, he presented me with my Qualified Weapons Instructor (QWI) badge upon completion of the arduous 6-month Tornado F3 QWI course. At the time, I was not aware of Peter's stellar flying career or his involvement in the Falklands Conflict as one of the eight original Harrier GR3 pilots. After a sabbatical of twenty years, and under the tenuous link that we were both Air War College graduates, I approached Peter to write the foreword for this book. He was gracious with his time and inputs; I could not have asked for more. Sir, thank you.

Finally, and most importantly, projects such as this require significant commitment and sacrifice. The author focuses on the former to the detriment of the latter, which they rarely see. As a result, the family bears the burden of the author's selfish pursuit of their passion. I am forever grateful to my wife Helen and our three children, Euan, Ellie and Maddie, who not only spent eighteen months on the Islands with me, but they have also been incredibly supportive and allowed me the freedom to research, think, write and review this project over the last few years. This book is as much yours as it is mine.

John Shields

Foreword

In April 1982, I was a squadron leader staff officer responsible for Harrier GR3 tactical development at the Central Tactics and Trials Organisation located at RAF High Wycombe. I had been in the appointment less than twelve months having returned from an exchange tour with the US Navy flying A-7E Corsairs, A-4M Skyhawks and AV-8A Harriers with VX-5, their operational test and evaluation unit based at China Lake in central California. Despite being on a staff tour, I was fortunate that I was also allowed to maintain my flying currency on Harrier GR3s with 1(Fighter) Squadron at RAF Wittering. Indeed, I had recently completed a Norwegian deployment with the squadron. Consequently, I was resigned to a period stuck in the office while the squadron deployed to Canada as part of Exercise Maple Flag. However, the Argentine invasion of the Falkland Islands changed everything. The squadron's participation in Exercise Maple Flag was cancelled and they immediately made arrangements for a South Atlantic deployment. As part of the preparations, I was seconded to the squadron and found myself leading the last wave of Harrier GR3s on a 9-hour transit from the UK to Ascension Island – a far cry from my staff duties and desk at High Wycombe. At Ascension Island, we transferred the aircraft to the ill-fated MV *Atlantic Conveyor* for the last leg of the journey to join our host for the remainder of the Conflict, HMS *Hermes*. Over the remainder of the Conflict, we learned many lessons, some the hard way. In my classified post-Conflict report, recently released in the National Archives, I suggested that my first lesson was, 'Don't volunteer for anything!' While a flippant comment, my experiences and the lessons I learned in the South Atlantic in 1982 would remain with me for the rest of my time in the Service.

Much has been written about the Falklands Conflict between the UK and Argentina, most of it by people personally involved, or as a result of interviews with people who were actually involved. This book, from a fellow Air War College graduate, offers a comprehensive analysis of the conflict by an author who was not involved but who brings his own expertise with an air-defence background to that analysis. I opine that it offers an intellectually neutral view of events. I do not want to pre-empt this book by writing a lengthy foreword based on my experiences and, possibly, prejudices. However, I will offer just a couple of my own thoughts and experiences as background.

The Vulcan 'Black Buck' attack on the airfield at Port Stanley was strategically important – it demonstrated the UK's ability to reach mainland Argentina, even if the intent and will was not present. As a result, air defence fighters were retained for the defence of the mainland, and after the first air-to-air encounter on 1 May 1982, to the best of my knowledge, no Argentinian missile-armed fighter flew over the Islands. This was a tactical error by the Argentinians allowing the Sea Harriers and attack Harrier GR3s to operate freely in the upper airspace over the Islands with no concern about looking out for escorting fighters armed with missiles. This was important for the Sea Harriers which did not have great overtake speed advantage over Argentinian attack aircraft without trading height for speed once a formation was spotted. If a delay searching for escort fighters had been necessary before committing, then some, maybe many, successful engagements may have been missed.

The ground attack Harrier GR3s were similarly advantaged by not having to scan for Argentinian fighters and could concentrate on the difficult task of searching for targets from ultra-low level whilst avoiding the many surface threats against them.

The Battle of Goose Green was an amazing achievement by the numerically inferior 2 Para and according to conventional wisdom should not have been possible against a numerically superior defending force. I led a close air support mission to attack air-defence artillery at Goose Green, and that attack had a significant effect on the will of the Argentine forces to continue their resistance against a fatigued attacking force which was becoming short of ammunition. That success by 2 Para set a belief of victory amongst UK forces and, probably, defeat amongst the mostly conscript Argentinian forces. This was an important mindset for ground forces embarking on some subsequent very difficult battles.

It was only at the closing stages that precision-guided weapons from the air could be brought to bear against Argentinian targets – a restriction that limited the effectiveness of the UK's ability to attrit the Argentinian ground forces.

Enjoy this independent analysis of the conflict – it brings a less parochial view of the event than much that has preceded it.

Air Vice-Marshal (Retired) Peter V. Harris AFC

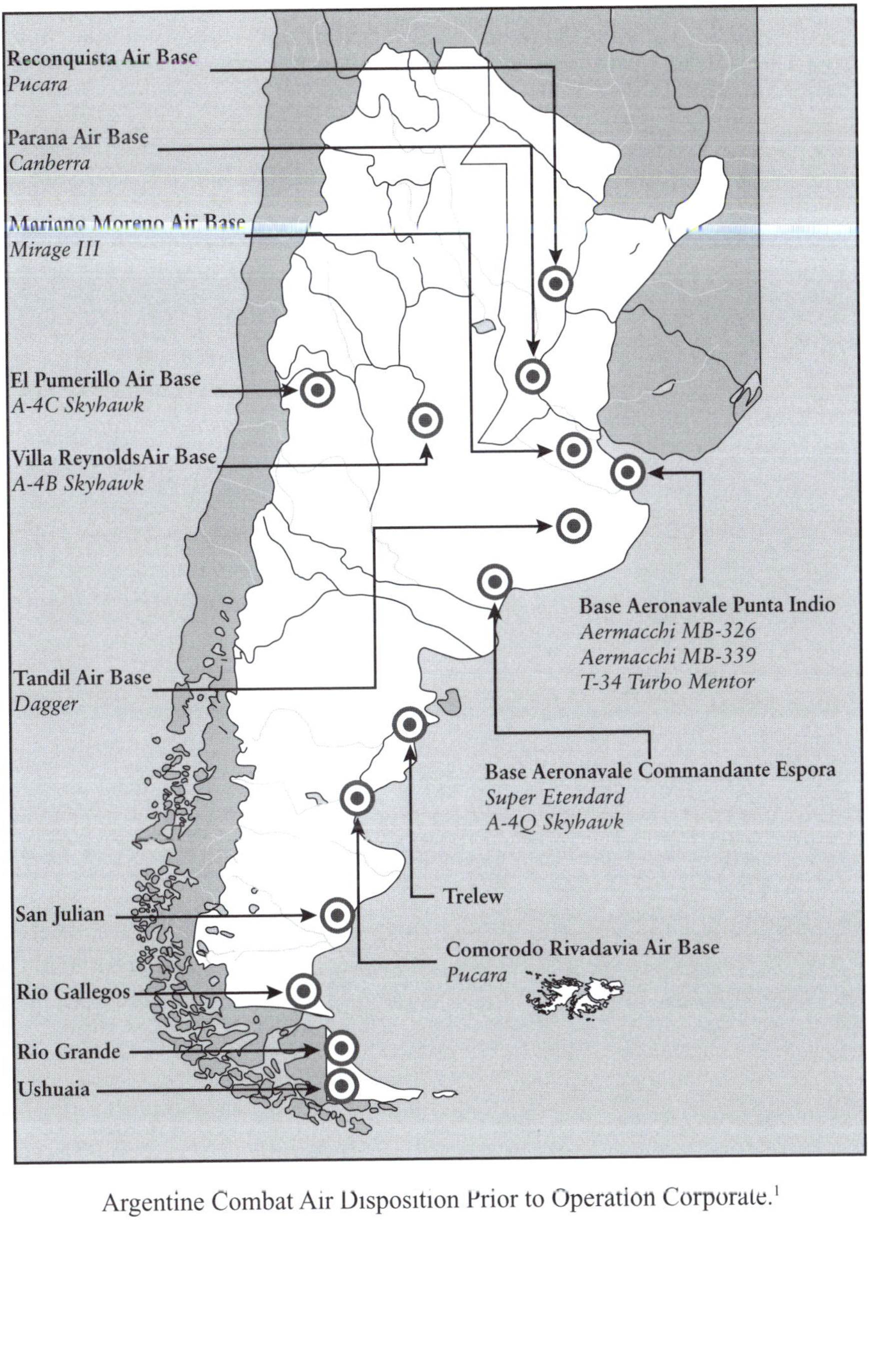

Argentine Combat Air Disposition Prior to Operation Corporate.[1]

Chapter 1

Introduction

'One captured A4 [Skyhawk] pilot admitted to being turned back three times by Sea Harriers before eventually penetrating the AOA [Amphibious Operating Area] and getting shot down on his 4th sortie.'

Lieutenant Commander Nigel Ward
Commanding Officer 801 Naval Air Squadron.[1]

Ward used the above example in his official post-Falklands Conflict report to highlight the Sea Harrier's dominance throughout the campaign.[2] Although Ward did not name the pilot nor the cause of his demise, the only Argentine fast jet pilot to be captured during the Conflict was *Teniente* Ricardo Lucero, an A-4C Skyhawk pilot from *Grupo 4 de Caza*. On 25 May 1982, Lucero was indeed shot down by British forces during his fourth mission.[3] However, Lucero was successfully engaged not by a Sea Harrier but by a combination of land and maritime-based anti-aircraft weapons as he approached the British beachhead at San Carlos.[4] While he recovered from his injuries in the British field hospital at Ajax Bay, Lucero spoke to a British journalist via an interpreter. Ian Bruce, the *Glasgow Herald* correspondent, reported that Lucero said, 'I was shot down in my fourth attempt to attack your beachhead … three previous attempts were aborted when your Harriers intercepted us over the sea.'[5] Research from a variety of British and Argentine sources confirmed that Lucero failed to drop any weapons during his first three missions on 1, 9, and 24 May, respectively. However, the aborted missions were due to an inability to find targets, poor weather, and, despite avoiding a Sea Harrier combat air patrol, the weight of ground fire.[6] Consequently, and contrary to Ward's assertion, not one of Lucero's missions failed due to Sea Harrier intervention. Was this incident unique, or was it indicative of a much broader issue where success was falsely attributed to the Sea Harrier to enhance its reputation?

In addition to the perceived Sea Harrier dominance during the air campaign, both protagonists have generated several other air power-related myths. As a result, there remains confusion surrounding the air power lessons of the operation. Indeed, many of the perceived lessons now appear to be beyond reproach. However, the steady release and access to new primary source material create an opportunity to review and challenge many of the enduring and entrenched views regarding the Conflict.

However, authors must consider the utility and benefit of further research into the Conflict. Sir Michael Howard disparaged the quality of the historiography of late twentieth century conflicts. In particular, Howard suggested that the military history of the Gulf and Falklands War reaching the public domain was akin to 'scrapings from barrel bottoms.'[7] Howard's statement is a damning, if harsh, indictment. In addition to the issue of quality, Williamson Murray warned that not everyone embraces the benefits of military history:

> 'Throughout history, leaders and institutions have repeatedly manifested an almost willful ignorance of the past.'[8]

For example, in the early twentieth century, Admiral Sir Jackie Fisher suggested that 'every condition of the past is altered.'[9] Fisher's dismissal of military history as a learning mechanism was reinforced two decades later by Montgomery, who suggested 'those who think that because they have read a little military history, everyone else is an ignoramus.'[10] Arguably, these legacy views are redundant as the history of warfare is now a core part of professional military education for the modern officer cadre. However, the contemporary position faces challenges. Citing Vietnam, Panama, and Iraq as examples, Murray claims that 'few current civilian and military leaders seem willing to indulge in systematic reflection about the past.'[11] Consequently, to avoid perpetually failing to learn from the mistakes of previous campaigns, there is an enduring utility in the study of military history. Nevertheless, military history acolytes must be wary of how to use their reflections. Michael Howard warned that one of the characteristics of military history 'is its parochialism. It was all too often written to create and embellish a national myth, and to promote deeds of derring-do among the young.'[12] Therefore, and perpetuated by ambivalence, enduring myths, and a desire to maintain reputations, there is an apparent reluctance to challenge the established narrative.

To offer something better than 'scrapings from barrel bottoms,' this book has adopted a revisionist approach. Consequently, the book will demonstrate that the established positions from both participants are an eclectic mix of tales that are overly optimistic, partially correct, or misleading. As a result, this book will demonstrate that the operational outcome was a function of Argentine failings rather than British successes. However, several common deficiencies impacted both sides during the prosecution of their respective air campaigns, such as ineffective air command and control. To assess the campaign from an Argentine perspective, the campaign has three distinct phases that reflect the changing British campaign priorities. A similar approach is then adopted to view the British prosecution of the Argentine operational centre of gravity. The book proposes three research questions to assess the air campaign. First, the book reviews the Falklands Conflict operational centres of gravity, both from a British and Argentine perspective. Second, the book analyses the effectiveness of Argentine and British air power in attacking and defending the stipulated operational centres of gravity. Lastly, the book examines the factors affecting the prosecution of both the Argentine and British air campaigns and reviews how these impacted the existing myths of Operation Corporate – the name given to the Falklands Conflict by British military planners.

The Established Position

On 27 May, John Nott, the British Secretary of State for Defence, informed his fellow Cabinet colleagues that 'British air defences, both the Harriers and the missiles, were performing with great effectiveness.'[13] Nott's statement following the successful completion of Operation Sutton, the amphibious assault at San Carlos, sets the tone and direction for what would become one of the enduring legacies of the Conflict. Buoyed by the recent success of the amphibious assault, Nott, perhaps unwittingly, exaggerated the utility of British air defence capabilities during the crucial phase of the Falklands Conflict. Reinforcing his point, conceivably, to offset the recent loss of the Type 42 destroyer, HMS *Coventry,* and the supply ship MV *Atlantic Conveyor*, Nott also suggested that over fifty Argentine combat aircraft were shot down by British forces.[14] Although the total figure is accurate, the cause of their demise is more complicated. Eleven aircraft, including non-combat aircraft, were destroyed during the Special Air Service raid on Pebble Island. Airfield attacks at Stanley and Goose Green, as well as strafing missions, account for the remaining losses.[15] In contrast, his assessment at the Cabinet meeting two days previously was more subdued, but arguably more accurate, and reflected the extensive usage rather than the utility of the deployed British air defence capabilities. Nott told the Cabinet that 'the Sea Harrier and the Rapier surface-to-air missile had proved effective in combat, and the Sea Harrier had shown a remarkably high rate of operational readiness.'[16] There is no doubt that the Sea Harrier and Rapier played an important role in the British campaign. Still, there appears to be a level of ambiguity regarding their actual performance and decisive contribution to the campaign outcome. However, the British were not the only participants to benefit from campaign-related myths.

From an Argentine perspective, they also received flattering praise for their performance, particularly during the battle for San Carlos. Aided and abetted by the first narratives of the Conflict, both sides quickly perpetuated the lore that the Argentine pilots were worthy and competent opponents who, if it were not for bad luck, had the potential to defeat the British. Although ultimately defeated in battle, at the end of the campaign, military analysts rightly considered Argentine air power to be the *primus inter pares* of the Argentine military components. During Operation Sutton, the Argentine air arms' intervention ensured a lasting reputation, both nationally and globally, as a credible force. The post-Conflict situation was a significant change from their position during the planning stages of Operation *Azul/Rosario*, the Argentine operation to invade the Falkland Islands when the *Fuerza Aérea Argentina* were excluded from initial campaign planning by its army and naval counterparts.[17] However, some commentators considered Argentine pilots to be 'capable and well trained' as well as 'professional and proficient.'[18] Others suggested that the pilots were merely 'the cream of Argentine polo-playing aristocracy, and had nerve, honour and the traditional macho image to maintain to the full.'[19] Nevertheless, the robustness of Argentine air power has now become the established norm. However, was this perception truthful or merely a polite but inaccurate platitude to mollify a defeated foe? Alternatively, did the positive reflection on the Argentine pilots obscure the real deficits in the other components of their military capability, which, when combined, demonstrated the true capability of Argentine air power?[20] Ultimately, was Argentine air power effective and efficient in its ability to deliver the required effects against the British deployed force?

Some commentators suggest that the Conflict is already extensively documented.[21] Therefore, what benefit does this book add to the extensive library of Falklands air war narratives? This proposition will suggest that one critical area of research is missing. The vast majority of the Falklands Conflict narratives focus on the tactical level outputs of the campaign rather than reviewing the joint and operational level outcomes – the ability of each side to strike the decisive blow against their opponent and achieve a military victory. The *Gulf War Air Power Survey*'s authors articulated the outputs and outcomes concept in their seminal analysis of Operation Desert Storm. They contended that campaign outcomes, or effects achieved, should be the measure of success, rather than merely reporting their outputs, such as the number of sorties flown, the number of targets attacked, or bombs dropped.[22] Therefore, this book aims to understand the linkages between force structure, outputs, and outcomes during the Falklands Conflict. By conducting this form of analysis, this narrative addresses the veracity of many of the Conflict's myths. For example, and as suggested by Admiral Sir 'Sandy' Woodward, the British Carrier Battle Group Commander during the Conflict, did the introduction of the AIM-9L Sidewinder air-to-air missile tip the balance of the air war in favour of the Sea Harriers?[23] Or, as posited by Cordesman and Wagner, were the Argentine unexploded bombs a significant burden to British maritime operations?[24] Also, was the perception that the Argentines diverted their Mirage IIIs from the Falklands operation in order to defend Buenos Aires from potential Vulcan raids correct? A claim which subsequently infuriated 'Sharkey' Ward.[25]

The myths have a consequence. They become the established position and beyond reproach. A point reiterated by Woodward, 'in the years since, opinions and assessments have been considerably refined, and some "facts" have been cast in stone when they should have been cast on the rubbish tip.'[26] However, Woodward was himself guilty of generating one of the key myths of the campaign that would also become the origin for this book.

The Centre of Gravity Argument

The genesis of this book surrounds the debate of what actually constituted the British operational centre of gravity during the Conflict. Today, the centre of gravity concept is a key component of military doctrine, used explicitly in campaign planning and execution.[27] However, neither participant explicitly used the centre of gravity term and construct during the 1982 Falklands

Conflict. Moreover, the Conflict 'was fought without the benefit of two factors today taken for granted – formal doctrine and institutionalised jointery.'[28] As highlighted by Sheffield, British Cold War military doctrine was, 'semi-formal at best; was centred around one individual commander or existed in a specific set of circumstances, and was not necessarily easily transferable elsewhere, and in some cases it was more honoured in the breach than the observance.'[29] Although Sheffield's comments were land-centric, air power doctrine was in a perilous condition. 'Doctrine in the RAF went into hibernation from 1968 when the fourth edition of AP1300 *RAF War Manual* was last amended and then subsequently withdrawn as "obsolete" in the early 1970s; doctrinal thinking did not re-emerge until 1990.'[30] Consequently, the British were guilty of failing to embrace the last element of Holmes' edict that suggested 'doctrine is not just what is taught, or what is published, but what is believed.'[31] So what doctrine or methodology did British military staffs use to plan and execute the Falklands Conflict?

Post the Second World War, two warfighting cultures emanated from the British Army – Montgomery's attrition and tidy battlefield philosophy and Slim's manoeuvrist approach.[32] Sheffield highlighted that 'in practice, Montgomery cast a long shadow over the Army in Europe. Many of his protégés were placed into important positions, and the Monty method prevailed until the 1980s.'[33] In 1982, with the operational level of war yet to be embraced by NATO, the commander's flair was deemed to be a key determinant in how wars were planned and executed. Today, that philosophy remains valid, but it supports rather than drives the formal doctrinal science used in contemporary operational-level planning.

The initial British planning focus for the Falklands campaign was on the complex task of getting the force embarked and deployed.[34] The more detailed campaign planning was subsequently conducted and refined during the passage south. The 1982 product of the British planning effort, and in line with its established planning processes, was the Appreciation of Situation.[35] Many of the activities identified in the British Appreciation of Situation have commonality with the modern operational-level planning methodology. However, in contrast to the contemporary approach, the Appreciation of Situation placed greater emphasis upon the Commander's judgement and intuition. Additionally, the relative importance, vulnerability, and sequencing of the various tasks are less well understood when using the Appreciation of Situation methodology. The use of modern doctrine in the book is not to critique the 1982 commanders or their ways of working. They were guilty of no more than implementing the established procedures of that time. Ultimately, the key benefit of using the current doctrine is that it enables a significantly greater depth of understanding and analysis. This approach clarifies the campaign execution by articulating what might have been defended or attacked, rather than limiting the investigation to the more narrow construct in use in 1982.

Contemporary British doctrine uses the Falklands Conflict as a mechanism to explain the centre of gravity concept. The doctrinal example also reinforces Woodward's view, in his book *One Hundred Days*, that the aircraft carriers were the British operational centre of gravity. However, this book will suggest that the British operational centre of gravity is more complicated than merely focusing on the British aircraft carriers. To develop an alternative perspective of the critical British military capabilities, a deeper understanding of the campaign's centres of gravity has been developed using Professor Joe Strange's work at the United States Marine Corps University.[36] The centre of gravity concept is not new. Over two centuries ago, Clausewitz explained that the centre of gravity was the 'hub of all power and movement, on which everything depends.'[37] The centre of gravity principle came to military prominence once again, nearly a decade after the Falklands Conflict. Colonel John Warden of the United States Air Force, informed by his earlier thinking from his book, *The Air Campaign*, used the term extensively during the early planning phases ahead of the 1991 Operation Desert Storm.[38] As part of the Checkmate organisation in the Pentagon, Warden identified three centres of gravity as part of his *Instant Thunder* campaign plan that aimed to strike decisive blows against the Iraqi regime.[39]

Following Operation Desert Storm, Strange developed the centre of gravity construct further. Frustrated by the eclectic mix of definitions and interpretations for centre of gravity across the American military fraternity, he introduced a process to identify the centre of gravity and introduce the concept of several related supporting terms: critical capabilities, critical requirements and critical vulnerabilities, as shown and defined in Table 1A.[40] It is essential to understand the relationship between the four parts to comprehend what elements undermine the enemy. Freedman reinforced Strange's views when he stated that 'hitting an enemy system in exactly the right place would cause it to crumble quickly, as the impact would reverberate and affect all the interconnected parts.'[41] Strange informed that the 'right place' is the critical vulnerabilities, as they are:

> 'Weaknesses which can be exploited to undermine, neutralize and/or defeat an enemy center of gravity. By definition, a center of gravity cannot also be a critical vulnerability.'[42]

Therefore, if planners identified and negated the enemy's critical vulnerabilities while they protected their own critical vulnerabilities, then campaign success would follow. As Freedman suggested, 'by the late 1980s, these various strands came together to form a distinct doctrinal form embedded in Western military establishment.'[43] Today, Strange's work continues to provide the backbone for NATO's planning doctrine to ensure that the 'determination of one single, overarching enemy centre of gravity at each level of war remains an ideal, but not always a practical goal.'[44]

Term	Contemporary Doctrine Definition
Centre of Gravity	The actor's primary element of power.
Critical Capabilities	The capabilities on which the centre of gravity depends.
Critical Requirements	Those conditions, resources or means that are essential to the realisation of critical capabilities.
Critical Vulnerabilities	The weaknesses, gaps or deficiencies through which the centre of gravity may be influenced or neutralised.

Table 1A – Contemporary Centre of Gravity Definitions.[45]

However, the centre of gravity concept is not without its critics. For example, Freedman suggested that 'for a simple, symmetrical shape finding its centre of gravity was straightforward. Once an object had moving parts or changes its composition the centre would be constantly shifting.'[46] Consequently, Freedman believed that the Clausewitzian *schwerpunkt* mantra is an overly simplistic model that fails to comprehend that the enemy and the situation can adapt and change.[47]

Despite the criticism, the centre of gravity construct has enduring value as a military planning tool. With the contemporary trend of ever reducing military force sizes, Strange's construct offered the military commander the opportunity to maximise the efficiency of his fighting force against the opponent's weaknesses. However, failure to embrace the concept means that the likely consequence is a long, expensive, and bloody battle of attrition. If used correctly, the centre of gravity analysis could achieve the nirvana that the attacker strives for: to quickly identify and effectively prosecute an exposed and valuable critical vulnerability. At the other end of the spectrum, the attacker's folly is to waste its finite and precious resources on a vigorously defended target that adds limited value to defeating the opposition. Adolf Galland, the Second World War

Luftwaffe 'ace' and *Fuerza Aérea Argentina* advisor in the late 1940s to the mid-1950s, suggested that 'he who wants to protect everything, protects nothing.'[48] Looking at Galland's assertion through the lens of 'critical vulnerability' and by replacing the word 'protect' with the word 'attack' shows that the contrary position is also true. The latter situation is, arguably, a more applicable view to the 1982 context.

The contemporary doctrinal view of the British centre of gravity during the Falklands Conflict, as shown in Figure 1.1, reflected Woodward's view that the aircraft carriers were fundamental to the success of the campaign. However, Woodward later contradicted himself on the importance of both aircraft carriers. His initial proposition suggested that significant damage to either aircraft carrier 'would probably cause us to abandon the entire Falkland Islands operation.'[49] Nevertheless, he later stated that the loss of [HMS] *Invincible* would mean that the 'operation is at least jeopardised. Lose [HMS] *Hermes* and the operation is over.'[50] Although Woodward's latter view undermined his earlier statement regarding the loss of a single aircraft carrier would ultimately lead to defeat, he reinforced the perception that the aircraft carriers were the British centre of gravity. It would appear that the argument for the aircraft carriers to be the centre of gravity was due to their ability to furnish control of the air via the Sea Harrier capability. Moreover, the key advantage that HMS *Hermes* had over HMS *Invincible* was that it could carry Woodward's command team and an additional number of Sea Harriers.[51] However, during a 2002 seminar, Woodward refined his views further by suggesting that 'lose one aircraft carrier before the landing, before we got a strip ashore, which was 6 June' and the operation was over.[52]

Critically, Woodward's immediate superiors back in Britain had a different perspective on the importance of the aircraft carrier throughout the campaign. Admiral Sir Henry Leach, the then Chief of the Naval Staff, agreed with Woodward's most recent view by suggesting that the issue was more complicated than a simple binary response:

> 'It depended so much on the timing, did the loss or damage occur to one or to both, permanent or temporary, before, during or after the initial assault landing and so on ... If both carriers had gone before the landing, then I think that serious consideration to cancelling the operation would have been given. If it had been after the landing … I think we would have pressed on and taken the risk.'[53]

Supporting Leach's statement is that on 2 April, the Prime Minister consulted the Service Chiefs about the suspected casualties and losses that the British could face during the campaign. Admiral Sir John Fieldhouse, Woodward's immediate superior as Commander-in-Chief Fleet, suggested that the losses could be as high as up to 3000 people, four to six escorts, and an aircraft carrier.[54] However, it appeared that Fieldhouse's risk appetite was not as robust as that of his own superior, Leach. Leach would have tolerated the loss of twice as many escorts.[55] Moreover, Fieldhouse suggested that if they lost a carrier before D-Day he would not have recommended going ahead with [Operation] Sutton.[56] Woodward was unsighted on the details of the debate discussed at meetings back in Britain as he had deployed south with the Task Force. Consequently, Woodward's view that the operational centre of gravity was the aircraft carriers throughout the campaign reflected elements of information provided to him by his immediate superior rather than the more comprehensive views of the Chief of the Naval Staff. Intriguingly, three senior military officers who were in the same command chain generated three different perspectives on the risk appetite associated with the loss of one or both British aircraft carriers. However, statements by individuals who are neither accountable nor responsible for the decisions generate confusion in the campaign's historiography; that ambiguity has endured.

At the strategic level, how much political will did the British Prime Minister have for the campaign, and what level of risk would she have tolerated? Thatcher's biographer suggested that:

> 'Throughout the crisis, Clive Whitmore had made it his business to remind Mrs Thatcher that she needed to make some sort of private calculation, grim though it was, of how many British deaths the government could sustain. She refused to put a figure on it but was interested in his answer. He told her a maximum of a thousand.'[57]

Although her Private Secretary's response was significantly less than her senior military advisors' view on casualties, Thatcher's private calculation was never made public.

Margaret Thatcher's reputation as the 'Iron Lady' was renowned. Indeed, the United States Secretary of State's diplomatic negotiations in April reinforces her political commitment. However, she felt that Al Haig's shuttle diplomacy between Argentina and Britain was ultimately futile as she 'never really believed that a military government could withdraw.'[58] Unpopular in the polls at home, untested in major military operations and unsure of her own, never mind national, risk appetite on casualties, Thatcher was potentially vulnerable. Nevertheless, she felt that she must do the right thing – 'to restore the freedom of the Falkland Islanders.'[59] She admitted to being 'desperately anxious about casualties,' particularly during the early stages of the campaign.[60] Thatcher's emotions during Operation Paraquet, the British operation to recover South Georgia in late April, ranged from, 'near despair to confident reassurance.'[61] Thatcher's latter emotion reflected the safe recovery of special forces personnel following two Wessex helicopter crashes on Fortuna Glacier. However, Admiral Sir John Fieldhouse wanted the Prime Minister to realise that the campaign 'wasn't going to be risk-free.'[62] As a result, and as Freedman notes, the grim benefit of losing HMS *Sheffield* and the deaths of twenty sailors was that 'the country at large now realised the seriousness of the situation and the meaning of war.'[63] Moreover, it blooded, tested, and hardened the resolve of the Prime Minister. Nonetheless, she was never immune to the concerns of potentially large-scale British casualties. For example, in the planning for Operation Sutton, she expressed that 'the prospect of losing a ship carrying a large number of troops was terrible.'[64] In addition to the support from the Service Chiefs, who had all served during the Second World War, her Cabinet contained a significant number of individuals with military experience from the Second World War as well as National Service commitments. Indeed, two of her Cabinet received gallantry medals.[65] Although a group of experienced former and current military personnel mentored the Prime Minister, there was a fleeting opportunity for the Argentines to exploit Thatcher's concerns over casualties. Yet, as the campaign matured and the desired British end-state became increasingly assured, the consequences of significant losses were likely to reduce.

So, what actually constituted the British and Argentine operational centres of gravity during the Conflict? In its purest form, NATO doctrine calls for a single centre of gravity at each level of warfare – a single centre of gravity at the operational level and a further centre of gravity at the strategic level.[66] This book will focus on the operational centres of gravity. Space has precluded the inclusion of detailed strategic centre of gravity analysis into this book, which may be an area for fruitful research in the future.

Centre of Gravity in the South Atlantic

Argentinian forces invaded the Falkland Islands on 2 April 1982. Britain responded rapidly by dispatching a task force to reoccupy the Islands.

The Argentinian armed forces had 220 jet aircraft. The British Task Force had thirty-four, all of which were Harriers. Control of the air was vital to enable amphibious landings and provide freedom of manoeuvre for surface forces. Initial planning showed that even after a successful reoccupation of the Islands, the Royal Navy would have to retain two aircraft carriers in the South Atlantic for several weeks, and probably longer. The only hard surface runway in the Falklands, at Stanley, was not long enough to operate fast jet aircraft and could not be easily extended.

The Royal Navy had two aircraft carriers: HMS *Hermes* and HMS *Invincible*. HMS *Illustrious* had been launched but was not yet operational. The deduction was simple: for control of the air, the Task Force could not afford to lose a carrier.

That premise shaped the naval campaign. The Falklands lie 300 miles east of Argentina. Placing two carriers east would keep them out of range of enemy aircraft. That had implications for the availability of air cover; the Harriers had to make relatively long transits to and from their operating area. Because relatively few aircraft were available, they could only keep on station for short periods. British planners intended to build a forward operating base to accommodate twelve Harriers once land operations got underway. However, the loss of much of the stock of perforated steel planking on the *Atlantic Conveyor* limited the capability to only four aircraft.

HMS *Illustrious* joined the task force later in the year, but only after the reoccupation of the Falkland Islands. If viewed through today's operational planning methodology, two functioning carriers would arguably have been the Task Force centre of gravity. The Argentinians knew how vital the carriers were and repeatedly tried to find and sink them.

Figure 1.1 – Doctrinal View on the British Centre of Gravity during the Falklands Conflict.[67]

Due to its static, defensive and reactive nature, the Argentine operational centre of gravity for the entirety of the campaign was the Argentine fielded forces that surrounded and protected the campaign's vital ground – Stanley, the capital of the Falkland Islands. In contrast to the Argentines, the British had to build, sustain, and operate their force at range before conducting offensive and contested land operations for the vital ground. As a result, it is possible to identify several British operational centres of gravity during the campaign. From a NATO doctrinal perspective, multiple centres of gravity are an acceptable proposition.[68] In contrast to Warden's three centres of gravity that ran in parallel during Operation Desert Storm, it is the contention of this book that there were three sequential British operational centres of gravity during the Falklands Conflict.

Contemporary UK doctrinal analysis of the Falklands Conflict centre of gravity rightly identifies the importance of control of the air, the *primus inter pares* of the four enduring air power roles, in delivering campaign success.[69] This position assumes that the British were facing a competent opponent who understood air power and would employ its assets in the same manner as any other modern air power protagonist. However, if the Argentines did not approach the air campaign through the expected course of action, the British could, in theory, win an uncontested victory in the air but face the prospect that the Argentines still controlled the vital ground around Stanley. Ultimately, in the Falklands Conflict, control of the air could not deliver the required military end-state as it is an enduring supporting, rather than a decisive, effect. The critically important activity that control of the air produces is the freedom of manoeuvre to the action it supports. Therefore, the operational centre of gravity must be capable of taking and securing the vital ground of Stanley. Consequently, once the decisive force was in the operating area, control of the air became a critical requirement and not an operational centre of gravity. Likewise, the aircraft carriers were a critical vulnerability that enabled the control of the air critical requirement.

Consequently, the aircraft carriers, arguably, constituted the operational centre of gravity during the initial phase of the campaign before the arrival of the amphibious assault force. Moreover, there is a contention that the aircraft carriers formed part of the British strategic centre of gravity construct – political will. However, to preserve the strategically important political will at home, mass British casualties needed to be avoided. With the aircraft carriers carrying a significant number of personnel on board both HMS *Hermes* and the smaller HMS *Invincible,* public opinion on the British endeavour may have wavered if either vessel suffered substantial casualties or damage.[70] Sensitivity regarding the impact of mass British casualties also percolated into amphibious assault planning. The transfer of personnel between ships before Operation Sutton also highlighted the importance of preserving the critical land forces. This force would be needed to contest, defeat, and retain the decisive Argentine-held ground in and around Stanley.

To deliver the UK's stipulated end-state of 'bring[ing] about the withdrawal of Argentine Forces from the Falkland Islands and dependencies, as quickly as possible,' the UK military forces would need to undertake an action to retake the Argentine-held ground in the Falkland Islands, particularly around Stanley.[71] To deliver the required outcome against a demanding timeline, the UK had limited viable options to project military force ashore. The only realistic option available to the British was to conduct an amphibious assault. The British had considerable experience in amphibious assault operations to assist in their planning to retake the Falkland Islands. Consequently, the enduring amphibious operation lessons from Gallipoli, Dieppe, Normandy, and Suez, in rank order, were [control of the air] during the assault, [control of the air] after the assault, logistical support, intelligence, as well as command and control at the operational level.[72] As a result, British military history reinforces the importance of control of the air as a critical requirement during the prelude and execution of Operation Sutton.

With the arrival of the amphibious force in the South Atlantic, the British operational centre of gravity switched to the British amphibious force. However, once the beachhead at San Carlos was secured and the breakout commenced, it can be determined that the British operational centre of gravity transferred for the last time. Up until the Argentines eventually capitulated on 14 June, the final operational centre of gravity compromised the fielded British land forces as they moved from San Carlos to Stanley. With the British operational centres of gravity now clarified, there is a need to understand the strategic air power context that each participant faced during the prelude to the Conflict.

Strategic Air Power Context

From a British perspective, 1982 saw their air arms focused on the vital North Atlantic alliance, a point reiterated in the 1981 Nott Defence Review. Naval aviation's critical task was to keep the North Atlantic sea lanes open with particular emphasis on anti-submarine warfare. In contrast, the RAF was fixated on home-based operations from extensive, well-supported hardened facilities in the UK and RAF Germany to support operations within North West Europe. Consequently, retention of existing and procurement of new air defence interceptors allowed the RAF to continue to contribute to British and European air defence. The attack role also received significant investment: the single-seat Jaguar aircraft was kept in service, bolstered by the continuing introduction of the two-seat, all-weather Tornado GR1 fighter bomber and a commitment to a new Harrier variant.[73] However, this philosophy was to the detriment of expeditionary air warfare that was now limited to small-scale but frequent deployments such as those conducted by the Harrier and Jaguar to support NATO's flanks.[74] The emerging concept of UK air operations in 1982 appears to be remarkably similar to that employed during the Korean War – a Cold War proxy conflict requiring air expeditionary operations. Air power during the Korean War faced identical challenges. Stephens suggests that 'Air force commanders tended to focus on the war they thought they would have to fight – namely, a massive confrontation with the Soviet Union on the plains of Western Europe.'[75] Consequently, Grove argued that the RAF 'was neither mentally nor physically prepared for the operations in the South Atlantic.'[76] As a result, flawed command and control arrangements were among the many lessons that emanated from the campaign.[77] These lessons chimed with the Korean campaign. As Stephens again highlighted, 'Korea marked the point at which the command and control of air assets became the central challenge for *the* effective conduct of joint warfare.'[78]

The Argentine air power context is perhaps less well documented and understood. However, Hobson suggested that 'the armed forces were in a better state of readiness and had more operational experience than most in the region, as conflict with Chile was never far from the surface and guerillas within Argentina had been active in recent years.'[79] Therefore, it could be perceived that the Argentines were well equipped and practised in operations in southern Argentina. Access to the Buenos Aires-based British Defence Attaché's files before the Conflict provides a more telling perspective. In his December 1981 report, the Defence Attaché observed:

> 'All told one gets a picture of a very alert national defence trying to make up in enthusiasm what it lacks in modern equipment and skill. Whilst one can only guess at its overall effectiveness if called upon to fight, it is certain that its capability will increase year by year. The speed of the process will largely depend upon the money.'[80]

Burden reinforces the Defence Attache's views, who suggested that the Argentine configuration and effectiveness was sub-optimal at the start of the Conflict. Indeed, the *Fuerza Aérea Argentina* 'began by establishing a revised command structure to meet the circumstances of the emergency.'[81] Ultimately, it would appear that neither participant's air power capabilities were funded, configured, equipped, nor trained for the battle that it was about to face. The ability to rapidly adapt their nation's air power capabilities would be a key determinant in the successful outcome of the Conflict.

Literature Review

There is a vast array of literature concerning the Falklands Conflict and its associated air war, with narratives spanning tactical to the grand strategic. To develop a compelling argument and methodology for the book, it was imperative to understand the strengths and weaknesses of the various key document sets that enabled the book.

A key challenge for this book was developing a methodology to compare and contrast the success or otherwise of the various combat air missions. Most narratives discussed sortie rates as a measure of success. However, the metric is applied inconsistently across all the aircraft involved in the campaign. Most narratives looked at the campaign from a single Service, unit, or aircraft type perspective rather than using the mechanism across the totality of each nation's air power capability. Moreover, the ability to launch a sortie does not have a direct correlation to mission success. Many commentators identified this factor and consequently mapped the aircraft's location as an indicator of mission effectiveness. This methodology remains flawed, as the physical location of the aircraft still does not ensure mission success. Some aircraft are more capable than others due to factors such as payload, range, speed, avionics, and aircrew experience. Therefore, the difficulty was to identify a mechanism that demonstrated that the required operational effect was delivered. Most narratives fall into the trap of measuring outputs, such as sortie rates, rather than analysing the outcome or effect that the attack missions were trying to achieve. To destroy the various operational centres of gravity, air power had to understand the sequencing of priority targets throughout the campaign, find and identify the targets before physically attacking them to deliver the required effects. Therefore, the weapon's journey, rather than the attack aircraft carrying them, had to be mapped to understand the effect or outcome. Consequently, the literature needed to provide a robust and credible data set of the weapon's journey that could be subsequently analysed. So, what documents were available? What level of fidelity did they provide? And what was their integrity?

At the strategic level, both sides conducted high-level reviews in the post-Conflict period. In July, the British Prime Minister directed a committee under the chairmanship of Lord Franks 'to review the way in which the responsibilities of Government in relation to the Falkland Islands and their Dependencies were discharged in the period leading up to the Argentine invasion of the Falkland Islands on 2 April, taking account of all such factors in previous years as are relevant; and to report.'[82] Upon publication in January 1983, the Franks Report 'was widely seen to let the Government off the hook, but also spared the previous Labour Government embarrassment.'[83] The Argentine equivalent of the Franks Report was the *Informe Rattenbach*.[84] Of note, the report was released into the public domain in 2012 but, as yet, there is no English translation. Nevertheless, both reports are of limited value to this book as they both deal with the strategic causal factors rather than reviewing the operational prosecution of the Conflict.

Both nations produced official histories of the Conflict. However, there has been debate regarding the utility of official accounts. Christina Goulter suggested that 'all good military historians go through a *rite de passage,* the point at which they realise that the official histories are not necessarily gospel.'[85] Jeffrey Grey went even further as he described official histories as 'frequently synonymous with "cover up", where not indeed with official lying.'[86] Peter Gray provided a more nuanced position. He described the challenges faced by the author of an official history as the balance between the much-vaunted lack of academic freedom and independence to meet a master's intent versus the privileged access to files, documents, and other materials that authorities deny to other researchers.[87] From a British viewpoint, Freedman's two-volume *The Official History of the Falklands Conflict* provides a broad insight into the military campaign as well as the diplomatic and strategic issues.[88] Although Sheffield has described Freedman's work as a '*tour de force*' that rectified many of the errors contained within the 23-year-old initial official government report, *The Falklands Campaign: The Lessons*, it was not beyond reproach.[89] While Freedman aimed to focus primarily on 'British policy and strategy', this approach left only a 'modest proportion' allotted to the land and air campaigns.[90] Consequently, the military campaign narrative was concise and 'sparing on the tactical detail.'[91] Moreover, in contrast to other official histories, Freedman deliberately avoided including the impact individuals had on events. Freedman justified this approach because he felt that 'it has expressly not been my task to highlight the failures of individuals.'[92] However, Sheffield commented that 'it would be instructive to know the rationale behind the decision … whether this is the result of official policy, or a self-denying ordinance on the part of the author.'[93] Nevertheless, Sheffield also praised Freedman for tackling areas of controversy and contention. From an air perspective, the challenges included command and control issues as well as the Rapier surface-to-air missile system's woeful performance that was in sharp contrast to its elevated status in the immediate post-Conflict aftermath.[94] Ultimately, Sheffield commended Freedman's work 'as an essential text, which is both bold and authoritative, to which future generations of historians will surely be indebted.'[95]

In contrast, the Argentine official history was split along Service lines when the *Fuerza Aérea Argentina* and the *Comando de Aviación Naval* both generated independent narratives. In contrast to the British publication, both Services produced detailed tactically-orientated narratives that were devoid of the higher level strategic thinking.[96] From the perspective of developing the book, the Argentine official histories provided significant mission detail, which helped refine the hypothesis. However, it became apparent that the documents suffered from a few notable omissions. Consequently, both participants' official histories accurately reflected Robin Higham's comment that 'official histories are best understood as the first word, not the final word.'[97] As a result, the official histories make an excellent starting point. However, the documents lacked detail, either through policy, accidental oversight, editorial decisions, or classification. Consequently, any detailed analysis on the Falklands air war had to be supported by alternative, credible data such as the seminal research conducted by Ethell and Price, *Air War South Atlantic*, as well as Burden *et al's Falklands Air War*.[98] With access to Argentine pilots and combat reports, their work in the mid-eighties challenged the British Government's initial optimistic claims regarding enemy aircraft losses. Several more recent books were equally engaging and further bolstered the academic position. Notably, Cordesman and Wagner's *The Lessons of Modern War Volume III*, Bicheno's *Razor's Edge*, and Hobson's *The Falklands Air War* all provided a rich source of information on the air war.[99] Nevertheless, their narratives were all subtly different, but all added value to the book.

Beyond the academic realm, several Falklands Conflict veterans have written and spoken about the subject matter. At the higher command level, large anniversary-related events provided a rare opportunity to reunite key players to discuss events. For example, in 2002, a major conference was held at the Royal Military Academy Sandhurst that re-examined the events of 1982. Given the passage of time and the perceived need to preserve legacies, events such as these usually perpetuated the existing position. Indeed, Woodward informed the audience that he attended 'less in the hope of learning anything new than to try to ensure that history did not get changed in order to drive "new" lessons.'[100] Nevertheless, the opportunity to gather such a distinguished and broad group of individuals and have their perspectives captured was invaluable.[101]

One of the first of the practitioners' accounts to be released post-Conflict was Lieutenant Commander Nigel 'Sharkey' Ward's narrative, *Sea Harrier over the Falklands: A Maverick at War*.[102] The book contained an insight into the exploits and issues associated with his tenure as the commanding officer of 801 Naval Air Squadron on board the smaller of the two British aircraft carriers, HMS *Invincible*. The book also contained several bold proclamations regarding the Sea Harrier's performance during the campaign. Additional Harrier pilot memoirs were to follow, but over a decade after Ward's account, as the Conflict approached its 25th anniversary. Squadron Leader Jerry Pook's book, *RAF Harrier Ground Attack – Falklands*, provided a vociferous viewpoint on the integration of the Harrier GR3 force onto HMS *Hermes*.[103] Flight Lieutenant Dave Morgan, a Royal Air Force exchange officer, flying with 800 Naval Air Squadron on board HMS *Hermes*, produced a more balanced perspective of Harrier operations in the South Atlantic in his book, *Hostile Skies*.[104] From the three books written from a British operator's perspective, there is ambiguity regarding the utility of Harrier operations in the South Atlantic. Each individual flew a different aircraft type or operated from a different ship during the Conflict. Therefore, it is unsurprising that their perspectives were markedly different. Narratives written by people who were at the heart of the action can be compelling. However, individuals who produce these tactical perspectives can, at times, be too close to the activity to be truly objective. Nevertheless, by virtue of the timing of its publication, Ward's book had primacy in the historiography and public perception. As a result, many of his views are now the established position and appear sacrosanct and echo Whitmarsh's comment that 'once lodged it is difficult to shake out a myth.'[105]

From an Argentine viewpoint, there is a limited number of articles written in English to counter the dominant British narrative. Indeed, British authors write many of the early Argentine accounts of the Conflict, such as Middlebrook's book, *The Argentinian Fight For The Falkland Islands*.[106] Consequently, these documents could be construed incorrectly, as aiding the British cause. Nevertheless, there is a small group of native Spanish-speakers that have written in English on the subject matter. At one extreme, Moro, a Falklands Conflict veteran himself, wrote *The History of the South Atlantic Conflict*.[107] Moro's book is an interesting take on the Conflict. Many of his opinions and views are unique, unsupported by a full range of evidence, and contrast sharply with the British view of the Conflict. Several native Spanish-speakers take a more balanced and credible approach to the Conflict; authors include Huertas, Briasco, Hafes, Cicalesi, and Rivas in their numerous articles and books such as *Tabanos at War, Falklands – Witness of Battles* and *The Fight for 'Las Malvinas.'*[108] Although the Spanish-speaking authors' work provided a detailed insight into the various units' activities during the Conflict, their work tended to focus on the tactical level and show limited analysis at the operational level. Nevertheless, their extensive data proved useful to verify and bolster the official Argentine narratives. Indeed, Rivas' book, *Wings over the Malvinas*, provided the trigger for this book's methodology. Rivas provided a near-comprehensive picture of the number of aircraft, aircraft type, weapon loads, locations, and results of Argentine sorties.[109] Written in English, Rivas' book was based on the Argentine official histories but bolstered by interviews with participants that added additional detail and insight into the more sensitive and recently declassified missions.[110] A further benefit of Rivas' narrative is, after interviewing the aircrew involved, he identified some erroneously omitted missions from the original official histories.

Research for this book also took advantage of several online resources. In particular, three websites are noteworthy. First, the Margaret Thatcher Foundation provides an extensive online cache of documents relating to the British Prime Minister's tenure.[111] The documents about the Falklands Conflict range from digitalised documents from The National Archives to Thatcher's handwritten account of the Conflict. Second, the RAF Historical Society web pages offered a wide range of data from those at the tactical, operational and strategic levels during the lead-up and prosecution of the Conflict.[112] From an Argentine perspective, the *Fuerza Aérea Argentina* website provided a useful insight into the air force's activities on a day-by-day basis.[113] Although the website was not exhaustive in its detail, it remains a complementary tool to the Argentine official history narrative as well as the other secondary source perspectives on the Argentine air battles.

The rising popularity of the podcast has added to the oral history portfolio. However, when dealing with oral histories, 'care has to be taken to analyse critically the story that unfolds for the veracity of the account, any exaggeration (not that aircrew in particular are prone to this), self-justification or self-depreciation.'[114] Indeed, analysis of interviews with various Falklands Conflict veterans highlighted that their positions vary wildly over time, perhaps reflecting their release from the constrained tether that was once their senior military position. Also, it was evident that oral histories made individuals prone to potentially make inaccurate assertions that did not benefit from the editor's pen. Nevertheless, access to the Imperial War Museum oral history catalogue provided a gateway to a broad spectrum of veterans over an extensive post-Conflict period. Of note, the Imperial War Museum's oral history catalogue includes several individuals who have not written about their experiences; these include Moore and Curtiss, the British Land and Air Commanders during the Conflict.

Understanding air power's contribution to the broader campaign, including its support to the other environments, was a fundamental part of this book's research. From the maritime perspective, and in particular the amphibious assault viewpoint, the number, types, dates, and names of the ships used during the campaign are well known. The maritime force used to protect and convey the British assault forces to San Carlos is well established in the vast majority of the key books covering the Conflict. Likewise, the spearhead infantry forces and their assault ships are also well understood. These forces were put ashore in the first few hours of the assault. However, some ships with their embarked cargo and personnel remained in San Carlos for several days awaiting disembarkation. An effective Argentine air attack against these vessels could have had a detrimental, if not disastrous, effect on the campaign. However, a clear picture of what constituted the critical second wave of forces and what these ships carried is less readily available in the secondary source material. Surprisingly, neither Clapp and Southby-Tailyour in *Amphibious Assault Falklands* nor Thompson in his *3 Commando Brigade in the Falklands* narrative provided a comprehensive solution.[115] Although the follow on forces were predominantly embarked on Royal Fleet Auxiliary ships, there are few books and little detail on Royal Fleet Auxiliary activities beyond the initial offload at San Carlos. Neither Johnson-Allen's *They Couldn't Have Done It Without Us*, nor Puddlefoot's *No Sea Too Rough* provided the required level of detail of Royal Fleet Auxiliary activities.[116] Therefore, the primary source material clarified the situation. Consequently, the 3 Commando Brigade files held at The National

Archives articulated which units were embarked upon which ship during the amphibious assault.

From a British land forces stance, significant secondary source material has been written on their journey south, the amphibious assault and the battles at Goose Green and the hills surrounding Stanley. The views of those who were there were the most compelling of these. Consequently, the works by Vaux, Gardiner, Van der Bijl, and Southby-Tailyour all provide beneficial insights into British and Argentine air power's impact on the progress of the land campaign.[117] However, there is little insight from two of the key British protagonists: the Land Component commander, Major General Jeremy Moore, and the commander of 5 Infantry Brigade, Brigadier Tony Wilson, neither of whom published memoirs. Consequently, access to primary source material such as their Record of Proceedings, War Diaries, and oral histories helped to fill this void.

Many of the elements required to develop and build this book's methodology were available through secondary sources. Again, British primary source material helped to fill several voids. Gray suggests, 'that primary source materials are the lifeblood of original research,' but caution must be applied.[118] To a novice researcher, primary source material could be the nirvana that will answer the full gamut of research questions. The reality is somewhat different. It can be a 'time-consuming and frustrating occupation' researching in an archive.[119] However, unexpected opportunities do arise, seldom used files, such as the air attaches' annual reports from the British Embassy in Buenos Aires, were available. The attaches' files, spanning thirty years before the Conflict, provided a rare insight into the culture, ethos, and problems of the developing *Fuerza Aérea Argentina*.[120] Nevertheless, seeking a full set of documents that provided all the answers associated with the book is a forlorn hope. For example, the release of documents relating to the Conflict into the public domain is ongoing; others remain redacted. Those documents that are available may have elements that are missing or simply do not provide the anticipated level of detail.

By way of example, secondary source material associated with the Sea Harrier and Harrier GR3 sorties was far from comprehensive. Consequently, access to primary source material was required to attempt to clarify the position. Unfortunately, the primary source information at the Fleet Air Arm Archives was disappointingly limited. Elements of the Sea Harrier squadrons' Flight Authorisation Sheets, Record of Proceedings and Fair Flying Logs were accessible.[121] However, not all of the desired documents were available. Some were incomplete, with crucial pages missing, or simply lacked the desired degree of detail. As a result, it was not possible to build up the required level of information to build a more comprehensive picture of Sea Harrier operations. Research on the Sea Harrier squadrons stalled until the release of several critical files from The National Archives. Of note, the 801 Naval Air Squadron report was particularly detailed and insightful.[122]

As with the Sea Harrier files, the release of the 1 (Fighter) Squadron combat reports occurred during the research period.[123] However, the reports appear to have been written significantly after the events in the South Atlantic. As a result, the documents added confusion rather than clarity to the Squadron's activities. The rapid Harrier GR3 deployment, on a high tempo and unusual contingent operation, may account for the apparent reverse-engineered combat reports. As a result, the Harrier GR3 mission reports force the researcher to rely upon a set of non-contemporaneous information regarding 1 (Fighter) Squadron's mission performance and its operational narrative rather than being able to rely upon a timely, raw, but accurate source of mission reporting. Complicating the issue further is the fact that there are two versions of 1 (Fighter) Squadron's combat reports that are subtly different and contain contradictory information. The first version resides at The National Archives, while the second version is part of the Scientific Evaluation Team's report.[124] Consequently, and somewhat surprisingly, building the picture of British combat air mission outputs and outcomes was achievable but significantly more difficult than generating the Argentine equivalent. However, producing the Argentine version was not without its challenges.

Due to time, cost, and distance constraints, this book could not make use of or access Argentine primary source material. In mitigation, translating the Argentine official histories from Spanish into English helped to fill in many of the voids. Any ambiguity, nuance, or technical detail was clarified and verified using secondary source material and the support from two Argentine military historians.[125] Consequently, the amalgamation of several sources allowed the corroboration of Argentine data. As a result, it was possible to develop a unique and unified picture across all the Argentine attack platforms and their weapons. In turn, the book was able to establish the Argentine's ability to achieve its outcomes. Consequently, the basis of the argument focuses on a logical and auditable process that provides an arbitrated, rather than explicit, picture of the causal factors for success and failure during the defence and attack of the various operational centres of gravity in the South Atlantic.

Despite the extensive writing on the campaign, there remain several further gaps in the air campaign that need to be addressed in the future once the information becomes available. Several elements of the air campaign remain classified and subject to much speculation. For example, the participation of 51 Squadron's Nimrod R1s and the Canberra PR9s of 39 Squadron remains ambiguous. Both units appear on the Conflict's roll of honour, but there is little documentation in the public domain on their actual contribution. However, upon release of these currently redacted files from The National Archives, it will be possible to glean a better understanding of the units' role, basing, activities and support to the broader British campaign.

Admiral Harry Train (United States Navy), the Supreme Allied Commander Atlantic in 1982, questioned the relevance of the Conflict. He believed that the campaign was a 'failure of deterrence' and that the 'the strategic dynamics of the Falkland Islands conflict were more of two ships passing in the night than a head-to-head politico-military confrontation.'[126] Nevertheless, this book will demonstrate that there are a significant number of tactical and operational level air power lessons that remain relevant today and in the future. Moreover, in the enduring dilemma of balancing the ends, ways, and means associated with United Kingdom Defence, the correct lessons must be drawn from campaigns to ensure that future capability investments are coherent and balanced. This book is a unique opportunity to review the efficiency and effectiveness of a small cadre of combat air assets to strike and defend a broad spectrum of targets under demanding conditions, both environmental and at the extremities of its support chain while utilising new weapon capabilities. Consequently, identifying the true causal factors behind inefficiency and ineffectiveness is paramount for any future air arm to consider. To conduct the necessary campaign analysis, the following chapter articulates the methodology used to scope the remainder of the book.

Chapter 2

Methodology

'One of the guiding principles of fighting with an air force is the assembling of weight, by numbers, of a numerical concentration at decisive spots.'

Lieutenant General Adolf Galland,
Second World War Luftwaffe fighter pilot with 104 victories
and *Fuerza Aérea Argentina* Advisor 1948-1955.[1]

To analyse if Galland's Argentine acolytes and their opponents adhered to his principle, it is crucial to establish the timing, location, participants, desired outcomes, and measures of success for the operation. As a result, this chapter articulates the 'where, when, who, what, why, and how' factors that will be analysed further in subsequent chapters.

Where and When?

Although Argentine forces invaded the Falkland Islands and South Georgia on 2 April and Operation Paraquet, the successful British operation to recapture South Georgia concluded on 28 April, the book will focus on the military campaign on the Falkland Islands themselves and review the campaign from the start of British combat air operations on 1 May until the Argentine surrender on 14 June.[2] Within that timeframe, there are three distinct phases to the British campaign to recover the Falkland Islands. Each step is analysed separately and in greater depth in Chapters 3, 4 and 5, respectively. The campaign fulcrum or tipping point of the British campaign occurred during the second, and arguably the most critical, of the three phases.[3] Therefore, by defining the timeframe of Operation Sutton, the amphibious assault, the first and last phases of the operation, can also be specified.

H-Hour, the time of the physical landing of British military forces on the Falkland Islands, occurred in the early hours of 21 May. However, 0900 Greenwich Mean Time on 20 May was, in effect, the amphibious assault force's first point of vulnerability.[4] At this point, the amphibious assault force left its loitering position 140 nautical miles north-east of Stanley. The British force moved towards the landing site via a circuitous northern route to avoid detection by Argentine aircraft in the vicinity of Stanley and from the suspected submarine operating off the north coast of the Falkland Islands.[5] Operation Sutton culminated on 26 May when Brigadier Julian Thompson, the commanding officer of 3 Commando Brigade during the Conflict, declared he had sufficient force and support to break out from the beachhead.[6] Although it would take another three weeks for the amphibious group to land the divisional headquarters and 5 Infantry Brigade, the British operational centre of gravity switched from the amphibious forces to the British fielded land forces. The change occurred when the British troops started to disperse from their concentrated location at San Carlos and dilute as they dispersed eastwards towards Stanley.[7] This transfer of the British operational centre of gravity occurred on the evening of 26 May as the Second Battalion of the Parachute Regiment (2 PARA) left its positions. Under the command of Lieutenant Colonel H. Jones, 2 PARA left the high ground of Sussex Mountains, overlooking San Carlos, and headed south towards Goose Green, the first land battle of the campaign.[8] Chapter 4 discusses the implications for combat air during Operation Sutton, whereas Chapter 5 highlights the lessons learned during the land campaign.

With the operational centres of gravity established for the last two phases of the British campaign articulated, it is crucial to consider the first phase of the British operation. Spanning the period 1 - 19 May, the British Task Force's roles were to blockade the Total Exclusion Zone, conduct special forces reconnaissance and direct action tasks.[9] By enforcing the self-proclaimed 200-mile Total Exclusion Zone around the Falkland Islands, and by definition achieve the desired level of control of the air and ensure sea control, the British Task Force could create the conditions that would facilitate a successful amphibious assault. Consequently, the key force elements that could deliver the task were the two British aircraft carriers. Therefore, the British operational centre of gravity for the first phase of Operation Corporate was HMS *Hermes* and HMS *Invincible*. The decisive force, the amphibious assault ships, did not arrive in the vicinity of the Falkland Islands until 18 May.[10]

Who and What? – The British Combat Air Protagonists

Inter-Service rivalry, the introduction of new weapons and roles, missions conducted at significant range from regular operating bases, and the adaptation of their military capabilities to meet the emerging challenges were all factors that both Argentine and British air arms had to contend with during the Conflict. Before discussing the three British combat air capabilities deployed during Operation Corporate, it is important to understand the strategic context that the British units were operating in during 1982.

Reflecting on the existing policy of the 'East of Suez' retrenchment, supporting NATO in a European Cold War context was the focus of British military plans. Defence expenditure was 5.2 per cent of Gross Domestic Product (GDP), a comparatively luxurious position compared to contemporary levels of Defence funding but still less than the 6.5 per cent of GDP in 1964 in the prelude to Denis Healey's series of Defence Reviews.[11] However, the reality was that the recently elected Conservative government inherited an unbalanced and unaffordable Defence programme from its predecessors and realised that 'we cannot go on as we are.'[12] The causal factors for the 1981 Defence Review conducted by John Nott were enduring. In his memoirs, Healey suggested that 'ever since the [Second World] war, Defence had been under exceptional economic pressure, since technology increased the cost of new equipment much faster than the increase in the nation's wealth.'[13] In a similar vein to Nott in 1981, Healey blamed previous incumbents for the difficult decisions he made in his own Defence Reviews.[14]

The 1981 Defence Review determined that Defence had, 'four main roles: an independent element of strategic and theatre nuclear forces committed to the [NATO] Alliance; the direct defence of the United Kingdom homeland; a major land and air contribution on the European mainland; and a major maritime effort in the Eastern Atlantic and Channel.'[15] Although there was consideration for military operations beyond the NATO area, the Defence Review contained a simple and weak one-liner, 'our Forces will also continue as necessary to sustain specific British responsibilities overseas, for example in Gibraltar, Cyprus, Belize, and the Falkland Islands.'[16]

The British vision for sustaining interests overseas, specifically the Falkland Islands, was compromised by two major decisions. First, the plan to phase out the specialist amphibious ships HMS *Fearless* and *Intrepid* by 1982 and 1984 respectively would have had long-term consequences for the Falkland Islands' recovery if implemented.[17] Also, the Falkland Islands-based ice patrol ship, HMS *Endurance,* was due to be decommissioned and not replaced – a further signal to Argentina that the British had disinvested in the Falkland Islands. In an endeavour to mitigate the decisions, the Defence Review suggested that it intended 'to resume from 1982 onwards the practice of sending a substantial naval task group on long detachment for visits and exercises in the South Atlantic, Caribbean, Indian Ocean, or further east.'[18] However, the scale, tempo, and duration of these operations were not specified. Therefore, it is no surprise, and as stated by Air Marshal Sir John Curtiss, the Air Commander for Operation Corporate, that 'no one had envisaged a UK out-of-NATO-area operation, indeed it had been ruled out by successive Defence White Papers.'[19] Consequently, the limited number of British combat air assets available and suitable to conduct Operation Corporate is a reflection of the European-centric British Defence Policy. In contrast to the eclectic mix of Argentine combat air assets, only three types of British combat aircraft were capable of operating in the remote and challenging South Atlantic – the Fleet Air Arm's Sea Harrier as well as the RAF's Harrier GR3 and Vulcan.

The most numerous of the British combat air assets was the Sea Harrier. Initially, and in contrast to the RAF's viewpoint, the Fleet Air Arm had little interest in the Harrier capability. During the 1960s, the Royal Navy 'stuck determinedly to their requirement for a two-seat, radar-equipped, supersonic, all-weather fighter to be catapult-launched from their carriers, [HMS] *Victorious*, *Eagle*, *Ark Royal*, and the projected new 50,000-ton attack carrier CVA01.'[20] In particular, the Fleet Air Arm wanted to order the American McDonnell-Douglas F-4 Phantom to equip the Royal Navy's aircraft carriers.[21] However, as part of Denis Healey's 1966 Defence White Paper, the CVA01 programme was cancelled as it did not give 'sufficient operational return for our expenditure.'[22] Consequently, much to the chagrin of the Royal Navy, and particularly the Fleet Air Arm, it was decided 'that the tasks for which carrier borne aircraft might be required in the late 1970s can be more cheaply performed in other ways. Our plan is that, in the future, aircraft operating from land bases should take over the strike/reconnaissance and air defence functions of the carrier on the reduced scale which we envisage that our commitments will require after the middle of the 1970s.'[23]

As a result of the CVA01 cancellation, the Fleet Air Arm's F-4 Phantom would solely serve on board HMS *Ark Royal* and HMS *Eagle*. Consequently, only forty-eight F-4K Phantoms were ordered by the British Government for the Fleet Air Arm, rather than the original plans for 140.[24] However, following the 1972 cancellation of HMS *Eagle's* refit, twenty-two F-4K

Phantoms initially intended for the Royal Navy were transferred directly to the RAF.[25] The net result was that the Fleet Air Arm was left with a single operational squadron of F-4K Phantoms to embark on the aged HMS *Ark Royal*, which was rapidly approaching its out of service date. With no new aircraft carrier investment, there was a palpable fear within the Fleet Air Arm that British embarked fixed-wing aviation was about to wither and die. The fear became a reality when 892 Naval Air Squadron's F-4K Phantoms, and their Buccaneer counterparts from 809 NAS, were transferred to the RAF after the decommissioning of HMS *Ark Royal* in 1979.[26] This transfer of capability did not help to soothe the inter-Service rivalry that already had a reputation of being 'truly poisonous' during the CVA01 debacle.[27] Indeed, the former Chief of the Imperial General Staff, Field Marshal Sir Gerald Templer, described the relationship in equally appalling terms in his 1965 report on the rationalisation of air power. 'We believe the present state of feeling between these two Services at the Whitehall level is deplorable.'[28]

In the eyes of the Royal Navy and the Fleet Air Arm, the net winner of Healey's 1966 Defence White Paper decisions was the RAF. Healey's decision to invest in the RAF's aspirations to purchase fifty General Dynamics F-111 long-range, multi-role aircraft rather than carrier aviation created enduring friction between the Fleet Air Arm and the RAF.[29] However, the RAF's perceived victory over the senior Service was short-lived. Due to continued financial pressures, a series of further defence expenditure reviews were undertaken 'in July 1967 and finally the most fundamental changes of all in December 1967 and January 1968 when the decisions to leave East of Suez and to cancel the F-111 were taken.'[30] As a consequence, and with a direct bearing on the 1982 Falklands Conflict, the RAF retained the Avro Vulcan in service to fill the long-range attack role until the eventual replacement for the F-111, the Panavia Tornado, could enter service.[31]

The retirement of HMS *Ark Royal* in the late 1970s with its embarked combat air capability and enablers left a significant capability gap for the Royal Navy to attempt to backfill. Consequently, the Royal Navy needed to review its manned fighter capability and embrace the Harrier as a self-funded, low-cost, low-risk solution to meet the combat air demands of the new generation of the Royal Navy's deliberately ambiguously titled 'through deck cruisers.' The RAF was not opposed to the concept of embarked fixed-wing combat air power.[32] Indeed, following company and military test pilot trials on board HMS *Blake* and *Eagle,* 1 (Fighter) Squadron conducted a deployment on board HMS *Ark Royal* in the early 1970s.[33] However, the

RAF's concerns about Sea Harrier related to the relative cost and priorities rather than the 'philosophy' of the platform.[34]

In early 1970, Naval Staff Requirement 6451 stipulated the need for a force of twenty-five aircraft to fulfil the emerging task.[35] The new platform's objective was to provide the Royal Navy with an organic capability for air intercept, reconnaissance, and limited surface attack based on the Harrier aircraft. With the Royal Navy 'concentrated on anti-submarine warfare in the high priority area of the Eastern Atlantic and Channel,' it was imperative that the Fleet maintained its freedom of manoeuvre to deliver the required deterrence effect, in concert with or without United States Navy support.[36] As a result, there was a need to deny Soviet aircraft from gathering intelligence on the Fleet's disposition. Therefore, the Maritime Harrier's focus was to counter the threat posed by the large, long-range, fast, but subsonic, Tupolev Tu-95 reconnaissance aircraft (or more commonly known by the NATO reporting name of Bear D) operating at medium to high altitudes.[37] The then Chief of the Air Staff, Air Chief Marshal Sir Denis Spotswood 'was never convinced of the operational effectiveness of the Maritime Harrier, although he recognised that the aircraft could just meet the limited requirement that had been stated.'[38] At the same meeting, the Deputy Chief of the Defence Staff (Intelligence) representative reinforced the Maritime Harrier's narrow requirement set by stipulating that 'the wider aspects of the totality of the Soviet air threat had not been considered.'[39] In response, Vice Admiral John Treacher, a former Fleet Air Arm pilot and captain of the recently decommissioned aircraft carrier HMS *Eagle*, informed the group that he 'was confident that the Harrier could meet the requirements of the Navy and would provide a proper balance of forces within the Fleet.'[40] Nevertheless, its own Service recognised during the Sea Harrier's inception that it was a limited platform.[41] However, the Royal Navy was also cognisant of the lessons of history that demonstrated the folly of operating a maritime force with inadequate air support. As a result, the Sea Harrier was seen by some as 'a good all-rounder with one pre-eminent virtue – it is there.'[42] The acrimonious relationship between the RAF and Royal Navy during the mid-1960s and early 1970s concerning carrier aviation would have consequences in the South Atlantic in 1982 and generate a number of the Conflict's myths.

The primary physical constraining factor on Sea Harrier design and force size was the size of its operating platform – the aircraft carrier. As a result and compared to the Phantoms and Buccaneers that it supplanted, the Sea Harrier was slower, carried a smaller payload, and had a reduced operating range. Additionally, the second-order effects of the diminutive new class of aircraft carriers meant that there was insufficient space to field either organic air-to-air refuelling or airborne early warning enabling capabilities. Both of these enabling capabilities, previously available on the now de-commissioned HMS *Ark Royal,* would be key in delivering persistence and situational awareness to the Sea Harrier. Devoid of the key enablers, a small force of embarked manned fighters was likely to find the effective and efficient delivery of control of the air challenging. Nevertheless, the new aircraft also had a few benefits. For example, as the Sea Harrier was a development of the RAF's existing Harrier GR3 aircraft, it was perceived to be a low-risk technical solution. Moreover, the Sea Harrier's key sensor, the Ferranti-manufactured Blue Fox radar, was based on the existing Sea Spray radar planned for the Lynx helicopter and was also deemed a low-risk proposition.[43]

The Sea Harrier's proposed radar performance 'would have a capability not dissimilar to the Lightning' – the aircraft that the F-4 Phantom had replaced in RAF service, and thus a downgrade in capability.[44] One of the deployed Sea Harrier pilots reinforces the point on the radar's poor performance. Lieutenant Commander Dave Braithwaite remarked that the radar's actual performance was akin to the De Havilland Sea Vixen – an aircraft that was retired from the Fleet Air Arm in 1972 in favour of the F-4K Phantom.[45] Nevertheless, for an anticipated 1 per cent of its budget, the Sea Harrier was imperfect but an affordable and low-risk solution to the problem of protecting the Royal Navy in the Eastern Atlantic against the Soviet Bears into the 1980s.[46]

The Sea Harrier first flew in August 1978 and entered front-line service with 800 Naval Air Squadron on 31 March 1980.[47] The second front-line squadron, 801 Naval Air Squadron, formed on 28 January 1981.[48] By the end of March 1982, both front-line squadrons and the training squadron, 899 Naval Air Squadron, were operational and operated the vast majority of the now extended purchase of thirty-four aircraft.[49] However, not all aircraft were available to the front line units. One aircraft crashed pre-Conflict, and two were awaiting manufacture. Additionally, four of the remaining Sea Harrier fleet were allocated to critical clearance and trials work. The Aeroplane and Armament Experimental Establishment at RAF Boscombe Down retained three Sea Harriers, while British Aerospace operated one aircraft at Dunsfold.[50] Consequently, the Royal Navy was able to muster an initial force of twenty Sea Harriers for deployment to the South Atlantic. 800 Naval Air Squadron embarked twelve aircraft on board the larger of the two aircraft carriers, HMS *Hermes*, whereas 801 Naval Air Squadron took eight Sea Harriers onto the smaller HMS *Invincible*. A further eight replacement Sea Harriers eventually joined the Task Force before Operation Sutton on board MV *Atlantic Conveyor*.[51]

During the Conflict, the key air defence weapon of the new Sea Harrier was the latest variant of the United States-designed Sidewinder air-to-air missile – the AIM-9L Sidewinder. The development of this, the third-generation Sidewinder, 'was shaped by air-to-air missile problems in the Vietnam War.'[52] In 1977, the Raytheon-built AIM-9L Sidewinder beat competition from the French-manufactured Matra 1 missile and a British development missile to meet the British military requirement for a stockpile of 1370 short-range air-to-air missiles with an introduction to service by 1980/81.[53] The new missiles would allow the RAF to bring its stockpile up to 2500 short-range air-to-air missiles, thus enabling the RAF F-4 Phantom squadrons to deliver six days of intensive flying rates in wartime.[54] The AIM-9L Sidewinder stockpile would expand later to 2500 missiles to replace the existing AIM-9G Sidewinder stockpile and encompass RAF attack aircraft; the order would also incorporate the Royal Navy requirement for 264 AIM-9L missiles.[55] The fielding plan for the Sea Harrier would see the initial tranche of seventy-four missiles delivered by mid-1980 to enable the first embarked Sea Harrier operations from HMS *Hermes*. The second tranche of ninety missiles was required by 1981 to meet the deployment schedule of HMS *Invincible*.[56] However, to offset the impact of procuring a United States-manufactured weapon, it was decided that the missile would be built under licence by a European weapons consortium headed by BGT (Bodenseewerke Gerätetechnik) who had experience in the manufacture of earlier Sidewinder variants.[57] As early as 1977, the Chief Scientific Advisor became aware of concerns about BGT's ability to deliver the missiles on time.[58] Therefore, the British adopted a parallel risk-mitigation process to directly approach the United States to procure an early batch of missiles.[59] The risk materialised in 1982, and the mitigation plan failed to deliver the necessary stockpile in time. Due to the limited British AIM-9L Sidewinder inventory, the Sea Harrier force left Portsmouth on 5 April with a stockpile consisting solely of the older and less capable AIM-9G Sidewinders.

Both aircraft carriers deployed with a small stockpile of AIM-9G Sidewinders; HMS *Invincible* held thirty weapons, whereas HMS *Hermes* stored forty missiles, with the remaining thirty-three missiles held on board RFA *Resource*.[60] The limited British stockpile of AIM-9L Sidewinders was initially transferred to HMS *Hermes* as it transited past Ascension

Island over the period 16-18 April.[61] Consequently, the British Task Force departed south from Ascension Island with 160 AIM-9G [Sidewinders] and 109 AIM-9L [Sidewinders].[62] HMS *Invincible* belatedly received its AIM-9L Sidewinder stockpile on 21 April and conducted missions with the missiles six days later.[63] Nevertheless, the perception was that the initial upload of missiles was insufficient to meet the longer-term needs of the Task Force. Consequently, British concerns led to requests to the United States for 300 AIM-9L Sidewinders from their own stockpiles.[64] Therefore, following United States approvals, the delivery of the first 100 missiles to Ascension Island occurred on 14 May.[65] Subsequently, a long-range C-130 Hercules mission was flown to airdrop a number of the missiles to the Fleet in the South Atlantic before 23 May.[66] Ultimately, the Sea Harrier community had introduced a new weapon onto the platform, albeit an evolution of an existing and known system. As a result, the Sea Harrier force's initial tactics, training, and doctrine reflected its legacy weapon system. The Sea Harrier's ability to adapt to the new weapon system would be critical to Operation Corporate. However, the two deployed Sea Harrier squadrons took an individualistic, rather than a collegiate approach to their tactics.[67]

Delivery of control of the air through manned fighters is not merely a function of the platform's capability. Several enabling functions must support the aircraft. For example, the ability to see, understand, and react rapidly to an enemy approach was critical in the successful outcome of the Battle of Britain. In 1940 the RAF used the *Chain Home* radars to provide sufficient early warning to the finite Fighter Command resource to concentrate the small force at the right place and at the right time.[68] However, over four decades later, the Task Force deployed to the South Atlantic with limited intelligence, surveillance, and reconnaissance assets, in particular without an airborne early warning capability. The previous naval airborne early warning capability, the Fairey Gannet, was retired at the same time as HMS *Ark Royal*.[69]

Broadly in line with the policy of having one-third of the Sea Harrier squadrons manned by RAF pilots, the deployed Sea Harrier force included seven RAF pilots. Additionally, the junior Service's contribution to carrier-based combat air came in the guise of the Harrier GR3s of 1 (Fighter) Squadron, commanded by Wing Commander Peter Squire.[70] During routine operations, the Squadron was 'declared to ACE Mobile Force (Air) and SACEUR's Strategic Reserve (Air) with deployment options ranging from north Norway to eastern Turkey.'[71] Consequently, all three Harrier GR3 front line squadrons were familiar with operating in austere and remote conditions in the field and from deployed operating bases. However, they had no recent experience of operating from aircraft carriers.[72] Nevertheless, on 8 April, the Assistant Chief of Air Staff (Operations) tasked 1 (Fighter) Squadron for 'details of operational requirements needed to prepare the squadron for possible involvement in the South Atlantic.'[73] Moreover, the RAF Harriers' explicit task was to operate in the attack and reconnaissance roles. Yet, they were to deploy to the South Atlantic as attrition replacements for the anticipated Sea Harrier losses. The Harrier GR3s were to serve in an unfamiliar embarked air defence role flown by pilots with limited exposure to the task.[74]

On reflecting on the efforts to prepare his Squadron for Operation Corporate, Squire noted the considerable support required from a multitude of agencies to enable the ambitious expedition, including the Ministry of Defence Procurement Executive, the Ministry of Defence, RAF Germany and Industry.[75] However, he also highlighted his frustrations regarding the initial ambiguous command and control arrangements. Squire said the squadron was 'reacting to inputs from four sources, Ministry of Defence, Strike Command, 18 Group and the Navy, with 38 Group kept very much in the dark.'[76] Nevertheless, the efforts to turn an expeditionary land-based attack squadron into an embarked air defence capability in a tight timeframe were impressive. Aircraft were rapidly modified to ensure that they could operate from an aircraft carrier. Modifications included 'the fitting of shackles to the outriggers for lashing down purposes, a modification to allow active nosewheel steering and an engineering design to provide a means of aligning the aircraft's INAS (Inertial Navigation and Attack System) on a moving deck.'[77] Additional modifications involved the fitment of 'an I-Band transponder for bad weather recoveries, hardened limiters for the engine control system and an anti-corrosion treatment.'[78]

Harrier GR3 flying training before the deployment included ski jump training at Royal Naval Air Station Yeovilton between 14 and 23 April.[79] Additionally, air combat training was conducted against RAF Lightnings and Hunters as well as French *Armee de l'Air* Mirage IIIs and *Aeronavale* Super Etendards. The training gave the Harrier pilots an insight into the capabilities of the Argentine aircraft they would face in the coming weeks over the South Atlantic.[80] Moreover, the Squadron conducted a useful end-to-end test of the new control of the air capability when five of the six AIM-9G Sidewinders were launched successfully at the Aberporth weapons range, off the west coast of Wales, on 30 April.[81] However, the control of the air role was not the sole focus of the squadron's work-up. The Squadron conducted ultra-low level flying down to 100 feet and dropped twenty-eight cluster bombs against a splash target.[82] There were also further reviews of expanding the Harrier GR3 capability. RAF staff instigated work to integrate anti-radiation missile and precision attack capabilities onto the Harrier GR3. Additionally, providing the aircraft with a self-protection capability against enemy air and ground threats received significant attention.[83] The latter capabilities would be available in the latter stages of Operation Corporate but not in time to support the initial Harrier GR3 deployment or Operation Sutton.

On 19 April, the Squadron received its movement instructions. The initial task was to deploy nine aircraft; six aircraft would join the Task Force while the three remaining Harriers stayed at Ascension Island to conduct air defence duties.[84] Over the period 2 - 6 May, the nine aircraft deployed from their home base at RAF Wittering to Ascension Island. They used a combination of air-to-air refuelling and refuelling stops at RAF St Mawgan in Cornwall and Banjul in Gambia to reach their destination.[85]

Planning assumptions suggested that after twenty-one days of operations, the Sea Harrier force could be as low as fourteen aircraft.[86] The need to replace only the aircraft (and pilot) rather than the total capability meant that 1 (Fighter) Squadron deployed with a skeleton engineering staff of only eighteen personnel. Although initial plans called for thirty-eight engineers to prepare for the deployment, this figure is still some way short of the manning levels required to support the aircraft during normal operations. Of note, the ten Harrier GR3 aircraft detachment based in the Falkland Islands post-Conflict would require 200 support staff, i.e. twenty personnel to cater for a single airframe.[87] However, due to a command edict to limit sleeping quarters to above the waterline, living space was at a premium on board HMS *Hermes*.[88] Consequently, and despite the limited number of RAF engineering personnel, they slept 'in hammocks and camp beds erected in passageways where some routine movement continued throughout the quiet hours.'[89] The net result was additional pressure on the existing Sea Harrier engineering staff to support a similar, but different, aircraft type.

The third and last aircraft to consider as part of the British combat air contribution to Operation Corporate is the Avro Vulcan. At the start of the Conflict, the aircraft was in its last few months of military service. The operational conversion unit, the squadron responsible for training Vulcan aircrew, closed in August 1981, and three operational squadrons had retired within the previous three months.[90] The three remaining operational squadrons based at RAF Waddington were due to be disbanded by 30 June.[91]

The origins of the Vulcan date back to the 1947 B 35/46 requirement for a new medium-range bomber. In response to the need for a bomber capable of 500 knots at 50,000 feet with a range of over 3,350 nautical miles while carrying a 20,000 pound (lb) payload, Avro's chief designer and creator of the iconic Lancaster bomber, Roy Chadwick, conceived the futuristic delta-wing design.[92] Initially known as the Avro 698, the Vulcan first flew in 1952, and the B1 variant entered RAF service in May 1957 as part of what became the V-Force triad alongside the Handley Page Victor and Vickers Valiant bombers.[93]

For the vast majority of its career, the Vulcan was a nuclear-armed bomber. The Vulcan's initial role was to act as Britain's first line of defence as part of the independent nuclear deterrent capability. To meet this task, a pre-determined number of Vulcan crews and their nuclear-armed aircraft were kept at very high readiness 24 hours per day, 365 days of the year. The Vulcan B2 variant carried either the Yellow Sun or Red Beard free-fall nuclear weapon.[94] An air-launched ballistic missile was to be carried under each wing on a weapons pylon in an attempt to give the aircraft greater stand-off and survivability against increasingly dense and sophisticated Soviet defences. Following the termination of the Anglo-American Skybolt programme, three Vulcan squadrons from February 1963 fielded the less ambitious Avro-built Blue Steel missile.[95]

However, Blue Steel's front-line tenure was short-lived as 'the medium bomber force was formally stood down from QRA (Quick Reaction Alert) at midnight on 30 June 1969.'[96] As a result, and due to the introduction of Polaris-armed submarines, 'responsibility for the strategic deterrent passed from the RAF to the Royal Navy.'[97] With the loss of its primary role, some might have questioned the Vulcan's continuing utility to Britain's defence. However, the Vulcan received a reprieve following the cancellation of the F-111 programme. With minor airframe modifications, a new weapon, minimal investment, and change from high to low altitude operations, the Vulcan, along with surplus Fleet Air Arm Buccaneers, would provide a solution to the long-range nuclear attack capability gap. A gap that would exist until the Panavia Tornado entered service. Consequently, until the Vulcan retired, it planned to be a low-level tactical nuclear bomber using the WE177C free-fall nuclear weapon. With no 'East of Suez' commitment in place, there was no requirement for the Vulcan to continue air-to-air refuelling nor, from 1976, the need to continue to train for the secondary conventional bombing role.[98] After nearly a quarter of a century dedicated to the nuclear attack role against a known Warsaw Pact threat, the Vulcan force prepared for a long-range conventional attack against Argentine-held territory – a role that was beyond the comprehension of most British military planners. As a result, the Vulcan force was neither trained nor equipped to cater for a long-range conventional attack on the Falkland Islands.

Of note, Argentina considered purchasing all three British combat air platforms used during the Falklands Conflict for use by their armed forces. The issue of exporting military equipment to Argentina was 'not without political delicacy.'[99] At its inception, the *Fuerza Aérea Argentina* was 'largely British equipped, standards are British and doctrine Royal Air Force.'[100] However, this was not necessarily through choice, but since 'Great Britain owed Argentina a huge debt for its continuous supply of food during the [Second World] War. Unable to offer a full financial settlement, the United Kingdom offered to pay it with weapons, offering its more modern systems. Among the material thus received from 1947 were 100 Gloster Meteor F Mk 4 fighters, thirty Avro Lincoln and fifteen Avro Lancaster bombers, fifteen Bristol 170 Freighter and twenty-four Vickers Viking transports, twelve Airspeed Consul and seventy de Havilland Dove light transports, and 100 Percival Prentice trainers.'[101] However, and until the mid-1960s, the fledgling independent air arm struggled to carve its niche within the Argentine military construct. According to the British Air Attaché's report, and as a result of struggling to maintain obsolete aircraft, the ramifications of a failed coup and holding limited sway with its two more senior Services, 'at the end of 1955 the air force is clearly in an unhappy and disturbed state.'[102] Five years later, the position was no better. 'It is difficult to see how the Argentine Air Force can ever acquire the self-confidence and prestige which it must acquire in order to hold its own on a footing of equality with the two longer established services.'[103] By 1963, due to the 'parlous state into which the Argentine Air Force had fallen' as well as a national budget which 'is in a state of continuous deficit,' the Air Attaché held the view that 'the Argentine Air Force in its present state cannot be considered as an operational force of any consequence.'[104]

However, two years later, in 1965, there was a ray of hope. In October 1956, the United States Air Force set up a Mission in Argentina with the intent 'to co-operate with the Argentine Air Force in an advisory capacity with a view to increasing its technical and functional efficiency' paved the way for the procurement of the first batch of second-hand A-4 Skyhawks nearly a decade later.[105] However, the Air Attaché noted presciently that 'the re-equipment with US material will put the Argentine Air Force in a position of having to support US policies or go short of spares and replacements.'[106] As a result, the Argentines came to regret their procurement decision some seventeen years later during the Conflict.

Much to the dismay of the British Air Attaché, the French were also becoming influential in Argentina. With the local manufacture of 'a small French jet trainer and communications aircraft,' it was clear that the British domination of supply of military aircraft to the *Fuerza Aérea Argentina* was beginning to wane.[107] The British were partially guilty in their own downfall by initially offering over-priced, second-hand Canberra and Hunter aircraft.[108] Additionally, this promising period of re-equipping the *Fuerza Aérea Argentina* 'was clouded as a result of our ban on meat imports from countries where foot and mouth disease was endemic … the Reed Report (which pointed a finger at Argentine mutton as the probable cause) touched Argentine pride to the quick and caused some hysterical outbursts of wrath.'[109] Ultimately, the Argentine military aircraft inventory would be modernised and become more internationally diverse.

From a British export perspective, both the Embassy in Buenos Aires and the British Defence Industry actively pursued further sales to Argentina, but defence export policy became increasingly restrictive. As noted by the Defence Sales Organisation:

> '…throughout the period successive [British] Governments have tried to strike a balance between the economic benefits to be expected from Defence sales, the need to maintain good relations with Argentina, concern over human rights and the possibility of a direct military threat to the Falkland Islands.'[110]

Reflecting on the existing frictions between Argentina and Chile, Lord Chalfont, a minister in the Foreign and Commonwealth Office, felt an 'ineradicable distaste for a policy that involves selling weapons of an advanced type in an area like Latin America – especially to two countries involved in territorial disputes.'[111]

Elements of the Argentine Navy showed interest in procuring up to a fleet of twelve of the fledgling Harrier aircraft in early 1970.[112] The requirement was met by the significantly cheaper, more numerous, but second-hand American A-4 Skyhawks. Nevertheless, with an expected lifespan of five years, some saw the aged Skyhawk as a temporary solution.[113] From a Defence Sales Organisation perspective, 'the indications are, however, that a purchase of Harrier has been postponed rather than cancelled.'[114] As a result, the British saw an opportunity to sell the yet to be built Sea Harrier to Argentina. However, after initial Embassy and Defence Sales Organisation staffing in late 1981, the Foreign and Commonwealth Office responded with,

> 'Although it is clear that neither an aircraft carrier nor Sea Harrier would have any implications for internal repression in Argentina, it is equally clear that both would be capable of use against the Falkland Islands. They would fall foul of our second guideline for arms sales to Argentina.'[115]

The adoption of a more restricted defence sales policy by both the United Kingdom and the United States in the prelude to the Conflict meant that the Argentines would eventually purchase the French Super Etendard rather than the Sea Harrier.[116] Consequently, and as highlighted by the Defence Sales Organisation, 'if the Argentine Navy were to purchase Sea Harrier we would have some considerable hold over them in that the aircraft could only be kept flying with logistic support from the UK.'[117] The net result was that the British had to invest considerable time and diplomatic efforts in an endeavour to constrain the Super Etendard capability during the Conflict.

In a similar timeframe to the Sea Harrier enquiries, the Argentines also considered the purchase of Vulcan aircraft. In early 1982, the *Fuerza Aérea Argentina* was 'firmly interested in acquiring Vulcan in 1983 despite recent publicity about cuts in defence expenditure. They require between six and twelve aircraft which would form a new unit which would be additional to present strengths.'[118] The Defence Attaché in Buenos Aires, perhaps naively, added that he had 'been unable to identify a specific role for these aircraft but is convinced that they would be inappropriate for use in any adventure against the Falkland Islands. We can only assume, therefore, that the Vulcan would be purchased either as a deterrent or for operations to the West.'[119] However, it was an industrial decision that eventually scuppered the potential sale of Vulcans to Argentina. On 3 February, less than two months before the Argentine invasion, and 'despite earlier interest, BAe [British Aerospace] have now decided at Aircraft Group Board level that, for commercial reasons, they do not wish to become involved in the modernisation and ongoing support of this type of aircraft.'[120]

So, cost, British export policy, and industrial interests ensured that the Argentines fielded only one British combat air platform during the 1982 Conflict. So what was the Argentine air power situation in 1982?

Who and What? – The Argentine Combat Air Protagonists

To understand the fighting components of the Argentines' combat air capability, it is crucial to understand the force's development and configuration. The inter-Service rivalry between the RAF and the Fleet Air Arm is well known. However, the antagonistic relationship between the two British Services was contained, mostly, to within the corridors of Whitehall. In sharp contrast, the battles between the *Fuerza Aérea Argentina* and the *Comando de Aviación Naval* were, at times, physical and lethal. In his 1960 report, the British Air Attaché noted that,

> 'Although the Argentine Air Force has so far had little success in re-equipping itself with modern aircraft, it has largely succeeded in preventing its bitter rival, the flying arm of the Argentine Navy, from doing any better. The rivalry between these two arms has also so far stultified any attempt to set up an Air Force equipped and trained to deal with submarines, although it is now the determined policy of the Navy to concentrate chiefly upon that role. The Argentine Air Force will not agree to the Navy taking responsibility for maritime air defence and the Navy for their part have so far succeeded in blocking aspirations of the Air Force to set up something akin to the Royal Air Force's Coastal Command.'[121]

However, the Argentine national strategy changed between 1955 and 1962 when the emphasis moved from national defence to national security. The key concern became the need to counter any internal communist growth. Consequently, 'counterinsurgency was the policy the air force had to adopt to survive in the new hostile environment.'[122] With the loss of the counter-maritime capability to the *Comando de Aviación Naval*, the *Fuerza Aérea Argentina* acquired assets that were suitable only for 'short-ranged ground support missions.'[123]

The dilemma faced by the Argentines in the 1960s echoes with those faced by the United Kingdom. However, it appears that the Argentines fell for the demands of furnishing their short-term needs rather than adopting a more pragmatic and balanced force that would meet their long-term requirements. The consequences of an Argentine decision to generate a niche combat air arm would prove to be a flawed strategy in the South Atlantic some two decades later. There is an argument that the Argentines lost the war due to this doctrinal change some two decades before the war started.

The divisive relationship between the two Argentine air arms can be traced back to June 1955 when the two Services were predominantly on opposing sides of a failed *coup d'état* to overthrow President Juan Peron.[124] The most notorious element of the revolution occurred on 16 June 1955, with a *Comando de Aviación Naval* air raid on a pro-government rally in Plaza de Mayo in central Buenos Aires and home of the Presidential palace, *Casa Rosada*. The strike involved thirty Argentine naval aircraft and accounted for over 300 civilian deaths. The attack remains the largest aerial bombing ever faced by the Argentine mainland. The *Fuerza Aérea Argentina* participation was also involved:

> 'Air Force action was confined to the fighter base at Moron on the outskirts of Buenos Aires. In the first phase Meteors from this Base operated on the Loyalist side in defence of the Capital, and actually shot down one of the attacking Naval planes. Later in the day Moron was captured by junior officers of the Base who defected to the rebel side ... a small number of Meteors subsequently operated with the rebel forces and shot up various targets in the city.'[125]

During the 1970s, and as highlighted by the Foreign and Commonwealth Office, the issue continued:

> 'The armed forces have remained under a Ministry of Defence since the coup of 1976. Despite an outward show of unity, there is considerable inter-service rivalry for political influence, particularly between the Army and the Navy. The Army greatly resents the increased power and influence gained by the Navy in particular at the time of the [1976] coup.'[126]

In 1982, Argentine combat air capability encompassed ten different platform types spread across the *Fuerza Aérea Argentina* and the *Comando de Aviación Naval*. British assessments suggested that Argentine squadrons were well manned at a ratio of three pilots per airframe.[127] Additionally, the aircrew were 'well motivated, and skilled, with high levels of skills and experience in squadron commanders and operations officers. Flying hours in peacetime were considered compatible with maintaining aircrew efficiency.'[128] However, in the thirty years preceding the Conflict, the British Air Attaches in Buenos Aires provided alternative insights into the flying discipline and morale issues of the *Fuerza Aérea Argentina*. In 1952 it was reported that 'there is a general lack of "guts," *esprit de corps*, and enthusiasm for the Service.'[129] The 1960 report noted that two civilians died and a further five injured due to ricochets during an Air Week firepower demonstration. The Air Attaché was shocked that 'nobody seemed perturbed, however, over this blatant example of bad flying discipline.'[130] The 1965 report did not hold back on its criticism, and used terms based on stereotyping as much as rational analysis:

> 'As a body of fighting men, the Air Force comes fairly low down in the World scale. The Argentines, with their strong intermixture of Italian blood, are not a warrior race.'[131]

In the 1968 and 1971 versions, the tone avoided gross stereotyping. Still, the message was equally damning: 'flying skill is generally of a high standard in the AAF [*Fuerza Aérea Argentina*] but airmanship would be better if more self-discipline could be imposed.'[132] Approaching the Conflict, the 1977 report reiterated that 'too many pilots were irresponsible and exceeded the limitations of either themselves or their aircraft.'[133] Nevertheless, in the final annual report before the Conflict, the British Embassy in Buenos Aires appositely noted that the *Fuerza Aérea Argentina* performance, 'despite equipment weaknesses, indicates that they would make dangerous enemies.'[134] Ultimately, the historical and the post-Conflict views of Argentine pilots were inconsistent, although the immediate pre-Conflict narrative should have raised concerns.

The backbone of the Argentine combat air capability was the McDonnell Douglas A-4 Skyhawk. Initially, fifty former United States Navy A-4B Skyhawks were procured for the *Fuerza Aérea Argentina* between 1966 and 1970 to generate *Grupo 5 de Caza* of the *V Brigada Aérea* based at San Luis, near Cordoba.[135] Due to the Vietnam War, the initial A-4 Skyhawk force build-up was slower than anticipated. The priority supply of weapon racks and gunsights focused on the United States Navy's Skyhawks rather than Argentina's needs. As a result, the A-4B Skyhawks were initially unable to perform their primary attack role.[136] Limited access to A-4 Skyhawk spares would occur again in the lead up to the Conflict. However, Argentina overcame the Vietnam War-related supply issues, and a further sixteen refurbished A-4Bs, designated as A-4Q Skyhawks, were delivered to the *Comando de Aviación Naval* in 1971 and 1972 and formed *Tercera Escuadrilla Aeronaval de Caza y Ataque*.[137] Although normally operated from *Base*

Aeronaval Commandante Espora, at Bahia Blanca, the A-4Q Skyhawks were also capable of being deployed from the sole Argentine aircraft carrier, *ARA Veinticinco de Mayo*.

The last tranche of twenty-five refurbished A-4C Skyhawks was delivered to Argentina in 1976 to create *Grupo 4 de Caza* of the *IV Brigada Aérea* based at Mendoza.[138] The A-4C Skyhawks were superior to the A-4B Skyhawk variant as they incorporated 'five weapon stations, in lieu of three, [a] better gunsight, and a somewhat more complete avionics fit.'[139] However, by May 1982, attrition had reduced the now ageing and increasingly obsolete force down to twenty-four A-4B Skyhawks, seventeen A-4C Skyhawks, and eight A-4Q Skyhawks.[140] Indeed, the British assessment of the Argentine Skyhawks suggested that 'despite the simplicity of the aircraft, the Argentines have been unable to maintain an adequate spares back-up with the result that half of the aircraft remain unserviceable; however, some of these could be pressed into service in a wartime situation.'[141]

The Argentine A-4 Skyhawk force was limited to the use of 'dumb' free-fall weapons. The *Comando de Aviación Naval* Skyhawks exclusively used the American-built Mark 82 500lb bomb. In contrast, the *Fuerza Aérea Argentina* aircraft used the *Explosivos Alaveses* (Expal) 250-kilogramme bomb, either with conventional or parachute-retarded tails, the latter for low-level weapons delivery.[142] However, as of 11 May 1982, the *Fuerza Aérea Argentina* Skyhawks had clearances to use the larger British Mk 17 1000lb bomb, typically used by their Canberra force.[143] Additionally, the *Grupo 4 de Caza* aircraft with their extra wing hard-points allowed the carriage of the Israeli-provided Shafrir 1 infra-red air-to-air missile. The Shafrir 1 was limited to a stern sector engagement due to its seeker sensitivity and was similar in capability to the AIM-9G Sidewinder.[144] Moreover, the Argentines deployed the three Skyhawk variants across three different operating bases for most of the campaign. Consequently, from the outset of the campaign, their scarce logistics network was being stretched needlessly.

In numerical terms, the second most significant Argentine attack force was the Israel Aerospace Industry Dagger – a copy of the French-designed Mirage V. The fighter-bomber was known initially as the Nesher during its brief operational career in the Middle East. However, the aircraft was known as the Dagger for the export market. The *Fuerza Aérea Argentina* acquired thirty-nine Daggers in 1978, with the last aircraft's delivery in February 1982.[145] One observer suggested that the aircraft's brief appearance in Israeli service 'reflects its pedigree – a development design towards the definitive Kfir.'[146] However, from an Argentine perspective, the key advantage of the Dagger, and unlike the more numerous Skyhawk, was that it was not subject to the problems of 'embargoed spare parts and shortages of operational equipment' from the United States.[147] Although in technically excellent condition, the aircraft was new in service with 'several pilots on strength with little experience of the new aircraft' and austerely equipped for its primary and secondary roles of air defence and ground attack.[148] However, the problem of using inexperienced pilots on South Atlantic operations was not unique to the Argentines. Godden noted that 'one pilot was only one-third of the way through his Sea Harrier training' before being deployed to the South Atlantic.[149] The thirty-seven remaining Daggers in service were integrated into two squadrons and formed *Grupo 6 de Caza* as part of *VI Brigada Aérea* at Tandil Air Base near Buenos Aires.[150] Following the invasion, the Daggers deployed south and operated from two separate locations: San Julian and Rio Grande.[151]

The smallest fleet of air combat air assets available to the Argentines was the French-built Dassault Super Etendard. However, the aircraft, when paired with the Exocet anti-ship missile, was also the most potent as it was the sole precision attack weapon available to the Argentines. The *Comando de Aviación Naval* ordered the aircraft in late 1979 to replace its ageing A-4Q Skyhawk fleet.[152] The Argentines intended to form a ten-aircraft squadron, *Segunda Escuadrilla de Caza y Ataque,* based at *Base Aeronaval Commandante Espora* alongside the A-4Q Skyhawk squadron, with the remaining four aircraft held in reserve.[153] However, the second batch of five aircraft and five missiles, which were due to be delivered in April 1982, was curtailed when, following extensive British diplomatic pressure, the 'French ceased all military related activities once hostilities broke out.'[154] By this stage, the delivery of the first five aircraft and five Exocet missiles to Argentina occurred in November 1981. However, the full integration of the missile to the aircraft was incomplete.[155] While the Super Etendard pilots and support personnel trained in France between November 1980 and August 1981, the pilots had limited time on the aircraft and no tactical training on the use of the Exocet missile.[156] Nevertheless, the French assessed the Argentine pilots to be good.[157] Extensive British diplomatic pressure meant that as 'spare parts for the [Super] Etendards were cut off by the NATO arms embargo, the [*Comando de Aviación Naval*] decided to hold one of the five fighters in reserve and use it for spares to support the remaining four aircraft.'[158] The key question was whether a small, niche, but inexperienced force was capable of finding and striking the British operational centre of gravity using its modern, precision stand-off capability and tip the balance of the Conflict in Argentina's favour?

Following a 1952 Canberra Goodwill Flight commanded by Air Vice-Marshal Dermot Boyle, the Argentines showed initial interest in procuring Canberra bombers in 1955.[159] However, the Argentine proposal caused significant debate in the United Kingdom. The Defence Sales Organisation suggested that 'it is most unlikely that the Argentines contemplate the use of these aircraft against us in the Falkland Islands Dependencies.'[160] In contrast, the Foreign Office highlighted that the 'Canberra are pretty devastating weapons – and with their great range and bomb-load they are an even greater menace than an aircraft carrier – and they would greatly increase local Argentine military superiority over us in the Antarctic area.'[161] Despite the concerns, Argentina eventually procured twelve second-hand Canberras from the United Kingdom in the early 1970s.[162] The Canberra procurement appears to be at odds with the *Fuerza Aérea Argentina* mission of focussing on counter-insurgency activities and, perhaps, shows an attempt to procure a more balanced, rather than a niche, force. However, and since 1947, the Argentines had always fielded a long-range attack capability. Specifically, the Argentines used Avro Lancaster and Lincoln bombers in the attack role.[163] Archive evidence suggests that British officials thought Argentine interest in the Canberra might have reflected internal and external prestige needs; Argentina was keen to be seen as a leading state within Latin America and a mechanism for the government to keep favour with the *Fuerza Aérea Argentina*.[164]

In early 1982, the ten surviving Canberras were part of *Grupo 2 de Bombardero, II Brigada Aérea*, and operating from Parana Air Base in the north of Argentina.[165] Although an aged platform, the key advantages that the Canberra had over its smaller and nimbler combat air brethren were its considerable range and ability to carry a significantly larger, albeit non-precision, payload. Due to its extended range capability, the Canberra force operated from a base located a considerable distance away from the operational area. Therefore, and before the start of the Conflict, eight Canberras deployed to Trelew.[166] Consequently, valuable ramp space was available at the forward operating bases closest to the Falkland Islands so that the fuel-critical Daggers, Mirages, Super Etendards, and Skyhawks could reach the Falkland Islands unassisted. Nevertheless, some operators raised concerns about operating such a large, slow and obsolete aircraft against a sophisticated opponent.[167]

Building on the French influence that started with the procurement of the jet trainer and communications aircraft in the early Sixties, Argentina selected the French Mirage III as its new air defence fighter. From 1972, the Mirage III force, *Grupo 8 de Caza* of *VIII Brigada Aérea*, was based near Buenos Aires and deployed twelve of its sixteen available aircraft in support of the Argentine operation.[168] The assets retained at their home base of Mariano Moreno were used for alert duties to protect the mainland from a possible Vulcan strike against important strategic targets.[169] Three aircraft were deployed to Comodoro Rivadavia in southern Argentina and were also used only for homeland defence. The remaining nine fighters were based at Rio Gallegos and were used to support Falkland Island operations.[170] Of note, the Mirage IIIEA variant used by the Argentines was not capable of conducting attack missions. Consequently, the aircraft was employed solely in the control of the air role. As the aircraft could not carry out strikes against the aircraft carriers, amphibious assault force, or British land forces, the Argentine mission analysis against the various British operational centres of gravity excludes the Mirage III sorties.

The North American F-86 Sabre, famed for its performance with the United States Air Force over MiG Alley during the Korean War, was in its twilight years of service with the *Fuerza Aérea Argentina.* The Argentines procured twenty-eight second-hand F-86F Sabres with deliveries commencing in September 1960.[171] However, two decades later, only eleven aircraft remained in service with *Grupo 4 de Caza*.[172] Due to its limited utility, the Argentines elected not to deploy the F-86 Sabre during the Conflict. As a result, any further analysis excludes the F-86 Sabre.

Of the three Argentine combat air assets deployed to the Falkland Islands, the most capable aircraft was the indigenously designed and built *Fábrica Militar de Aviones* Pucara. The two-seat turboprop entered service with the *Fuerza Aérea Argentina* in the late 1970s and operated in the counter-insurgency role. In 1980, and in an effort to secure a contract to supply the aircraft with upgraded machine guns, Douglas Bader, the former Second World War RAF fighter pilot, opined that the Pucara's primary role would preclude its use if a Falkland Islands conflict materialised.[173] In reality, the Pucara's close air support capability and its ability to operate from rough, semi-prepared operating surfaces, meant that the opposite was true. Although *Fábrica Militar de Aviones* had built sixty Pucaras at their Cordoba facility, only thirty-five aircraft were in active use or under overhaul on the charge of *Grupo 3 de Ataque* at Reconquista.[174] The remaining aircraft were exported, lost in accidents, tasked for test and evaluation needs, or awaiting acceptance. *Grupo 3 de Ataque* elected to deploy south and retained mainland operating bases in southern Argentina at Comodoro Rivadavia and Santa Cruz, which allowed for easier access to the Pucara contingent based on the Falkland Islands.[175] The Falkland Islands-based Pucaras, due to the lack of protection shelters, were left out in the open and subsequently suffered heavily during shelling by the Task Force, and from airfield attacks. Moreover, the boggy Falkland Islands terrain proved troublesome for Pucara ground operations, including suffering damage during take-off and landing incidents.[176] With a limited logistical support capability forward deployed to the Falkland Islands, many of the damaged aircraft were unable to return to service. Despite some notable performances, the Pucara's limited outputs and effects against the British operational centres of gravity exclude the Pucara from further analysis.[177]

The *Comando de Aviación Naval* procured ten Aermacchi MB-339s that entered service over the period 1980-1981 and were operated by *1 Escuadrilla de Ataque* at *Base Aeronaval Punto Indio*.[178] The unit was dual-tasked both as a light attack and an advanced flying training unit and was still engaged in development work with the aircraft at the outbreak of the war. Although capable of carrying 250 and 500lb bombs, there were concerns that the 'aircraft's unsophisticated bomb release mechanism was considered potentially dangerous.'[179] As a result, the six Aermacchi MB-339s deployed to Stanley used machine gun pods and Zuni rockets as their default weapons during Falkland Island operations.[180] Although an Aermacchi MB-339 was the first aircraft to find and attack the amphibious assault force on 21 May, the Aermacchi MB-339's limited effect has removed it from further consideration in this book.[181]

The last and least capable combat air platform to consider is the Beech T-34 Mentor. The *Comando de Aviación Naval* had a fleet of fifteen aircraft used for primary and intermediate pilot training and co-located with the Aermacchi MB-339 squadron at *Base Aeronaval Punto Indio*. Although initial plans called for deploying eleven serviceable aircraft to the Falkland Islands, only four aircraft arrived at Pebble Island after the proposed operating base at Goose Green was deemed inadequate.[182] The aircraft focused on the counter-land role. Consequently, the aircraft were lightly armed and capable of carrying machine gun pods as well as rocket launchers on four under-wing hard-points.[183] However, the pilots had no previous weapons experience on the aircraft.[184] Moreover, following the Special Air Service raid at Pebble Island on 15 May, all four aircraft were destroyed.[185] Therefore, the T-34 Mentor's limited outputs and effects on the British operational centres of gravity have forced its elimination from the campaign analysis.

Why and How? – Measuring the Outcome not the Output

With the timeframe and the constituent parts of the various combat air capabilities established, the next step is to address the scale and success of their effectiveness in striking their opponent's centres of gravity. Many historians and participants of the Conflict make some form of reference to the number of Argentine missions flown during the period of interest.[186] Most narratives focus on the days of significant aerial activity rather than take a more holistic perspective. Alternatively, several articles focused solely on a specific aircraft type or squadron's activities during the Conflict. In particular, many narratives concentrate on the outputs of the unit involved, such as missions flown, numbers of bombs dropped, or the percentage of aircraft arriving in the target area. The data contained within a few reports resonated with those used in this book, but they failed to analyse the data or demonstrated the process behind their generation. Consequently, no single document measures the totality of the effect delivered across the panoply of air assets. This book aims to fill that void by articulating the resources associated with missions: planned, launched, that arrive in the target area, that penetrate the British defences, or employ their weapons against the target and those that delivered the required effects against the various operational centres of gravity. This case study has adopted a different measure of effect from the traditional output-based rule of using sortie rates to gauge the operational outcome.

The contention here is that the aircraft is merely the delivery platform and does not create the operational effect. The weapon, not the delivery platform, produces the required operational effect. Therefore, this book aims to articulate the journey of each air-to-ground weapon during the Conflict. There is an assumption that each weapon delivered the same level of effect. This binary approach recognises that the Argentines used four different weapons that span both precision weapons as well as various types and weights of 'dumb' bomb. Nevertheless, evidence from the Conflict suggested that there was only one case where the detonation of a weapon in the target vessel caused significant casualties but did not cause the destruction of the intended target.[187] Therefore, and in addition to measuring the journey of each weapon, the book will explore the causal factors behind the success or failure of the delivery of the weapon. Supporting the book deductions is a series of annexes that show the detailed evidence and its source. Not all commentators agree on the tactical details of each action. The different viewpoints of a tactical action, overzealous accounting, deliberate manipulation of the events, or memory fade caused by the passing of time generate friction, confusion, and a lack of clarity. The conflicting views are articulated and arbitrated in the associated footnotes within each annex. Likewise, on the rare occasion where there is no primary or secondary source data detailing the weapon load, the issue is highlighted. Moreover, an assumed weapon load is used and explained in the footnotes. Typical weapon loads carried by the aircraft type and its operating location form the basis for assumed weapon loads.

The net results of the analysis, shown in the various annexes, provide a unique insight and deliver an unseen perspective of the Falklands Conflict as well as present a compelling argument for the operation's outcomes. With the methodology for the book now articulated, the following chapter reviews the use of air power during the first phase of the Falklands Conflict.

Chapter 3

Air Power prior to Operation Sutton – *Bautismo de Fuego!*[1]

'Vulcan aircraft refuelled by Victor tankers attacked the Port Stanley airfield during the night. Subsequently at dawn Sea Harriers carried out further attacks. Both operations were successful. All aircraft and personnel involved have now returned. There are no casualties.'

Ministry of Defence Press Statement,
1 May.[2]

In the early hours of 1 May, the British gambit heralded a new phase in the South Atlantic campaign. However, this was not the Argentines' first experience of the Avro Vulcan. The initial Vulcan attack on Stanley airport also coincided with the 24th anniversary of a twin Vulcan fly-past over Buenos Aires as part of the inauguration ceremony for the newly elected Argentine President, Doctor Arturo Frondisi.[3] Two years later, two Vulcans from 101 Squadron, the same unit that would go on to conduct the Black Buck 1 raid, also participated in a multi-national fly-past over Buenos Aires to mark the 150th anniversary of Argentine independence.[4] The symbolism of Operation Black Buck, and the possible threat presented by the Vulcan, were not lost on the Argentine government.

With the arrival of the British naval force off the Falkland Islands, and following a successful repossession of South Georgia during Operation Paraquet, any hope of a diplomatic solution between the two nations had dwindled rapidly. However, the British Task Force poised off the Falkland Islands, at that time, lacked the key military elements in sufficient scale to seize and hold the vital ground of Stanley. On 1 May, the British amphibious force that contained the required assets to achieve the recapture of the Falkland Islands was located in the vicinity of Ascension Island and scheduled to arrive off the Falklands on 16 May.[5] The initial British force was therefore required to blockade the 200-mile Total Exclusion Zone around the Falkland Islands. By enforcing the blockade, the British aimed to achieve control of the air and sea to reduce the risk to the subsequent amphibious assault.[6]

The attacks on the airfields at Stanley and Goose Green were merely the signals of the start of the military campaign 'to repossess the Falkland Islands as quickly as possible.'[7] British planners did not expect the Vulcan nor the subsequent Sea Harrier raids to be a decisive, campaign-winning move. The British motive for the attacks was to generate an early and decisive battle for control of the air and remove the numerical advantage of Argentine air power.[8] Nevertheless, the Argentines had a choice of where and when they contested their battles. The Argentine options ranged from aggressive counterattacks, or deliberately avoiding a battle of attrition and simply preserving and concentrating their assets to strike where, as Clausewitz described, the opposition 'mass [was] concentrated most densely' – the critical amphibious assault.[9] The Argentine response in their first military campaign, their *bautismo de feugo*, would determine the outcome of the first phase of the Conflict.

The British planners accurately assessed the Argentine response in their outline concept of air operations for the repossession of the Falkland Islands. In the document, British planners suggest that the Argentines would 'in the short term, maintain the recce [reconnaissance] effort and to nibble at the UK TF [Task Force] while maintaining attack and fighter aircraft for committal at the most opportune moment most probably as the landing commences. This course will include attempts to identify a relatively soft target, for example a resupply ship, with a view to a disruptive pre-landing attack.'[10] This chapter articulates the key British and Argentine combat air participants; identifies the British operational centre of gravity; Argentine and British combat air outputs; the level of Argentine success achieved during their attack against the British operational centre of gravity as well as the outcomes of the period 1 - 19 May.

The Key Participants of the *Bautismo de Fuego*

Argentine Combat Air Participants. Despite gaining knowledge of his fellow *Junta* leaders' plans for Operation *Azul/Rosario*, the Argentine invasion of the Falkland Islands, in late December 1981, Brigadier General Lami Dozo was able to conceal *Fuerza Aérea Argentina* preparations for the upcoming operation.[11] For example, up until 6 April British technicians, working for Marconi Avionics and installing Dagger modifications at the Rio Cuarto air base, 'had not seen any indication in the maintenance unit concerning preparation for conflict.'[12] *Grupo 4 de Caza* deployed five A-4C Skyhawks, as part of a routine exercise – *Operativo Gélido II*, at Rio Gallegos in southern Argentina during the period of the invasion.[13] However, the unit and the other *Fuerza Aérea Argentina* combat air assets played no direct part in the invasion of the Falkland Islands. The remainder of April was a frantic period for the eclectic mix of Argentine combat air assets as they prepared, trained and deployed their fleets of aircraft from the various bases around Buenos Aires and northern Argentina to the austere forward operating bases approximately 1200 nautical miles away in Patagonia. The scale of the initial deployment reflected the capacity at the forward operating bases and the difficulties in generating the full complement of aircraft due to the limited spares pool as well as knowledge of recently acquired aircraft such as the Super Etendard and Dagger.

<table>
<tr><th>Author</th><th>Dagger</th><th>Mirage III</th><th>Canberra</th><th>A-4B Skyhawk</th><th>A-4C Skyhawk</th><th>A-4Q Skyhawk</th><th>Super Etendard</th></tr>
<tr><td>Rivas[14]</td><td>14</td><td>12</td><td>8</td><td>12</td><td>11</td><td>8</td><td>4</td></tr>
<tr><td>Freedman[15]</td><td>24</td><td>8</td><td>6</td><td>18</td><td>14</td><td>12</td><td>5</td></tr>
<tr><td>Ethell & Price[16]</td><td>26</td><td>16</td><td>9</td><td colspan="3">76</td><td>5</td></tr>
<tr><td>Hobson[17]</td><td>19</td><td>8</td><td>7</td><td>12</td><td>12</td><td>8</td><td>4</td></tr>
<tr><td>Burden[18]</td><td>24</td><td>8</td><td>6</td><td>18</td><td>14</td><td>8</td><td>4</td></tr>
</table>

Table 3A – Argentine Order of Battle as at 1 May.

Analysis of the array of secondary sources highlighted, as shown in Table 3A, that there is a debate regarding the number of deployed Argentine combat air assets on 1 May. Although most commentators simply state the figures, Rivas provides additional detail by identifying the airframe movements on a daily basis. Rivas has created a clear audit trail for the vast majority of Argentine combat air movements and progress throughout the campaign; thus, this book uses Rivas' position as the baseline for the Argentine combat air order of battle during the Conflict.

The reality is that the figures also reflected that the deployed force size ebbed and flowed throughout the campaign as aircraft deemed unserviceable at the start of the campaign became available and deployed south. At the same time, some were lost in combat while other aircraft were returned to their home units to undergo battle damage repair. The key benefit of the Argentine strategy was that they were able to replace their losses and maintain their deployed force size to meet the expected amphibious assault by the British. Consequently, there was a steady flow of air traffic between north and south Argentina. Several sources misinterpret the continuous flow of aircraft as aircraft leaving the South Atlantic operating area to defend key elements of national infrastructure. This situation would become one of the enduring myths of the campaign, not helped by the British Air Commander, who believed that the Vulcan raids caused 'the Argentines to withdraw their Mirage III aircraft back to Buenos Aires to defend the capital against a perceived attack.'[19]

While this was an exaggeration, in reality, the Argentines retained a small cadre of Mirage III and Dagger aircraft at their home bases near Buenos Aires throughout the campaign to mitigate against such a British attack.[20] Nevertheless, the Argentines had a finite resource of aircraft, and the implications of running out of available assets would have a detrimental effect during the latter stages of the campaign.

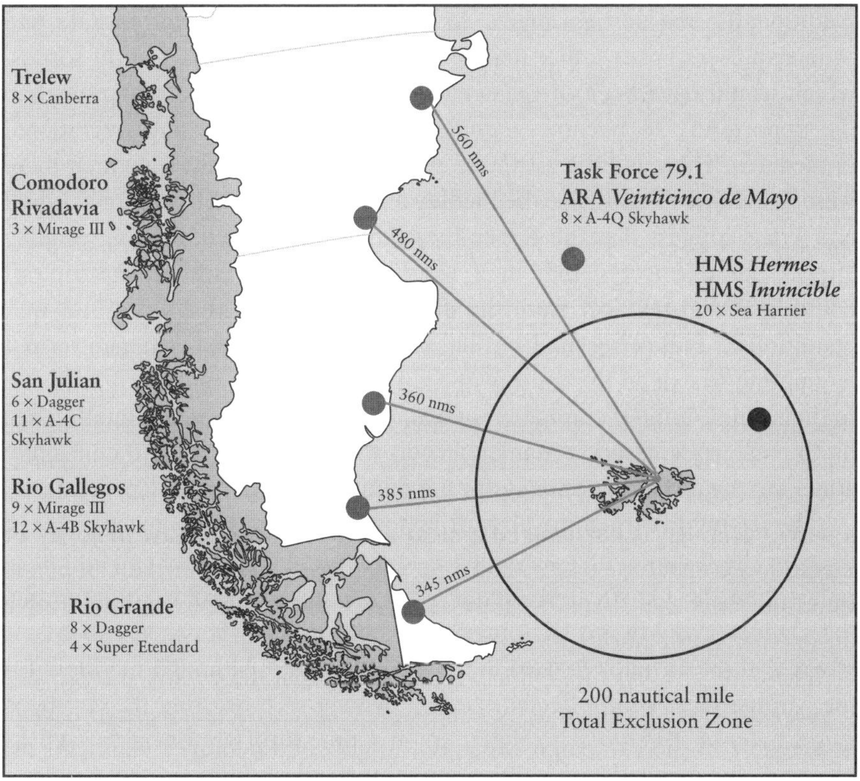

Figure 3.1 – Combat Air Dispositions as at 1 May.

Once fielded in southern Argentina, the various combat air units conducted some form of joint training, albeit with limited success.[21] For example, and contrary to its agreed concept of operations, *Fuerza Area Argentina* A-4B Skyhawks practised anti-shipping attacks with unguided bombs, colloquially known as 'dumb' bombs (in contrast to guided, 'smart' weapons). However, the beached ship was unable to manoeuvre defensively and incapable of firing back at its attackers – a very different prospect to what the Argentine pilots would face in the coming weeks.[22] Daggers planned sweep, escort, and attack training missions alongside their naval counterparts, but they failed to find the designated targets or suffered from aircraft serviceability issues.[23] If the Argentines could have developed these nascent training missions into successful attack sorties during the Conflict, then the massed raids would have proven problematic for the British fleet to deal with effectively.

As part of their training programme before the Conflict, the Argentines flew several combat air sorties over the Falklands.[24] However, these familiarisation missions appear to be ad hoc rather than deliberate planning. Additionally, the sorties appear to have been designed for morale and propaganda purposes rather than as mandated area familiarisation sorties, which would have been of greater value. Therefore, only a few pilots had the opportunity to become acquainted with the terrain and operational procedures. There is little available evidence to support the view that there were Argentine plans to use the Stanley airport for fast jet operations. Ethell and Price suggest that the Super Etendard force looked at using Stanley airport but discovered that in a war-fighting configuration, the aircraft could land and take off from the diminutive airfield in dry, but not wet, conditions.[25] Following the Conflict, the Argentines faced criticism for not attempting to extend the runway at Stanley airport and making it available to their range-limited combat air assets. The lack of up-to-date intelligence on the resources based at Stanley airport forced the British into constantly attacking the airfield at Stanley for the duration of Operation Corporate.

The basing of Argentine aircraft in southern Argentina appears to have been on a first-come, first-served basis and centred on Service and unit lines rather than the logistical challenges that the aircraft faced. For example, the Dagger and Mirage III forces were both divided between two bases, whereas three airfields housed the A-4 Skyhawks.[26] Although the logic for the Mirage III basing reflected its dual tasking of protecting the deployed *Fuerza Aérea Argentina* headquarters at Comodoro Rivadavia as well as meeting the demands of conducting escort missions over the Falkland

Islands. However, the rationale behind the division of the attack units is less clear. As a result, Argentine units shared their limited spares pool, bespoke to type weapons, and engineering experience across southern Argentina's airfields. The incoherent fielding plan degraded the efficiency and effectiveness of the Argentine combat air assets. This situation was a missed opportunity by the Argentines to concentrate and sustain their force and was ultimately a poor application of one of the key principles of war.[27] Nevertheless, and based on Rivas' figures, Figure 3.1 shows the disposition of British and Argentine combat air assets as of 1 May.

British Combat Air Participants. On 1 May, the deployed Sea Harrier units were limited to a force of twenty aircraft with no prospect of an uplift in aircraft and pilot numbers until the arrival of 809 Naval Air Squadron on board MV *Atlantic Conveyor* on 18 May. Therefore, the force had to conduct the first phase of Operation Corporate within its current resource. There was considerable angst that the outnumbered Sea Harrier force could lose a significant number of aircraft in the heavily anticipated battle for control of the air. Nevertheless, and unlike their Harrier GR3 and 809 Naval Air Squadron counterparts, the aircraft carrier-embarked Sea Harriers had the luxury of conducting flying training during their passage south, thus enabling them to hone their air defence and attack skills. Flight Lieutenant Ian Mortimer, an RAF officer, serving on 801 Naval Air Squadron, commented that during the passage south 'we trained a lot, planned attacks on various targets like vessels and airfields. We dropped a few bombs and did lots of intercept work.'[28] The latter skill set would be critical in achieving the desired level of control of the air before the amphibious assault. The task should have unified the Sea Harrier community. However, there appeared to be a disparity in how each aircraft carrier was planning and conducting Sea Harrier operations.[29] As a result, and before the start of combat operations, there was a level of friction between the aircraft carriers with little opportunity or desire to harmonise their outputs and tactical procedures. Complicating the issue further was the debate within the Ministry of Defence of how to make the best use of the Sea Harrier. Some suggested that the Sea Harrier should focus on the defensive counter-air role. However, other commentators claimed that this was too narrow a perspective. For example, the Chief of the Air Staff, Sir Michael Beetham, was an advocate of offensive counter-air operations and 'expressed his frustration at the Royal Navy's planned use of the Sea Harrier or, indeed, the apparent lack of any air plan.'[30]

On 1 May, the Harrier GR3s of 1 (Fighter) Squadron remained at their home base of RAF Wittering. However, the groundcrew deployed that day to Ascension Island via RAF Brize Norton while the aircraft started their deployment to Ascension Island the following day.[31] Following the arrival of MV *Atlantic Conveyor* at Ascension Island on 5 May, the Harriers landed onto the converted MV *Atlantic Conveyor* on 6 May in calm conditions. Nevertheless, Wing Commander Squire noted that 'most pilots approached their first VL (vertical landing) onto a deck with some apprehension.'[32] The Harrier GR3s were not the sole occupants of the MV *Atlantic Conveyor*; they would be joined on the journey south by the eight Sea Harriers of the newly-commissioned 809 Naval Air Squadron as well as four Chinook and six Wessex helicopters.[33] After a 12-day transit, four of the six Harriers were flown from MV *Atlantic Conveyor* to HMS *Hermes* on 18 May, a mere two days before the start of Operation Sutton, with pilots who were unfamiliar with aircraft carrier operations.[34] The remaining two aircraft joined their compatriots over the following two days.[35] Ultimately, the Harrier GR3s would not participate in the first of the three phases of the operation to repossess the Falkland Islands. However, significant activity had taken place to plan, prepare, deploy, and sustain the force.

Unlike the much smaller Sea Harrier force that deployed enmasse, the larger Harrier GR3 community was not fully committed to the Falklands Conflict. Although 1 (Fighter) Squadron was the lead Harrier GR3 squadron for Operation Corporate, it was not a full squadron deployment. Nevertheless, the deployment still had ramifications across the whole Harrier community. The two remaining operational Harrier GR3 squadrons, 3 (Fighter) and 4 Squadron operated from RAF Gutersloh in West Germany. Both squadrons maintained their normal routine wherever possible in support of their main effort – NATO operations in Central Europe. Consequently, the Harrier GR3 squadrons participated in the four-week Tactical Leadership Programme in West Germany and Exercise Maple Flag 9, a major multi-national exercise in Canada, conducted the critical NATO Tactical Evaluation (TACEVAL) assessment and practised field deployments. Moreover, the units sent two pilots on a significant post-graduate training programme – the Harrier Qualified Weapons Instructor course.[36] However, the Harrier GR3 detachment conducting a deterrent role in Belize was unaffected during Operation Corporate.[37]

Nevertheless, the RAF Germany Harrier squadrons and the Harrier Operational Conversion Unit, located alongside 1 (Fighter) Squadron at RAF Wittering, provided extra pilots and aircraft to support the 1 (Fighter)

Squadron deployment.[38] Also, the RAF Germany Harrier squadrons provided pilots with previous air defence experience to rapidly convert to the Sea Harrier.[39] Additionally, 4 Squadron deployed three pilots to Ascension Island over the period 17 – 26 May to provide a limited air defence capability.[40] The Harrier GR3s were replaced in the Ascension Island air defence role on 26 May by Phantom FGR2s of 29 (Fighter) Squadron.[41] April and May were a hectic period for the Harrier GR3 force as it prepared for its own baptism of fire. Still, it demonstrated that the Harrier force had sufficient resilience and depth to meet both its long-term enduring and short-term emerging tasks.

Defining The British Operational Centre of Gravity during the *Bautismo de Fuego*

With the combat air capability stipulated for both sides at the start of the military confrontation, attention must turn to the targets that the Argentines needed to strike to achieve a decisive military victory. Argentine intelligence-gathering assets ascertained the timing, size, and composition of the British fleet. Argentine merchant vessels, including the *Rio de la Plata,* passed within four miles of Ascension Island over the period 25 – 27 April.[42] Additionally, Argentine Air Force Boeing 707s shadowed the British ships as they sailed south from Ascension Island towards the Falkland Islands. The initial Boeing 707 reconnaissance missions were conducted over the period 21 – 25 April and made regular contact with both aircraft carriers and between six and eight escorts.[43] Due to the Boeing 707 missions, the Argentines should have gleaned a good understanding of the British force composition and capabilities. However, there appears to be some confusion amongst Argentine commentators regarding the British intentions on 1 May. For example, Moro believed that the Argentines repelled several British attempts at a direct landing against Stanley.[44] However, Table 3B shows the constituent parts of the British Task Force 317 as it sat poised off the Falkland Islands. Of note, the Task Force had sufficient resources to deal with the repossession of South Georgia against an Argentine occupying force of 137 personnel. However, the initial British maritime force was incapable of repossessing the Falkland Islands, where 13,000 Argentine soldiers, sailors and airmen were ensconced.[45] The size, role, and intent of the initial British Task Force of aircraft carriers, destroyers, and frigates, as well as Royal Fleet Auxiliary vessels, was to deliver sea control and control of the air as its primary outputs. Moreover, the British force did not contain the required amphibious assault ships and troops to project a ground force ashore. Task Force 317 would not receive further naval assets until the arrival of the amphibious force on 18 May, which included six Landing Ship Logistics as well as both Landing Platform Docks.[46] Additionally, the British force had yet to secure control of the air or sea control. To conduct all three activities concurrently would have been an ambitious and fraught affair as well as contrary to prudent doctrine. Therefore, Moro's claims regarding repelling the landings on 1 May are flawed.

Aircraft Carriers	Destroyers	Frigates	Royal Fleet Auxiliaries
HMS *Hermes*	HMS *Glasgow*	HMS *Alacrity*	RFA *Resource*
HMS *Invincible*	HMS *Coventry*	HMS *Arrow*	RFA *Olmeda*
	HMS *Sheffield*	HMS *Plymouth*	
	HMS *Glamorgan*	HMS *Yarmouth*	
		HMS *Broadsword*	
		HMS *Brilliant*	

Table 3B – British Task Force 317 as at 1 May.[47]

Task Force 317 was assigned to enable the amphibious assault, not to conduct it. To do so, they had approximately three weeks to deliver the required levels of control of the air and sea control before the amphibious assault. The key ships were the two aircraft carriers of the fourteen vessels initially deployed, and as shown in Table 3B. Each aircraft carrier had an embarked force of Sea Harriers and Sea King anti-submarine warfare helicopters. Both assets would be key to the delivery of the control of the air and sea control tasks. However, they were not the sole means of delivering and enabling the required operational outcomes.

Developing a timely and accurate assessment of what was happening in the air around the operating area was essential if the British were to use their limited number of aircraft efficiently to deliver control of the air. The previous generation of British aircraft carriers had their own organic airborne early warning capability in the guise of the Fairey Gannet. The new generation of aircraft carriers was explicitly designed to operate Sea Harriers and helicopters and had no means of launching or recovering conventional take-off and landing aircraft. Consequently, legacy carrier-borne aircraft, such as the Gannet, were incompatible with the new fleet of Invincible-Class aircraft carriers. Moreover, even if an improvised solution could be found for the larger HMS *Hermes* to operate Gannets, this would have been at the cost of several Sea Harriers.

The task of providing a localised air picture for the Task Force fell predominantly to the three Type 42 destroyers (HMS *Glasgow*, *Coventry*, and *Sheffield*). The destroyers' surveillance radars were able to produce a credible situational awareness picture. When coupled with the destroyers' long-range Sea Dart surface-to-air missile capability, the ships' radar could, in theory, deliver a potent level of control of the air for the British Task Force. However, the limited number of sea-based surveillance radars could not provide the comprehensive wide-area air picture that an airborne early warning asset could deliver. With the destroyers' radar located on the host ship, rather than thousands of feet in the air, the curvature of the earth curtailed a long-range, low-level detection capability. As a result, the sea-based radar's line of sight was limited. Moreover, the Type 42s' radar also had a limited over-land detection capability. The technical shortcomings had operational consequences.[48] To maximise detection range and reaction time forced the Type 42 destroyers to conduct their air surveillance task closer to the threat than perhaps was prudent. As a result, the Type 42 destroyers were vulnerable and at an increased risk to attack from Argentine air power, in particular the Exocet-armed Super Etendards. Moreover, the Argentine Navy had also procured two Type 42 destroyers.[49] Therefore, the newly acquired Argentine Super Etendards had practiced attack missions against their own Type 42 destroyers and knew how to avoid the Type 42 destroyer's strengths and exploit its weaknesses.[50]

Although the Type 42 destroyers provided the critical outer layer of defence with its Sea Dart long-range, surface-to-air missile capability, each of the frigates and the remaining destroyer had its own self-protection capability that would aid the control of the air task.[51] The older generation of surface combatants vessels used the first generation of surface-to-air missiles, which were of questionable utility. Nevertheless, the most capable frigates were the two modern Type 22 ships armed with the short-range Sea Wolf surface-to-air missile.[52] Due to their modern and capable self-defence capabilities, the Type 22 frigates acted as the aircraft carriers' 'personal bodyguards' during the early stages of the Conflict. However, close protection of the aircraft carriers was not the Type 22 frigates' sole task during the campaign. They would also work in combination with the Type 42 destroyers as well as act as the personal protection for the amphibious assault force.

The Type 22 frigate was designed from the outset, not as an air defence asset but as a specialist anti-submarine warfare vessel. Consequently, the loss of a Type 22 frigate would have had an impact across the spectrum of

Centre of Gravity	**Critical Capabilities**
British Aircraft Carriers	1. The ability to enforce blockade. 2. The ability to contest control of the air. 3. The ability to establish sea control. 4. The ability to endure in location.
Critical Vulnerabilities	**Critical Requirements**
1.1.1. Robust and timely communication links. 1.1.2. A clear chain of command. 2.1.1. Limited number and capability of Sea Harriers. 2.1.2. Maritime Force Air Defence limitations. 2.2.1. Lack of Airborne Early Warning. 2.2.2. Type 42 Destroyers in Picket Role. 2.3.1. Robust and timely communication links. 3.1.1. Sufficient Anti-Surface and Anti-Submarine Warfare helicopters. 3.1.2. Sufficient Anti-Surface and Anti-Submarine Warfare Frigates. 3.1.3. Sufficient Anti-Surface and Anti-Submarine Warfare submarines. 3.2.1. Lack of persistent intelligence, surveillance, reconnaissance capability. 4.1.1. Royal Fleet Auxiliary ships. 4.1.2. A safe location to conduct Replenishment at Sea.	1.1. Effective command and control. 2.1. A high-readiness and capable air defence force. 2.2. A robust Recognised Air Picture 2.3. Effective command and control. 3.1. A high-readiness and capable Anti-Surface and Anti-Submarine Warfare force. 3.2. A robust Recognised Surface Picture. 4.1. The need to replenish frequently.

Table 3C – British Operational Centre of Gravity prior to Operation Sutton.

operations in the run-up to the amphibious assault. In contrast, the Amazon-Class Type 21 frigates, HMS *Alacrity*, and HMS *Arrow* were relatively cheap, general-purpose escort vessels. However, the Type 21 frigate's self-defence capability was limited to the increasingly obsolete Sea Cat surface-to-air missile. The Type 21 frigate's utility was in its ability to exploit its multi-role capabilities. As a result, the Type 21 frigates became increasingly used in the naval gunfire support role that saw them conduct multiple operations throughout the campaign and often put them in harm's way.

To sustain the fleet at sea, the Royal Fleet Auxiliary deployed two ships: a Fleet Oiler and a Fleet Replenishment vessel.[53] Both vessels conducted multiple replenishment at sea tasks each day and exploited their embarked helicopters to ferry stores to keep the deployed British fleet topped up with fuel, stores, and weapons throughout the campaign.[54]

Building on the narrative of the component parts of the British Task Force 317, Table 3C presents the hypothesis that the British operational centre of gravity before Operation Sutton was the aircraft carriers. The corresponding boxes, containing the critical capabilities, requirements, and vulnerabilities, breaks down the centre of gravity's supporting elements into their constituent parts. Prior to the amphibious assault, the British needed to enable and protect their critical vulnerabilities. In contrast, how effective would Argentine air power be at striking these targets?

The change of the operational centre of gravity as Operation Sutton occurred is not a reflection on the diminished importance of control of the air, or for that matter, sea control. Controlling both the sea and air environments were enduring campaign requirements, but their demotion reflects that their relative importance reduced the closer the British forces got to their desired end-state. For example, reflecting the dwindling importance of the aircraft carriers, their traditional bodyguards, the Type 22 frigates, were both used to protect the amphibious force during its transit into the amphibious operating area around San Carlos during the critical amphibious assault.[55] Indeed, during the initial stages of Operation Sutton, HMS *Invincible* transited with the amphibious assault force to protect them with her long-range Sea Dart surface-to-air missile capability.[56]

Both aircraft carriers were critical to the enabling phase of Operation Corporate. Although they remained relevant throughout the campaign, their relative importance to the success of the British campaign reduced as the campaign reached its latter stages. Nevertheless, would the Argentines comprehend the significance of the aircraft carrier during the initial stages of the Conflict and target it appropriately? Equally important, would the Argentines understand the changing British priorities as the campaign matured and adapt their targeting accordingly?

Bautismo de Fuego Outcomes

The first air attacks of the campaign on 1 May as well as the loss of ARA *General Belgrano* on 2 May and the Type 42 destroyer HMS *Sheffield* two days later created global headlines. However, it is rare to see these tactical events as part of the broader context of the phase or the Conflict. By way of example, there were several less well-known events during the first weeks of the Conflict that generated cumulative effect and pressure on both participants. As a result, the operational outcome is, perhaps, less well understood. For example, on 12 May, another of the Type 42 destroyers, HMS *Glasgow*, was forced to withdraw from the campaign after an unexploded bomb damaged the ship.[57] The operational impact of losing HMS *Glasgow* was the equivalent of losing HMS *Sheffield*. However, the event did not generate the same level of global media interest as the ship remained afloat, and the only casualty on board HMS *Glasgow* was one man who suffered from shock.[58] Nevertheless, the net result was that a single Type 42 destroyer, HMS *Coventry*, was left to fill the role once occupied by three air defence ships. Fortunately, the British had resilience in their force structure, and two further Type 42 destroyers, HMS *Cardiff* and HMS *Exeter*, as well as the bespoke Type 82 destroyer HMS *Bristol*, were en route to the South Atlantic. However, the replacement destroyers would not arrive in theatre until after the initial amphibious assault on 22 and 26 May.[59] To exacerbate the situation further, the Sea Harriers lost three, or 15 per cent, of its force during the first week of the campaign. During an airfield attack at Goose Green on 4 May, Argentine ground fire accounted for the loss of one aircraft, and a further two Sea Harriers disappeared in what appeared to be a mid-air collision on 6 May.[60] More importantly, the Sea Harrier force lost all three pilots along with their aircraft. However, their task had not changed. The remaining cadre of Sea Harrier pilots and aircraft shared the constant operational burden. As a result, and with only minimal activity from the Argentines, gaps were starting to appear in the British ability to deliver control of the air.

From an Argentine air power perspective, they lost several aircraft during the first three weeks of combat operations, including six A-4 Skyhawks, two Mirage IIIs, a Dagger, and a Canberra, as well as expending 40 per cent of their precious Exocet stockpile. However, what had Argentine air power achieved to compensate for its material losses? More importantly, did the Argentine activities impact on the British centre of gravity or its opposition's desire to achieve an effective blockade before the inevitable amphibious assault?

Although there is extensive documentation of the key events during the significant days of air operations, the quality and depth of reporting on the scale, participants, role, and the success of Argentine air power during its *bautismo de fuego* is more varied. As shown in Annex A, the

Argentine combat air assets flew a total of 130 missions over the period 1 – 19 May, an average of fewer than seven sorties per day. However, the daily sortie rate was sporadic, with 1 May accounting for just less than half of the total missions for the nineteen-day phase. The Argentine outputs were significantly less than those anticipated by the British, who expected the Argentines to generate 60 per cent aircraft serviceability for their fighter aircraft during the Conflict, deliver three sorties per day per airframe, and up to 150 missions per day.[61] In mitigation, and as shown in Annex A, the weather did have a detrimental impact on Argentine air operations. Over the period 2 – 11 May, the daily weather was assessed to be poor at either the southern Argentine airfields or over the Falkland Islands. Consequently, it is perhaps not surprising that Argentine outputs were inconsistent during this period. However, in the week before the British amphibious assault, the Argentines only flew a total of six combat air sorties despite the weather assessed as poor only on the afternoons of 18 and 19 May. Therefore, the Argentines were evidently preserving its combat air capability to counter the inevitable amphibious assault. However, was this a prudent measure or a missed opportunity to apply greater pressure on the British Task Force, given the damage inflicted upon the control of the air capability?

To assess the success, or otherwise, of the Argentine combat air capability, it is essential to understand the number of attack missions planned and executed during the lead up to the amphibious assault. However, the actual number of missions planned and flown by the Argentines on the first day of battle is unclear. Freedman, Burden, as well as Ethell and Price suggest that Argentina planned fifty-six missions comprising sixteen A-4B Skyhawks, twelve A-4C Skyhawks, six Canberras, twelve Daggers as well as ten Mirage III sorties.[62] In contrast, Cordesman states that 'fifty-four attack sorties out of seventy-two sorties were flown against the task force.'[63] Complicating the issue even further is the *Fuerza Aérea Argentina* website, which suggests that they launched fifty-eight sorties on 1 May.[64] However, each narrative focused solely on the activities of the *Fuerza Aérea Argentina* and omitted the events of its sister Service – the *Comando de Aviación Naval*. Moreover, and beyond the actions of 1 May, few commentators discuss the Argentine flying activities before the start of Operation Sutton in any depth.

Rivas provides a more comprehensive picture of Argentine combat air activity on 1 May. Analysis of his work, the basis for the data contained within Annexes A, C, and D, shows that on 1 May, the *Fuerza Aérea Argentina* and the *Comando de Aviación Naval* planned sixty-four combat air sorties. However, only sixty missions were launched successfully from the Argentine mainland.[65] Of the sixty missions flown, there were thirty-two attack missions and twenty-eight control of the air tasks. Therefore, as shown in Figure 3.2, Argentine combat air apportionment was 53 per cent towards attack and 47 per cent to control of the air tasks. Rivas' figures contradict Cordesman's view that the weighting was significantly biased towards the attack role. The disparity between Rivas' and Cordesman's position may be because, unusually, several Daggers, A-4C and A-4Q Skyhawks conducted control of the air missions on 1 May. Post the initial action, the number of Argentine aircraft that conducted control of the air missions rapidly dwindled to such an extent that between 7 May and the start of Operation Sutton, no control of the air missions were flown over the Falkland Islands. The Daggers and A-4 Skyhawks became dedicated attack platforms, and control of the air missions became the sole responsibility of the Mirage III force. However, after a disappointing debut on 1 May, and the loss of two Mirage IIIs as a consequence of a Sea Harrier engagement, the Mirage III subsequently played a minor role during the Conflict even when it returned to operations on 21 May.[66] The Mirage III's failure to influence the campaign and compete against the Sea Harriers for control of the air was due, in part, to their inability to remain in the operating area. The Mirage's limited endurance was compromised further by its inability to conduct air-to-air refuelling due to the lack of an air-to-air refuelling probe.

As mentioned previously, there is a misconception that following the initial raids, Argentine Mirage III aircraft withdrew from operations to protect Buenos Aires from a potential Vulcan raid.[67] However, Rivas alluded to an event that may be the causal factor for the misunderstanding and the generation of one of the enduring myths of the Falklands Conflict. On the evening of 29 April, A-4C Skyhawk and Dagger aircraft launched from their San Julian deployed operating base and flew north, relocating to Comodoro Rivadavia to protect the aircraft after an unidentified radar contact approached the airfield.[68] The scare was a false alarm, and the aircraft returned in time to respond to the British air raids on 1 May.[69]

In contrast to Freedman's information which simply stated that thirty-five of the combat air missions arrived in the vicinity of the target area, the breakdown of Argentine combat air resource between attack and control of the air missions provided the ability to analyse the success, or otherwise, of the attack or control of the air missions.[71] Moreover, as shown in Figure 3.2, the apportionment between attack and control of the air changed as the campaign matured. By increasing their focus on the attack mission to the

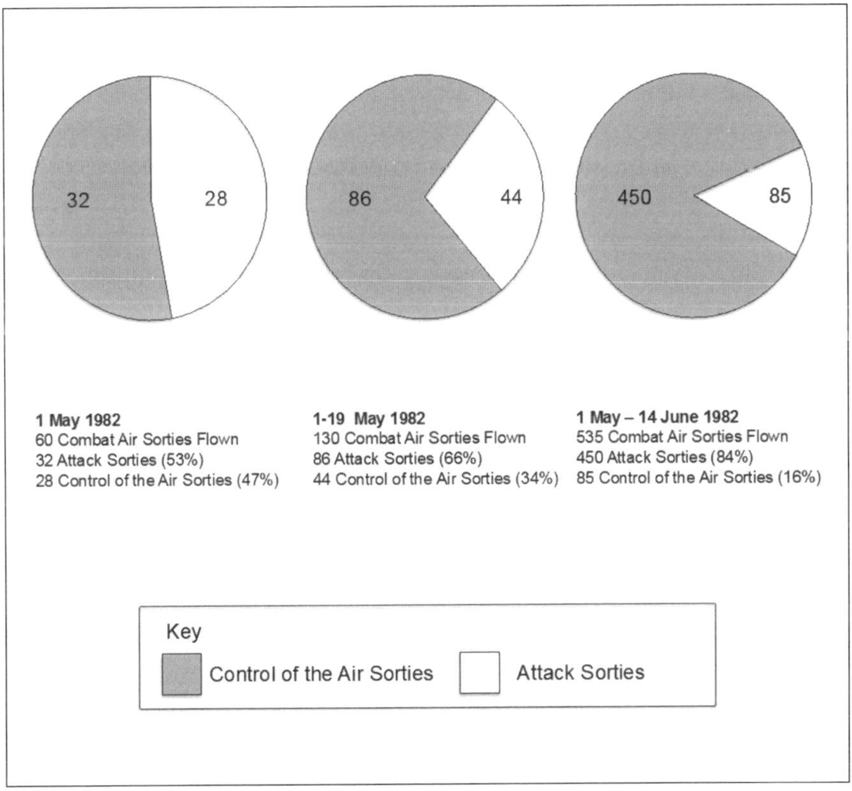

Figure 3.2 – Argentine Combat Air Apportionment during Operation Corporate.[70]

detriment of control of the air without establishing the required level of air superiority was a critical Argentine mistake. As the *Fuerza Aérea Argentina*'s former mentor, Adolf Galland, suggested, 'to use a fighter-bomber when the strength of the fighter arm is inadequate to achieve air superiority is putting the cart before the horse.'[72] Ultimately, the lack of Argentine investment in gaining an ability to achieve control of the air handed a *gratis* advantage to the British that the Argentines struggled to recover from.

The British would not achieve their desired air superiority before Operation Sutton. However, it was not for the lack of trying. In contrast to its Argentine counterparts, and as shown at Annex B, the much smaller Sea Harrier force flew 386 sorties over the same period, an average of over twenty sorties per day and a near 300 per cent increase in outputs when compared with its Argentine counterparts.

In mitigation, the British aircraft operated much closer to the combat area than their opponents, which allowed reduced transit times and aircraft to be regenerated for subsequent missions significantly quicker. However, the Sea Harriers without the benefit of airborne early warning, air-to-air refuelling or a forward operating base had limited situational awareness, endurance, and time on task.[73] Therefore, the small Sea Harrier pilot cadre spent a considerable number of hours either on patrol, transiting to and from the carriers, or sat in their cockpits on alert. As a result, the HMS *Hermes*-based pilots flew an average of fifty-seven operational missions each during the forty-five-day deployment.[74] On 801 Naval Air Squadron, Ward informed that most of his pilots had 'sixty war missions under their belt.'[75] However, it appears that Ward overstated his Squadron's performance. In his post-Conflict report to the Captain of HMS *Invincible,* Ward stated that the original and surviving pilots of 801 Naval Air Squadron flew an average of 53.25 operational missions during the Conflict, only Ward flew sixty missions.[76]

With each Sea Harrier mission lasting over an hour, the pilots were flying at over twice the rate envisaged in the original Sea Harrier requirement of 225 hours per annum.[77] Moreover, the airborne time does not include the mental and physical demands of sitting hours on end in the Sea Harrier cockpit conducting quick reaction alert duty. Consequently, the cumulative effect of their efforts started to take a toll on the pilots and accounted for several aircrew errors that began to creep into later air operations. For example, one senior pilot inadvertently released an AIM-9L Sidewinder instead of dropping a bomb.[78] Although the incident was embarrassing, it was not fatal. However, Ward suggested that fatigue was 'a definite contributory factor' for the death of another pilot on 23 May on his thirtieth operational mission.[79] The demise of an invaluable aircraft and its experienced pilot after crashing into the sea immediately after a night carrier launch vividly demonstrated the consequences of having insufficient pilots. Reflecting on the campaign, the Captain of HMS *Invincible* suggested that 'in this type of operation a ratio of no less than 1.5 aircrew to aircraft is the minimum required to sustain efficiency. 1.75 to 1 would have been ideal.'[80] The initial manning ratio of 801 Naval Air Squadron was 1.375 to 1.[81] As will be demonstrated in Chapter 5, the Argentines were at the other end of the experience/fatigue spectrum.

As the campaign progressed, the lack of airborne early warning and the reduction in the Type 42 destroyer fleet would be mitigated, to a certain extent, by non-traditional methods. For example, the use of Chilean air traffic control radars at Punta Arenas provided timely information on Argentine assets launching from their bases in southern Argentina.[82] Additionally, and as part of Operation Fingent, a British Type 95 radar and personnel were deployed in May to the Chilean airfield at Balmaceda, located on the Argentine border and 180 nautical miles west of Comodoro Rivadavia, to provide additional radar coverage.[83] Moreover, British special forces and submarines operating around Argentine coastal airfields provided a similar detection and warning capability.[84] With the scale of operations undertaken by both participants now understood, it is now time to understand how effective Argentine attack missions were and the causal factors behind these missions' relative success.

Analysing the Outcomes of the *Bautismo de Fuego*

As shown in Figure 3.3, the data contained within Annex C shows that of the ninety-three planned weapons for use during the Argentine attack sorties on 1 May, not one was employed against (never mind strike, detonate or sink) the British operational centre of gravity – the aircraft carriers. Moreover, although the Argentines planned to strike the fourteen ships that made up Task Force 317, not one British ship was hit by an Argentine bomb during the raids of 1 May. Nevertheless, not all commentators agreed with this position. For example, Juan Carlos Sapolski, a Dagger squadron commander, asserted that 'the English pilots shunned combat' and 'after getting back to base, we agreed that it was almost easy. There was no resistance, we dropped our ordnance without any problem.'[85] Furthermore, Moro suggested that, specifically, a British Type 42 destroyer suffered heavy damage during the action on 1 May.[86] The British version of events highlighted that there were no Type 42 destroyers involved in the action of 1 May. The Argentine misidentification of HMS *Glamorgan* for a Type 42 destroyer is perhaps unsurprising given the *Fuerza Aérea Argentina's* lack of exposure to the maritime environment. This issue of poor ship recognition by the Argentines would be a recurring theme throughout the Conflict.

As shown in Figure 3.3, the 1 May raids started well for the Argentines with most of the planned Argentine weapons successfully launched from the mainland. Only two of the planned ninety-three weapons failed to get airborne from the Argentine airfields. During the transit, weapon numbers reduced to eighty-three, or 89 per cent of those planned and 91 per cent of the weapons that managed to get airborne. However, breaching the British defences caused a significant reduction in capability with only twenty-three weapons successfully avoiding the layered defences (equating to 25 per cent of the successfully launched bombs and 28 per cent of the weapons that reached the Islands). In the target area, only six weapons were employed (6 per cent of the planned weapons and 7 per cent of those launched from the mainland) and targeted against HMS *Glamorgan*, HMS *Alacrity*, and HMS *Arrow*.[87] Although the bombs registered a few near misses, and contrary to some Argentine claims, the bombs failed to hit any of the British ships.[88]

The analysis of Argentine combat air activities on 1 May would suggest that it was a dismal performance. When coupled with the loss of four aircraft, the lack of a tangible return from the attack missions was disappointing. Freedman described the Argentine response as 'inadequate.'[89] However, Moro claims that the Argentine performance on 1 May was 'a great victory.'[90] Nevertheless, the analysis shown here tells a stark story – the Argentine aircraft allocated to control of the air missions jettisoned more of their external fuel tanks than their attack aircraft counterparts dropped bombs on 1 May.[91]

The results of the 1 May attacks would infer that the British perception that Argentine pilots were 'professional, proficient and pretty gutsy when

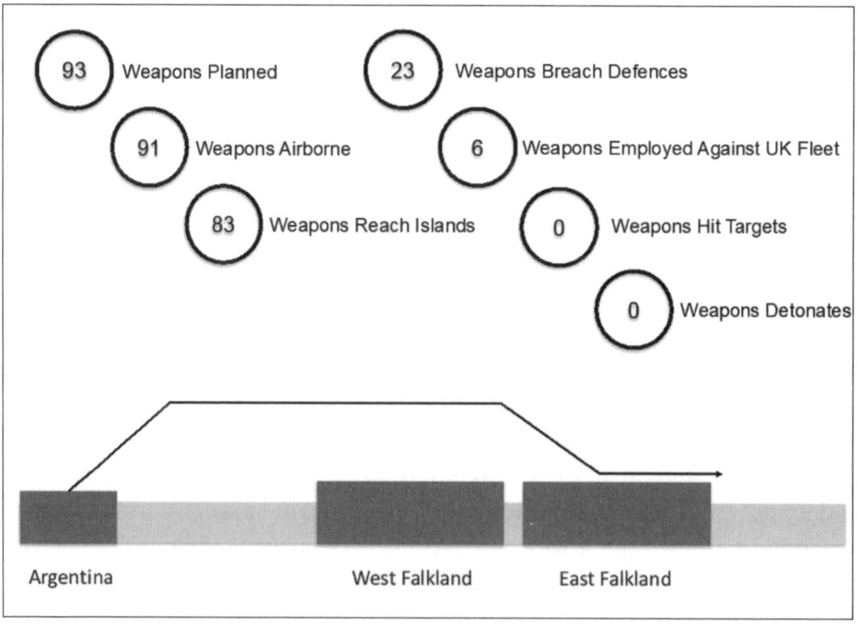

Figure 3.3 – The Utility of Argentine Weapons on 1 May.

it comes to flying and fighting the aircraft, prepared to take risks' was not necessarily the case.[92] From a British perspective, the initial analysis is more gratifying. Of the eighty-three bombs that arrived over the Falkland Islands, only twenty-three weapons eluded British defences. The Sea Harrier deserves much of the credit as thirty-two of the ninety-three Argentine weapons failed to reach their target due to the mere presence of Sea Harrier combat air patrols, with a further four weapons failing to reach their intended targets due to the loss of a Canberra to the Sea Harrier/AIM-9L Sidewinder combination. Although dominant in protecting the British ships on 1 May, would the Sea Harrier be able to deliver the same level of performance for the remainder of the phase and throughout the campaign? Endeavouring to answer these questions by merely looking at the activities of 1 May in isolation is flawed. Although 1 May was the most active day of the opening phase of Operation Corporate, any deductions drawn from these initial events could distort the outcome of the first phase as they do not demonstrate the Argentines' ability to adapt following their inauspicious start.

As a result, Figure 3.4, derived from data contained within Annexes C and E, shows the complete Argentine attack picture over the period 1–19 May. Prior to Operation Sutton, the Argentines managed to launch an impressive 204 out of the planned 206 weapons (or 99 per cent). During the transit to the Falkland Islands, the number of weapons reduced to 170, which equates to 83 per cent of those planned and those weapons that managed to get airborne (a reduction of 7 per cent and 8 per cent respectively when compared with the same activities on 1 May). The diminished performance, albeit small, driven by increasingly unserviceable aircraft, was a trend that would continue to worsen as the campaign progressed. Nevertheless, 107 weapons managed to breach the British defences. This figure equates to 52 per cent of the successfully launched bombs, a significant increase in the 25 per cent figure attributed to 1 May activities. Moreover, this figure also accounts for 63 per cent of the weapons that reached the Islands. In the target area, Argentine air power employs fifteen weapons against the fleet. This figure equates to 7 per cent of the planned weapons, 7 per cent of the bombs that managed to get airborne. These figures are comparable with similar activities on 1 May, with only two hitting the target (less than 1 per cent of those planned and 13 per cent of those dropped). Table 3D breaks down the journey of each Argentine weapon even further by articulating the causal factors, and their relative importance behind the success or failure of the weapon. As a result, thirteen causes can be identified and quantified.

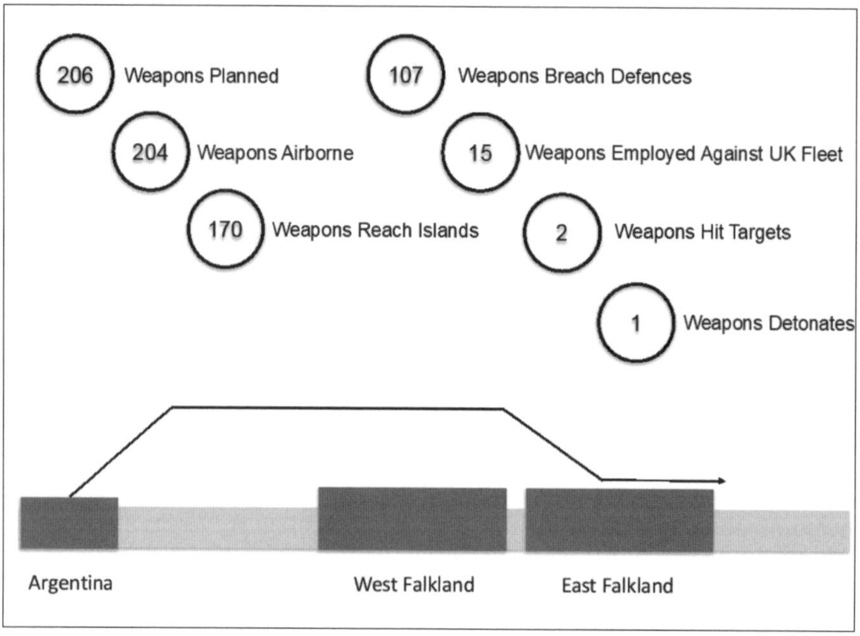

Figure 3.4 – The Utility of Argentine Weapons over the period 1 - 19 May.

Ranking	Causal Factor	Scale (out of 206)	Percentage
1	Weapons not dropped	90	44
2	Sea Harrier – Soft Kill[97]	32	16
3	Mission Cancelled	24	12
4	Serviceability – Air Abort	22	11
5	Weapon Employment – Missed Target	13	6
6	Maritime Force Air Defence – Soft Kill	12	5
7	Sea Harrier – Hard Kill[98]	4	2
8	Crashed before dropping Weapon[99]	2	<1
=9	Serviceability – Ground Abort	2	<1
=9	Target Mis-Identified	2	<1
=11	Weapon Employment – Unexploded Bomb	1	<1
=11	Maritime Force Air Defence – Hard Kill	1	<1
=11	Successful – Hit and Detonates	1	<1
	Total	206	100

Table 3D – Causal Factors for Failure to Deliver Weapons during 1–19 May.

To understand the activities or lack of, that influenced their impact on the first few weeks of the Falklands campaign, the following section will review the top five causal factors. The most significant causal factor, and by a considerable margin, is that Argentine attack sorties failed to drop their weapons. This factor is not a reflection on weapon serviceability but indicates the Argentine inability to find and attack one of the fourteen vessels that made up Task Force 317. The inefficient use of 45 per cent of the weapons was a result of the lack of effective Argentine intelligence, surveillance, and reconnaissance platforms. The Argentines did have a limited number of maritime patrol aircraft. However, only two P-2 Neptune remained airworthy at the start of the Conflict. Moreover, the Argentines withdrew both aircraft from operational use on 15 May. The driver was not only reliability issues but concerns over its vulnerability and obsolete status in a modern battle.[93] Five S-2E Trackers were subsequently transferred from the now redundant aircraft carrier, ARA *Vienticinco de Mayo*, to Rio Grande in an endeavour to mitigate the capability gap, but they were unsuitable to support attack missions, in particular Super Etendard missions.[94]

Another problem to contend with was that both the P-2 Neptune and S-2E Trackers were owned, and operated by, and trained exclusively with the other assets from the *Comando de Aviación Naval* in accordance with the national doctrine that determined responsibility for sea warfare rested solely with naval forces. Consequently, the *Fuerza Aérea Argentina*, who owned the majority of the attack platforms, had limited opportunity to integrate with the *Comando de Aviación Naval* intelligence, surveillance, and reconnaissance platforms. As the campaign progressed, the Argentines would mitigate the issue to a certain extent, and the following chapter addresses the issue. Nevertheless, Argentine reconnaissance and attack assets were unable to discern the correct target to attack. As a result, the Argentine ability to strike the British aircraft carriers was down to luck rather than diligent planning and execution.

Although the intelligence, surveillance, and reconnaissance platforms were the key mechanism to cue attack platforms onto their prey, they were not the sole mechanism. A few Argentine platforms had their own on-board sensors such as the Agave radar on the Super Etendard. Although the Argentines fully exploited the Agave radar's capability during the Exocet attacks of 4, 25, and 30 May, Super Etendards needed intelligence from an external source to know where to look and enable a covert low-level approach to maximise the surprise of their attack. Without such a cue, the success of the attack was likely to be limited. For example, on 23 May, a pair of Super Etendards was unable to find the British fleet.[95] Moreover, even when they could find a target, the Super Etendard's radar could not discern what type of vessel it was about to attack.

Consequently, poor doctrine, inadequate equipment, a lack of joint approach to the air war, and an inappropriate balance of air power roles were all drivers in the Argentines' inability to drop weapons on the British Task Force during the opening weeks of the Falklands Conflict. However, and although it was the leading cause, it was not their only deficit.

The second most relevant factor is the Sea Harrier's ability to deter the attacking force. Accounting for 16 per cent of Argentine weapons, the Sea Harrier's 'soft kill' capability is still some way short of the 44 per cent of the main causal factor. Nevertheless, was the outcome a measure of a successful Sea Harrier defence or a reflection of an inexperienced force that gave its opposition too much respect? Alternatively, did the Argentines deliberately adopt a low-risk approach to preserve their force for easier or more critical missions in the future? The latter point is at odds with the commonly held view that 'Argentine pilots earned the respect of their enemies and most of the world with their skill and bravery.'[96] Therefore, the former, rather than the latter point, is a more likely conclusion.

Further analysis of the data reinforces the notion of changing Argentine risk appetite throughout the campaign. For example, the evidence proved that the Sea Harrier was highly successful and influential during its activities on 1 May. However, the Sea Harrier does not sustain that level of success over the period 1 - 19 May. As a result, the Sea Harrier had limited influence on Argentine combat air power over the period 2 - 19 May. This assessment is at odds with the widespread perception that the Sea Harrier was dominant throughout the campaign. In mitigation, Argentine activity levels were low during the latter stages of the opening phase of the campaign. However, one day of successful activity does not assure campaign success, but it can create the genesis of a myth and an enduring legacy.

The third most influential factor reflects the cancelled missions, equating to 12 per cent of the total planned missions. On 3 May, the Argentines tasked two flights of four A-4B Skyhawks with an anti-shipping mission. However, en route to the target area, it was discovered that the ships were Argentine, forcing the cancellation of the task.[100] Once again, the lack of an effective intelligence, surveillance, and reconnaissance capability had hindered Argentine air power. Compounding the factor further is that the aircraft, due to their limited range, are unlikely to be capable of being re-tasked onto another target, even if the Argentines could identify one.

The fourth most influential causal factor to contend with is the number of air aborts, accounting for 11 per cent of the total weapons planned during the phase. Factors influencing air aborts included technical failures of the attack aircraft themselves or with their enabling asset. Highlighting limited exposure or experience in the task, some attack assets struggled to complete air-to-air refuelling successfully. On another mission, a fuel leak on board the KC-130 Hercules air-to-air refuelling aircraft compromised the mission.[101] Another area of concern was that attack aircraft were misidentified by their controlling agency as control of the air assets and vectored towards a Sea Harrier combat air patrol.[102] With insufficient range and endurance to return to their original anti-shipping mission, Argentine pilots had no option but to abort their mission. The attack missions were reliant on their enablers to achieve mission success. However, and as demonstrated by the number of air aborts, the enablers can also become a significant constraint if they are unavailable or if the attack pilots have limited exposure to their utility.

The last of the causal factors to be reviewed reflects the 6 per cent of the weapons that missed their intended target. Other than the Super Etendard with its Exocet missile, the remaining Argentine combat air aircraft were constrained to non-precision attacks through the use of 'dumb' bombs. As a result, Argentine attack aircraft mitigated their lack of precision by dropping multiple weapons in a single attack against a single target to increase their probability of success. Although an inefficient use of its weapon stockpile, it was a practical solution to the Argentines lack of precision. Indeed, a British Defence Intelligence assessment of Argentine air power was broadly accurate when it stated that 'aircraft delivering free fall bombs are likely to achieve less than a 5 per cent chance of achieving major damage against the range of ships deployed.'[103] The lack of precision during attack missions was not solely constrained to the Argentines. During the Black Buck missions against Port Stanley airfield, the Vulcan conducted its bombing run thirty degrees off the runway heading to maximise the chances of successfully hitting the runway. Even with a bomb load of twenty-one weapons, the probability of dropping a single bomb on the runway was 90 per cent with a 75 per cent probability of hitting the runway twice.[104]

So what did the Argentine air activities achieve before Operation Sutton? The initial surge of activity on 1 May was described by Burden as 'a bad day for the [*Fuerza Aérea Argentina*] in virtually all respects with none of the combat units having achieved any significant success but suffering losses and, in certain cases, some considerable embarrassment.'[105] Although Argentine combat air activity for the remainder of the phase could be described, at best, as moderate, it did achieve some notable success despite the best endeavours of the South Atlantic weather systems to hinder its progress. However, the lack of effective intelligence, surveillance, and reconnaissance meant that Argentine forces were unable to neither find nor strike the British operational centre of gravity, the aircraft carriers, during the prelude to the amphibious assault.

The subsequent, but infrequent, harassing raids had an impact on the British fleet. The loss of two of their three Type 42 destroyers was a significant blow. Arguably, the British ships were merely the first vessels that the attacking aircraft found rather than being specifically targeted to negate the British control of the air capabilities. Frustrating the British planners further was that although the Sea Harrier was very effective on 1 May, its ability to influence the campaign in the weeks before the amphibious assault was extremely limited. However, the Sea Harrier's impact was not a self-induced limitation. The causal factor was the Argentine refusal to conduct a decisive air battle before an amphibious assault. By preserving their force and waiting to contest the crucial amphibious assault, Argentine air commanders bought themselves time to think and plan for future operations. Additionally, they could create much angst and apply significant pressure upon British planners at all levels.

In contrast to their *Fuerza Aérea Argentina* and *Comando de Aviación Naval* counterparts, the maritime surface fleet became a fleet-in-being in the run-up to Operation Sutton. Chastened by the loss of ARA *General Belgrano* on 2 May, the Argentine Navy avoided direct confrontation with the British fleet and elected to remain in littoral waters for the remainder of the Conflict. As a result, the Argentines yielded de facto sea control with minimal effort to the Royal Navy. At the strategic level, the removal of his key force elements from the Conflict suggested that the commander-in-chief of the Argentine Navy, Admiral Jorge Anaya, was thinking long term and ensuring he remained prominent in the post-Conflict power struggle. Operationally, the implications were that sustaining the Falklands garrison would be by air power alone. Despite the air embargo, Argentine transport aircraft, including C-130 Hercules, Fokker F-28 Fellowships, and Lockheed Electras flew forty-five sorties, predominantly at night, to provide 470 tons of supplies and over 500 passengers into the Falkland Islands garrison while returning over 300 personnel to the mainland.[106] These resupply missions would be conducted up to and including the last night of the Conflict.[107] However, and although the air transport cargo and passenger numbers vary marginally between commentators, it is apparent that the resupply level was insufficient to maintain the garrison in the longer term.[108] Brigadier General Mario Menendez, the Argentine Governor of the Falkland Islands, estimated that his garrison's daily requirement to be 17 tonnes of food and 9.5 tonnes of fuel.[109] Ultimately, Argentine air transport only delivered '41 per cent of the requirement.'[110] With the Austral winter fast approaching, the British simply could not wait for the blockade to take full effect and starve the Argentine garrison into submission.

In many respects, the military activities of the first three weeks of May in the South Atlantic were a phoney war, merely a series of opening moves before the arrival of the key players that would determine the outcome of the Conflict. Despite the Argentine swing towards attack missions to the detriment of contesting control of the air, neither side won the opening round outright. Both participants were blooded and damaged, but, critically, both had survived in sufficient strength to contest the critical phase of the campaign – Operation Sutton and the amphibious assault.

Chapter 4

Air Power during Operation Sutton: *Muerte Negra* or *Los Moscardones*?

'Perhaps the most important task of a commander is to identify and strike appropriate enemy centres of gravity.'

Colonel John A. Warden III,
United States Air Force.[1]

Warden's observation demonstrated the seemingly simple task confronted by Argentine air power during Operation Sutton. Facing them was a fleeting opportunity to mass its husbanded combat air power and strike the British operational centre of gravity. The amphibious force was confined to a defined fleet of ships in a concentrated space, advancing slowly to the point that would represent its closest approach to the South American mainland. To exploit this opportunity, and given the ambivalent attitude taken by its army and maritime counterparts, Argentine air power had to find and strike the enemy with the full force of its air power capabilities. In order to articulate the effectiveness of Argentine air power against the amphibious force, it is vital to understand the condition of both air power protagonists as they approached the critical phase of the campaign. Additionally, this chapter will clarify the operation's timeframe as well as identifying the vessels and their cargo that constituted the British amphibious force. The net result of this analysis is a more profound and auditable understanding of the causal factors that affected the Argentine air power response to the British landings.

The Key Participants of Operation Sutton

Although the embarked Sea Harrier force had dwindled from its original twenty aircraft to seventeen aircraft, including the loss of all three pilots, the embarked combat air power of the British fleet was rejuvenated and reached its peak before the start of Operation Sutton.[2] The arrival of MV *Atlantic Conveyor* on 18 May bolstered the Sea Harrier force by a further eight aircraft.[3] The aircraft from the hastily re-formed 809 Naval Air Squadron, commanded by Lieutenant Commander Tim Gedge, were split equally between the two aircraft carriers and integrated into the existing Sea Harrier squadron structures.[4] In addition to the new aircraft, a new tranche of Sea Harrier pilots joined the force, thus creating a total of thirty-four Sea Harrier pilots, with the majority, twenty-one, embarked on board HMS *Hermes*.[5] However, the new cadre of Sea Harrier pilots had a mixed experience level. Although some of the pilots had previous Sea Harrier or embarked air operations experience, few were fully qualified on type as they had joined the unit from exchange tours, staff appointments, or rapidly converted from Harrier GR3 units. Consequently, the increase in manpower was exacerbated further by the fact that there was no opportunity to fly during the long transit south. Indeed, one rapidly converted RAF pilot, Flight Lieutenant Steve Brown, nearly crashed his Sea Harrier during the take-off from MV *Atlantic Conveyor* before transferring the aircraft to one of the aircraft carriers.[6]

Also on board the MV *Atlantic Conveyor* were the six Harrier GR3s and eight pilots of 1 (Fighter) Squadron.[7] The Harrier GR3s, unlike 809 Naval Air Squadron, remained a formed unit on board HMS *Hermes*. Initially planned as an attrition replacement for the Sea Harrier in the air defence role, the Harrier reverted to its traditional attack role due to fewer Sea Harrier losses than anticipated. However, the integration and tasking of the Harrier GR3s in conducting the attack role caused enduring friction throughout the campaign between the unit and its embarked command chain.[8] Although the 1 (Fighter) Squadron pilots had experience on the Harrier GR3, their exposure to maritime operations was extremely limited. Again, and in a similar vein to the additional Sea Harriers, the operational benefit of the extra Harrier GR3s had to be offset with an increased operating risk.

The Sea Harriers and Harrier GR3s would be protecting and supporting the British operational centre of gravity, the amphibious force, during the landing phase of Operation Corporate. Following its hasty assembly in the United Kingdom, the amphibious force departed Ascension Island on 7 May to join the Task Force.[9] Throughout the journey, the crews made frantic efforts to ensure that the ships were loaded correctly. Even so, when the amphibious force joined the carrier battle group on 18 May, the transfer of manpower and equipment had not been completed.[10]

Nevertheless, the British operational centre of gravity for Operation Sutton had arrived off the Falkland Islands. The British military objectives for Operation Sutton were stipulated in Operation Order 3/82 and released on 12 May by Admiral Sir John Fieldhouse.[11] The instructions to the military commanders were 'to repossess the Falkland Islands as quickly as possible.'[12] However, as a precursor to the amphibious assault, local sea control and air superiority had to be achieved before the main amphibious assault could begin. If unsuccessful, the British would conduct the initial landings at night. The relative lack of activity by the Argentine combat air assets during the first few weeks of the Conflict meant that there was no guarantee that the British forces could achieve the required level of control of the air during the landings. However, the mitigation plan to offset any control of the air deficit reflected that the Argentines had a minimal night attack capability.[13] Consequently, the ability to conduct the initial assault during the hours of darkness was a subtle mitigation factor that most commentators miss. Nevertheless, British politicians and senior military officials were understandably uncomfortable with the prospects of conducting a week-long amphibious assault without an assured level of control of the air.

During the War Cabinet meeting on 18 May, the Service Chiefs shared a unified view on the necessity of the proposed landings.[14] Along with his fellow Service Chiefs, Air Chief Marshal Sir Michael Beetham 'was in full support of an immediate landing.'[15] However, and along with the Permanent Under-Secretary, Sir Frank Cooper, Beetham was concerned about the 'weakness of the air defence of our ships.'[16] Moreover, Beetham acknowledged the risk that the Argentine air force remained a viable organisation and to expect losses.[17] His naval counterpart, Admiral Sir Henry Leach, was also worried about the lack of air superiority but judged it to be an acceptable risk.[18] Fieldhouse had also previously expressed concerns regarding 'the limitations of the Sea Harrier in air combat at low levels.'[19] Nevertheless, time was pressing. Applying further pressure to the situation was the rapidly approaching austral winter and the embarked amphibious assault force that had already spent two weeks at sea with minimal training opportunities. Consequently, at 1145 on 18 May, 'the authority to execute Operation Sutton was given by the Chief of Defence Staff.'[20]

With their land forces fixed in static defences around the vital ground of Stanley and the fleet confined to territorial waters, air power was the sole mechanism available to the Argentines to counter the British amphibious assault. The ambivalent attitude of the Argentine maritime and land components during the amphibious assault was in sharp contrast to that of the Argentine air services. Indeed, Margaret Thatcher commented that 'enthusiasm for a fight turned out to be in inverse proportion to fighting spirit.'[21] This lack of coherency between the Argentine armed forces did not augur well for joint operations in the next and key phase of the campaign. Reflecting on the importance of the impending step was the level of effort expended by the Argentines. Indeed, and as shown at Annex A, the Argentine combat air response to the landings on 21 May produced its highest number of sorties for a single day during the whole campaign. However, could the Argentines turn their outputs into the desired outcomes?

Attack on Landing Platforms and troops
Troop Transports
Active Air Defence against aircraft and helicopters
Aerial coverage of air transport aircraft
Attack beachhead and/or columns of troops

Table 4A – *Fuerza Aérea Argentina* Combat Air Priorities.[22]

The *Fuerza Aérea Argentina* had planned its response to a potential British amphibious assault and articulated its aims and priorities for the use of its combat air assets as part of Operation Plan 2/82 – *Mantenimiento de la Soberania* as early as 7 April.[23] Moro suggested that the document stated that the priority targets were the landing craft and troops on the beach, with troop transports as a secondary priority.[24] As an alternative, and where intelligence on the location of targets was lacking, the Argentine operational plan gave formation leaders broad initiative to select targets as they emerged.[25] However, as shown in Table 4A, Operation Plan 2/82 stipulated five combat air priorities. Although Moro identified the first two elements, he failed to capture both control of the air requirements, the need to attack the beachhead area as well as troops breaking out from the landing area.

The effectiveness of the Operation Plan 2/82 would be in its thorough dissemination and the level of understanding by those executing the Operation Plan over a month later. However, as will be seen later, the *Comando de Aviación Naval* adopted its own unique targeting priorities that bore little similarity with those embraced by their air force counterparts.

Analysis of Rivas' work suggests that rather than reducing their combat air footprint in southern Argentina post the initial air battles, the Argentines were able to increase the number of their deployed combat air assets. By comparing Figure 4.1 and its equivalent in the previous chapter, it shows that despite the loss of seven aircraft and aircrew, Argentine combat air

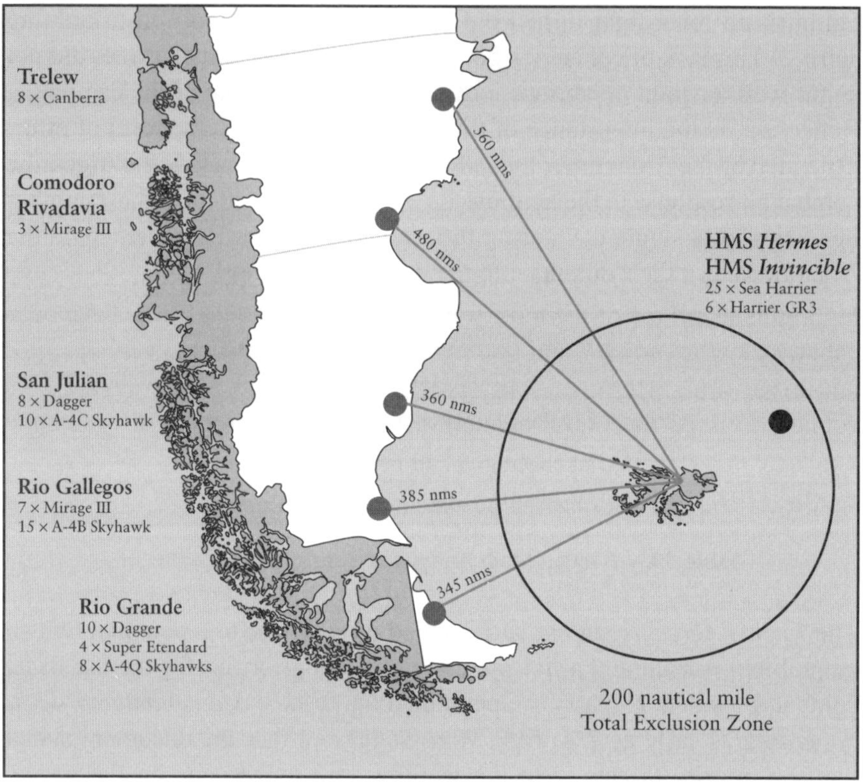

Figure 4.1 – Combat Air Participants at the start of Operation Sutton.

capability in southern Argentina increased from seventy to at least seventy-three aircraft.[26] The reason for the slow build-up and increase in capability was the time taken to bring long-term unserviceable aircraft up to operational readiness and deploy them to the airfields in southern Argentina. The net result was that Argentine air power had survived its *bautismo de fuego,* increased its force size, achieved some success, and frustrated British plans. It was all generated with relatively minor levels of effort.

Defining the British Operational Centre of Gravity during Operation Sutton

With the entry standards to Operation Sutton of both participants now understood, the next stage is to appreciate the constituent parts of the British operational centre of gravity during Operation Sutton – the amphibious force. The critical requirements, critical capabilities and critical vulnerabilities incorporated within Table 4B used Professor Strange's reviews of the United States Marine Corps Pacific Island campaigns during the Second World War.[27] Additionally, the book utilises contemporary British amphibious doctrine and applied military judgement to create a British operational centre of gravity analysis for Operation Sutton.

Comparison of Table 4B with the Argentine Operational Plan 2/82 highlights that three of the most important critical requirements have been captured by the primary and secondary target sets – troops, landing craft, and troop ships. However, there is an argument that the Argentine plan contained a superficial level of analysis as well as ambiguous direction and guidance to the tacticians that had to implement it.

With the British operational centre of gravity for Operation Sutton now outlined, it was now in the hands of the Argentine military to find and attack the British fleet that, if successful, would significantly contribute to the outcome of the Falklands Conflict. To quantify how effective the Argentines were in their quest to strike the British ships, there is a need to ascertain the vessels that constituted the amphibious force and their precious cargo. The British operational centre of gravity during Operation Sutton formed a fleet of twelve ships, as shown in Table 4C.[28] Seven Royal Navy destroyers and frigates protected the amphibious force during its approach to San Carlos as well as act as its last line of defence throughout the remainder of Operation Sutton.[29] With the British amphibious force structure, its contents, and defence now articulated, it is important to understand how the British intended to project their amphibious capability ashore. The plan saw the assault force come ashore in three waves. The first two waves contained the spearhead assault troops of 3 Commando Brigade bolstered by two battalions from the Parachute Regiment. Led by the Landing Platform Docks, HMS *Fearless* and *Intrepid,* smaller landing craft projected the troops ashore. During the second wave, the landing craft offloaded the assault troops from MV *Norland* and SS *Canberra*. Of note, the British completed the first two waves before Argentine air power could respond to the landing. However, with the assault troops ashore, the third wave was vulnerable to attack. The third and last wave included the fleet of Landing Ships Logistic vessels tasked to bring key enablers and supplies to sustain the force ashore. Of note, the third wave would also take significantly longer to disembark than the first two.

Centre of Gravity	**Critical Capabilities**
British Amphibious Force	1. The ability to select targets. 2. The ability to project power at range. 3. The ability to parry enemy threats en route to and in the target area. 4. The ability to project power from ship to shore. 5. The ability to suppress/destroy enemy defensive firepower. 6. The ability to capture heavily defended objectives.
Critical Vulnerabilities	**Critical Requirements**
1.1.1. Timely and accurate intelligence disseminated to and from decision-makers. 2.1.1. Sufficient assault ships available. 3.1.1. Persistent and effective Sea Harrier capability. 3.1.2. Effective ground-based air defence. 3.1.3. Robust maritime force air defence. 3.1.4. An enduring aircraft carrier capability. 3.2.1. Sustainable anti-surface/ submarine warfare capability. 4.1.1. Landing craft availability. 4.2.1. Sufficient landing craft crews. 4.3.1. A capable land combat force in sufficient strength. 5.1.1. Frigate and Destroyer availability. 5.2.1. Timely and accurate response from the Harrier GR3 force. 6.1.1. Rapid and sustainable distribution capability. 6.2.1. Sufficient support helicopters.	1.1. Intelligence on enemy capability and intent. 2.1. Long-range troop ships. 3.1. Control of the air in the area of interest. 3.2. Sea control in the area of interest. 4.1. Sufficient, suitable landing craft. 4.2. Trained landing craft crews. 4.3. Trained assault troops in sufficient strength. 5.1. Naval Gunfire Support. 5.2. Close Air Support. 6.1. Ship-to-shore logistical support. 6.2. Rapid manoeuvre capability.

Table 4B – British Operational Centre of Gravity during Operation Sutton.

Commodore Mike Clapp, Commander Amphibious Warfare and the individual responsible for the planning and execution of the amphibious landing, intended to offload the third wave as quickly as possible to minimise their exposure to Argentine air power. His view was 'that one bomb into a logistics ship could ruin thousands of tons, whilst one bomb into a dispersed Beach Support Area would have less of an adverse effect.'[30] Indeed, the design of the five Landing Ships Logistic bore this concept in mind. The ships 'could land equipment and vehicles directly on to beaches through a bow door.'[31] However, only one of the Landing Ship Logistic Masters had ever carried out a beach landing, and the crews lacked recent practice in this type of offload.[32] As a result, the unloading of supplies would be slower than anticipated and complicated even further as the ships had higher priority items stowed, incorrectly, to facilitate a bow discharge directly onto the beaches.[33]

The intent was to provide the land component with two days of supplies ashore and create a floating supply base within San Carlos. At the beachhead, two Landing Ships Logistic, RFAs *Sir Galahad* and *Sir Percivale* would be configured 'with two days of supplies for the brigade, consisting mainly of ammunition, packed fuel and rations. Another four days of supply would be on [RFA] *Stromness*, with sixteen additional days on [MV] *Elk*. These two ships would keep reserve supplies available at the edge of the Total Exclusion Zone for re-stocking [Landing Ships Logistic] as required.'[34] Consequently, after the initial assault, the plan was to have supplies distributed between the beachhead, afloat in the Amphibious Operating Area, and in bulk at the edge of the Total Exclusion Zone. The plan mitigated the threat of having a single large stockpile of stores ashore that could be easily targeted and negated by a successful Argentine attack. Moreover, the idea meant that supplies could be fed into the landing area quickly and when required.

The plan suggested that it would take two days to get immediately required stores ashore, and seven to eight days to complete the amphibious assault.[36] However, several factors affected the timing of the offload. The Landing Ships Logistic resupply run to MV *Elk* on the edge of the Total Exclusion Zone would take twenty hours to complete the transit one-way. Moreover, the Masters of the slow-moving ships preferred to transit at night to minimise their exposure to an air attack.[37] Following concerns over the vulnerability of ships in San Carlos, Fieldhouse directed that SS *Canberra*, MV *Norland*, and RFA *Stromness* sail towards the safer waters outside of the Total Exclusion Zone on the evening of 21 May.[38] Although a prudent measure, the ships sailed with significant supplies remaining on board. For example, the SS

Ship	Role	Embarked Force
HMS *Fearless*	Landing Platform Dock	Headquarters 3 Commando Brigade 3 Commando Brigade Signal Squadron 3 Commando Brigade Air Squadron D Squadron, 22 Special Air Service RL Detachment, 30 Signal Regiment 47 Air Despatch Squadron, Royal Corps of Transport Air Defence Troop, Royal Marines Y Troop, Royal Marines RAF Special Forces Detachment 8 Commando Battery 40 Commando
HMS *Intrepid*		3rd Battalion, The Parachute Regiment
RFA *Sir Galahad*	Landing Ship Logistic	59 Commando Engineer Regiment First Raiding Squadron Landing Ship Logistics Detachment Echelons of 3 Commando Brigade Signals Squadron
RFA *Sir Geraint*		T Battery, 12 Air Defence Regiment, Royal Artillery 29 Commando Regiment Air Maintenance Group Landing Ship Logistics Detachment
RFA *Sir Lancelot*		Commando Logistics Regiment Landing Ship Logistics/Mexeflote Detachment
RFA *Sir Percivale*		Headquarters Company 45 Commando 7 Commando Battery, Royal Artillery 8 Commando Battery, Royal Artillery Landing Ship Logistics/Mexeflote Detachment
RFA *Sir Tristram*		X and Y Company, 45 Commando Elements of Headquarters Company 45 Commando Landing Ship Logistics/Mexeflote Detachment
RFA *Stromness*	Fleet Stores Ship	45 Commando 3 Special Boat Squadron Echelons of 3 Commando Brigade Signals Squadron
RFA *Fort Austin*	Fleet Replenishment Ship	Anti-Submarine Role with embarked Sea Kings.

Ship	Role	Embarked Force
SS *Canberra*	Ships Taken Up From Trade	42 Commando
MV *Europic Ferry*		29 Battery, Royal Artillery
MV *Norland*		2nd Battalion, The Parachute Regiment

Table 4C – British Amphibious Force Composition.[35]

Canberra contained 90,000 rations, enough to feed the Brigade for eighteen days.[39] Ultimately, the supply ships were always planned to be present in the landing area throughout the period of the assault and vulnerable to attack, particularly in the first few days of the amphibious assault. However, would Argentine air power be able to exploit this opportunity?

Most commentators limit their analysis of Operation Sutton to looking at activities starting on the morning of 21 May. However, as stated previously, Operation Sutton began at 0900 on 20 May.[40] The first detection of the amphibious force by the Argentine forces occurred 26.5 hours after it set sail and by a ground patrol near the landings. Consequently, after several false alarms, the mainland-based Argentine air commander realised that the amphibious assault was underway at San Carlos. The first Argentine strikes from the mainland left Rio Grande at 1225 and entered the [Falkland] Sound near Swan Island at 1325 – six hours after the initial landings and over twenty-eight hours since the start of the operation.[41] Argentine intelligence assets failed to detect the amphibious assault force and cue Argentine strike assets to attack the British when they were most vulnerable.

As a result of failing to deploy a timely and useful intelligence, surveillance and reconnaissance capability that could find and track the amphibious assault force, the Argentines were unable to send their most capable asset, the Exocet-armed Super Etendards, to strike the amphibious force in open and the most vulnerable of waters. Moreover, by failing to understand their local environment, the Argentines handed the British twenty-eight hours of advantage and allowed them to progress unmolested to the intended landing area. Thus, the British were able to exploit freedom of manoeuvre in all three environments, maintain their initiative, and dictate the tempo of future operations.

By failing to understand British intentions, the Argentines doomed themselves to a reactive strategy dictated by British decisions for the remainder of the campaign – all for the sake of a useful intelligence gathering capability. The causal factor behind this situation links back to the 1969 decision to give 'exclusive jurisdiction to defend Argentina from sea attack to the Navy.'[42] Therefore, intelligence gathering at sea was a naval task, and the air force 'was specifically prohibited from developing or acquiring any capability suitable for operations over sea.'[43] This decision would have wide-ranging implications for the campaign, particularly the air force's ability to strike maritime targets successfully. However, the retirement of the two remaining P-2 Neptunes meant that the task fell to the much smaller and shorter-range S-2E Tracker, a carrier-based intelligence-gathering asset. After the Argentine aircraft carrier withdrew from the campaign in early May, 'five of its S-2E Trackers deployed to Rio Gallegos in order to continue reconnaissance and anti-submarine duties.'[44] The Trackers flew three missions on 20 May and were operating to the north-west of the Falkland Islands. However, their only success was on one of the missions when they achieved intercepts of British fleet radar emissions, but there was no radar detection of the fleet due to the Tracker's limited range.[45]

Of note, and to enhance their intelligence capability, Brazil supplied two Embraer EMB-111A Banderiante patrol aircraft to *Comando de Aviación Naval* in early May. Although they had greater range than the Tracker, the Banderiante was limited to a fleet of two aircraft, with minimal crew training, and flew its first mission on 22 May.[46] Therefore, the Banderiante capability arrived too late to inform or influence the outcome of Operation Sutton and 'provided no true substitute for the long-range mission profile of the Neptune.'[47] With the amphibious assault force taking a convoluted route to avoid detection from the ground-based radars at Stanley, the Argentines completely missed the opportunity to exploit the transit of the amphibious force. Consequently, the Argentines were now reliant on successfully striking the amphibious force as it landed ashore.

Operation Sutton Outputs

The Sea Dart-armed HMS *Invincible* initially escorted the amphibious force. However, the aircraft carrier peeled away from the amphibious assault group at 1415 on 20 May to return to the safer waters of the eastern Total Exclusion Zone.[48] Despite concerns regarding the location of the Argentine submarine ARA *San Luis*, the amphibious force's approach to San Carlos remained undetected and uncontested.[49] Due to a navigational error and a technical issue on board HMS *Fearless*, the lead vessel, the force arrived at its landing point at 0730 on 21 May, one hour later than the planned H-Hour.[50] Nevertheless, the last of the assault troops, the Third Battalion of the Parachute Regiment (3 PARA), landed at 1130.[51] The amphibious assault ships were arrayed around San Carlos Water and protected by the surrounding high ground. In contrast, the seven escort ships, and RFA *Fort Austin*, were located further west in the more open waters of Falkland Sound and acted as the inner defensive screen.[52] Three Sea Harrier combat air patrols were located up threat by a further fifty miles to act as the outer screen.[53] A further layer of defence was occasionally added by the British when a Type 42 destroyer operated to the north of the Islands. The Sea Dart-armed destroyer worked alongside a Type 22 frigate that acted as the destroyer's protector with its Sea Wolf short-range surface-to-air missile.

Although the British combat air assets were outnumbered by over three to one, as shown in Figure 4.1, they were able to deliver a significantly higher number of sorties than their opposition. Although the British aircraft operated much closer to their aircraft carriers than the four hundred nautical mile radius transits faced by their Argentine counterparts, this does not fully explain the quantum difference in outputs between the two forces. Nevertheless, and as shown in Annexes A and B, would the British near 250 per cent advantage in outputs over their foe during the period of Operation Sutton provide the British forces with the outcomes they desired?

Annex F articulates the various Argentine attacks of 21 May, the largest Argentine combat air contribution of the whole Conflict. In contrast, Annex G reviews the remaining period of Operation Sutton, 20 and 22-26 May. Both annexes look at the Argentine mainland-based combat air assets, their weapon load, and their ability to get their weapons from the planning stage, airborne, into the operating area, breach British defences and strike their intended targets successfully. One deliberate omission in the annexes is the missions that were planned but not flown due to weather constraints at the forward operating bases.

The weather has always been a significant constraint in military air operations. Moreover, the South Atlantic weather patterns can be unforgiving to the unwary aviator. Jorge Columbo, the commanding officer of the Super Etendard squadron in 1982, stated that 'May, June, July and even August are the worst months of the year in Rio Grande as far as flying is concerned: 90 per cent of the time it is cloudy, rainy, foggy and icy with a low or very low cloud base and visibility usually below one hundred feet or (at the best) a quarter of a mile, not to speak of strong cross winds that were always present in Rio Grande.'[54] Columbo's views, although limited to his own forward operating base at Rio Grande, provided a pessimistic view of the typical winter weather patterns that impact not only Patagonia but also the Falkland Islands and its surrounding waters. Southby-Tailyour provides an alternative perspective; he suggested that the weather in the Falkland Islands is akin to 'Dartmoor surrounded by the sea' or 'the Hebrides but sunnier and windier.'[55] Moreover, Southby-Tailyour highlighted that the wind was the 'single most dramatic difference' with the average wind speed over four times the British norm.[56] The weather was more demanding than the British faced at home and certainly more extreme than the Argentine aircrew encountered at their home bases in northern Argentina. The weather would have a significant influence on air operations throughout the campaign.

The British military analysis of the weather forecasts throughout Operation Sutton, as shown in Annexes A and B, suggested that apart from the morning of 25 May, the weather assessment was no worse than 'fair' for both participants.[57] However, although the British report is comprehensive, detailed, and covers the full campaign, it is, at times, optimistic in its assessment of the weather at the southern Argentine airfields. For example, Argentine air power employment on 22 May was particularly poor and had dropped from the previous day's high of seventy-two sorties down to a mere fourteen sorties.[58] An analysis of the British meteorological archive evidence would suggest that the weather in Southern Argentina was no worse than 'fair.' As a result, the deduction is that the causal factor for the poor performance of Argentine air power was not the weather. In contrast, Ethell, Burden, Rivas, Moro, and the *Fuerza Aérea Argentina* website all provided a significantly more pessimistic viewpoint and indicated that the weather was the driving factor behind the low level of activity on mainland airbases on 22 May.[59] A similar issue arose on 23 May, where weather hampered, but did not ground, mainland air operations.[60] However, beyond the disparities associated with mainland weather on 22 and 23 May, there is a general consensus that the weather was suitable for air operations for the majority of Operation Sutton.

The rationale for the lower quality weather assessments at the Argentine airfields traces back to the fact that British meteorologists had the benefit of actual weather observations to support their assessments of the weather over the Falkland Islands and the British fleet. In contrast, weather observations for the large number of Argentine airfields scattered over several hundred miles were not available. The net result is that the British assessment of the weather over Argentine airfields was less accurate than those stated for the Falkland Islands and British fleet. Consequently, with the weather factor and the need to preserve the force removed, deficits in the Argentines' ability to generate and deliver air power outputs were starting to materialise. Ultimately, the fast-moving and volatile weather systems in the South Atlantic did influence air activities but it was not the driver that some may have suggested. As a result, the Argentines averaged twenty-four sorties per day during Operation Sutton.

Although the British aircraft operated in the same volatile weather conditions as the Argentines, the weather impact on embarked Sea Harrier operations was less of a limitation to British air operations. Ward highlighted that the unique operating characteristics of the Sea Harrier aircraft allowed the aircraft to operate in conditions beyond conventional carrier-based aircraft capabilities.[61] In fact, despite the high tempo and rapidly changing weather systems, the Sea Harriers and Harrier GR3s increased their outputs from sixty-one sorties on 21 May to sixty-six the following day. They averaged fifty-seven sorties per day over the totality of Operation Sutton.[62] The average figure is all the more impressive, given that there was minimal flying conducted on 20 May to prepare the force for the upcoming surge in flying associated with protecting the amphibious assault.

Analysing the Outcomes of Operation Sutton

As shown in Figure 4.2, the data shows that of the planned 172 Argentine weapons on 21 May, not one struck any of the twelve amphibious assault ships that made up the British operational centre of gravity. Moreover, only 128 out of the planned 172 weapons (or 74 per cent) managed to get airborne from mainland Argentina. During the transit, weapon numbers reduced to seventy-three, equating to 42 per cent of the planned weapons and 57 per cent of those that made it airborne. Sixty-three weapons breached British defences (equating to 50 per cent of the successfully launched bombs and 87 per cent of the weapons that reached the Islands). In the target area, the Argentines employed forty-five weapons against the British warships with only eight hitting a target (5 per cent of the weapons planned, 6 per cent of the bombs that managed to get airborne and 18 per cent of those dropped).

Of the eight weapons that hit a target, four bombs (50 per cent) failed to detonate but caused significant damage to HMS *Antrim* and HMS *Argonaut*. Both warships were conducting escort duties in the northern approaches to the Falkland Sound and the mouth of San Carlos Water, respectively; a single bomb hit HMS *Antrim* while two weapons struck HMS *Argonaut*. The fourth unexploded bomb hit HMS *Ardent,* which was the most southerly of the escort ships. The ship was conducting naval gunfire support against Goose Green in support of Operation Tornado, the deception plan to mask the true location of the British landings. However, all four weapons that detonated struck HMS *Ardent*. With the loss of twenty-two sailors, HMS *Ardent* eventually succumbed to her mortal wounds and sank in the early hours of 22 May.[63]

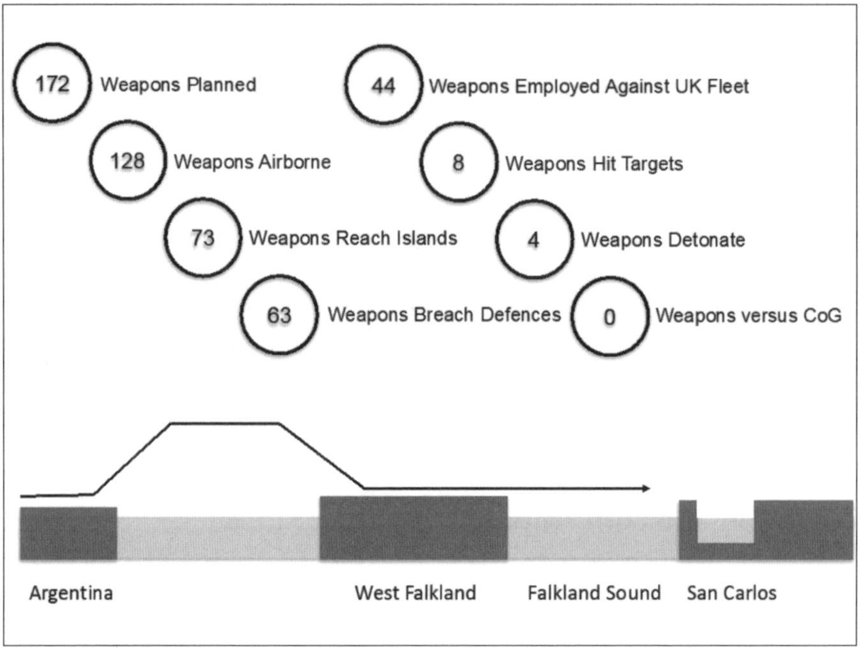

Figure 4.2 – The Utility of Argentine Weapons on 21 May.

While the Argentines dropped only one of every four bombs they planned, only one weapon in every eleven dropped struck and detonated against a target. Moreover, only one weapon in every forty-three struck and exploded against a British warship. The results associated with 21 May suggest that the perception that the Argentine pilot cadre was highly capable is questionable, if not a fallacy. From a British perspective, the initial analysis is no more gratifying.

Of the seventy-three bombs that arrived over the Falkland Islands during the initial landing period of Operation Sutton, sixty-three weapons managed to elude British defences. This figure equates to 87 per cent of the weapons that made it to the Islands evaded combat air patrols as well as negating maritime and land-based air defences. This figure notably contradicts Ward's perception that the Sea Harriers 'enjoyed command of the skies over the Islands.'[64] However, by solely focussing on 21 May, the most active day of Operation Sutton, it could be argued that the results are misleading. Moreover, the figures also ignore the possibility that performance could improve while in contact with the enemy, or captured the lessons from a high intensity and focused campaign conducted over an extended period. Consequently, Figure 4.3 shows the complete picture encompassing the period 20 - 26 May.

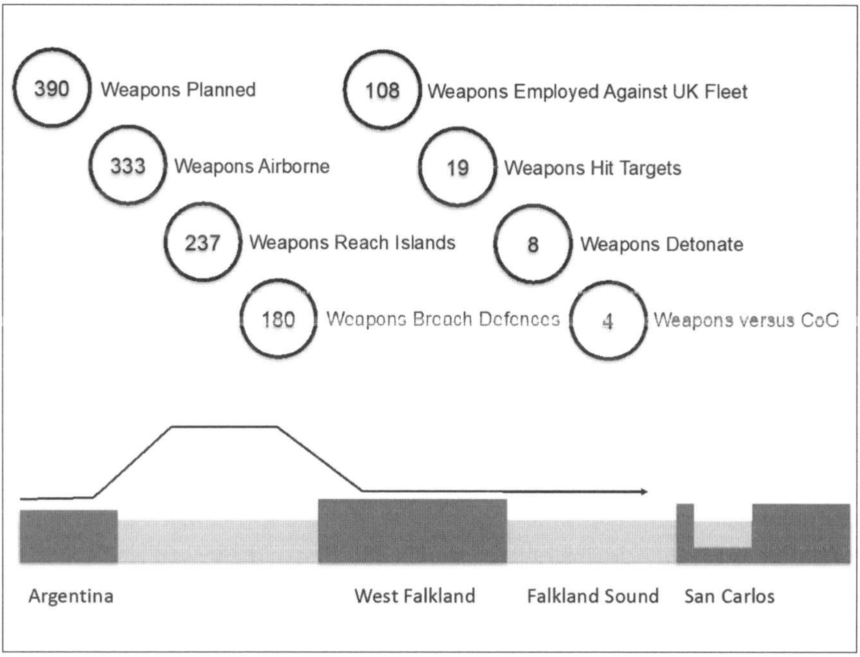

Figure 4.3 – The Utility of Argentine Weapons over the period 20–26 May.

In response to Operation Sutton, the Argentines managed to launch 333 out of the planned 390 weapons (or 85 per cent), an 11 per cent improvement over 21 May activities. The improved response is a reflection of a more effective and reliable command and control capability. Put simply, the 'fog of war' had now been removed, and the location of the amphibious assault was now common knowledge. Even so, and highlighting their lack of familiarity with the Falkland Islands, several Argentine attack formations were unable to find and attack targets in the days immediately following the amphibious assault.[65]

During the transit, weapon numbers reduced to 237, equating to 61 per cent of the planned weapons and 71 per cent of the successfully launched weapons (an improvement of 19 and 14 per cent respectively when compared with the same activities on 21 May). The improved performance is, again, a result of improved command and control – 180 weapons managed to breach the British defences (equating to 54 per cent, a minor improvement in comparison to 21 May, of those bombs that made it airborne and 76 per cent of the weapons that reached the Islands). In the target area, the Argentines employed 108 weapons against the fleet with only nineteen hitting the target (5 per cent of the weapons planned, 6 per cent of the bombs that managed to get airborne and 18 per cent of those dropped). These figures are, again, comparable with similar activities on 21 May. Of the nineteen weapons that hit targets, eleven bombs (57 per cent, compared with 50 per cent on 21 May) failed to detonate. Still, they caused damage to three of the Royal Fleet Auxiliary ships, which notionally constituted 25 per cent of the original British operational centre of gravity. By this stage, Operation Sutton was now four days old.[66] Therefore, it is perhaps not surprising that one of the two supply vessels attacked, 'had almost finished unloading.'[67] Nevertheless, it took time before the damaged ships were operationally capable again. As Freedman highlighted, 'it took [RFA *Sir*] *Galahad* until 28 May 1982 before it became fully operational while [RFA *Sir*] *Lancelot* was not ready until 7 June 1982.'[68]

During Operation Sutton, the Argentines planned to use a total of 390 weapons, with 21 May accounting for 44 per cent of their activity. Of note, not one of the weapons was able to destroy a member of the initial amphibious assault force. However, and in addition to the loss of HMS *Ardent* on 21 May, Argentine air attacks accounted for the loss of HMS *Antelope*, *Coventry*, and MV *Atlantic Conveyor*. The common perception of the British landings was that it was a simple battle of attrition, where Argentine combat air losses balance against British shipping losses. In many respects, the perception is correct – the Argentines lost nineteen mainland-based aircraft during the period of Operation Sutton, whereas the British lost four ships with several other ships damaged. The loss of the Royal Navy ships and members of the ship's company, while damaging to the British effort, was not significant in the overall campaign as the Royal Navy had sufficient resilience to have all three warships replaced. However, by merely measuring outputs without recourse to the outcomes delivered can lead to a skewed perspective of the Operation. For example, the loss of MV *Atlantic Conveyor* did have consequences in the broader campaign's prosecution. Although the intended target was one of the British aircraft carriers, effective countermeasures defeated the Exocet. However, the decoyed missile was able to re-acquire another large surface target. It struck MV *Atlantic Conveyor*, loaded with 'six Wessex, one Lynx and three Chinook helicopters, tents for five thousand troops and the material to build a mobile airstrip for the Harriers.'[69]

Indeed, the loss of MV *Atlantic Conveyor* was, arguably, the most significant British loss during Operation Sutton, if not the whole campaign. Twelve personnel, including the ship's Master, were killed in the Exocet attack, and the material loss had a significant impact on the British scheme of manoeuvre.[70] So much so, some Argentine commentators have suggested that MV *Atlantic Conveyor*, rather than an aircraft carrier, was the intended target.[71] From a British point of view, the loss of the helicopters, one of the critical requirements, meant that British commanders had to adapt their plan for the breakout from San Carlos.[72]

So, are the Argentine air operations of 21 May reflective of the broader Operation Sutton timeframe? Barring the issue regarding ineffective command and control on 21 May, there appears to be a general similarity in Argentine success rates over the two periods. Having mapped the various journeys of Argentine weapons, the next section will review and analyse the causal factors that influenced the prosecution of Argentine air power.

As shown, the vast majority of Argentine weapons were able to breach British defences. Therefore, was the Sea Harrier the scourge of the Argentines as many analysts suggest? Ward argued that the platform was so successful that it gained the '*Muerte Negra*' nick name.[73] In contrast, Rivas suggested that the British misinterpreted the Argentine communications, and the Argentines referred to the Sea Harrier by the significantly less endearing sobriquet of '*Los Moscardones* (the botflies).'[74] By articulating the causes and their relative importance in the prosecution of the Argentine attack of the British amphibious force addresses the dichotomy of views.

Ranking	Causal Factor	Scale (out of 390)	Percentage
1	Mission Cancelled	91	23
2	Weapon Employment – Missed Target	88	23
=3	Serviceability – Air Abort	52	13
=3	Weapon Employment – No Drop	52	13
5	Navigation Errors	21	5
6	Serviceability – Weapon Employment	20	5
7	Serviceability – Ground Abort	13	3
8	Sea Harrier – Hard Kill	12	3
=9	Sea Harrier – Soft Kill	11	3
=9	Weapon Employment – Unexploded Bomb	11	3
11	Weapon Employment – Hit and Detonates	8	2
12	Ground-Based Air Defence – Soft Kill	7	2
13	Target Mis-Identified	3	<1
14	Maritime Force Air Defence – Hard Kill	1	<1
	Total	390	100

Table 4D – Causal Factors for Failure to Deliver Weapons during Operation Sutton.

Analysis of Table 4D shows that the top five causal factors for the Argentines failing to deliver the required effects against the British operational centre of gravity are: weapons that missed their intended target, missions cancelled during execution, aircraft serviceability, failure to drop their weapons and serviceability issues when endeavouring to drop the weapon. Of note, two notable attributes are missing from the leading five causes – the Sea Harrier and unexploded bombs. Both characteristics are commonly associated with British success and Argentine failure during the Conflict. However, the Sea Harrier capability, generated by combining both Sea Harrier 'hard' and 'soft' kills, would reside in fifth position on the list with a score of twenty-three (or 6 per cent). As for the unexploded bombs, it is the joint ninth most influential factor with a score of eleven. Next, the book will review the top five causes in priority order.

The most significant factor for the failed use of Argentine weapons is the cancellation of attack missions. Although the analysis discarded pre-take-off weather cancellations, evidence shows that cancelled missions accounted for ninety-one (or 23 per cent) of the total Operation Sutton weapons. Of note, the two platforms that could carry the most significant number of weapons, the Canberra and A-4Q Skyhawk, accounted for eighty-eight of the ninety-one weapons that suffered due to mission cancellations. Moreover, all of the mission cancellations occurred on 21 May, the first and most significant day of combat operations.

The mission cancellations highlight the confusion in the Argentine command and control function regarding the location of the British amphibious assault and the priority targets. The source of the 'fog of war' can not only be traced to the lack of effective intelligence, surveillance and reconnaissance assets to detect and track the British fleet, but also to the distinct lack of jointery between the Argentine Services. This inter-Service enmity percolated down to the operational level where joint planning was the responsibility of an organisation colloquially known as the 'Pantheon,' a perceived retirement home for senior officers who were not competitive for further promotion but too young to be retired.[75] As a result, the endorsed plan appeared to lack credibility with the individual Services. During the Conflict, the deployed *Fuerza Aérea Argentina* assets were commanded by the *Fuerza Aérea Sur* at Comodoro Rivadavia, located closer to San Carlos than it was to its *Comando de Aviación Naval* counterpart at Rio Grande. Despite repeated requests from the *Fuerza Aérea Argentina*, there would be no co-located air component headquarters. The lack of unity of effort and command subsequently compromised the flow of information.

Following the attacks of 1 May, Argentine air power outputs were meagre as they were prudently preserving its force until the critical British assault on the Falkland Islands took place. Moreover, the Argentine Operation Plan 2/82, which was written six weeks before Operation Sutton, was distributed to all units, but it was either misunderstood or ignored. Even the *Fuerza Aérea Argentina* official history fails to capture all five of the priority tasks correctly.[76] At the tactical level, the confusion was evident. One captured A-4 Skyhawk pilot informed his hosts that he had been 'specifically ordered to attack the warships.'[77] In contrast, and on 21 May, the tasking for the other *Fuerza Aérea Argentina* Skyhawk unit was to 'execute bomb and gun attacks on landing ships and transport vehicles, and on warships as second [priority].'[78] Another pilot from the same Skyhawk unit, Ernesto Ruben Ureta, noted that his attack priorities were: aircraft carriers, logistical support (aircraft and ships), ships close to land, other aircraft/helicopters and warships.[79]

From an Argentina *Armada* perspective, its operational directive stipulated a generic and broad naval mission and execution for all of its units. Consequently, it failed to identify specific target priorities for its air arm.[80] However, the *Comando de Aviación Naval* articulated its targeting priorities in the lower level document – *Plan de Operaciones de la Fuerza de Tareas 80.* The *Comando de Aviación Naval* was required to neutralize the amphibious assault capacity of the enemy naval force; priority targets included aircraft carriers, transport, and logistics vessels as well as missile-equipped vessels.[81] Nevertheless, at the tactical level, the *Comando de Aviación Naval* pilots believed that their priority was a straightforward one. One A-4Q Skyhawk pilot informed that 'our primary objective was to look for the aircraft carriers, of course.'[82] Ultimately, none of the Argentine operators' views accurately reflected the Argentine operational plans. Consequently, confusion reigned, and Argentine air power lacked the required focus to be truly useful. To some British observers, it appeared 'that no clear aim had been given to the attacking pilots, except (with very limited time) to engage the first target they saw.'[83] Freedman says that 'while conserving for [the Operation Sutton] battle, the Argentine Air Force did not appear to have planned for it.'[84] In contrast, it appeared that the operational plans existed, but there was inadequate coordination and poor communication between the operational and tactical levels. Moreover, the Argentines' continual desire to prosecute the British aircraft carriers highlighted that they were unable to comprehend the fluid and agile nature of the Conflict and the relative importance of the various targets as the campaign matured. Consequently, it is unsurprising that Argentine air power was unable to exploit its numerical advantage during the early and critical stages of Operation Sutton.

The second most influential factor affecting the delivery of Argentine weapons during Operation Sutton was weapons that were dropped but missed their intended target. With 23 per cent (or 88 of the 390 weapons planned) missing their intended targets, the Argentines were rueing its lack of investment in a precision capability.

Compounding the issue even further was the lack of exposure to the demands of anti-ship attack missions. With the *Fuerza Aérea Argentina* constitutionally restrained from conducting the maritime attack role, anti-shipping training conducted before Operation Corporate was of limited benefit in the restricted time available. Moreover, it may also account for the fact that 'many bombs hit the water aft of the ship suggesting that the Argentine pilots aimed for the middle of their targets without compensating for the vessel's forward speed.'[85] Compromising Argentine attacks were the limited training against a niche target set, the lack of precision weapons, and a contested battlespace that forced the Argentine pilots to employ their weapons from a less than ideal attack profile. Therefore, it is inevitable that a large number of Argentine weapons missed their intended targets.

The joint third most influential cause for the Argentine failure to deliver the required effect against the British amphibious force was aircraft serviceability rates and inability to drop weapons. When ground abort, air abort, and technical failures during weapon release are combined, it comprises fifty-two (or 13 per cent) of the 390 weapons planned during Operation Sutton. Three key factors influence this predicament: sanctions, ageing equipment, and the location of assets. The only new aircraft in the Argentine fast jet inventory was the Super Etendard, with the remainder consisting of ageing, second-hand, and increasingly obsolete British, American, French, and Israeli-manufactured aircraft. Due to human rights concerns during the Carter administration, the United States had imposed the 'Humphrey/Kennedy Amendment that involved an embargo on the sale of warlike equipment to Argentina.'[86] The sanctions affected all three Skyhawk variants used by the *Fuerza Aérea Argentina* and the *Comando de Aviación Naval*. A US embargo on new deliveries and spare parts initially stalled the Argentine aspiration to procure a fourth tranche of twenty-nine A-4B Skyhawks and thirty-two additional J65 engines in the late 1970s and early 1980s.[87]

The thawing of American and Argentine diplomatic relations during the early days of the Reagan presidency raised new hope. However, the outbreak of hostilities quickly quashed the burgeoning relationship, much to the surprise of the Argentines. Indeed, the procurement of United States-supplied A-4 Skyhawk engines received British Prime Ministerial attention during the Conflict.[88] As a result, the lack of spares in the Skyhawk force had forced Argentina to manufacture its own spare parts for the aircraft. However, the indigenously produced components were 'blamed for two known Argentine Air Force A-4 Skyhawk losses in late 1981.'[89]

The sanctions meant that the A-4 Skyhawk force was constrained to using 'time expired ejection seat rocket boosters.'[90] Consequently, the fatality rate amongst A-4 Skyhawk pilots ejecting from their aircraft was significantly higher than that of their more modern and Israeli-supported Dagger compatriots. The aircraft's weapon system was also affected by the weapons embargo; the twin 20mm cannons fitted to the A-4 Skyhawks suffered from a '12 per cent probability of working properly without jamming.'[91] Ongoing financial constraints meant a reduced A-4 Skyhawk availability rate, which manifested itself as limited flying hours for the pilots.[92] The parlous state of the A-4 Skyhawk capability is at odds with Fursden's view that 'the Argentines certainly did not lose the war because of bad equipment.'[93]

Although not assisted by its late introduction into the Operation *Azul*/*Rosario* plans, the *Fuerza Area Argentina* was reliant on external support to maintain its capability. With aircraft sourced from several nations, the Argentines needed assured access to spare parts and weapons to sustain their outputs. While the United States continued their embargo, Argentina's neighbour, Peru, provided Mirage fuel tanks and eventually a squadron of Mirage Vs to offset the Dagger attrition.[94] Likewise, Libya provided additional missiles and other spares that were delivered by *Fuerza Aérea Argentina* Boeing 707 during the Conflict.[95] Despite extensive lobbying from the British, 'there was an overwhelming amount of evidence that the Israeli government was involved in arms negotiations with Argentina throughout the crisis.'[96] The Israeli position perhaps was not a surprise as 'Israel's Prime Minister, Menachem Begin [was] a known Anglo-phobe.'[97] Consequently, Israel delivered fuel tanks and fuses to the Argentines.[98] Nevertheless, the British were more successful in securing French support against military sales to Argentina, in particular the access to the remaining five Exocets ordered before the Conflict.[99] President Francois Mitterand's 'staunch' support throughout the campaign particularly pleased Margaret Thatcher.[100] The lack of assured access to a sustainable capability compromised Argentina's ability to deliver outputs and outcomes. Therefore, one of the major lessons of the Conflict is the need to maintain operational sovereignty of your own capabilities.

In equal third position, also accounting for fifty-two (or 13 per cent) of the 390 weapons, serviceable aircraft breached the British defences and arrived in the target area, but for reasons other than a technical failure, they were unable to drop their weapons. Factors affecting the prosecution of the target include poor target selection during the planning phase or the inability to positively identify the target. The first issue harks back to understanding what constitutes the enemy's centre of gravity. Once recognised, the attacking force's full weight should focus on striking the centre of gravity. However, any ambiguity or misunderstanding of what constitutes the critical target set will lead to the attacking force hitting targets with limited or no connection to the centre of gravity. The Argentine attacks on suspected, but spurious, radar sites and troop concentrations located a significant distance away from the amphibious landing areas are an excellent example of their confusion over what constituted the critical targets.[101] The second issue highlights the fact that the Argentines were a day, good weather attack force. Due to a lack of sensors, either on board the attacking aircraft or carried by a supporting intelligence, surveillance, and reconnaissance asset, the ability to prosecute a target at night or in poor weather was extremely limited. The key lessons here are to understand and strike the enemy's centre of gravity, use the enabling air power assets to cue the attacking force into the target area, and then use the attacking aircraft's on board sensors to refine the attack further to deliver a precision strike capability.

In fifth place were the twenty-one (or 5 per cent) of the 390 weapons that failed to make it to their intended target due to navigation errors. Despite the use of the Fenix Squadron communications aircraft to act as pathfinders for the attack aircraft, several occasions remained when the Argentines could not find the target area, their designated tanker, or pathfinder aircraft.[102] As a result, navigation errors forced the Argentines to abort several missions. The vast majority of Argentine attack aircraft were simple platforms that lacked the required precision navigation systems or sensors required to find, intercept, and fly alongside other aircraft in poor weather conditions. Although some aircraft received modifications to carry the Omega navigation system, it was not a fleet-wide embodiment.[103] In terms of lessons, future capabilities must be equipped and trained to function in all of its intended operating environments.

Comparing the causal factors during Operation Sutton with the period 1 – 19 May shows that four out of the five major causal factors are common between both phases. Air aborts, cancelled missions, weapons missing their intended targets and not dropping the weapon are included in both lists as the key causal factors. However, the Sea Harrier's influence on the Argentine pilots' ability to employ their weapons successfully waned during Operation Sutton. After a strong showing in the first phase of Operation Corporate, the Sea Harrier's performance dropped from a respectable second place down to joint seventh during Operation Sutton. The Sea Harrier's actual performance questions Ward's assertion that 'air superiority was achieved' during the Conflict.[104] Consequently, weapon serviceability replaces the Sea Harrier in the top five most influential factors during Operation Sutton. The high tempo of operations and an increase in the number of Argentine weapons appears to be applying pressure to the Argentine's ability to sustain their force. However, as the campaign approached its culminating phase, would these trends continue?

With a bridgehead secured on East Falkland as well as the move of 2 PARA from Sussex Mountains towards Goose Green, Operation Sutton culminated on 26 May.[105] As a result, Argentina's fleeting opportunity to strike the concentrated British military force located in and around San Carlos closed. Following the successful completion of the amphibious assault, the British aspiration to achieve their desired end-state of repossessing the Islands was becoming increasingly viable. However, the lack of air manoeuvre capability, the austral winter, and a larger enemy force sitting in wait on the high ground in prepared defensive positions around Stanley meant that Operation Corporate's outcome was by no means assured. The next chapter reviews both participants' prosecution of the concluding phase of the campaign.

Chapter 5

Air Power Post-Operation Sutton – Stanley or Bust!

'We'll have to bloody well walk!'

Lieutenant Colonel Andrew Whitehead, Royal Marines
Commanding Officer 45 Commando
25 May.[1]

At the conclusion of Operation Sutton, 5500 British military personnel were now ashore at San Carlos.[2] During the period of the assault, the British lost one destroyer and two frigates from their outer ring of defences with several others damaged. Critically, Argentine air power failed to penetrate the British inner sanctum, where the landing ships were offloading the spearhead forces and critical support infrastructure, early enough in the operation or with sufficient conviction. However, the loss of MV *Atlantic Conveyor* in the latter stages of Operation Sutton with its cargo of helicopters adversely impacted the tempo of the last phase of Operation Corporate – the British advance to Stanley. The amphibious assault location was forty-five nautical miles west of Stanley, and the British planners knew that as they were 'at the end of a long logistics pipeline, the force could not afford to get bogged down in protracted operations. The only prudent course is to plan for a short, sharp, decisive campaign.'[3] Devoid of the necessary helicopters to move their force rapidly towards Stanley, the British troops faced a march across difficult terrain, made all the more arduous when burdened with carrying their own equipment and a quickly approaching austral winter. Consequently, could Argentine air power influence the outcome of the final phase of the Conflict?

With the perception that political pressure was building in Britain to break out from the beachhead at the earliest opportunity, the senior military leaders sought a quick win. Consequently, Admiral Fieldhouse ordered Brigadier Thompson 'to re-activate the Goose Green raid and move out of San Carlos.'[4] Thompson faced the dilemma of meeting his superiors' demands that 'more action was required all round' while balancing these needs against the backdrop of a new superior who was incommunicado.[5] The Commander Land Forces Falkland Islands, Major General Jeremy Moore, was still travelling to the South Atlantic and had not yet released his plans for Stanley's future investment. Concurrently, Thompson had to deal with the need to build sufficient resilience ashore and generating contingency plans to mitigate the helicopter deficit. This idea was succinctly articulated by a command team member, as noted in the introduction to this chapter.

Although Thompson was responsible for the amphibious assault and securing the beachhead, he was not responsible for the planning or execution of the remainder of the land campaign. Thompson had been directed by Moore on 12 May to 'push forward from the bridgehead area so far as the maintenance of its security allows, to gain information, to establish moral and physical domination over the enemy, and to forward the ultimate objective of repossession.'[6] His remit and available forces constrained Thompson's offensive options. Consequently, the task of planning and executing the repossession of the Falkland Islands fell to Moore. However, at the start of the third and final phase, Moore was still with the 3000 men of 5 Infantry Brigade on board SS *Queen Elizabeth II*. Moreover, the recently and rapidly installed secure satellite communication suite on board *SS Queen Elizabeth II* was ineffective.[7] As a result, communication between Moore and Thompson was limited and meant that understanding any emerging ideas and issues was problematic. To build connections with his new command team as quickly as possible, Moore transferred from SS *Queen Elizabeth II* to HMS *Fearless* on 29 May, via a 2-day stint on board HMS *Antrim*. Moore subsequently took control of the land battle on 30 May.[8]

To reduce the exposure of the luxury liner to enemy action, the follow-on British forces would transfer from SS *Queen Elizabeth II*. SS *Canberra*, MV *Norland*, and RFA *Stromness* received their new passengers in the safer waters at South Georgia before depositing them at San Carlos over the period 31 May to 2 June.[9] As a result, there was an apparent hiatus in British land operations that led to further exposure of troops and equipment to air attack at San Carlos. The frustration over the lack of progress while subject to air attack was palpable amongst the ground troops at the beachhead. Lieutenant Colonel Nick Vaux, the Commanding Officer of 42 Commando, commented that 'the only time morale became a worry was when we waited impatiently for the breakout at San Carlos.'[10] With the land forces in varying degrees of disorder, what was the condition of both British and Argentine combatants at the start of the Conflict's last phase?

The Key Participants Post-Operation Sutton

As with the previous phase, the Argentine navy's input during the last part of the Conflict was minimal. The major Argentine surface vessels remained within territorial waters and played no role in the remainder of the Conflict. However, the Royal Navy was unable to locate the Argentine submarine force. As a result, the Royal Navy maintained the high tempo and focus of anti-submarine warfare for the remainder of the campaign. Despite the Royal Navy's anti-submarine warfare expertise, honed by years of competition against the Soviets, the British were unable to find or fix the Argentine submarine capability. However, it was not for the lack of effort. The deployed anti-submarine force of twenty Sea King helicopters flew a near-constant three aircraft anti-submarine screen. The Sea Kings flew an impressive total of 2,253 flying hours during Operation Corporate.[11] When coupled with the surface fleet contribution to the anti-submarine role, the effort was considerable. However, the lack of a persistent maritime patrol aircraft capability was notable from an air power perspective. The Ascension Island-based Nimrod maritime reconnaissance aircraft had rapidly introduced an air-to-air refuelling capability to allow them to operate in the South Atlantic. Despite, flying 111 Operation Corporate-related missions, the Nimrod's influence on the anti-submarine, and for that matter the anti-surface, warfare battle was limited.[12]

Consequently, the small Argentine submarine force had the potential to cause significant damage to the British deployed force if the Argentine Naval commanders were so inclined. In reality, the Argentine submarine force comprised only three submarines. After the harrying by several Fleet Air Arm helicopters and ultimate scuttling of ARA *Sante Fe* at Grytviken in South Georgia on 25 April, the Argentine submarine force consisted of two modern, German-built boats that were fast and very quiet.[13] However, the torpedo armament of ARA *Salta* and *San Luis* was very unreliable.[14] Despite the Royal Navy's best efforts to deter the Argentine submarine threat, the Type 21 frigate HMS *Alacrity* was attacked, albeit unsuccessfully, by a torpedo fired from ARA *San Luis* during the Type 21 frigate's high speed run through the Falklands Sound before Operation Sutton on 11 May.[15]

The ARA *San Luis* returned to port immediately after the event. Moreover, the sole remaining Argentine submarine, ARA *Salta*, was reported to have 'experienced torpedo fire-control problems as well as noise problems and undertook no operational patrols' during the period of the Conflict.[16] Despite the minor activity levels of the Argentine submarines, the British maintained sea control for the remainder of the campaign. However, control of the air was by no means assured for the British as the *Fuerza Aérea Argentina*, and the *Comando de Aviación Naval* continued to play an active role in the campaign.

From a British perspective, their depth of defence capability was about to be tested and ably demonstrated. The loss of four frigates and destroyers, as well as damage to other ships, had been offset by the arrival of several replacement Royal Navy vessels from 21 May, including the destroyers HMS *Bristol*, HMS *Cardiff*, and HMS *Exeter,* as well as four Type 21 and three older Leander-class frigates.[17] However, the focus of the campaign had swung away from purely protecting the aircraft carriers and their ability to deliver control of the air as well as sea control. These enduring roles remained important, but they were enabling functions rather than drivers to support the continued logistics build-up on the Falkland Islands. These functions would be required to protect the ground force as it moved eastwards from San Carlos to Stanley. As a result, the aircraft carriers would remain a lucrative and relevant target for the remainder of the campaign. Consequently, the British aircraft carriers seized the attention of the Argentine senior leadership as well as their air arms. Nevertheless, and as discussed previously, the loss of an aircraft carrier in isolation during the last phase of the campaign was unlikely to have curtailed the British outcome. Reinforcing this point further was the small airstrip at San Carlos, capable of supporting Harrier operations, which was declared operational on 5 June.[18] As a result, there is an argument that as the campaign developed, there were more valuable British targets that would have yielded higher returns for the Argentines.

With 3 Commando Brigade now safely ashore, Commodore Mike Clapp's role as Commander Amphibious Warfare, was far from over. Although the frantic pace of operations during the amphibious assault had reduced, there was a continuous demand for stores into San Carlos to sustain the force ashore. Consequently, there was a continual flow on the British logistical supply chain that reached back to Britain and transited via Ascension Island, South Georgia and the Logistics Loitering Area, located at the edge of the Total Exclusion Zone, before heading to the beachhead at San Carlos. With Moore considering his options for moving and sustaining the force closer to Stanley, there was increased pressure on the limited number of logistic supply ships, landing craft, and support helicopters. With demand outweighing resources, tolerating risks proved necessary to meet the campaign needs. As the British troops could not rely upon helicopters to cover the difficult terrain between San Carlos and the high ground surrounding Stanley, the alternative solution to walk was a challenging prospect, but deliverable. However, airlifting the equipment that the troops could not carry was required due to the poor to non-existent road infrastructure. As a result, the lack of helicopters meant that lower priority items, such as personal equipment, was delayed and it took some time before reuniting rucksacks and spare rations with their owners.[19] Consequently, morale in the front-line troops diminished but, critically, was not destroyed. As an example, senior commanders offered their subordinates an option to retreat from their forward positions to provide their troops with respite. However, field commanders unanimously rejected the opportunity as they felt that this would have a detrimental effect on the troops.[20] The net result was that the supply platforms, equipment, and locations were all critical elements for supporting the British advance to Stanley. Therefore, from an Argentine air power perspective, the British amphibious fleet remained profitable targets for the remainder of the campaign. If Argentine air power had shut off or delayed the onward flow of troops and stores to the front line, the progress of the British ground forces towards Stanley could have been interrupted or even halted.

The arrival of 5 Infantry Brigade brought the British component on the island up to a strength of 8,500 personnel. Nevertheless, the Argentine land component still outnumbered its British counterparts. Freedman suggested that of the 13,000 Argentine military personnel garrisoned on the Falkland Islands, the Argentines positioned two of their eight Argentine regiments on West Falkland at Port Howard and Fox Bay with 1,000 personnel at each location.[21] Additionally, Freedman notes that the Argentine forces on West Falkland were 'effectively useless as they lacked the size, firepower, and mobility to cope with any British operation on West Falkland.'[22] With a garrison at Goose Green consisting of 1,007 military personnel, the remaining Argentine military personnel were located at Stanley and contained a bayonet-strength of between 5,000 and 6,000.[23] However, although the number of soldiers remained in favour of the Argentines, they were a mixed group of poorly trained and led conscripts supported by a small cadre of professional soldiers. Consequently, and despite opinions that the Argentines had many technical advantages and material comforts in comparison to their British opposition, Moore believed that 'the Argentinians lacked the "stomach" to fight in the "high, arid, bitterly cold area" beyond their outer defensive perimeter around Stanley.'[24] Moore's views reflected those made during the 22 April War Cabinet when a Deputy Chief Defence Staff (Intelligence) briefing suggested,

> 'This leads me to the crux – morale ... the environment is inhospitable, the weather harsh, the people unfriendly, living conditions primitive and food barely adequate. We now reckon 80 per cent are young – very young – conscripts ill prepared for the rigorous life they face. If reverses elsewhere are rammed home and if, above all, the garrison is subjected to a vigorous campaign of harassment – from the ground (by special forces) and from the air – its will to fight will be sapped. It will feel isolated and perhaps even abandoned.'[25]

Nevertheless, if the British were to achieve their objectives, they would have to break one of the basic tenets of defeating an enemy ground force. Prudent planning suggested that an attacking force should outnumber the defending force by a ratio of 3:1.[26] At best, the British had parity in numbers, but only if they were able to maintain their force size during the journey from San Carlos to Stanley. Therefore, the outnumbered British ground forces could not tolerate significant casualties en route to achieving their end-state. As a result, there was an opportunity for Argentine air power to enhance their land force's numerical advantage further. Even in the latter stages of the campaign, Argentine air power might have made a decisive contribution by finding and striking British fielded forces, their supporting equipment, and its logistics. It did not.

Moore finally clarified the British plan to move their land forces from San Carlos with the stated intent 'to secure Port Stanley' at 0415 on 1 June.[27] 3 Commando Brigade would take a northerly axis via Teal Inlet and Mount Kent, whereas 5 Infantry Brigade would take the southern approach via Fitzroy, Bluff Cove, and Mount Challenger. Both brigades would then contest the high ground to the west of Stanley before moving onto Stanley. However, the British held one of their eight land units in reserve at San Carlos – a disappointed 40 Commando had the unenviable task bestowed upon them. 45 Commando had started the move to Stanley several days earlier when at first light on 27 May, they departed Port San

Carlos on foot for Teal Inlet.[28] From a British viewpoint, the parallel lines of advance challenged an already stretched logistics chain. From an Argentine air power perspective, the dispersal of British land forces across two lines of approach meant that they would be increasingly difficult to find, identify, and strike. The lack of intelligence, surveillance, and reconnaissance aircraft, and an army focused on static defence with a limited probing capability meant that Argentine combat air assets would be attacking with limited, dated, or incorrect information on the British disposition. The Argentine attack aircraft would need to find, identify, and attack camouflaged, and concealed targets dispersed across East Falkland with limited assistance. With aged and basic platforms that lacked organic sensors to cue the aircraft onto targets and a lack of precision weapons to deliver the required effects, the already battered Argentine combat air assets faced a significant challenge. However, if the Argentines could locate and attack enemy troops or logistics, then the British operational tempo could be adversely affected.

From a British combat air perspective, they had lost one Sea Harrier and a single Harrier GR3 during Operation Sutton. As a result, they would approach the final phase of Operation Corporate with a force of twenty-four Sea Harriers and five Harrier GR3s, as shown in Figure 5.1. However, due to their high-risk, low-level attack missions, the number of Harrier GR3s routinely available for tasking suffered due to extensive battle damage and attrition. Nevertheless, and unlike their Sea Harrier counterparts, the Harrier GR3 force deployed further aircraft to sustain its attack capability. On 1 June, two replacement Harrier GR3s flew an eight and a half hour mission from Ascension Island to HMS *Hermes*, supported by Victor air-to-air refuelling aircraft.[29] The squadron conducted a similar mission a week later.[30] However, these missions were not without their detractors. The commanding officer of HMS *Hermes*, Captain Linley Middleton, believed that Operation Bowsprit, the Harrier GR3 replacement plan, was merely a 'publicity stunt by the RAF.'[31] Despite Middleton's reservations regarding the risk associated with the long over-sea transit, the missions went ahead. So, what benefit did the 'RAF publicity stunt' bring to the British campaign?

The four new aircraft not only allowed the Harrier GR3 output to increase but also introduced several new capabilities to the campaign. Following the successful completion of Trial Puritan, the aircraft now had clearance to use laser-guided bombs.[32] Additionally, an ALE-40 chaff and flare dispenser, as well as a self-protection radar jammer, were now available for use.[33] Also, as part of Trial Athene, one aircraft was modified to use the Shrike anti-radiation

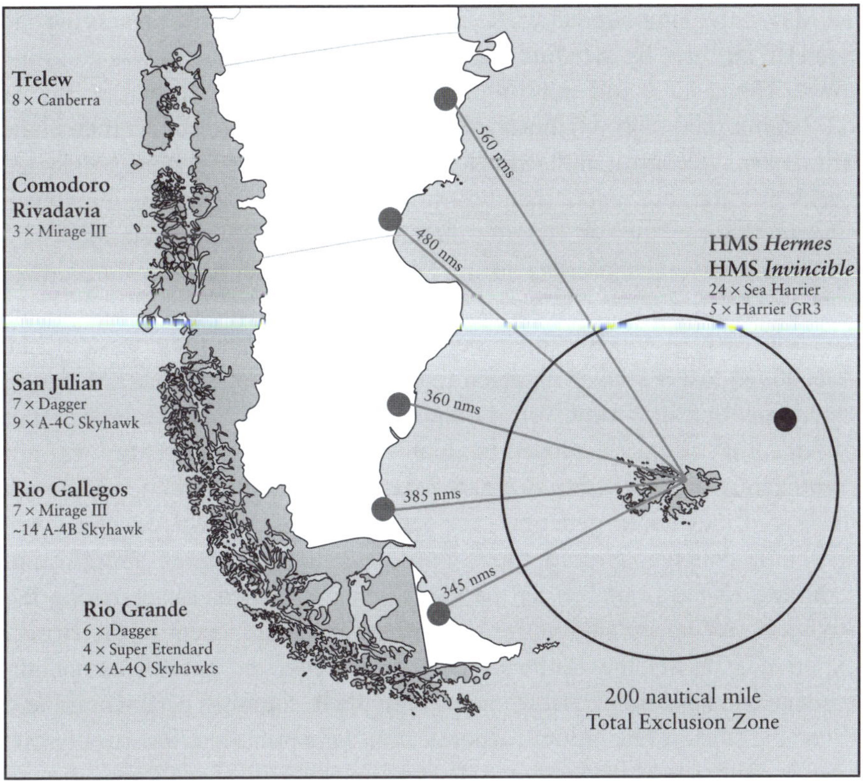

Figure 5.1 – Combat Air Participants Post-Operation Sutton.

missile, the same missile used on two of the Vulcan's Operation Black Buck missions.[34] Consequently, the British task force delivered a sustainable and enhanced attack capability throughout the remainder of the campaign. If the additional Harrier GR3s travelled solely by sea-based transport, the next opportunity for an increase in capability would be the arrival of MV *Contender Bezant*. However, the cargo ship and its consignment of a further four Harrier GR3s would not arrive until 14 June – the day of the Argentine surrender.[35] In parallel, 3 (Fighter) Squadron was identified as the follow-on replacement for 1 (Fighter) Squadron and, after some uncertainty, eventually commenced its deployment to the South Atlantic, post-Conflict, on 30 June with eight pilots and thirty-six engineers.[36]

In contrast to the Harrier GR3 force, the Sea Harriers were fully committed to the Falklands Conflict and had little spare capacity to generate fully trained manpower or equipment. The loss of one of the few Sea Harriers left in Britain on a test and evaluation sortie at Yeovilton on

17 May only compounded matters further.[37] Consequently, preserving the Sea Harrier force by avoiding the high-risk, low-level attacks was an astute move. The assured and enduring attack capability provided by the Harrier GR3 community allowed the smaller Sea Harrier force to concentrate on its primary role – control of the air. However, both Sea Harrier units conducted attack missions but predominantly from the safer confines of medium level. Chapter 7 covers the Sea Harriers' contribution to the attack role.

Despite several successes during Operation Sutton, Argentine air power was on the precipice of a rapid decline in capability. In addition to the seven aircraft lost in the three weeks before the amphibious assault, the Argentines lost a further nineteen mainland-based combat aircraft during Operation Sutton.[38] However, as shown in Figure 5.1, the total number of Argentine aircraft deployed in Southern Argentina on 27 May was not significantly different from that at the start of Operation Sutton.[39] Although the Argentines could generate replacement aircraft to replace shot down and battle-damaged aircraft, the resource was finite and fewer aircraft were returning to the front line as the campaign progressed. Exacerbating the Argentine air power situation even further, and reminiscent of the British experience during the Battle of Britain in 1940, the loss of campaign-hardened and experienced aircrew was rapidly becoming a pertinent issue.[40] Since the start of Operation Corporate, the Argentines had lost twenty-one aircrew. The Sea Harrier pilot fraternity, and typical of the global fighter community, was rife with black humour. One of its number suggested that any silent period could be described 'as quiet as a Mirage crew room.'[41] Ironically, the Sea Harrier pilot attributed with the comment was killed following a night take-off from the aircraft carrier during the latter stages of Operation Sutton.[42]

As the number of combat air platforms began to dwindle, the Argentines belatedly co-located their combat air assets. The remaining A-4B and A-4C Skyhawks merged into a single unit based at San Julian from 9 June.[43] In a similar timeframe, the surviving Daggers were brigaded together at Rio Gallegos.[44] However, there was no tangible benefit from the move as the campaign only had five days to run until the Argentine surrender. Moreover, the endeavours to simplify Argentine logistics and concentrate their combat air capabilities were limited to a single Service rather than an air component perspective. An earlier and joint perspective on co-located combat air operations could have benefitted the Argentines in the delivery of efficient air power.

The Argentine authorities reintroduced some of the perceived less capable aircraft in an attempt to offset the losses of the main Argentine attack assets. After a sabbatical that encompassed the period 4 - 20 May, the Canberra returned to combat operations. The initial raids on 1 May exposed the platform's vulnerability. Consequently, the temporary withdrawal from operations allowed the aircraft to focus on training for night attacks that included both low and medium-level attack options. However, of the eight aircraft in the fleet, only three aircraft were equipped with radar.[45] Without night vision goggles, forward-looking infra-red sensors, precision navigation systems, or fleet-wide embodiment of radar, the Canberra's new night attack capability was going to be, at best, a token effort. Despite the benefits of a large payload, the Canberra's outputs were of limited value. During the thirty-three Canberra missions planned during the last and the most intensive phase of Operation Corporate, the Canberra planned to drop 162 weapons against British forces.[46] Moro suggested that several attacks were successful. However, it would appear that not one of the Canberra weapons struck a British target.[47] Indeed, on watching one of the Canberra's night attacks on 4 June, Southby-Tailyour commented on the Canberra's lack of precision as 'a delightful waste of their ordnance.'[48] Much like the medium-level Sea Harrier bombing runs against Stanley airfield, the Canberra raids, at best, caused a nuisance effect against British forces by applying pressure outside the regular daytime working hours of Argentine air power. Consequently, the parochial and naïve Argentine approach to the application of air power limited their outputs and, as the remainder of the chapter will demonstrate, their desired outcome.

Defining The British Operational Centre of Gravity Post-Operation Sutton

During the last of the three phases of Operation Corporate, the Argentines had three distinct sets of targets to choose from: the carrier battle group, the amphibious assault force, or the land force making its way from San Carlos to Stanley. However, only one of them could constitute the centre of gravity. This book contends that at this stage of the campaign, the British strength lies with their ground force, a capability that could physically seize and hold Stanley and, therefore, deliver the British end-state of repossessing the Falkland Islands. However, the aircraft carriers and the amphibious assault force both enabled the British land forces and, thus, discarding them as an irrelevant target set is flawed. Damage or destruction of either would curtail the British campaign, albeit the impact would vary depending on the breadth and depth of the attack. The waning importance of the previous centre of gravity, the amphibious assault force, was highlighted by Southby-Tailyour when he returned to San Carlos during the last phase of the operation to see that it 'was fast becoming a mere maintenance and stores area.'[49] The reduced relevance and activity levels at San Carlos are a far cry from its centrality during Operation Sutton. However, some participants suggested that the amphibious assault ships still retained primacy over the land forces during the last phase of the operation. Even as late as 5 June, Captain Dingemans, the commanding officer of HMS *Intrepid*, believed that his ship, one of the two Landing Platform Docks, was more vital to the campaign than his cargo – the 600 men of the Second Battalion, Scots Guards.[50]

Land Forces Falkland Islands Major General Jeremy Moore, Royal Marines	
3 Commando Brigade Brigadier Julian Thompson, Royal Marines	**5 Infantry Brigade** Brigadier Tony Wilson
40 Commando, Royal Marines	Second Battalion, Scots Guards
42 Commando, Royal Marines	First Battalion, Welsh Guards[51]
45 Commando, Royal Marines	First Battalion, 7th Duke of Edinburgh's Own Gurkha Rifles
2 PARA[52]	
3 PARA	

Table 5A – British Land Forces Falkland Islands – Task Group 317.1.

With the British land force now identified as the centre of gravity for the last phase of Operation Corporate, it is now important to understand the infantry units that would provide its strength. Consequently, Table 5A identifies the command team, the two Brigades, and the eight subordinate fighting units deployed to the South Atlantic that would make up the key elements of the British land component and the last of the three British centres of gravity for Operation Corporate.

For the British to achieve their desired end-state, they had to defeat the Argentine fielded forces that held Stanley. The only component that could achieve this outcome was the British land forces. Consequently, Table 5B distills the British land forces' attributes as the operational centre of gravity and critical capability for the post-Operation Sutton phase of the Conflict. In keeping with previous chapters, by analysing the critical capability further, the critical requirements and critical vulnerabilities can be deduced. The land force needed to be supported by the other components to bring additional firepower to bear against the enemy. Therefore, artillery, close air support, as well as naval bombardment, are needed to offset the deficit in force size.

Additionally, sustaining the force's logistical needs would also be vital to maintain the tempo of operations and pressure upon the Argentine forces. Lastly, air and sea control were required to provide the other components with the necessary freedoms to conduct operations when and where needed. The associated risks with the British scheme of manoeuvre were considerable. Force size, range, speed, and capability were all attributes that influenced Sea Harrier availability. This critical vulnerability had to be understood, masked, and mitigated to achieve the desired British campaign end-state. However, did the Argentines understand the British needs and associated issues? If so, could they exploit them deliberately, or were the Argentines purely reliant on luck and arbitrary targeting to see them through to the end of the campaign?

Following the first two phases of Operation Corporate, Argentine air power switched from a predominantly maritime to a mixed target set that encompassed both land and maritime-based targets. As doctrine restricted training in the counter-maritime role, it is perhaps not surprising that the *Fuerza Aérea Argentina* stumbled through the first two phases of the campaign. However, the introduction of counter-land operations as part of the latest phase of the operation was an area that should have been more familiar and successful for the *Fuerza Aérea Argentina.* Therefore, was a paradigm shift in Argentine outputs and outcomes about to occur as a result of the new series of emerging targets? Alternatively, were the issues that beset the previous phases of the Conflict simply too significant to rectify?

Although the Argentine plan to deal with the amphibious assault was set and distributed a month before the actual execution of Operation Sutton, there seems to have been less rigour applied to the use of Argentine air power following the amphibious assault. Indeed, neither Rivas nor Moro highlighted the likely targets or priorities, let alone the planned apportionment between maritime and land-based targets. Moro suggested that to preserve its aircraft, the Argentine Air Force South Command deliberately avoided using its aircraft in the high-risk ground support missions.[53] However, Moro's remarks contradict the Argentine operational order that suggested that the secondary target set included the fielded force.[54]

The Argentine command's view is coherent with the philosophy of not attacking the enemy's strength, or centre of gravity, directly. However, it appears that Argentine air power outputs were predominantly reactive and increasingly low-risk in nature with little or no thought given to the more vulnerable and easier to strike targets that made up the critical capabilities and critical vulnerabilities of the British ground forces. By fighting a series of sporadic, bespoke, tactical engagements rather than a series of integrated, deliberate, planned attacks, achieving the desired outcome became an ambitious, if not impossible, goal for the Argentines. So, what did Argentine air power achieve during the British advance to Stanley?

Centre of Gravity	**Critical Capability**
British Land Forces Falkland Islands.	1. The ability to defeat Argentine fielded forces on the Falkland Islands to seize and hold Stanley.
Critical Vulnerabilities	**Critical Requirements**
1.1.1. Force size in comparison to opposition. 1.1.2. Predictable direction of approach to Stanley. 1.1.3. Reduced speed of manoeuvre. 1.1.4. Approaching Austral winter. 1.2.1. Limited reach of artillery. 1.2.2. Significant artillery logistics burden. 1.3.1. Vulnerability of frigates during naval gunfire support. 1.4.1. Lack of precision strike. 1.4.2. Lack of night attack capability. 1.4.3. Reduced Harrier GR3 availability. 1.4.4. Limited Sea Harrier attack capability. 1.4.5. Forward Air Controller capability restricted. 1.5.1. Limited Sea Harrier availability. 1.5.2. Lack of intelligence, surveillance. reconnaissance. 1.5.3. Limited Maritime Force Air Defence capability. 1.5.4. Ground-Based Air Defence limitations. 1.6.1. Lack of support helicopters. 1.6.2. Long and vulnerable lines of communication. 1.7.1. Sustainable Anti-Submarine/Anti-Surface Capability.	1.1. A land force with tactical and moral advantage over Argentine counterparts. 1.2. Artillery Support. 1.3. Naval Gunfire Support. 1.4. Close Air Support. 1.5. Control of the Air. 1.6. Logistical support. 1.7. Sea Control.

Table 5B – British Operational Centre of Gravity Post-Operation Sutton.

Post-Operation Sutton Outputs

Despite the static Argentine ground defences, the British build-up, breakout from the beachhead, and transit to the hills surrounding Stanley was a slow affair. Even with a full complement of support helicopters, the British expected the build-up of forces at San Carlos to take seven days. The loss of the MV *Atlantic Conveyor* and its support helicopter payload slowed both the offload and the onward movement of troops and their equipment to the key battles. Additionally, Argentine air raids only compounded the slower than anticipated offload as non-essential supply ships sought the safer waters outside of the Total Exclusion Zone. The perceived lack of activity and progress caused concerns at the strategic level. The net result was that 2 PARA under the command of Lieutenant Colonel 'H' Jones was dispatched to capture, rather than raid (the initial plan), Goose Green. The battle was controversial as it committed one of the five available British battalions to a battle that was not directly supporting the end-state of the campaign and, as Thompson himself argued, was 'off the line of march.'[55] However, the command team back in Britain believed that 'the capture of Goose Green and Darwin was essential to protect the beachhead from a flanking attack.'[56] From a strategic perspective, and cognisant that Moore and the force required to deliver the investment of Stanley were still days away from the Falkland Islands, the battle for Goose Green maintained campaign momentum and public support.

As with the previous phases, the weather was a constraining factor in the planning and execution of missions. However, and as shown in Annexes A and B, it was not an asymmetric advantage to either air component as the weather affected both participants in equal measure and only for a brief period in early June. Beyond the period of 2 - 4 June, the weather was generally acceptable to conduct the various missions. Ultimately, the weather was not a significant constraint in generating combat air outputs for either participant.

The period between the completion of Operation Sutton and the eventual Argentine surrender on 14 June saw several Argentine air power events – some successful, some less so. However, did the Argentine air arms make the best use of their air power? Analysis of Annex A shows that the Argentines flew 213 combat air sorties throughout 27 May – 14 June, which equates to an average daily sortie rate of eleven per day. However, the daily profile varied considerably, ranging from zero to thirty-six. The average Argentine daily flying rate following the amphibious assault was significantly less than the twenty-four sorties per day flown throughout Operation Sutton, and less than a third of the British sorties during the last phase of the Conflict.[57] Once again, and despite having the larger inventory, the Argentines were unable to better British outputs. Moreover, although there was only a minor difference in the number of Argentine combat air assets deployed between the start and the end of Operation Sutton, the daily outputs reduced by over 50 per cent. The change in these levels reflected initial British intelligence assessments that 'aircraft availability would drop sharply after a short period of intensive operations.'[58] However, what were the Argentines able to achieve with the sorties that they were able to generate?

Complicating the Argentine attack plan further was the expansion of its target set. With the British now ashore and advancing towards Stanley, the counter-land campaign was the prime target for Argentine air power. Consequently, the amphibious force and the carrier battle group were still relevant targets but were now secondary and tertiary targets. As shown in Figure 5.2,

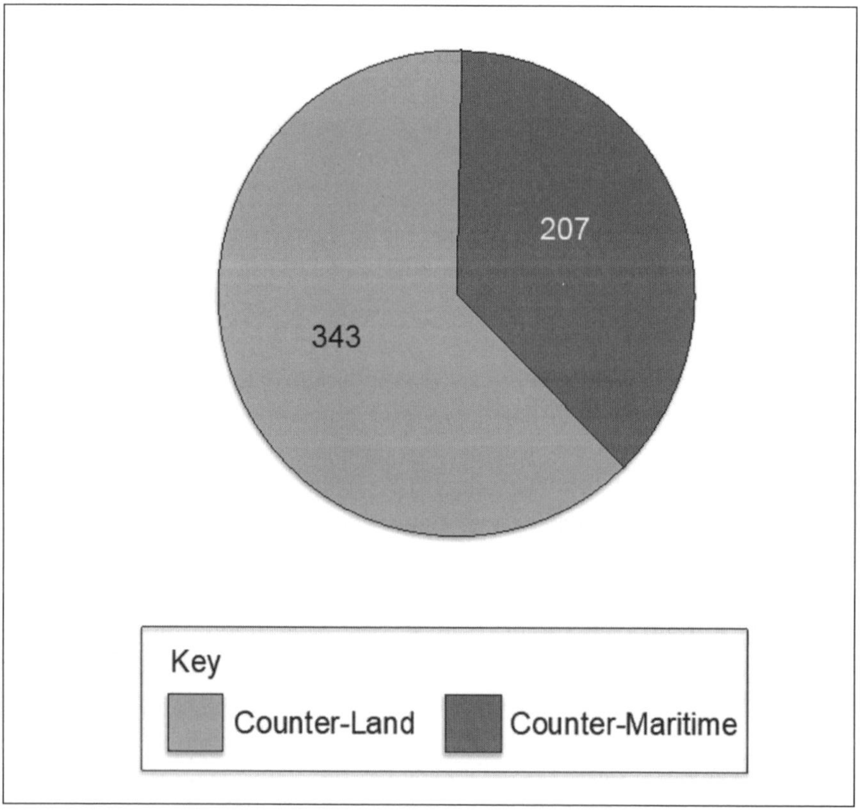

Figure 5.2 – Argentine Attack Weapon Apportionment Post-Operation Sutton.

the 213 combat air missions in the last phase of Operation Corporate generated 550 weapons. The weapons were split 207 (38 per cent) towards maritime targets, with the remaining 343 (62 per cent) allocated to land-based targets. Given that the British weight of effort now focused on the land campaign, it would seem that the Argentines could have apportioned additional assets to support the counter-land task. During the last phase of the Falklands Conflict, five Argentine attack missions stand out in terms of their achievements and lessons against the prosecution of the British centre of gravity.

The first event to consider occurred on 27 May on the same day that 2 PARA advanced from Sussex Mountains for its upcoming battle at Goose Green. Argentine air power was to make the first of several successful raids during the Conflict's last phase. Two formations, each comprising three A-4B Skyhawks, attacked ground targets in the San Carlos area. In a rare case, photographic reconnaissance from an earlier Learjet mission cued the attack mission.[59] Four of the six allocated aircraft reached the intended target area. Two aircraft attacked the eastern shore and achieved some success against 40 Commando's echelon area, killing one Royal Marine and wounding several others.[60] In contrast, the A-4B Skyhawks that attacked the western shore of San Carlos struck the Brigade Maintenance Area, located near the old refrigeration plant at Ajax Bay and consisted of an equipment dump, a cookhouse, and a hospital complex.[61] Although several weapons did not explode, including two bombs that embedded themselves in the refrigeration plant housing the medical facility, several weapons hit their targets and detonated.[62] The net result of the raid was six killed and thirty injured.[63] Beyond the human casualties, the material damage was minimal, although the destruction of the weapons stockpile was spectacular. However, the destroyed mortar ammunition, allocated to 2 PARA to support their imminent Goose Green attack, was quickly replaced, and its substitution did not impede the tempo of operations.[64] From an Argentine perspective, the intelligence-led attack proved to be successful, if costly. Argentine air power delivered a strong and effective attack against a British critical vulnerability. However, the attack in the San Carlos area of operations was overdue and had limited impact. Moreover, the loss of one aircraft and damage to the remaining three A-4B Skyhawks applied further pressure on aircraft availability and aircrew morale.

The second notable event occurred during the 36-hour battle for Goose Green, the only major land battle of the campaign that took place during daylight.[65] As neither the British nor the Argentines had a robust night attack capability, Goose Green was the only battle where air power directly supported the land battle. Although poor weather affected air power's early contribution to the battle, air power did play a significant role in the latter stages of the battle. From a British perspective, and viewed through participants' eyes, the introduction of the Harrier GR3 in the latter stages of the battle was:

> 'A textbook example of a close air support mission: a hard-hitting attack against a target of great importance to the enemy. Launched at a crucial time in the land battle, whose results were clearly seen by the ground troops – thus strengthening the resolve of those on one side and demoralising those on the other.'[66]

Major Chris Keeble, who commanded 2 PARA during the latter stages of the battle following the death of its commanding officer, commented that 'the attack gave a great boost to the morale of our troops.'[67] While the British air power contribution was timely, accurate, useful, and impacted on both sides' morale, the Argentine air power contribution was less effective. Before the British attack, two *Comando de Aviación Naval* Aermacchi MB-339s and two *Fuerza Aérea Argentina* Pucaras endeavoured to conduct close air support missions. However, in contrast to the later Harrier GR3 mission, the Argentine missions were ineffective, weapons missed their intended targets, British defences shot down two of the four aircraft with one pilot killed, and the other captured.[68] Compromised by attrition during continued air raids at Stanley and the successful special forces attack at Pebble Island, Argentine air power was unable to deliver effective close air support missions. It failed to provide the required level of support to the land component. Consequently, the credibility of Argentine air power was compromised.

The next Argentine mission is the most contentious of the campaign in the eyes of Argentine commentators. On 30 May, a rare mixed formation comprising two *Comando de Aviación Naval* Super Etendards and four *Fuerza Aérea Argentina* A-4C Skyhawks flew an anti-shipping mission. This unique, joint mission intended to use the last remaining Exocet missile to strike one of the British aircraft carriers and use the Skyhawks to provide additional firepower. The controversy regarding the mission was not about the only joint Argentine mission or its intended target, but its outcome.

The Argentine version of events suggests that the formation of six aircraft attacked and damaged HMS *Invincible*. In contrast, the British narrative is that the last Exocet missile in the Argentine inventory missed its target, and the follow-on force of four A-4C Skyhawks attacked a Type 21 frigate. During the attack, Sea Darts fired from HMS *Exeter* shot down two A-4C Skyhawks and the two remaining aircraft, both flown by relatively junior and inexperienced pilots, untrained in maritime operations or ship recognition, dropped their weapons against – but missed – HMS *Avenger*. The fact that HMS *Invincible* returned to the United Kingdom after the Conflict has not prevented some Argentine commentators from believing that they had sunk HMS *Invincible*, and the loss covered up by the British.

Irrespective of this bizarre controversy, it illustrates a continued Argentine fascination with the British aircraft carriers, which was an unnecessary effort at this late stage in the campaign. The aircraft carriers played host to many of the British critical vulnerabilities, and any successful attack would have damaged the British campaign as well as providing the Argentines with a propaganda coup. As discussed previously, any attack on the British aircraft carriers was unlikely to have been a fatal blow to the British campaign, particularly in the period after Operation Sutton. Consequently, the Argentines should have allocated their precious air power resources to strike more appropriate and weaker critical vulnerabilities rather than a well-defended aircraft carrier. As a result, the last Super Etendard/Exocet mission was a poor allocation of resources that ultimately neutered the Super Etendard capability and was responsible for the loss of two A-4C Skyhawks and their experienced pilots.[69]

The most significant event during the phase, and the single largest loss of British life during the entire Conflict, occurred at Fitzroy on 8 June. According to Southby-Tailyour, the attacks on RFAs *Sir Galahad* and *Sir Tristram* were entirely avoidable.[70] Nevertheless, the military and political levels felt the loss of fifty-four sailors and soldiers and a further fifty-seven wounded.[71] In her memoirs, Thatcher's reaction to the news of the attack was 'how many more?'[72] From a military perspective, amongst those on board the vessel were elements of the First Battalion, Welsh Guards, a key component of the 5 Infantry Brigade's southern push towards Stanley. Consequently, the attack by five A-4B Skyhawks meant that although the battered Welsh Guards remained as a fighting unit following the attack, it had to be bolstered by two companies of Royal Marines from 40 Commando.[73] Even so, the British held the unit initially in reserve.[74] However, at the operational level, the Welsh Guards were only one of the eight British battalions allocated to the land campaign and one of the seven battalions assigned to the upcoming battles around Stanley. Although the British mapped all seven units to Argentine hilltop positions to capture, the strongest and more capable units took on the initial and more critical battles. The allocation of the later and least likely to occur battles went to the weaker or more politically sensitive units. As a result, neither the Welsh Guards nor the Gurkha Rifles had to fight for their designated objectives, Mount William or Sapper Hill, as the Argentines capitulated before the battle for the last two hills surrounding Stanley.[75] Ultimately, the Argentines, once again, attacked an element of the British operational centre of gravity, but it was not struck with sufficient ferocity to do anything more than delay the British advance by two days.[76]

From a broader campaign perspective, the British operated two Forward Brigade Maintenance Areas: one at Fitzroy supporting 5 Infantry Brigade on the southern flank and the other at Teal Inlet dedicated to 3 Commando Brigade and its northern approach.[77] Consequently, and as previously stated, the relevance of San Carlos diminished as the campaign progressed. Although the Argentines attacked San Carlos and Fitzroy, the support base at Teal Inlet appeared to have been neither identified nor attacked. The lack of emphasis on intelligence, surveillance, and reconnaissance once again denuded Argentine planners with an opportunity to strike British critical vulnerabilities.

The last attack to consider occurred on the penultimate day of the Conflict and targeted the 3 Commando Brigade headquarters on the western slopes of Mount Kent. In fact, the headquarters was subject to two air attacks on 13 June, one by a Canberra in the early hours of the morning and the second later in the day by seven A-4B Skyhawks.[78] Neither raid caused casualties, but there is a disparity regarding the physical damage caused by the A-4B Skyhawk attack. Cervera, one of the Argentine pilots involved in the raid, claimed to have seen four or five helicopters destroyed.[79] Moro, in a more reflective mood, suggested that the Argentines only obliterated three helicopters.[80] In contrast, making use of official British figures, Freedman states that three light helicopters were damaged.[81] Irrespective of the number of helicopters damaged or destroyed during the attack, the proximity of the helicopter park to the headquarters compromised the 3 Commando Brigade's command team.[82] The numerous helicopter movements in the area provided Argentine observers with an insight into the importance of the area. Although the headquarters only suffered a shredded tent, the damage could have been severe as the 3 Commando Brigade command team were due to hold a meeting at the time of the attack.[83] However, as Freedman pointed out, the raid 'was generally inconsequential.'[84] The Argentines were able to find and attack the 3 Commando Brigade headquarters, but it did so on the evening of the last of the already prepared land battles – too late for the desired campaign-winning effect. Unable to deliver the desired outcome, Argentine air power was, again, guilty of delivering too little, too late.

Although all seven variants of Argentine combat air assets participated in the last phase of the Conflict, their ability to sustain their outputs varied considerably. Due to their enforced sabbaticals following their losses on 1 May, the Mirage III and the Canberra forces were able to maintain a level of output until the end of the Conflict. After 1 May, but before their reintegration into the campaign during Operation Sutton, the Mirage III force concentrated on defensive counter-air missions over the southern Argentine air bases rather than sweep and escort sorties over the Falkland Islands.[85] However, several forces were not so fortunate. The small but potent Super Etendard force flew its last mission and fired its last Exocet missile on 30 May, over two weeks before hostilities ceased. On completion of its last mission, the Super Etendard force recovered north to its home, *Base Aeronaval Commandante Espora,* on 1 June to conduct night training.[86] According to Rivas, the Super Etendards received orders on 13 June to deploy to Rio Grande for an attack mission with bombs.[87] However, the end of the Conflict prevented further Super Etendard involvement. The issue of combat air sustainability for the *Comando de Aviación Naval* worsened when the A-4Q Skyhawk force flew its last mission on 12 June, on the day that the critical night battles around the hills of Stanley commenced.

The responsibility for the delivery of Argentine combat air now fell solely to the *Fuerza Aérea Argentina.* However, were the units ready for the challenge? Given the heavy attrition of its assets during Operation Sutton and the enduring serviceability issues across the fleets, it is not surprising that these issues started to take its toll on the force's outputs. With the Mirage III force dedicated to the control of the air role, the responsibility for the remaining attack missions fell to the Canberra, A-4 Skyhawk, and Daggers. Despite fair weather over their airfields and operating area, the Argentines flew no attack missions from the mainland on 11 June. However, were the Argentines preserving their force once again for a surge of activity during the latter stages of the campaign? Activity levels for 12 and 13 June would suggest that this was the case. Despite poor weather on the morning of 12 June, the Argentines mustered eighteen sorties. A further twenty-eight missions were flown on 13 June, significantly more than the average of eleven missions per day for the phase of operations. Moreover, the

Argentine combat air output over the last few days of the campaign appears all the more impressive, given the fact that four of the seven combat air units were unable to participate. However, comparing this figure with what the Argentine combat air arms delivered just three weeks prior provides an insight into the demise of Argentine air power. On 21 May, the Argentines achieved a campaign peak of seventy-two combat air missions in a single day. Additionally, what did the surge in the last few days actually achieve?

Analysis of Annex H shows that the missions over the period 12 and 13 June, with the previously described notable exception, achieved very little in terms of getting Argentine weapons onto their designated or vital targets. Indeed, there was a sharp increase in the number of Argentine aircraft deterred by British defences. However, given the fact that the British defensive contribution had not increased significantly in terms of capability or volume, it leads to the assumption that the Argentine risk appetite had decreased considerably from that seen earlier in the campaign.[88]

One of the Falklands Conflict's enduring perspectives is that Argentine pilots were brave, utterly dedicated, and a direct reflection of Argentine pride, ethos, and culture. Vaux's view is a typical statement on the virtues of Argentine aircrew: 'few assessors had anticipated that the Argentine pilots would prove as resolute and tenacious as they turned out to be.'[89] However, their reduced performance in the latter stages of the Falklands Conflict sheds a slightly different and more human view. Perhaps Clapp offers a more balanced and accurate view when he suggests that 'if their aircrew were any guide to the rest of their armed forces there was certainly determination, but there was an equally clear will among some of the pilots to survive ... they would be a patchy enemy.'[90] Therefore, had the reduction in Argentine combat air participants, British campaign advances as well as cumulative aircraft and aircrew losses finally taken its toll on the *Fuerza Aérea Argentina* moral component?

Analysing the Outcomes Post-Operation Sutton

As in previous chapters, this section seeks to identify the causal factors, in priority order, for the failure of Argentine weapons to reach their intended targets. Figure 5.3 shows pictorially the data contained within Annex H and demonstrates that the Argentines planned to use a total of 550 weapons over the period 27 May to 14 June. In response to the British breakout from San Carlos, the Argentines launched 506 of the planned weapons (or

92 per cent), a minor 6 per cent improvement over the activities during Operation Sutton. During the transit, the number of weapons reduced to 442, equating to 80 per cent of planned weapons and 87 per cent of the launched weapons (a 17 and 14 per cent improvement respectively when compared with the same activities during the amphibious assault). Nevertheless, 361 weapons managed to breach the British defences (equating to 71 per cent, also a significant improvement in comparison to Operation Sutton, of the successfully launched bombs and 82 per cent of the weapons that reached the Islands). Although marginal, the improved performance is perhaps surprising given the parlous state of the mainland-based combat air capability. However, the introduction of the Canberra in the low-level night attack role could account for the difference in performance between the two phases. Moreover, the British targets were geographically dispersed rather than focused in the San Carlos area, leading to a more diffuse defensive coverage. Nevertheless, could the Argentines sustain this level of improvement through to successful weapon delivery?

In the target area, the Argentines employed 178 weapons against the fleet with only eighteen hitting the target or target area (3 per cent of the weapons planned, 4 per cent of the bombs that managed to get airborne and 10 per cent of those dropped). In contrast to the earlier figures for this

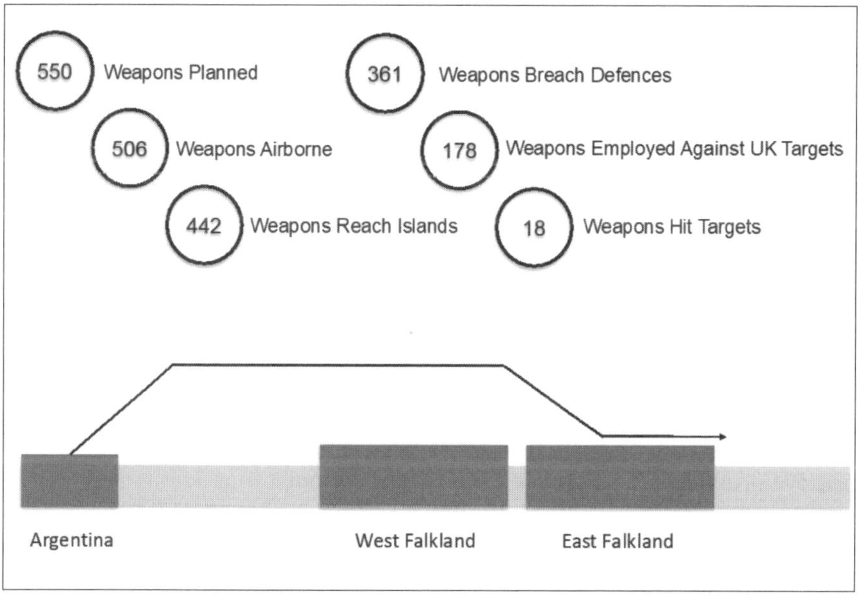

Figure 5.3 – The Utility of Argentine Weapons Post-Operation Sutton.

phase of operations, the weapon employment data shows a marked decrease in performance compared with Operation Sutton. So, if the Argentine targeting was ineffective during the last phase of Operation Corporate, what were the causal factors behind failing to deliver the weapons against their intended targets?

Drawn from analysis of Annex H, Table 5C identifies the reasons why Argentine bombs failed to strike their intended targets. When compared with the analysis in the previous chapters it can be seen that of the top five factors, three categories repeat in all three campaign phases: missed their target (31 per cent), failed to drop their weapons (27 per cent) and air aborts (16 per cent). All three factors were solely within the gift of the Argentines to resolve. Additionally, external forces, such as the British defence of their centre of gravity, do not influence the three factors. Moreover, neither of the common perceptions regarding the Conflict – Sea Harrier dominance and unexploded bombs – is included in the recurring themes.

Of note, included in the top five factors in the third phase of the campaign is the Sea Harrier's ability to generate a 'soft kill.' Consequently, a review of the analysis to date shows that the Sea Harrier's performance throughout the campaign was inconsistent. Following a strong showing during the first phase of the campaign, the Sea Harrier's accomplishments

Ranking	Causal Factor	Scale (out of 550)	Percentage
1	Weapon Employment – Missed Target	171	31
2	Weapons not Dropped	149	27
3	Serviceability – Air Abort	88	16
4	Sea Harrier – Soft Kill	44	8
5	Serviceability – Ground Abort	22	4
6	Maritime Force Air Defence – Soft Kill	20	4
7	Mission Cancelled	16	3
8	Serviceability – Weapon Employment	13	2
9	Weapon Employment – Hit and Detonates	11	2
10	Weapon Employment – Unexploded Bomb	7	1
11	Maritime Force Air Defence – Hard Kill	6	1
12	Sea Harrier – Hard Kill	3	<1
	Total	550	100

Table 5C – Causal Factors for Failure to Deliver Weapons Post-Operation Sutton.

ebbed significantly during the second phase. Nevertheless, the Sea Harrier did produce a stronger performance during the third and last phase of the campaign, where it was able to influence 8 per cent of the planned Argentine weapons. Some commentators, such as Ward, argued that the Sea Harrier's performance reflected its dominance throughout the campaign. However, the evidence suggests an alternative narrative. During the latter stages of the third phase, it is clear that Argentine aircrew were reluctant to engage or press home their attacks in a contested environment. Realising that their cause was rapidly becoming lost, Argentine aircrew understandably adopted a low-risk, life-preserving approach to their air operations. As a result, many Argentine aircrew elected to abort their missions rather than face an opposed attack – whether that be from Sea Harrier combat air patrol or from the variety of ground and maritime-based air defence systems. Therefore, many of the 'soft kills' attributed to the Sea Harrier community were not a reflection of the Sea Harrier's dominance or reputation but the self-preservation of a cadre of self-aware and soon to be defeated Argentine aircrew.

With the British armed forces moving inexorably towards their desired end-state, the Argentine aircrew continued to fly their tasked sorties. However, with failing equipment and significant losses in terms of both aircraft and personnel, Argentine aircrew morale appeared to be waning. Consequently, in the last few days of the campaign, Argentine aircrew may have been unable or unwilling to accept the risks required to turn these last few missions into the required outcomes. As a result, mission aborts due to the inability to find the target, aircraft serviceability issues, and the presence of Sea Harrier combat air patrols increased significantly. This change in ethos sits uncomfortably with the macho, passionate, and proud Argentine culture, as well as the global perception of the brave and heroic Argentine fighter pilots. Although Moro highlighted the criticism that 'the air force failed to operate during the last days of the conflict,' he failed to rebut or provide evidence to counter the allegation.[91] Consequently, Moro is content to retain the common perception of Argentine aviators as the valiant vanquished. Reinforcing the opinion is an Operational Research Branch report from Headquarters RAF Strike Command from September 1983 that stated, 'though they sustained considerable damage, it is fair to say that their air forces were not beaten and remained a viable force at the end of hostilities.'[92] However, the evidence tells a different story.

In an endeavour to capture the state of the Argentine air arm's moral component, it is useful to exploit the Argentine Army's views on what doctrinally constituted a broken military force. During the latter stages of the Conflict, General Galtieri told his Military Governor in the Falkland Islands, 'that the Argentine military code stipulated that a commander should fight until he has lost 50 per cent of his men and used 75 per cent of his ammunition.'[93] The Argentine leader's view chimed with the measurement of effectiveness figures used during Operation Desert Storm to assess Coalition success against the Iraqi Republican Guard.[94] Although the model is Army-centric, it does have utility in the air environment, particularly if the term 'aircraft and ammunition' replaces 'ammunition.' The model provides a suitable comparison to articulate the level of attrition in the physical component of Argentine air power as the campaign drew to a close. However, the model, as demonstrated in Annex I, is not without its flaws. First, it assumed that each air unit was fully manned and equipped at the start of the Conflict. Second, it does not take into account the quality of the pilots nor their platforms. Consequently, the assumption is that each pilot and aircraft can deliver the same capability. As a result, the analysis does not take into consideration individual experience, currency levels, or aircraft performance and payload. Last, from an engineering perspective, the logistics challenges faced by many of the platforms are unaccounted for. Nevertheless, there are several useful deductions drawn from the data contained within Annex I.

The first issue identified in Annex I is that no Argentine combat air unit flew on the last day of the Conflict. The last four remaining units flew their last missions the day prior. Of the seven Argentine combat air units that operated during the Conflict, only five were available for the start of the critical hilltop battles on the evening of 11 June. Of note, one of those five units, the A-4Q Skyhawk squadron, would cease operations on 12 June, amid the key land battles.

It is noteworthy that aircraft and weapon availability, rather than manpower, was the major constraint for all Argentine combat air units. Indeed, the parlous aircraft figures, shown in Annex I, are optimistic as they show the number of airframes available rather than aircraft that were physically capable of being used on operations. Indeed, Rivas suggests that at the end of the Conflict, of the eight available A-4C Skyhawks, only two were operationally capable.[95] Analysis of Annex I shows that by the end of Operation Sutton, three of the seven combat air units were already below the critical aircraft level of 75 per cent. This trend continued. By 1 June, only the Canberra unit, courtesy of its enforced sabbatical, had more than 75 per cent of its airframes available.

The Argentine units were well manned. Although the vast majority of units suffered losses, only one unit, the A-4C Skyhawk unit, came close to reaching the critical manning level of 50 per cent before ending its flying operations. The A-4C Skyhawk unit ceased combat operations on 9 June, five days before the surrender, and three days before the land battles for Stanley commenced.[96] However, the downside of a well-manned unit with limited flying assets was the lack of flying opportunities. Consequently, and in sharp contrast to the British situation, analysis of Rivas' work suggests that over 60 per cent of Argentine aircrew only flew three missions or less during the campaign; some way short of the Sea Harrier pilots who had each flown, on average, forty-five missions during the Conflict.[97] Moreover, further analysis of Rivas' work shows that the maximum number of operational missions flown by any Argentine combat air pilot during the Conflict was nine. In contrast, Flight Lieutenant Ted Ball flew the most Sea Harrier missions during the Conflict with sixty-four missions.[98] The Argentine flying rate was notably below the level which formed the mandate for the United States Air Force Exercise Red Flag. Based on Vietnam War experiences, where 'the first ten missions a pilot flew were his most dangerous, and that if he could survive this without getting shot down, then his chance of survival significantly increased.'[99] Consequently, the Nevada-based exercise aimed to provide aircrew with those first ten combat missions but in a peacetime training environment. The net result from an Argentine combat air perspective was that its corporate knowledge and experience levels during the Conflict were significantly lower than its British adversary. Argentine performance and survivability suffered as a result.

The evidence presented would suggest that the established image of brave Argentine pilots pressing home their attacks with vigour, while valid for the period of Operation Sutton, exaggerates the Argentine aircrews' contribution during the last days of the campaign.

Over the last three chapters, the focus has been on Argentine air power's ability to prosecute British forces during the three distinct phases of the Falklands Conflict: the initial preparation of the battle-space, the amphibious assault and, ultimately, the campaign to capture Stanley. The next chapter will look at the British contribution to the defence of the various centres of gravity throughout the campaign. Encompassing the air, maritime, and land contributions to the British delivery of control of the air, the next chapter builds on the issues already identified regarding the challenges of delivering the required level of control of the air. Consequently, the following chapter challenges many of the claims and lessons identified in early British official accounts of the Falklands Conflict.[100]

Chapter 6

Defending the British Operational Centres of Gravity – Sea Harrier: The Decisive Factor?

'It is now clear that a very high percentage of the Argentine attack missions never got through to their targets, and all of the credit for this deterrence must fall to the outer ring of defence, that is the three [Sea Harrier] Combat Air Patrols.'

Lieutenant Commander Nigel Ward,
Commanding Officer 801 Naval Air Squadron.[1]

The previous chapters have explicitly looked at the Argentine prosecution of British forces throughout the campaign. The analysis so far highlights that the British defensive influences on the campaign were not as convincing as many observers, such as Ward, have suggested. Consequently, this chapter reviews the British defence of their various centres of gravity throughout the campaign in greater depth and, in particular, their ability to deliver the required level of control of the air. As a result, this chapter will initially focus on the Sea Harrier's performance. Specifically, this chapter considers the much-repeated assertion that the Sea Harrier and the AIM-9L variant of the Sidewinder were fundamental to the defeat of the Argentines. However, the Sea Harrier was not the sole contributor to control of the air. Thus, the chapter will also examine the contributions of both British ground-based and maritime force air defences.

The dominance of the Sea Harrier with its rapidly introduced AIM-9L Sidewinder air-to-air missiles during the air battles is a much-quoted factor in explaining the successful British outcome of the Conflict. The notion permeated the strategic, operational, and tactical views of the Conflict. For example, at the grand strategic level, Thatcher suggested that 'without the

[Sea] Harriers, with their extraordinary manoeuvrability, flown with superb skill and courage, and using the latest version of the Sidewinder air-to-air missile supplied by Caspar Weinberger, we could not have retaken the Falklands.'[2] Likewise, at the operational level and used as the conduit to apprise the political level, participants such as Woodward concluded that 'it is now perfectly clear to me that without those AIM-9L [Sidewinder missiles] the Sea Harriers would not have been good enough.'[3] Moreover, within the land domain and embracing Ward's maritime and air viewpoint, key leaders such as Ian Gardiner, a company commander with 45 Commando during the Falklands Conflict, suggested that 'they [the Argentine air forces] could have won the war for Argentina, had it not been for the outstanding performance of our Harriers, and the Royal Navy ships, which stopped many aircraft from getting as far as us and our logistics.'[4] The perception of Sea Harrier and AIM-9L Sidewinder dominance is not limited to the British. The apologue has subsequently percolated to the United States. For example, T.R. Milton, a retired United States Air Force General, is quoted as saying:

> 'It was the AIM-9L Sidewinder air-to-air missile that caused the most envy. In the opinion of the Argentines, almost any airplane becomes something to be taken seriously if it has the AIM-9L [Sidewinder].'[5]

The Argentine Dagger pilot, Horacio Mir Gonzales, added weight to the argument that 'our main enemy was the Sidewinder; our main enemy was the Sea Harrier.'[6] Indeed, the Dagger force lost ten aircraft during the period of the landings, which included eight aircraft lost to the Sea Harrier and AIM-9L Sidewinder combination. The balance of the narrative is overwhelmingly in favour of the Sea Harrier and AIM-9L Sidewinder dominance. However, does the evidence support the assertion?

Supporting the established position, and as shown in Chapter 3, the Sea Harrier and AIM-9L Sidewinder combination made an impressive debut on 1 May. As a result, the Sea Harrier was the second most influential factor in stopping Argentine weapons during the prelude to the amphibious assault. However, the evidence suggested that the Sea Harrier's dominance in the air war was short-lived, and the aircraft's influence dwindled as the campaign progressed. Indeed, and as shown in Chapter 4, the aircraft's sway fell significantly during Operation Sutton to the joint fifth most influential factor in stopping Argentine weapons. Moreover, and as highlighted in the previous chapter, during the third and final phase of the campaign, the Sea Harrier's dominance marginally improved to the fourth most influential factor. Nevertheless, Argentine ambivalence may drive this latter position rather than Sea Harrier dominance. Throughout the three phases of the Conflict, the Sea Harrier was demonstrably the most influential British factor affecting the prosecution of Argentine weapons. However, the Sea Harrier's performance was some way short of fulfilling the post-Conflict praise heaped upon it. To understand the disparity, this chapter will review the effectiveness of the Sea Harrier capability as well as the broader British contribution to control of the air during Operation Corporate.

To better understand the Sea Harrier's strengths and weaknesses, it is essential to understand three distinct elements of its capability. As shown in Figure 6.1, the elements to be considered are the three key equipment components that make up the Sea Harrier capability: the platform, the sensor, and the weapon. All three components must be optimised and integrated seamlessly to exploit the capability's full potential. In isolation, a single component cannot deliver the required effect. By way of example, the recently introduced Super Etendard capability achieved an effective balance across all three components. However, the Super Etendard lacked the necessary numbers to sustain its outputs throughout the Conflict. Consequently, the Super Etendard was unable to deliver campaign-winning outcomes.

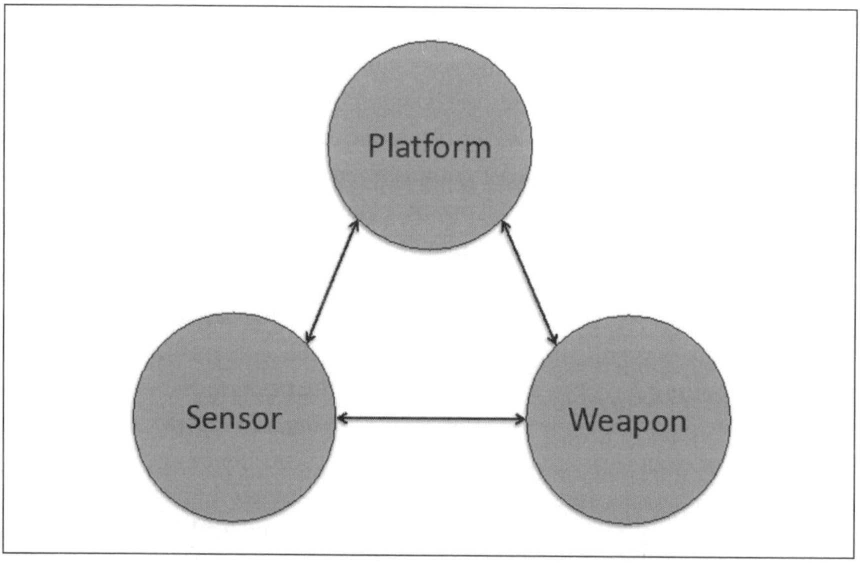

Figure 6.1 – The Sea Harrier Equipment Triumvirate.

The platform, or aircraft in this instance, should incorporate, at the very least, the core air power attributes of height, speed, and reach as specified in the United Kingdom Air and Space Doctrine.[7] In contrast, the weapon must be reliable, numerous, easy to use, lethal, and have a broad operating envelope to optimise its utility. Lastly, the purpose of the sensor is to aid situational awareness, prosecute the target to the attacker's advantage, and enable the weapon's full potential to be brought to bear against the enemy. Although the three components have an equipment focus, each component must also be supported by the remaining Defence Lines of Development so that the full capability can be fielded and used. This chapter will discuss each component in the context of the Sea Harrier and its impact on the prosecution of Operation Corporate.

Delivery of control of the air through manned fighters is not merely a function of the platform's capability. Several enabling functions must support the aircraft. However, the British Task Force deployed to the South Atlantic with a finite resource of Sea Harriers but, critically, no airborne early warning capability. The situation in 1982 was the polar opposite of the position desired by the Royal Navy in the mid-1960s following the CVA01 debacle.[8] Airborne early warning was perceived to be the priority capability furnished by future aircraft carriers.[9] However, a lack of hangar space and accommodation forced the deletion of the airborne early warning capability from the staff requirement during the detailed design phase for the new *Invincible*-class of aircraft carriers. The British forces would lament this decision in the South Atlantic during 1982.[10] Nevertheless, the rapid introduction of a Sea King airborne early warning capability benefitted from the retention of early Sea King-based airborne early warning designs. Consequently, after initial scoping meetings on 13 May, the Sea King airborne early warning capability was fielded on 30 July.[11] The rapid introduction into service was an impressive feat, but it was too late to influence the Falklands Conflict.

Unlike the previous generation of British naval aviation, the most recent batch of aircraft carriers had no indigenous air-to-air refuelling capability to provide the Sea Harrier combat air patrols with greater persistence. The lack of enablers meant that the Sea Harrier force was operating at a higher tempo and had limited situational awareness. An opponent who was willing to contest the air battle could have exploited the increased level of risk placed upon the Sea Harrier force. However, the Argentine planners elected to focus on the attack role to the detriment of control of the air and discarded one of their stipulated five campaign priorities – active air defence against aircraft and helicopters. Consequently, the Sea Harriers were able to intercept Argentine attack aircraft without worrying about Argentine fighter escorts.[12]

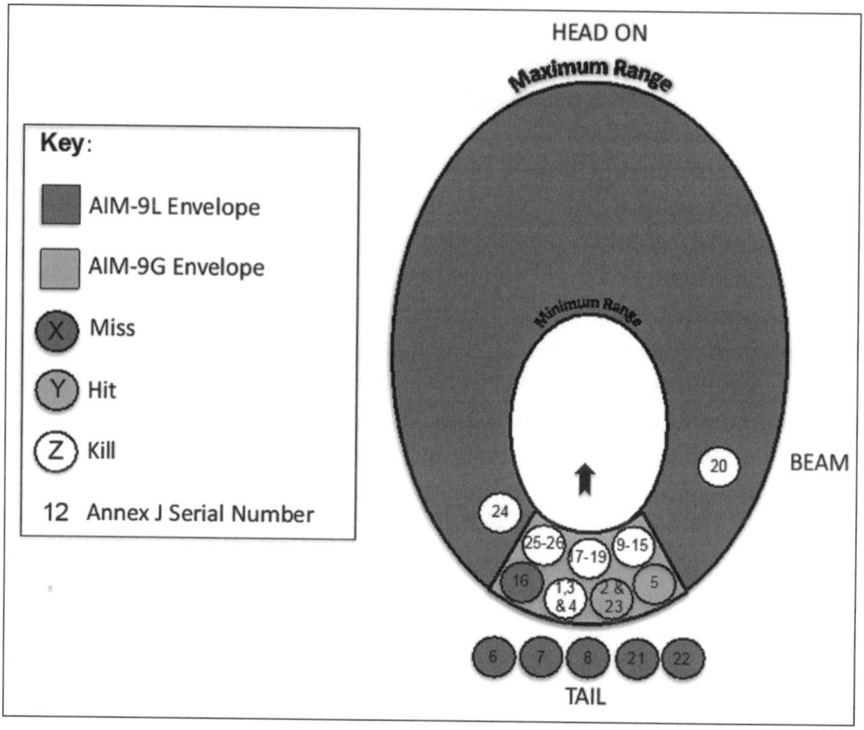

Figure 6.2 – AIM-9L Sidewinder Employment during the Falklands Conflict.[13]

From a weapons perspective, Figure 6.2 uses data contained within Annex J, is a pictorial representation of the various Sea Harrier and AIM-9L Sidewinder engagements against Argentine aircraft throughout the Conflict. The black arrow in the centre of the diagram represents the Argentine aircraft. The dark grey zone surrounding the target aircraft signifies the area where a Sea Harrier could effectively engage the target with the AIM-9L Sidewinder. When compared with the light grey zone, the stern only AIM-9G Sidewinder engagement zone, it can be seen that the AIM-9L Sidewinder provided significant kinematic and tactical advantages over its predecessor.[14] The evolutionary technological change that enabled the expanded weapon envelope of the AIM-9L Sidewinder was the introduction of a new seeker that allowed the missile to 'detect the longer wavelengths associated with warm aircraft parts, such as nose cones, giving the missile "all-aspect capability," including the long desired head-on shot.'[15] The level of success achieved reinforced the dominance of the Sea Harrier weapon system over Argentine aircraft. However, two factors limited the Sea

Harrier's ability to exploit the new generation of AIM-9 Sidewinder: The Sea Harrier's radar and training.

The Sea Harrier's radar enabled airborne interception as well as surface attack. In both roles, the radar was able to detect, track, and engage targets allowing the chosen weapon to be quickly cued and launched against its intended prey. Although the Blue Fox radar was effective in the clutter-free environment of medium to high altitude operations, it struggled in high clutter environments. The critical situations where the system toiled to detect targets occurred during operations at low altitude overland or when facing a significant height difference between the Sea Harrier and a target aircraft operating at a significantly lower altitude. However, the radar's practical performance had a direct correlation to the system's performance specification. The radar was optimised to operate between 15,000 and 35,000 feet as well as functioning effectively down to 5,000 feet.[16] In other words, the system focussed on the expected operating environment of its anticipated nemesis, the Soviet 'Bear D' reconnaissance aircraft. Moreover, each aircraft needed to have its own radar set to be effective. Nevertheless, and not for the first time in the Sea Harrier programme, there was a deficit in the number of radars available. Indeed, 'three of the reinforcement [Sea] Harriers that will be embarked on [MV] *Atlantic Conveyor* have a severely degraded air combat capability due to the lack of Blue Fox radars.'[17] Fortunately, the requisition of Blue Fox radars intended for the Indian Sea Harriers mitigated the deficits in radar numbers. Despite its inadequacies, advocates of the Sea Harrier believed that those who did not fully understand the system overstated the radar's limitations.[18]

As shown in Figure 6.2, only two of the twenty successful AIM-9L Sidewinder engagements were from beyond the legacy AIM-9G Sidewinder engagement envelope.[19] Nonetheless, elements of the Sea Harrier force had adapted its tactics in an endeavour to exploit the new enhanced head-on capability that the AIM-9L Sidewinder provided.[20] Consequently, the new tactics were used successfully on 1 May when two Sea Harriers engaged two Mirage III fighters. With both sets of aircraft operating in the clutter-free environment of medium altitude, the Sea Harriers executed their new radar-based tactics. As the aircraft rapidly closed towards each other, the lead Sea Harrier pilot attempted to achieve a missile lock. However, due to simple but effective Argentine countermeasures, the Sea Harrier pilots were unable to use the AIM-9L Sidewinder in the head-on engagement. Nevertheless, the Sea Harrier tactics were sufficiently flexible that the pilots quickly converted to a successful stern sector attack.[21]

Following the lessons of the first air battles on 1 May, the Argentines rapidly changed their operating procedures by focusing on attack missions using low-level, high-clutter overland routes. As a result, British air defences had limited situational awareness of incoming raids. The post-Conflict analysis shows that the British detected 109 of the ingressing high altitude Argentine raids and scrambled or provided initial vectors for Sea Harriers against the intruders.[22] Despite the early warnings, the raids would descend into the high clutter, low altitude environment for their final approach and attacks. The evolving Argentine tactics meant that the Sea Harriers struggled to detect the low-flying raids on their radars and, as a result, had few opportunities to achieve a full weapon system kill. Consequently, and as demonstrated in Figure 6.2, the Sea Harrier pilots needed to acquire and pursue the target visually. Inevitably, this tactic led to the Sea Harrier finding themselves in stern engagements using imprecise pilot-assessed ranges, rather than the more accurate radar-deduced ranges to employ their weapons.

Ward argued that even at low altitude, the Sea Harrier's radar remained effective. By way of an example, Ward cited his successful prosecution of an Argentine C-130 Hercules on 1 June.[23] However, analysis of the attack demonstrates both the good and the bad of the Sea Harrier capability. There is little doubt that the skilful manipulation of the Blue Fox radar allowed Ward to detect and close on his prey. Nevertheless, it is apparent that the pilot's range awareness diminished as he quickly closed on the large and slow-speed C-130 Hercules. Ward was aware that he was critically short of fuel and may have become visually fixated on the target to the detriment of monitoring the range to the target presented to him by his radar.[24] The net result was that Ward's first missile failed to intercept the target; it is highly likely that Ward fired the weapon beyond its maximum range. After rapidly closing on the C-130 Hercules, his second Sidewinder successfully found its target. However, the injured C-130 Hercules remained airborne. Consequently, Ward had to deliver the *coup de grace* with his 30mm Aden cannon.[25] The guidance offered that morning in a signal from Commander Task Force may have swayed Ward during his attack. The message suggested that 'shooting opportunities are at best fleeting. If you think you are in range always fire something. It might hit.'[26] The same signal then offered contradictory advice when it informed that in respect of the missile stockpile, 'conservation vital.'[27]

The Sea Harrier force was well versed and trained in fighter versus fighter tactics. Indeed, Ward informed readers of his memoir that the Sea Harrier achieved considerable success against the latest US fighters. During training missions against US Navy F-14 Tomcats and USAF F-15 Eagles, the Sea Harriers dominated their opposition and reputedly achieved kill ratios of 40:1 and 3:1, respectively.[28] However, there is little evidence to suggest that the Sea Harriers trained against a more eclectic and physically larger target set, such as the C-130 Hercules or Canberra.[29] As highlighted by Ward, the lack of Blue Fox radars during the early days of Sea Harrier operational training may be the rationale for the change in emphasis.[30] Forced to focus on visual manoeuvring against a fighter aircraft, where the use of radar is of secondary importance, the Sea Harrier pilots were able to hone their basic fighting skills. Conversely, the counter argument would imply that the lack of access to the Blue Fox radar might have compromised the Sea Harrier's ability to prosecute a larger target set more efficiently. At the maximum range of a missile, a large aircraft can appear to be significantly closer to the launch aircraft than a smaller fighter size target. As a result, unless the pilot is using accurate ranging from his sensor or is well trained and experienced in large aircraft intercepts, there is a possibility that a pilot may employ weapons outside of the kinematic envelope of the missile. Given that the Sea Harrier design requirement was to counter the large Soviet 'Bear D' threat, it is perhaps surprising that the Sea Harrier capability performed poorly against the larger Argentine aircraft. Consequently, reliance on inaccurate pilot-assessed, rather than sensor-deduced, distances between the fighter and its prey could account for the poor performance of the six AIM-9L Sidewinder missiles fired against larger Argentine aircraft for a return of only one kill. With much of the Sea Harrier's previous training focused against fighter aircraft, it is perhaps not surprising that the Sea Harrier's capability performed poorly against the Argentine Canberra formation on 1 May and the sole C-130 Hercules on 1 June. This issue may well be a case of a relatively new platform entering service with insufficient time to train for the full gamut of its proposed tasks. However, the alternative view would suggest that the Sea Harrier pilots correctly focused their training on the most dangerous threats and achieved, when able, considerable success against their fighter-sized counterparts.

The relatively small warhead contained within the Sidewinder missile further compounds the issue of engaging larger aircraft. Although effective against a small and agile fighter aircraft, the Sidewinder's warhead struggled to achieve a single shot kill against a larger aircraft, which has the benefit of numerous redundancy levels such as engines, electrical and hydraulic systems. Therefore, the fighter must be able to deliver multiple missiles to achieve the desired result – a 'hard kill.' Consequently, for a fighter aircraft, the quality and quantity of its weapon payload is a crucial parameter. This lesson was quickly rectified by the Sea Harrier community post-Conflict, rather than during as Corum suggested, when it doubled the aircraft's payload of AIM-9L Sidewinders from two to four following the introduction of a dual-missile pylon for each wing.[31] The issue was not only a payload concern but also the implications of multiple shots against a formation could cause a drain on the limited deployed AIM-9L Sidewinder stockpile. On 3 June, a signal from HMS *Hermes* reinforced the last point when it stated that one of its lessons learned was 'do not fire second missile unless sure first has missed.'[32]

As shown in Annex J, a total of twenty-six Sidewinders were fired during the Conflict, leading to twenty hits and seventeen kills, resulting in a probability of kill of 65 per cent. This figure is significantly less than the 87 per cent success rate quoted initially by Westrum, who then contradicted himself and broadly agreed with this book's analysis.[33] The airborne reliability of the AIM-9L Sidewinder was impressive; only one missile misfired.[34] However, on board the aircraft carriers the extended exposure of the missile to the vagaries of the South Atlantic weather systems caused issues where:

> 'Corrosion of fins, canards and their mountings was soon evident and the inadequacy of the missile covers soon became apparent. The issue was significant and forced HMS *Invincible* to return eleven of their first batch of twenty AIM-9L [Sidewinders].'[35]

Despite the relatively minor issues, the effectiveness of the AIM-9L Sidewinder during the Falklands campaign is significantly higher than the early generation of Sidewinders used during the Vietnam War. During the conflict in South-East Asia, Sidewinders were fired on 454 occasions but achieved only eighty-one kills, resulting in a dismal probability of kill of a mere 18 per cent.[36] To a certain extent, the limited training that the United States Navy and Air Force pilots had in weapon employment can account for a large proportion of the discrepancy. However, the performance of the later model AIM-9M Sidewinder with its improved countermeasure capability during the 1991 Operation Desert Storm is perhaps more surprising.[37] Despite the creation of the *Top Gun* programme and Exercise Red Flag to improve United States Navy and United States Air Force training capabilities, the AIM-9M Sidewinder performance during Operation Desert Storm was poor. Of the eleven AIM-9M Sidewinders employed, only six achieved kills, not twelve kills as claimed by Westrum. This situation led to a relatively disappointing probability of kill of 54 per cent.[38] The difference in performance reflected the more extensive array of countermeasures and tactics employed by the Iraqi air force jets. Nevertheless, the 1991 AIM-9M Sidewinder performance was disappointing when compared with the 1982 accomplishment.

During the Falklands Conflict, there were concerns regarding Sea Harrier pilots' knowledge of the new variant of Sidewinder's performance and its integration onto the platform.[39] Nevertheless, and despite exposure to the harsh climatic operating environment of the South Atlantic, the Sea Harrier/AIM-9L Sidewinder combination was effective when the target could be detected and intercepted. Analysis of Figure 6.2 demonstrates that the vast majority of the Sea Harrier AIM-9L Sidewinder firings were within the kinematic envelope of the legacy AIM-9G Sidewinder. This point reinforced the RAF's Central Tactics and Trials Organisation's view that one of the tactical lessons from the Conflict was that 'most missiles were fired from a visual acquisition in boresight and almost all were fired from close to the line astern position.'[40] An initial deduction would suggest that the older AIM-9G Sidewinder may have achieved a similar level of success as the recently integrated AIM-9L Sidewinder. This deduction is contrary to Woodward's assertion to Fieldhouse on the evening of 1 May that 'Mirage kills to date have been with AIM-9L with firings at extremities or outside expected [AIM-] 9G [Sidewinder] brackets. Live combat has proved that SHAR [Sea Harrier] needs improved performance of AIM-9L [Sidewinder] to counter Mirage speed superiority. It is essential that further Sidewinders supplied are Lima variant.'[41] However, corroborating Woodward's view is the post-Conflict report by the Scientific Evaluation Team. Reflecting on the ultra-low altitudes flown by the Argentines, the analysts suggested that 'it is unlikely that AIM-9G would have guided and fuzed to within a lethal distance in all of the circumstances under which the AIM-9L was successful.'[42] Therefore, the Sea Harrier was only able to exploit one element of the AIM-9L Sidewinder's capability. Ultimately, the enduring lesson is that when procuring a new weapon system, the user must be capable of exploiting it fully through an effective integration of both the platform and sensor.

The air-to-air kills against Argentine combat aircraft highlighted to date reflect those aircraft engaged before reaching their intended targets.

However, as yet, no account has been taken of the Argentine aircraft shot down during the egress from the target area. From Ward's perspective, his sister squadron's tactics did not deliver the required deterrent effect, and its engagements occurred following weapon release and with the Argentine aircraft escaping to the mainland.[43] However, the data contained within Table 6A refutes this claim. While it would be advantageous to engage Argentine attack aircraft before striking their intended targets and, in particular, the centres of gravity, there was a clear benefit to intercepting aircraft that were returning home following their attacks. Likewise, the ability to deter the ingressing force and achieve a 'soft kill' by forcing the opposition to jettison its weapons and abort its mission before reaching its intended prey was also advantageous. The mere presence of a Sea Harrier combat air patrol could achieve a 'soft kill.' Indeed Ward suggested that 'with respect to "frightening the intruders away," this is considered by the squadron to be the next best thing to shooting him down.'[44] As shown in the previous chapters, the number of 'soft kills' achieved is an indicator of the confidence, experience levels, and will to fight of the opposition.

In contrast to the 'soft kill,' the fighter pilot nirvana was the 'hard kill' and historically a highly prized result. However, a prudent measure is to take into consideration the timeliness of the 'hard kill.' For example, a 'hard kill' against an egressing Argentine aircraft that had already dropped its weapons did not assure the protection of a potentially critical British asset. However, the benefit of an egressing kill was that further attacks by that aircraft and its crew would cease. Moreover, such attacks sent a strong message to subsequent strike missions, particularly if they were from the same unit or operating base. In contrast, there is an argument that infers that a 'soft kill' against an ingressing Argentine bomber protected the British operational centre of gravity. Additionally, the 'soft kill' sent an equally strong message to the enemy. However, the 'soft kill' did allow the reconstitution of the attacking force for a subsequent attack. Moreover, survivors can disseminate lessons across the force to negate the threat.

Table 6A shows the Sea Harrier kills broken down between the two Sea Harrier squadrons over the periods of Operation Corporate as well as Operation Sutton. Despite Ward's protestations, the evidence shows that 800 Naval Air Squadron scored twice as many air-to-air kills during Operation Corporate and Operation Sutton than the HMS *Invincible*-based 801 Naval Air Squadron commanded by Ward. At first glance, the difference in performance could be attributed to the larger number of Sea Harriers embarked on HMS *Hermes*. However, by reviewing the activity levels or the outputs of both squadrons, as shown in Annex B, suggests that 801 Naval Air Squadron flew 598 sorties vice 800 Naval Air Squadron's 737 flights. Although the weight of effort of the outputs (55 per cent of the 1,335 Sea Harrier sorties during the Conflict) rests with, as expected, the larger of the two Sea Harrier squadrons, it is not as significant a margin as the number of air-to-air kills would suggest. Consequently, 801 Naval Air Squadron were more efficient at launching its aircraft on operational missions. Indeed, 801 Naval Air Squadron achieved a very impressive serviceability rate of 99.7 per cent and beyond the 93 per cent reliability requirement set in Naval Staff Requirement 6451.[45] Ultimately, 801 Naval Air Squadron provided 40 per cent of the Sea Harrier force but flew 45 per cent of the total missions: an achievement that the unit can be justifiably proud of.

	Operation Corporate Kills		Operation Sutton			
			Kills during Ingress		Kills during Egress	
	AIM-9L Sidewinder	Gun	AIM-9L Sidewinder	Gun	AIM-9L Sidewinder	Gun
800 Naval Air Squadron	12	2	6	2[46]	2	0
801 Naval Air Squadron	5	2[47]	3	1[48]	0	0
Total	17	4	9	3	2	0

Table 6A – Sea Harrier Squadron Air-to-Air Kill Comparison.[49]

However, 800 Naval Air Squadron was more efficient in turning its outputs into 'hard kills' by achieving 14, or 67 per cent, of the twenty-one Sea Harrier kills, which included two kills against Argentine aircraft egressing from the target area. All the more impressive given the fact that, and as shown in Annex K, 800 Naval Air Squadron was responsible for the vast majority of the Sea Harrier attack missions. Therefore, the disparity in the squadrons' operating procedures did not impact on the campaign outcome. However, the different operating procedures did generate friction between both Sea Harrier squadrons.

The AIM-9L Sidewinder is only one, albeit the primary weapon that allows the Sea Harrier to deliver its air-to-air capability. The aircraft also carried two 30mm Aden cannons and, as shown in Table 6A, accounted for four kills during the Conflict. The cannon provided a level of weapon effect resilience and utility, particularly if the pilot is low on weapons, had serviceability issues, or was unfamiliar with his primary weapon system.

The effectiveness of the Sea Harrier force could have improved further if both squadrons had adopted a common set of tactical procedures. The 800 Naval Air Squadron preference for medium-altitude combat air patrols meant that the Argentine radars around Stanley could detect them. Consequently, Argentine attack aircraft may have aborted their missions due to the presence of the exposed Sea Harriers. Likewise, early detection of the Sea Harriers operating at altitude and onward communication to the Argentine ingressing forces could have allowed the Argentine aircraft to modify their route away from the area of high-density British aircraft operations. In contrast, 801 Naval Air Squadron favoured the more difficult to detect low altitude patrols. The low altitude combat air patrol gave the Sea Harrier pilot greater control as many of the on board, and external sensors, as well as communication systems, offered limited assistance while operating in the low-level arena. Therefore, the low-level combat air patrol was reliant on the pilots visually acquiring, identifying, and prosecuting their prey. Moreover, the low altitude operating environment was more fuel-intensive and, as a result, considerably reduced the fighters' on-task time when compared with operations at higher altitudes. Also, air operations at low altitude, which were reliant on the Sea Harrier seeing its prey first, are a high-risk proposition. If the attacking force saw the defending fighter first, they could dictate the subsequent engagement, particularly if the Argentines had trained and equipped to contest the air battle.

The Argentines did provide a minimal control of the air capability during the Conflict. In the latter stages of the campaign, Mirage IIIs and Daggers flew on missions to decoy rather than engage the Sea Harriers. The post-Conflict analysis would suggest that Sea Harriers were successfully lured away by these missions on several occasions.[50] For example, on the morning of 8 June, Argentine fighters lured the Sea Harrier combat air patrol away from its Fitzroy patrol area. Consequently, a breach in the British defences allowed Argentine air power to attack the RFAs *Sir Tristram* and *Sir Galahad*.[51] Later the same day, the intervention of a decoy mission saved the last remaining A-4B Skyhawk egressing from Fitzroy.[52] Despite modest gains in the latter stages of the campaign, the Argentine investment in dedicated control of the air missions compromised their air campaign. Indeed, only eighty-five of the 535 Argentine combat air missions were dedicated to control of the air, with fifty-one of the sorties flown by the Mirage III fighter aircraft.[53] Ultimately, the Mirage III was limited in capability as well as output and failed to make a definitive contribution throughout Operation Corporate.

The A-4C and A-4Q Skyhawks, as well as the Daggers, were capable of carrying air-to-air missiles (albeit weapons which were at least a generation behind the AIM-9L Sidewinder) and were carried by some of the *Fuerza Aérea Argentina* aircraft during the initial air battles of 1 May.[54] However, for the remainder of Operation Corporate, the Argentines apportioned the vast majority of their assets towards the attack role and failed to provide their aircraft with adequate air cover. While recognising that the attack mission was the main effort, it was not the sole effort. A more prudent strategy would have been to provide a sweep or escort capability for attack missions. Air forces with platforms with a limited payload must choose wisely between the control of the air and attack roles. Operating at the extremities of their operating range, with limited air-to-air refuelling assets as well as a finite number of weapon stations on their fleet of attack aircraft, the Argentines' ability to re-role into the counter-air mission would mean that there were fewer weapons available to strike the British ships. However, the deficit in the number of available attack weapons must be balanced against the need to preserve their own force and effectively contest the air battle.

The Sea Harrier provided an impressive level of output throughout Operation Corporate. The key factor in its ability to furnish its outputs was the reliability of the Sea Harrier despite the harsh and unpredictable operating environment. Annex B also reinforces that the Sea Harrier was able to sustain its surged operating tempo throughout Operation Sutton and maintain its outputs throughout the broader Operation Corporate. In contrast, and as shown in Annex A, the Argentines were simply unable to sustain the required level of output even for the limited duration of Operation Sutton. Therefore, compromising Argentine outcomes was their inability to maintain the tempo of operations.

Although the AIM-9L Sidewinders used during Operation Corporate proved statistically more productive than their Operation Desert Storm counterparts, the outcomes of both campaigns were very different. Unlike the 1991 campaign, the Sea Harriers had insufficient numbers or available time on task to saturate the Falkland Islands airspace and deliver a decisive victory before, during, and after the critical battle around San Carlos. Consequently, the Sea Harrier force achieved a partial outcome. It was constrained to a localised, favourable air situation due to an inadequate force density, a lack of organic airborne early warning, on board sensor restrictions, and limited range and payload.

As shown in Table 6B and contradicting the belief that the Sea Harrier 'represented the single most effective deterrent to [Argentine] attack plans,' the Sea Harrier capability was responsible for stopping 106 (or 9 per cent) of the 1,146 weapons planned during the campaign.[55] As a result, the Sea Harrier is the joint fifth-highest influence on the Argentine prosecution of Operation Corporate. So, if the Sea Harriers were not as capable as predicted, did British planners miss an opportunity by not using the Harrier GR3s to support the Sea Harrier in delivering the control of the air task?

The Harrier GR3 could have bolstered the number of aircraft on combat air patrol in several ways. First, by creating a dedicated Harrier GR3 combat air patrol, thus giving greater coverage. Second, adding a Harrier GR3 to each pair of Sea Harriers on combat air patrol would provide additional firepower. Third, bolster resilience via the intermittent insertion of a pair of Harrier GR3s into the existing three Sea Harrier combat air patrol plan. With limited exposure to carrier-based air defence operations, these measures would have been unwise. The Harrier GR3s were, correctly, dedicated to the support of land forces for the remainder of the campaign. In particular, British planners were keen to attack Argentine helicopters in the lead up to the landings to deny the ability of Argentine forces to rapidly deploy forward and conduct a counterattack against the British assault.[56] Therefore, relieving the Harrier GR3 of the control of the air task was a prudent measure and ensured the full exploitation of the Harrier GR3 attack expertise as well as establish a balanced apportionment between the attack and control of the air roles. This division of responsibility meant that both Harrier communities could target multiple Argentine critical vulnerabilities simultaneously. Chapter 7 discusses the Harrier GR3's contribution to the attack air power role during Operation Corporate in further detail.

The Sea Harriers were demonstrably the most significant contribution to the British control of the air role. It is perhaps not surprising given the Sea Harrier's ability to exploit the core air power attributes of speed and reach that allowed it to operate freely across the Falklands battle space for the entirety of the campaign. However, ground-based air defence and maritime force air defence also helped deliver control of the air.

The Royal Navy's air defences operated from the first day of the campaign and in large numbers. Unlike their airborne brethren, the maritime systems functioned on board ships operating at relatively slow speeds and often in vessels prioritised for other campaign tasks. Moreover, the maritime force air defence capability consisted of several different weapon systems and host platforms, each with their own strengths and weaknesses, including range, serviceability, and lethality. Nevertheless, the maritime force air defence capability was active throughout the campaign as the ships carrying it were a focus of Argentine air attacks.

The Royal Navy deployed to the South Atlantic with four different air defence missile systems: Sea Slug, Sea Cat, Sea Dart, and Sea Wolf. Initial British official reports suggested that the missiles accounted for twenty-one kills and two probables.[57] Additionally, initial Carrier Task Group assessments of the missiles' capabilities suggested that Sea Wolf and Sea Cat were 'successful' and Sea Dart as 'reasonably successful.'[58] However, and in contrast to the accurate reporting made by the Sea Harrier aircrew, the ship-based air defence results suffered from optimistic reporting. Consequently, the initial assessment was eventually pared back to seven kills with a further four kills allocated to multiple weapon systems (including ground-based air defence systems).[59]

The legacy missile systems, Sea Slug and Sea Cat, were both used during the Conflict. However, both missile systems were obsolete and ineffective in their primary role. The only effective area defence weapon deployed by the Royal Navy was the Sea Dart on the Type 42 destroyers, the bespoke Type 82 destroyer, HMS *Bristol*, and the aircraft carrier HMS *Invincible*. However, when operating in the enclosed waters of Falkland Sound and San Carlos, the Sea Dart was constrained. As with the Sea Harrier/Sidewinder combination, Sea Dart struggled to exploit its kinematic advantage when denied the long-range situational awareness from its own sensor due to the limitations of the surrounding terrain. Nevertheless, the Royal Navy fired thirty-one Sea Dart missiles in sixteen engagements during the Conflict.[60] Preliminary evaluations suggested that Sea Dart was responsible for between seven and nine kills (equating to a probability of kill between 22.5 and 29 per cent).[61] The Ministry of Defence's formal assessment of the campaign refined this appraisal to eight kills (25.8 per cent probability of kill).[62] Although Ethell and Price's subsequent analysis suggested that kills attributed to Sea Dart were as low as five (16.1 per cent probability of kill), a more in-depth analysis shows that the Sea Dart was responsible for six Argentine kills.[63] Demonstrably, Sea Dart's actual performance during the Conflict was significantly less than its theoretical pre-Conflict predictions. Nevertheless, before the Conflict, the Sea Dart was held in high regard by the Argentine air arms. Mir Gonzales suggested that 'really our main concern, before 1 May, was the Sea Dart anti-aircraft missile system on board these ships. Every night, our dreams and nightmares were about the Sea Dart.'[64] Fuelling these fears was the 'conversations with Navy pilots who knew about the destroyers and frigates, they explained to us to attack a Type 42 destroyer would require at least seven aircraft going in together, and half of these aircraft would survive the attack – maybe! That made our calculations very easy.'[65] In contrast, Freedman suggested that the poor lethality issues with Sea Dart became well known as the campaign matured. As a result, with an assessed probability of kill of 35 per cent, it was recommended to use a salvo of two Sea Darts for each target aircraft.[66] Yet, limited embarked stockpiles meant that not all ships could adhere to this guidance. For example, HMS *Exeter* arrived with only thirteen warshot missiles, forcing the ship to adopt a single shot firing policy.[67]

With the Sea Dart's lethality issues understood and mitigated, the missile system proved to be particularly useful against a wide range of targets that operated at high and low altitudes. For example, on 9 May, HMS *Coventry* successfully engaged a Puma helicopter.[68] On the morning of 25 May, she also destroyed an A-4 Skyhawk flying at medium altitude and at long-range with Sea Dart.[69] HMS *Exeter*, one of the replacement Type 42 destroyers, used its Sea Darts on several successful engagements. On 30 May, *Exeter* destroyed, at long range, two out of the four low altitude A-4C Skyhawks that were supporting the last Super Etendard/Exocet attack.[70] Over a week later, on 7 June, *Exeter* conducted another successful long-range Sea Dart engagement against a high altitude Learjet undertaking a reconnaissance mission.[71] In the early hours of 14 June, a Sea Dart employed against a medium-altitude Canberra would claim the Conflict's last kill. However, there is some debate regarding which ship launched the successful missile. HMS *Exeter* and, another of the Type 42 replacements, HMS *Cardiff,* both fired weapons. Freedman and Brown allocated the kill to HMS *Cardiff.*[72] In contrast, Burden and Hobson stated that HMS *Exeter* was responsible for the victory.[73]

Despite its successes, Sea Dart was also responsible for several issues that had campaign-wide implications. Indeed, Admiral Fieldhouse 'made no bones ... about the short-comings of the Sea Dart air defence missile system.'[74] For example, during the 12 May engagements, HMS *Glasgow* was left practically defenceless when a salt-encrusted micro-switch failed.[75] On 25 May, Argentine Skyhawks attacked HMS *Coventry* while she was operating alongside HMS *Broadsword* to the north of Pebble Island. However, the Sea Dart system was unable to detect the four attacking A-4B Skyhawks that approached at low altitude over land.[76] The ship elected to prioritise the Sea Dart engagement over the fast-approaching Sea Harrier combat air patrol. Consequently, the protection of the Type 42 destroyer, one of the British critical vulnerabilities, was delegated to the Type 22 frigate and its modern point defence system – Sea Wolf.

Designed to meet Naval Staff Requirement 6522, the Sea Wolf missile system was required to deliver a 70 per cent probability of kill against a Mach

2 missile at a range of five kilometres as well engaging a second target within five seconds.[77] Although the Sea Wolf was responsible for the only maritime force kill during Operation Sutton, it had a poor campaign.[78] The Royal Navy fired seven Sea Wolf missiles during five engagements.[79] Initial assessments suggested that the five engagements led to five kills.[80] Once again, these figures are optimistic. Further research by Ethell and Price reported that Sea Wolf was actually responsible for only three kills.[81] Moreover, commanders found Sea Wolf to have 'little use inshore, contrary to expectation.'[82] As an example, several factors complicated HMS *Broadsword's* Sea Wolf weapon employment on 25 May, including failure to maintain clear fields of fire in a congested maritime environment, software glitches, and inability to track aircraft flying in close formation.[83] Consequently, HMS *Broadsword* was unable to engage the A-4B Skyhawk raid that attacked her and HMS *Coventry*. Although HMS *Broadsword* suffered damage during the attack, HMS *Coventry* was less fortunate – she would become the second Type 42 destroyer to be sunk during the campaign. Many of the issues identified during the loss of HMS *Coventry* on 25 May were similar to those identified thirteen days earlier during the attack on HMS *Glasgow*. Even before the loss of a second Type 42 destroyer, Woodward was clearly frustrated with the Sea Dart performance. 'I despair. The GWS 30 [Sea Dart] system appears to be totally unreliable. Altogether we are in a fairly desperate situation until Rapier comes good … No vital part of our capability has been lost (yet). But we still have a very long way to go before we can be sure the back of the Arg [Argentine] air force is broken.'[84]

Unlike their air and maritime compatriots, the Rapier, Blowpipe, and Stinger surface-to-air missiles would not make their campaign debut until the British established a beachhead on 21 May. Moreover, the ground-based air defence systems were operated in relatively small numbers, constrained by limited range and mobility due to terrain and inadequate transport infrastructure. Consequently, the ground-based air defence assets were used predominantly in the localised point-defence role. Nevertheless, expectations were high. As Thompson points out, 'Rapier was seen in some quarters as the main defence of San Carlos Water against Argentine air attacks from soon after first light on D-Day.'[85] However, would Rapier be able to deliver on Woodward and Thompson's aspirations?

Following the disembarkation of the spearhead infantry, the British now needed a protective umbrella over the beachhead. Therefore, the offload began of the twelve Rapier fire units operated by T Battery (Shah Sujah's Troop) from 12 Air Defence Regiment, Royal Artillery. Consequently, ten of the twelve fire units flew into their carefully computer-modelled firing positions surrounding San Carlos Water on 21 May.[86] However, the theory and reality soon diverged. British commanders quickly discovered that the system 'could not cope with the fast, low-flying, crossing targets, very difficult to see against a land background, and often several degrees below the horizontal so the Rapier was shooting at a sharp angle downhill.'[87] Consequently, 'several days were spent re-siting most of the launchers to make best use of their limited capability.'[88] The bedding in and refining the location of the Rapier capability took time and resources. Due to the nature of the Falklands terrain, a valuable helicopter had to be dedicated to move the units, irrespective of the fact that the new location was yards or miles away. However, the Rapier's woes were not over yet, the journey south on board RFA *Sir Geraint* meant that the 'system had been exposed to the rigours of a long sea voyage and was without its second-line support.' The latter remained at Ascension Island.[89] Therefore, the serviceability of Rapier was questionable. Additionally, Rapier was a significant logistics burden. At a time when helicopter support was limited, one support helicopter had to be devoted to the Rapier sites to supply them with 160 jerry cans of fuel per day to keep the generator-powered Rapiers running.[90] Moreover, although the unit deployed with the Field Standard A version of Rapier, it did not deploy with the associated Blindfire surveillance radar. With no sensor, the operators were unable to exploit the full capability of their system.

Ultimately, the Rapier capability fielded in San Carlos did not marry with the expectations placed upon it due to several factors. Woodward had put great faith in the Rapier capability. His diary entry on 20 May recorded that 'Rapier remains the king of trumps, I just hope the pack does not turn out to be missing that card.'[91] However, by 22 May, the reality was somewhat different, the capability was still days away from becoming fully operational, there were desperate pleas for spares and that first system ashore only managed to fire one missile which malfunctioned.[92] This situation was an early indicator of Rapier's performance for the remainder of Operation Corporate. This disparity between expectation and the reality of the Rapier capability caused friction between Woodward and Thompson.[93] This circumstance would not be the first time that concerns regarding localised air superiority and Rapier availability would be the subject of senior officer engagement.

The lack of air defence cover during Operation Sutton concerned Woodward and Clapp sufficiently during the planning stages of the amphibious assault that the deployment of an additional Rapier unit was requested. Senior British commanders approved the request on 16 May, but the second unit would not arrive until 5 June.[94] The arrival of an additional Rapier unit that specialised in the fixed defence of high-value assets, such as airfields, was an ideal opportunity to move the new arrivals into the role of protectors of the newly opened Forward Operating Base at Port San Carlos. However, with the operational focus and tempo moving away from San Carlos and towards Stanley, the site saw no action at the airstrip during the tenure of 63 Squadron, RAF Regiment.

Now freed from its San Carlos tasking, T Battery split its resources to cover the two-pronged infantry advance. Four fire units moved forward with 5 Infantry Brigade to Fitzroy. At the same time, a further four fire units supported 3 Commando Brigade at Teal Inlet. The transfer between locations was protracted and problematic due to the distance, challenging terrain, and scarcity of support helicopter assets. The delay in generating air cover caused Thompson sufficient angst to inform Moore of the situation.[95] However, Thompson's risk never became an issue as his window of vulnerability was brief, and the Argentines never challenged his predicament.[96] In sharp contrast, 5 Infantry Brigade would require the immediate use of its ground-based air defence assets at Fitzroy.

On the night of 7/8 June, the RFAs *Sir Tristram* and *Sir Galahad* moved the Rapier Fire Units allocated to 5 Infantry Brigade from San Carlos to Fitzroy.[97] The importance of achieving localised air superiority was well understood. As a result, the Rapiers received priority unloading from the ship. However, the helicopter transfer from ship to shore was still continuing when the A-4B Skyhawk raid attacked the RFAs *Sir Tristram* and *Sir Galahad* on 8 June. Despite the early offload, only two of the Rapier Fire Units were operational at the time of the raid. One of the two units had a temporary defect, whereas the other Fire Unit's position was in a less than ideal location.[98] Hobson suggested that the poor location of the Rapier Fire Unit was due to the need to protect the Brigade Headquarters rather than the ships offshore.[99] However, Southby-Tailyour added that the positioning of the unit with the temporary defect was to safeguard the 'eastern sea approaches.'[100] With the overhead Sea Harrier combat air patrol decoyed, the British simply did not have a resilient layered defence to protect their critical vulnerabilities.[101] As the Egyptians learned during their push east into the Sinai Desert in the 1973 Yom Kippur War, operating outside of an assured control of the air umbrella is fraught with risk.[102]

Freedman noted that 'initially [Rapier] came out of the campaign with a strong reputation.'[103] Indeed, official British post-Conflict analysis suggested that Rapier was accountable for fourteen kills and six 'probables' from sixty-one firings, giving a probability of kill of 25.5 per cent (or 36.4 per cent if the 'probables' are incorporated).[104] However, this performance was significantly below the initial requirement, GASR 3132/1, for a Rapier Single Shot Probability of Kill of 50 per cent.[105] Further analysis established that the missile's performance was significantly worse than expected and that Rapier was responsible for only one kill.[106] The net result was a rather dismal probability of kill of less than 2 per cent. Rapier was not the panacea that many had thought it would be. Indeed, the Battery Commander's assessment that 'Rapier more than proved its worth' was woefully optimistic.[107] The Rapier capability was fragile and compromised by a long sea passage, failed to field its Blindfire radar sensor, as well as reduced mobility, sighting, and reliability. Nevertheless, could the Rapier's shortfalls be compensated by their smaller, lighter man-portable air defence systems?

In addition to the Rapier capability, the British used two further ground-based air defence systems during the Conflict: the Blowpipe and Stinger man-portable air defence systems. The latter United States-built system was used exclusively by British special forces and accounted for the downing of a Pucara over Sussex Mountains on 21 May.[108] Both Argentina and Britain used the Blowpipe missile during the Conflict. In British hands, three units used the weapon, accounting for thirty-two fire units: Royal Marines embarked on several Royal Fleet Auxiliary ships, 2 PARA as well as the Royal Marine Air Defence Troop.[109] Between the three British units, they fired ninety Blowpipes during the Conflict.[110] However, and as with the Rapier capability, Blowpipe operators over-estimated their performance by initially claiming nine kills as well as two 'probables.'[111] As the system had an expected 20 per cent probability of kill against approaching targets, the Royal Artillery's initial assessment of Blowpipe's probability of kill was 'no cause for alarm.'[112] However, the subsequent analysis confirmed that Blowpipe would only achieve a single kill (representing 1 per cent probability of kill) during the Conflict, an Aermacchi MB-339 downed during the battle at Goose Green.[113] Again, and in keeping with the other ground-based and maritime force air defence systems, Blowpipe's performance was disappointing; it failed to deliver against its performance specification, and it was unable to provide the required campaign effect.

Despite the poor 'hard' kill performance by British air defence systems, there is a possibility that the volume of defensive fire may have contributed to several attackers being distracted during their bombing runs by forcing them to abort, fly too low or miss their intended targets. However, very few mission reports mentioned any detrimental effect of British ground fire on Argentine attack runs.[114] Therefore, British ground fire is a contributing, not driving factor.

Each environment should coordinate centrally to ensure that its contribution to the control of the air task is effective. The coordinating function falls under the auspices of the air command and control role. In sharp contrast to the reality faced in the South Atlantic in 1982, contemporary British doctrine highlights that,

> 'Effective command and control is essential to delivering air power. We vest command (of a force element, organisation, or operation) in an individual to assign direct authority, responsibility, and accountability. Control describes the coordination of the activities necessary to achieve the commander's intent. We can facilitate command and control by using common procedures and doctrine and by adopting communication systems that enable us to share information simply and quickly. Command and control is a human, not technical activity. Only individuals can be held to account for their actions. This means that the air commander's leadership, initiative, imagination, knowledge, judgement, and professionalism will ultimately determine success or failure.'[115]

In addition to coordinating and controlling the kinetic elements of the control of the air, the air command and control role looks to establish and utilise a theatre-wide air picture that aims to provide an accurate, real-time situational awareness picture. Typically, the air picture would fuse several inputs from a variety of sources such as intelligence, airborne early warning aircraft, air traffic control systems, as well as ground-based and maritime air defence radars. With an understanding of what is happening in the broader area of interest, the tasks to be conducted, and available assets, effective command decisions can be made regarding tasks, priorities, apportionment, and rules of engagement. Contemporary best practice would suggest that the Air Component Commander should be the single individual accountable for the air command and control function and direct the control of the air requirements along with the other air tasking requirements. However, if there are gaps or discrepancies in the air picture, the quality of decisions can be compromised, causing potential campaign consequences. So, did air command and control operate effectively and efficiently in the Falklands Conflict? The following paragraphs will highlight two factors that had a direct influence on British air command and control: picture and process.

Compromising the Air Commander's ability to make timely and correct decisions is the lack of a unified, real-time, and accurate view of what was occurring across the theatre of operations. From an air power perspective, the lack of airborne early warning capability and fleeting maritime reconnaissance assets only compounded the issue further. Despite mitigation factors such as access to United States satellite imagery and Chilean radar systems, the British had an incomplete understanding of what was happening or about to happen, on, over and around the Falkland Islands.[116] To offset the poor British situational awareness, the implementation, enforcement, and understanding of stringent processes ensured that effective control of the air could be established and maintained.

Although the British established many processes to ensure clear boundaries and responsibilities, not all of them were successful. Many of the tactical procedures were well developed after years of practice and experience in the NATO/Cold War environment. For example, the scrambling of Sea Harriers from the aircraft carriers to meet incoming raids was a well-honed drill. However, at the operational level, processes were needed to ensure cohesion and understanding, particularly, when units, environments, and components were operating simultaneously in time and space. As an example, deconfliction procedures were implemented between the maritime, land, and air elements overhead San Carlos during Operation Sutton to minimise the chances of fratricide.[117] However, when understanding, processes, and deconfliction broke down, calamity often ensued in the form of fratricide. On 5 June, HMS *Cardiff* shot down an Army Air Corps Gazelle helicopter with a Sea Dart missile.[118] Although HMS *Cardiff* had complied with the existing rules of engagement, the ship was unaware of Argentine and British dispositions at the time of the engagement.[119] The incident was avoidable, as Moore's staff on board HMS *Fearless* knew of the Gazelle's flight, but the information did not reach HMS *Cardiff*.[120] The lack of a universal, live, and accurate awareness of friendly activities meant that the British lost a valuable helicopter and four lives. Additionally, there were several other British near-fratricide incidents, all stemming from a lack of understanding and subsequent poor communication regarding what the other components or force elements were doing.[121]

From a control of the air perspective, British air command and control was unable to offset the deficits in the three environmental areas. Despite several mitigating factors, the British were unable to furnish a real-time and accurate picture of events. Ineffective operational level processes further restricted outputs. Consequently, timely decisions made by British military commanders used applied military judgement. Despite the vast experience of many British operators, poor choices, made with best intentions, led to painful mistakes. One of the key lessons identified by the RAF was that 'the Command and Control organisation was not as practised in peacetime exercises which caused confusion at unit level.'[122] Beyond the highlighted control of the air issues, British air command and control will be reviewed further in the next chapter.

Ranking	**Causal Factor**	**Scale (out of 1146)**	**Percentage**
1	Weapons not Dropped	291	25
2	Weapon Employment – Missed Target	272	24
3	Serviceability – Air Abort	162	14
4	Mission Cancelled	131	11
5	**Sea Harrier – Soft Kill**	**87**	**8**
6	Serviceability – Ground Abort	37	3
7	Serviceability – Weapon Employment	33	3
8	**Maritime Force Air Defence – Soft Kill**	**32**	3
9	Navigation Errors	21	**2**
10	Weapon Employment – Hit and Detonates	20	2
=11	Weapon Employment – Unexploded Bomb	19	2
=11	**Sea Harrier – Hard Kill**	**19**	**2**
13	**Maritime Force Air Defence – Hard Kill**	**8**	**<1**
14	**Ground-based Air Defence – Soft Kill**	7	**<1**
15	Aircraft Crashed before Dropping Weapon	2	<1
16	Target Mis-Identified	5	<1
	Total	1146	100

Table 6B – Causal Factors for Failure to Deliver Weapons during Operation Corporate.

The British ability to overcome their opposition was not as convincing as some commentators would depict. Expanding 3 Commando Brigade's concerns over the lack of Rapier and Blowpipe assets to encompass the majority of British control of the air assets is apposite.[123] Consequently, the high reliability of some British assets was insufficient to mitigate the lack of mass. As a result, the British were unable to cover, never mind saturate the airspace throughout Operation Corporate. The topography of the landing area and the surrounding high ground, while screening the amphibious force, also highlighted sensor limitations that compromised the ability to detect, identify, intercept and fully exploit the kinematic advantages of the various weapons used by the British forces. Ultimately, the British were unable to assure control of the air throughout Operation Sutton or the broader Operation Corporate.

Although Table 6B gives an aggregation of Argentine performance across all three phases, it is also an accurate reflection of the campaign with many of the trends and issues remaining consistent. As a result, Argentine failures rather than British victories dominate Table 6B. However, and given the disappointing performance of ground-based air defence and maritime force air defence, it is not surprising that the Sea Harrier was the most effective British contribution to the defence of Operation Corporate. However, the Sea Harrier only ranks as the fifth most effective source of negating the number of enemy weapons that reached the Task Force. Of note, the Sea Harrier's 'soft' kill capability performed better than its 'hard' kill capability. Arguably, the perception of the capability thus trumps the reality. Consequently, an active deception plan that feeds the enemy with a false impression of your capability or exploits their concerns and weaknesses will help to deliver the campaign end-state.

Combining British control of the air capabilities, the British defence of their centres of gravity accounts for the destruction or deterrence of 13 per cent of the 1,146 weapons. Ultimately, the outcome of Operation Corporate was assured, not by a dominant British defence of their centre of gravity against enemy efforts, but by Argentine air power failing to understand, find and attack the British centres of gravity. With the British ability to defend their centres of gravity now understood, the next chapter will assess the ability to understand, find, and strike effectively the Argentine operational centre of gravity. Additionally, Chapter 7 will also review the Argentine's ability to protect its own centre of gravity.

Chapter 7

Prosecuting the Argentine Operational Centre of Gravity – The British Fascination with Stanley Airport

'Argentine use of Port Stanley airfield and its surveillance radars constrains all our operations, enables redeployment and resupply of Argentine forces and maintains Argentine morale.'

Initial Plan for Operation Sutton,
Presented to Chiefs of Staff,
2 April.[1]

From the outset of the Falklands campaign, British military planners placed significant focus on neutralising Stanley airport as soon as possible. Despite notable British efforts to hinder air operations at Stanley airport throughout the campaign, damage to the runway surface was light. Consequently, the Argentines were able to use the airport right up until the evening before their surrender. Indeed, in the days immediately after the Conflict, it was reported that 'inspection of Port Stanley airfield by RAF LO [Liaison Officer] indicates full runway length of 4,100 feet to be serviceable but fuel handling equipment, ATC [Air Traffic Control] tower and hangars badly damaged.'[2] The British tactical failure to close down the airport led to significant post-Conflict debate. In response to a question from a Member of Parliament, the Permanent Under-Secretary of State for the Armed Forces stated that 'it is true that the attacks were not as successful as one would have wished, all the bombs dropped in its immediate vicinity and caused immense disruption and casualties to the Argentines.'[3] The limited success of the airfield attacks has led to substantial argument, mostly focused on the tactical utility of specific platforms. The debate does little to lessen inter-Service rivalry. However, perhaps British military leaders could have posed a more fundamental question during the initial planning phase of the campaign. Was there a need to attack the airfield throughout the campaign, or could the British attack resources have been put to better use on a different set of targets?

In his initial response to the proposed airfield attack, Admiral Leach said that it 'would be vital to deny Port Stanley airfield to the Argentines as soon as possible, and certainly before the Carrier Battle Group arrived.'[4] Therefore, the initial aspiration was to seek control of the air from the very outset of the campaign. Moreover, Leach's view also highlighted that the control of the air battle should begin even before the aircraft carriers arrived in theatre and beyond the reach of the embarked Sea Harriers. However, Leach's aspiration for a short, sharp, decisive blow against Stanley airport failed to take into consideration aircraft availability and capability. The inability of the combined Vulcan and Sea Harrier airfield attacks on 1 May to achieve this task meant that 'the decision to mount a further Vulcan attack was taken because reconnaissance had revealed that while the runway at Port Stanley was cratered, it was still possible for light aircraft, such as the Pucara, to use it.'[5] Consequently, the small airport became the target for a large number of British combat air attacks that lingered throughout the campaign.

Attacks on the airfield were not limited to those from the air. Significant effort was also invested in naval bombardment, starting on the afternoon of 1 May with HMS *Glamorgan*, *Arrow*, and *Alacrity* firing 154 rounds at the airfield infrastructure. As with the air attacks, the naval bombardment would continue throughout the campaign.[6] Nevertheless, the cost of the naval gunfire support effort would be significant. During the sixty-three bombardments, the ships suffered twelve air attacks resulting in one ship sunk, five severely damaged, and four slightly damaged.[7] Despite the combined British effort, the airport remained operational. Notwithstanding the effectiveness of British endeavours, was the British strategy appropriate and balanced?

To answer the question, this chapter reviews the key British combat air participants and their weapons. The following section articulates the various elements that constituted the Argentine operational centre of gravity. The next segment reflects on British air-to-ground weapon employment, before analysing the British combat air outputs as well as identifying the challenges in meeting the desired campaign outcomes. The chapter concludes with a look at the Argentines' ability to defend their operational centre of gravity.

The Key British Attack Participants

In addition to the Vulcan, Sea Harrier and Harrier GR3, recognition is also due to the British helicopter force's contribution to the attack role. However, helicopter attack missions were infrequent and minor in terms of outputs and outcomes. Therefore, the book discards these missions.

With the Vulcan in the twilight of its career, its utility in Operation Corporate was by no means obvious. However, the Vulcan's unique advantages were its range and large payload. Nevertheless, these positive attributes had to be offset by the Vulcan's lack of precision, limited crew training and experience in both the tactical bombing role and air-to-air refuelling. The strategic level also contemplated the utility of the Vulcan.

In addition to the airfield attack against Stanley airport, the British also considered the use of the Vulcan to strike Argentine mainland targets. As highlighted by Sheffield, the real value of the Black Buck missions 'lay in alerting Argentina to a possible threat to the mainland and thus tying down air assets that could have been deployed against the Task Force. Although not mentioned by Freedman, some suggest that the use of a nuclear-capable V bomber in the tactical role was a means of tightening the pressure on the Junta, by hinting at Britain's power and resolve.'[8] Despite the potential deterrence benefits of forcing Argentine air assets to defend their homeland, the concept did not become a reality. On 12 May, the Foreign Secretary concurred with the Defence department's view that it should rule out the expansion of the Vulcan's role in the campaign due to concerns over the continued need to maintain international support for the British position.[9] Additionally, there were more practical concerns, including Vulcan survivability and the ability to deliver the required tactical effect, a view based on the poor performance to date of the strikes against Stanley airport.[10] The decision to not strike the Argentine mainland was never made public. The Foreign and Commonwealth Office felt that 'the MOD's reluctance to renounce the option publicly is comprehensible, but it would be wise if the landing goes ahead to convey reassuring signals to the moderates in Latin America.'[11]

Nevertheless, even as late as 25 May, four days after the British amphibious assault at San Carlos, an internal RAF report reinvigorated the discussion. The granting of clearance on 21 May for the Vulcan to carry and release three 1000lb laser-guided bombs, coinciding with the Argentinian combat air surge to counter the British amphibious assault, may have resurrected interest in exploiting the Vulcan's potential.[12] The report suggested that 'attacks by Vulcan aircraft on the airfields at San Julian, Rio Gallegos, and Rio Grande are feasible, and that attacking aircraft could recover to Ascension if a reduced 1000lb bomb load or three laser-guided bombs were carried.'[13] The assessment of the plan is unknown. However, with Operation Sutton about to culminate and waning Argentinian combat air power, the extant risks at the tactical, operational, and strategic levels are likely to have significantly outweighed the benefits. Nevertheless, the Vulcan's broader campaign utility of delivering strategic effect was understood and considered but neither exploited nor denied in the public domain.

As for attacking Stanley airport itself, Beetham initially favoured the Sea Harrier option but soon became 'an extremely hawkish proponent of the idea' of the Vulcan's utility during the campaign.[14] However, Beetham's biographer perceived that the argument was not a Vulcan *vice* Sea Harrier debate. Beetham desired to see the full gamut of combat air missions being used rather than solely focus on the defensive counter-air mission.[15] At the initial Chiefs of Staff presentation on attacking Stanley airport, even the First Sea Lord suggested, 'only the Vulcan could do this, and in case, the Sea Harriers should be conserved to support the landing.'[16] However, there was a different naval perspective developing in the South Atlantic. The Sea Harrier force had developed its own plan to attack Stanley airport using ten aircraft in a joint night/dusk raid with the intent of rendering 'the majority of aircraft based at Port Stanley unserviceable or destroyed and to crater the main runway making it unusable for Argentine attack aircraft.'[17] Moreover, rather than seeing the Vulcan mission as an opportunity to preserve their small and outnumbered Sea Harrier force for the vital defensive counter-air role, the deployed Fleet Air Arm pilots saw the Vulcan raid as an 'expensive and cumbersome effort to achieve an uncertain result.'[18] The lack of trust, understanding, and cooperation between the RAF and Fleet Air Arm, as highlighted in the 1965 Templer Report, had manifested itself again.

Nevertheless, on 30 April, the British Task Force was informed that the Vulcan raid would precede the Sea Harrier attack.[19] Consequently, and with its retirement from service within sight, the Vulcan was about to have its baptism of fire. As specified in the Operation Corporate Air Operation Order 3/82, the mission was to 'impede Argentine air operations from Stanley airfield.'[20] The term 'impede' is perhaps a realistic reflection on the difficulty in delivering the task on a small target, thousands of miles away in an ageing bomber with a crew unfamiliar with the conventional role. Nevertheless, most analysts seemed to infer that the Vulcan was required to deliver a more robust effect, such as 'deny' or 'destroy.'[21] It would appear that the British practitioners were approaching the same task with two patently different views on the required outcome. There was a distinct lack of understanding and unity of effort between the planners in Britain and those in the South Atlantic when it came to the task and purpose of curtailing Argentine air operations from Stanley airport.

A small cadre of crews from across the three remaining Vulcan squadrons was selected to undergo specific training to prepare for potential South Atlantic missions. The requirement for Vulcan air-to-air refuelling missions had lapsed in the post-Polaris and 'East of Suez' period. Therefore, the crews had minimal experience in air-to-air refuelling, and the aircraft required modification to refresh the lapsed capability.[22] Consequently, the Vulcans conducted day and night tanking missions with the RAF Marham-based Victors from mid-April, supported by experienced air-to-air refuelling instructors.[23] Likewise, the crews practised their newly re-acquired conventional attack techniques in a similar timeframe.[24]

After years of neglect, and in addition to regenerating the Vulcan's air-to-air refuelling capability, the aircraft also required attention. The long oversea transit meant that the traditional method of radar navigation using ground features was not a viable option. Similarly, astronavigation was too inaccurate to deliver the level of precision navigation required. Carousel navigation systems scavenged from former British Airways Vickers VC10s, held in storage at RAF Abingdon, provided the required solution.[25] Another equipment area that required immediate attention was the on-board jamming systems. Although the system was effective against legacy Soviet equipment, it was ineffective against emerging Soviet threats and the more modern Western systems such as those used by the Argentines. The solution was to borrow a more modern AN/ALQ-101D jamming pod, as used by the RAF's Buccaneer force, and then to integrate it onto the aircraft via the defunct Skybolt missile external pylons.[26]

After an intensive training and engineering period, two Vulcans departed RAF Waddington and arrived at Wideawake Airfield on Ascension Island at 1800 on 29 April.[27] Aircraft parking space at the airfield was at a premium throughout the campaign. Air Vice-Marshal George Chesworth, the Chief of Staff (Air) at 18 Group, noted that 'because of a shortage of parking space at Wideawake, it was necessary to limit aircraft numbers based there.'[28] Therefore, careful orchestration of the number and type of aircraft held at Ascension Island was required to always launch the priority missions on time. As a result, the Vulcans were not permanent residents at Ascension Island throughout Operation Corporate.[29] When not in use, the aircraft would be flown back to RAF Waddington so that the higher priority tasks could use the airfield. As a result, Nimrod maritime radar reconnaissance missions and Hercules air drops, both requiring extensive use of the limited number of Victor air-to-air refuelling aircraft, could conduct their missions.[30] Consequently, two factors limited the Vulcan's output: available ramp space at Ascension and access to the required number of Victor air-to-air refuelling aircraft.

The second British aircraft type to conduct offensive combat air operations during the Conflict was the Sea Harrier. Although the Sea Harrier's focus was the defensive counter-air role, it was, by design, a multi-role combat aircraft. Consequently, the aircraft was used extensively during the Conflict in the attack role. However, and deliberately, there was a less than equitable split in the apportionment of attack missions across the Sea Harrier community. Ward said that 'the [HMS] *Hermes* air group would be biased towards ground/surface attack whereas [HMS] *Invincible* would act as the Anti-Air Warfare Control ship.'[31] As a result, 800 Naval Air Squadron on board HMS *Hermes* bore the significant brunt of the Sea Harrier attack missions.[32] According to Ward, the different modus operandi of the two Sea Harrier squadrons reflected the individual squadron's experience levels.[33] Additionally, there may also be more practical reasons why the two Sea Harriers adopted different approaches. First, the HMS *Hermes*-based Sea Harrier squadron was physically larger than its counterparts on board HMS *Invincible* and, as a result, could take on the additional tasking. Moreover, the aircraft carrier's physical design and capacity are another reason why 800 Naval Air Squadron was the lead unit for the attack role.

NSR 7097, the Naval Staff Requirement for the *Invincible*-class of aircraft carrier, stated that the air weapons stockpile requirement was 'forty AIM-9 Sidewinder air-to-air missiles, eighteen air-to-surface guided missiles, eighteen conventional 1000lb bombs and twenty-four Lepus flares.'[34] The small weapon stockpile allocated to the embarked combat air assets is a reminder of the anti-submarine warfare focus for the new class of aircraft carriers. Moreover, the stockpile requirement matched the limited combat air capability embarked, both in terms of the number of aircraft on board and the relative importance of the combat air role. By way of comparison, 'stowage in the volumetrically-similar [HMS] *Hermes* was 750 conventional 500lb bombs and considerably more guided weapons.'[35] As with the available ramp space at Ascension Island that affected Vulcan operations, the available infrastructure, whether land or sea-based, dictated and constrained the ways and tempo of working. Limiting the requirements at an early design stage, whether driven by lack of vision, cost, or political constraint, will ultimately constrain the platform's utility as it endeavours to adapt to the challenges of the contemporary environment beyond the drawing board.

The original specification for the Sea Harrier reflected that the aircraft procurement was 'to provide the Fleet with an organic capability for air intercept, reconnaissance, probe and limited surface attack.'[36] However, the surface attack capability was to support an anti-ship strike using air-to-surface guided weapons, rockets, bombs and 30mm cannon.[37] Of note, and reflecting the aircraft's maritime focus, there is no mention of a counter-land attack requirement in the original Sea Harrier specification. To facilitate the surface attack mission, the Sea Harrier's radar was to have an 'air-to-surface search capability against targets ranging in size from FPB [Fast Patrol Boats] to large cruisers.'[38] However, the requirement document also stated that the surface attack requirement 'should not be to the detriment, in cost or weight of the AI [Air Intercept] radar design.'[39] The last caveat, again, reflected that the Sea Harrier's focus was on the air-to-air role.

Despite recent software updates for the weapon-aiming computer, such as the 'Falk Loft 82' programme, the Sea Harrier lacked a precision attack capability.[40] However, many considered the Sea Harrier to be an effective attack platform. At the strategic level, the Chief of the Air Staff suggested that 'the Sea Harrier would be the most effective means of putting Port Stanley Airfield out of action; the Vulcans would also be effective, but carry a higher risk of causing civilian casualties.'[41] At the start of the Conflict, none of the deployed British combat air assets had a precision attack capability. Moreover, each aircraft type had limitations employing their 'dumb' weapons. Indeed, the Scientific Evaluation Team in its post-Conflict report noted that 'neither the Sea Harrier or [Harrier] GR3 were designed for [high altitude] attack and no appropriate bomb ballistic data was available. The drop accuracy achieved could not have been compatible with the damage radius of the bomb.'[42] In contrast, Ward states that the Sea Harrier could use its Blue Fox radar to update the NAVHARS [Navigation Heading Attitude Reference System] to conduct an effective medium-level attack.[43] Nevertheless, Ward played down the accuracy of such an attack when he suggested that the Sea Harrier was just as capable as a Vulcan.[44] However, the Sea Harrier's effectiveness as an attack aircraft did not achieve consensus throughout the Sea Harrier community. Indeed, 800 Naval Air Squadron aboard HMS *Hermes* had less confidence in the Sea Harrier's capabilities than its counterparts on board HMS *Invincible*.[45]

The lack of faith in the Sea Harrier's ability to operate effectively in the medium-level attack role is a reflection of the results that it was able to achieve. On listening to the radio communications of his sister squadron during medium level bombing raids against Stanley airport, Ward had 'heard calls of "1 mile short", "2 miles over" from the [HMS] *Hermes* boys.'[46] Pook also suggested that other Sea Harrier attack techniques were ineffective. 'In spite of the peacetime boasts of the Sea Harrier operators, their weapon system at that time was not capable of hitting a runway 4,000 feet long and 90 feet wide from a toss-bombing attack.'[47] Corroborating Pook's view is the Sea Harrier requirement document that stipulated that a bomb dropped from a Sea Harrier during a low level or toss attack should have a CEP (Circular Error of Probability) of 140 feet and 500 feet respectively.[48]

Ward's contention that the Sea Harrier was a more efficient platform than the fuel-intensive Black Buck missions is a difficult proposition to counter. Noting that he used different figures in his book and his official report, Ward suggested that for a single Vulcan bombing raid, the equivalent fuel would allow Sea Harriers to drop between 500 and 1,300 bombs.[49] However, Ward is guilty of simply measuring outputs and failed to take into consideration the operational effect required. Additionally, Ward does not highlight that a Sea Harrier with a full weapon payload would necessitate the removal of the external fuel tanks to cater for the additional weapons. Consequently, the Sea Harrier would be significantly short of fuel and suffer from a limited operating range. As a result, the aircraft carrier would have to be positioned unpalatably close to the Argentine threat to offset the deficit in aircraft range. Moreover, the Sea Harrier's focus on control of the air meant that it did not have sufficient aircraft, pilots, or time to fly the additional attack missions. Also, the extensive logistical support needed, both in terms of weapon stockpile and Royal Fleet Auxiliary ships to supply the additional fuel, was not available. Ultimately, Ward's assertion makes for an impressive headline but falls short when scrutinised more closely.

Nevertheless, the argument that the Sea Harrier was a more accurate attack platform has some theoretical basis. David Castle, a Vulcan navigator who participated in two Black Buck missions, stated that the CEP of a Vulcan medium-level radar attack was 1900 feet, some 700 feet greater than the Sea Harrier, as declared by one of the RAF exchange officers.[50] Additionally, primary source evidence also claimed that the Vulcan had a significantly poorer CEP during low-level attacks than the Sea Harrier. During the Vulcan work-up training, a 750-foot CEP 'is a reasonable estimate of delivery accuracy based on the trial results from Jurby and Garvie Island for low level delivery.'[51] However, the Sea Harrier operational analysis opined that 'four aircraft attacking the centre of the runway with five 1000lb bombs, 15 degrees off the centreline, would have a 95 per cent chance of cutting the runway given a delivery error of 100 feet CEP.'[52] Nevertheless, the reality would prove to be a very different prospect. Consequently, analysis of the British attack outputs and what they actually achieved will provide some form of clarity on the success or otherwise of the British attacks against Stanley airport.

The last British attack platform to be considered is the Harrier GR3. The RAF carrier-based attack capability was a belated, but timely, arrival in the Operation Corporate order of battle. Unlike the multi-role Sea Harrier, the Harrier GR3 was a dedicated attack platform. As part of its routine Cold War tasking, the Harrier GR3 was employed 'in the classic offensive air support role providing close air support, battlefield air interdiction and tactical air reconnaissance for the relevant army units.'[53] Consequently, the Harrier GR3 role was to attack targets that were 'second echelon Warsaw Pact armoured formations and mobile first echelon equipments where a rapid response for close air support was needed.'[54] By 1976, and to assist them with its task, the Harrier GR1 force received an upgrade to the GR3 standard. One of the enhancements was the distinctive thimble nose containing a laser ranging marked target seeker to provide accurate ranging between the target and aircraft.[55] However, and unlike the Sea Harrier, there was no sensor to cue the pilot onto the target itself. Therefore, the pilot was reliant upon seeing and identifying the target with his own eyes. Target identification was a significant challenge for a single-seat aircraft operating in a benign environment. During the Falklands Conflict, the problem was even more significant as the pilots were operating in contested airspace, at low-level, in poor weather and high speed against concealed as well as camouflaged targets. As a result, pilots were frequently unable to detect the target on their first pass. The lack of an on-board sensor also meant that the Harrier GR3 had no night or all-weather attack capability. Consequently, it is not surprising that, and as pointed out in a Number 38 Group report following the Conflict, medium-level and loft attacks in concert with a Sea Harrier and simultaneous dropping of weapons 'provided the better deliveries.'[56] As a result, the Harrier GR3 force was rarely able to provide adequate support to British land forces during the critical battles as its attacks 'were little more than nuisance value.'[57]

The Sea Harrier and the Harrier GR3 both had five weapon stations and two under-fuselage 30mm Aden cannon pods. However, the inboard wing pylons routinely carried 100-gallon fuel tanks. Consequently, a maximum of three weapon stations were available to carry weapons. Nevertheless, if the Harrier GR3 was carrying a reconnaissance pod on the centreline fuselage pylon or there was limited time to rearm the aircraft, the payload was usually limited to two weapons, one on each of the outboard wing pylons.[58] The British used five different air-to-ground weapons during the offensive air operations phase of the Falklands Conflict: the 1000lb bomb, the Royal Navy 2-Inch rockets, the BL755 cluster bomb, the Paveway laser-guided bomb, and the AGM-45A Shrike anti-radiation missile. The latter two weapons were precision-guided and rapidly introduced into service during the latter stages of the Conflict.

The 1000lb bomb was the only weapon carried by all three British attack platforms during the Conflict. Moreover, and as shown in Figure 7.1, the 1000lb bomb was also the most widely used British weapon. The 1000lb bomb could use several pre-set fuse settings to optimise the effect the weapon delivered against its intended target. The various fuses would allow the weapon to detonate on impact, at a pre-determined height above the ground, or at a pre-set time after impact. The 1000lb bomb could also use a free-fall or a parachute retard tail, the latter for low-level delivery.[59] Consequently, the 1000lb bomb had a broad utility if it could be delivered accurately. Low altitude and laydown attacks offered the most accurate results but meant that the bomb would strike the target at a sub-optimal angle and speed if penetration of the target was required; for example, breaking through a runway surface. Moreover, the attacking aircraft was more vulnerable to ground fire if it had to overfly the target area at low altitude. In contrast, medium-altitude, high-angle dive, and loft attacks provided greater survivability for the attacking aircraft and a better penetration angle, but this was to the detriment of precision.

Establishing the total number of weapons dropped by each of the British aircraft types was a relatively straightforward affair. Archival evidence clearly shows that 800 Naval Air Squadron dropped the highest number of 1000lb bombs during Operation Corporate; 144 in total.[60] In contrast, During its three bombing raids, the Vulcan dropped sixty-three 1000lb bombs, the Harrier GR3s used fifty-nine 1000lb bombs, and 801 Naval Air Squadron employed a further fifty-six bombs.[61] However, and despite the recent release of the primary source material, including combat mission reports, the specific weapon loads and usage per mission is more complicated to break down. Consequently, establishing the exact employment of each of the 322 British 1000lb weapons used during the Conflict is difficult to determine.

Adapting the 1000lb bomb into a laser-guided weapon was a relatively straightforward process from an engineering perspective. To turn the 'dumb' bomb into a smart weapon, it required the coupling of the legacy bomb to a 'well-proven American "Paveway" seeker head and guidance unit bolted on the front end. A set of flip-out stabilising fins was bolted on at the rear of the bomb.'[62] The conversion turned 'dumb 1940-vintage bombs into a piece of cutting-edge technology.'[63] However, the integration and employment of the new weapon were far more problematic. Prior to the Conflict, the Paveway laser-guided bomb was not part of the Harrier GR3 inventory. Nevertheless, the rapidly introduced weapon allowed the Harrier GR3 to attack with greater precision. C-130 Hercules flown from Ascension Island air-dropped the Paveway modification kits to the Task Force on 24 May.[64] Harrier GR3s used the weapons against Argentine targets six days later.[65] However, the lack of understanding of, and experience with, the new weapon soon became evident. There was confusion regarding how to deliver the required laser reflection from the designated target effectively. As a result, many of the initial weapons missed their target.[66] Nevertheless, once the air and ground parties had refined the procedures, the weapon was more effective during the latter stages of the land campaign. No. 1 (Fighter) Squadron dropped eleven laser-guided bombs during the Conflict, but only four guided successfully.[67] Ultimately, the weapons were responsible for direct hits on an artillery piece and a company headquarters.[68] Additionally, both the Vulcan in the United Kingdom and the Sea Harrier in the Falklands trialled the use of laser-guided bombs.[69] However, neither platform employed the weapons operationally.

Designed in the early 1970s, the Hunting Engineering BL755 cluster bomb countered lightly armoured targets and unprotected troops.[70] The cluster bomb incorporated seven bays, each containing twenty-one sub-munitions, creating a total of 147 munitions per weapon. However, there is a dispute concerning the weapon's usefulness. The Air Commander's Report highlighted that the weapon's 'utility was degraded against well dug-in defensive positions.'[71] In contrast, a post-Conflict Scientific Evaluation Team reported that 'interrogation of prisoners established quite unambiguously that air burst ammunition sapped their will to fight and that damage to weapons, machine guns was substantial.'[72] Nevertheless, both units on board HMS *Hermes* used the BL755 cluster bomb during Operation Corporate. Despite losing 240 cluster bombs, 30 per cent of the deployed stockpile, during the sinking of MV *Atlantic Conveyor*, 1 (Fighter) Squadron alone dropped eighty-three cluster bombs during the Conflict.[73]

In contrast, the HMS *Hermes*-based Sea Harrier squadron used twenty-one BL755 cluster bombs during Operation Corporate.[74]

During routine land-based operations, the Harrier GR3 force usually used the 68mm SNEB (*Societe Nouvelle des Etablissements Edgar Brandt)* rocket pod. The SNEB rockets were particularly effective against armoured fighting vehicles, bunkers, or soft targets. However, due to high electromagnetic forces on board ship, the SNEB rocket capability was not cleared for carrier-based operations.[75] Consequently, the Harrier GR3s had to rapidly adapt to the Royal Navy's equivalent capability – the Royal Navy 2-inch rocket pod.[76] After a hasty clearance process, permission to carry and fire the alternative weapon arrived on 26 April. Pre-deployment training was limited to one Harrier GR3 pilot deploying to Royal Naval Air Station Yeovilton to carry out a brief trial sortie only a few days prior to the Squadron's deployment to the South Atlantic.[77] However, the Royal Navy 2-inch rockets performed in a very similar manner to the SNEB rockets, albeit with a wider 'shotgun-like' distribution following launch.[78] Despite the lack of familiarity with the new weapons system, a shortage of cluster bombs compelled the Harrier GR3 force to use the Royal Navy 2-inch rockets.[79] Although the Royal Navy 2-inch rockets gave the Harrier GR3 force a degree of stand-off from the target, the weapon had a smaller footprint than the BL755 cluster bomb and suffered from a significant number of misfires.[80] Nevertheless, as the sole user of the capability during the Conflict, the Harrier GR3 force employed fifty-two pods of Royal Navy 2-inch rockets.[81]

To negate the Argentine surveillance radar systems, in particular, the Westinghouse AN/TPS-43 radar that provided long-range detection and early warning of British air activity to the Argentine attack force, the British required an effective suppression of enemy air defence capability. A secondary target set was the radars that supported the anti-aircraft artillery. The Vulcan was the most likely launch platform for the new mission. However, the weapon choice proved to be more problematic. Trials conducted in early May with the Martel anti-radiation missile, as used by the RAF's Buccaneer fleet, proved unsuccessful.[82] Therefore, the British requested United States permission to access and use their stockpile of AGM-45A Shrike anti-radiation missiles. As each AGM-45A Shrike had a specific seeker dedicated to searching a defined band of the radar spectrum, there were several missile variants to consider. The 'Dash 10' variant looked at the part of the spectrum where AN/TPS-43 early warning radar resided. In contrast, the 'Dash 9' option of the AGM-45A Shrike specifically searched for the Skyguard and Superfledermaus radars that supported the anti-aircraft artillery.[83] As a result, the Vulcan had to carry a mix of 'Dash 9' and 'Dash 10' AGM-45A Shrikes so that the British could attack the full spectrum of Argentine radars.

The supply of missiles, as well as aircrew and engineer training, was supported by the visit of AGM-45A Shrike-equipped USAF F-4G Phantoms from Spangdahlem Air Force Base in West Germany over the period 19 - 23 May at RAF Waddington.[84] Additionally, technicians from Naval Air Station China Lake, Nevada, assisted the endeavour.[85] The Vulcans were rapidly modified to carry a pair of AGM-45A Shrikes under each wing on the Skybolt wing pylons. However, due to the lack of time, aircrew training was minimal. Castle suggested that his crew's training was limited to testing the missile seeker against the air traffic control radar at RAF St Mawgan in Cornwall as they flew from RAF Waddington to Ascension Island on 26 May.[86] Nevertheless, a second Vulcan crew were more fortunate as 'the Shrike ARM [anti-radiation missile] was test fired on 27 May after a rapid feasibility study, and deployed to Ascension Island on the same day.'[87] After an aborted attempt on 28 May, the first of two successful Vulcan suppression of enemy air defence missions, Black Buck 5, was launched on 30 May.[88] Of the

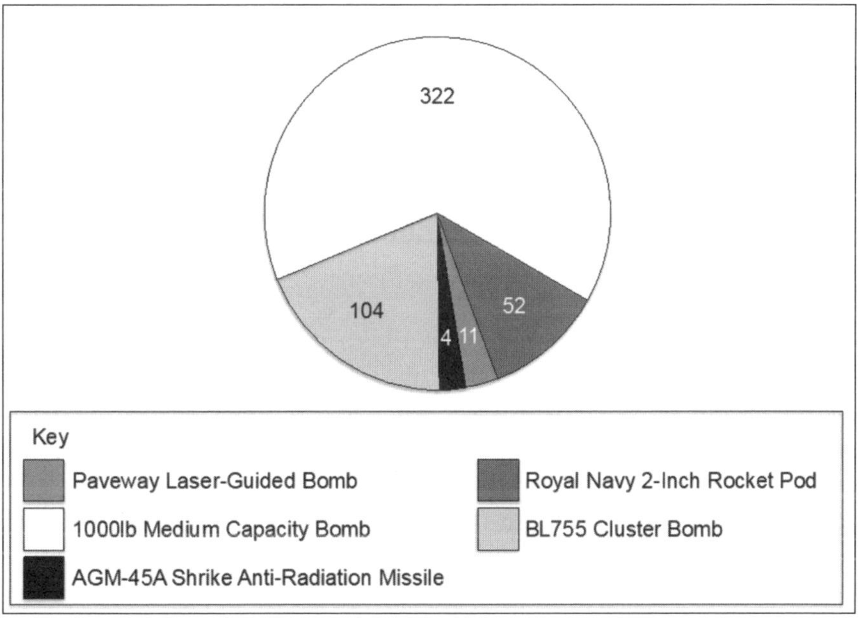

Figure 7.1 – British Attack Weapons Usage by Weapon Type.

eight AGM-45A missiles flown over the Falkland Islands during the Conflict, the Vulcans fired four with two missiles hitting or damaging targets.[89]

The British intent was to not limit the AGM-45A Shrike capability solely to the Vulcan. The Harrier GR3 also planned to be an AGM-45A Shrike platform. One of the replacement Harrier GR3 aircraft that arrived on board HMS *Hermes* on 8 June was capable of using the AGM-45A Shrike missiles.[90] However, the Harrier's AGM-45A Shrike capability was hampered by a lack of missiles, as the original weapons were not offloaded from a VC10 transport aircraft at Ascension Island as intended. Uruguayan authorities found and impounded the missiles during an aircraft inspection after it had been re-tasked with aeromedical duties to Montevideo.[91] Nevertheless, eight missiles, four launchers, and associated equipment were parachuted to the Task Force on 10 June by a C-130 Hercules on a 25-hour resupply mission from Ascension Island.[92] As a result, the Harrier force was AGM-45A Shrike–capable only from 13 June. The Argentine surrender 24 hours later thus precluded the missile's use during Operation Corporate.

As shown in Figure 7.1, the vast majority of weapons employed by the British during the Falklands Conflict were non-precision weapons. Of the 493 weapons used during the Conflict, only fifteen were precision weapons. Of note, the British rushed both types into service at short notice. Consequently, the success rate of the precision weapons was low and reflected the limited time the crews had to train and familiarise themselves with the nuances of their new systems.

Defining the Argentine Operational Centre of Gravity during Operation Corporate

It was imperative that the British attack forces understood their opposition's critical vulnerabilities and attacked the most susceptible and valuable targets. In contrast to the British forces that had to deploy, shape, and strike the Argentines to recover the Falkland Islands, the Argentines had the much simpler role of protecting and holding Stanley. The only forces that could achieve this task were the Argentine land forces. As a result, the Argentine operational centre of gravity throughout the Conflict was the Argentine land force located in and around Stanley. Table 7A shows the Argentine operational centre of gravity analysis. Of note, the study of the Argentine operational centre of gravity shows that the airfield at Stanley is a recurring critical vulnerability.

Centre of Gravity	**Critical Capabilities**
Argentine land forces in and around Stanley	1. The ability to hold ground. 2. The ability to defeat British land forces. 3. The ability to negate British air power.
Critical Vulnerabilities	**Critical Requirements**
1.1.1. Morale of land force. 1.1.2. Quality of troops. 1.1.3. Quantity of troops. 1.1.4. Shelter from environment. 1.2.1. Sea control to deliver goods by ship. 1.2.2. Stanley Airport to receive goods. 1.2.3. Freedom of manoeuvre on land to move goods. 1.2.4. Transport aircraft to deliver goods to the Islands. 1.2.5. Support helicopters to deliver goods around Islands. 2.1.1. Effective support weapons. 2.1.2. Shelter from enemy fires. 2.1.3. Quantity of troops. 2.1.4. Quality of troops. 2.1.5. Morale of land force. 2.2.1. Stanley Airport to support fast jet attack aircraft. 2.2.2. Available Argentine attack capability. 2.3.1. Reach of Argentine artillery and heavy weapons. 2.3.2. Effective Communications. 3.1.1. *Fuerza Aérea Argentina* to contest control of the air. 3.1.2. Ground-based air defence capability beyond Stanley. 3.1.3. Stanley Airport to support fast jet combat aircraft. 3.2.1. Surveillance radars for air command and control. 3.2.2. Strong leadership. 3.2.3. Effective communications. 3.2.4. Situational awareness.	Disciplined, well-led soldiers. Sustainable logistical support. 2.1. Strong defensive positions outside Stanley. 2.2. Attack capability. 2.3. Land fires capability. 3.1. Control of the air capability. 3.2. Effective command and control.

Table 7A – Argentine Operational Centre of Gravity during Operation Corporate.

The airfield at Stanley was the hub for Argentine logistics capabilities within the Falkland Islands. It was also the home to some, albeit limited, attack aircraft and had the potential to house more capable combat air assets. Consequently, it is right and proper that the British should attack the airfield during the campaign. Denying the airfield at Stanley would eventually bring about the Argentine land force's demise as it slowly ran out of resources to feed, fuel, and fight its various deployed capabilities. Moreover, during the early stages of British military planning, it was identified that 'Port Stanley airfield is most vulnerable to air attack.'[93] However, in parallel, it was apparent that 'a cardinal factor affecting operations will be the need to avoid, as far as possible, heavy fighting in the Port Stanley area. Severe loss of life among the small population, and widespread property destruction would defeat the operation's objective.'[94] However, quashing any fears of collateral damage was the operational analysis stating that 'there was no significant chance of a stray bomb impacting in Port Stanley Town.'[95]

However, the focus of British operations on Stanley airport was neither a quick nor a decisive solution to a campaign that faced significant time pressures. As shown in Table 7A, Stanley airport was not the sole critical vulnerability. Consequently, any subsequent analysis of the British prosecution of the Argentine operational centre of gravity needs to reflect on the number, efficiency, and relative importance of the targeting of the other critical vulnerabilities.

British Attack Outputs and Outcomes

Generating and articulating the British attack outputs and subsequent outcomes have proven to be more problematic than initially anticipated. Moreover, and perhaps surprisingly, it was a more complicated process than the creation of its Argentine equivalent. The key issue is that British primary source material is incomplete. For example, squadron authorisation sheets, flying logs, and operational record books are piecemeal, not available, lacking the required detail or contradictory. Although detailed primary source material supports the Vulcan and 801 Naval Air Squadron missions and weapon usage, there is no definitive set of Sea Harrier mission reports at The National Archives or the Fleet Air Arm Archives. Moreover, although the Harrier GR3 mission reports are available, they appear to have been written post-Conflict and contain several subtle inconsistencies with the Scientific Evaluation Team's subsequent work.[96]

Consequently, the broad spectrum of secondary source material fills the void left by the lack of primary source material. Even so, there are a small number of missions where the weapon used in the attack remains unresolved. The issue is relevant, but its impact is minor. Of the 493 air-to-surface weapons used by the British during the campaign, twenty weapons, or 4 per cent, cannot be attributed to a specific strike. As a result, there are likely omissions, errors, and frictions contained within the list of British attack weapons employed during Operation Corporate. While Annex K is likely to contain oversights and instigate debate, it still provides the most comprehensive list of data to date. It also provides a transparent and auditable foundation that can be tested and challenged as future narratives on the air war develop. Accordingly, the analysis of Annex K highlighted several noteworthy points.

First, due to the lack of Argentine combat air patrols and ground-based air defences focused around Stanley, it is clear that British attack aircraft had the luxury of freedom of manoeuvre from the aircraft carrier to the target area. When coupled with superior aircraft serviceability than the Argentines, British aircraft had a significantly more substantial probability of reaching their assigned targets than their Argentine counterparts. As a result, the British fast jet combat air assets were able to employ 493 weapons during the Conflict. Of note, the British weapon usage is significantly larger than the 301 weapons that its Argentine opposition was able to use in the same timeframe.

The second point to comment on is the apportionment and balance of the weapons amongst the British platforms. As mentioned previously, the *Hermes*-based 800 Naval Air Squadron flew the vast majority of the Sea Harrier attack missions. On board HMS *Invincible*, 801 Naval Air Squadron, in addition to its routine 'combat air patrol bombing' missions, only flew two dedicated attack missions. However, in terms of output, and despite arriving three weeks after the start of the campaign, 1 (Fighter) Squadron was the most prolific British attack unit. During the campaign, the Harrier GR3 dropped 205, or 42 per cent, of the British attack weapons. Collectively, the combined efforts of both Sea Harrier squadrons dropped marginally more weapons than the Harrier GR3 force. The reality of the Harrier GR3 force performance is contrary to the view of Lieutenant Commander Tim Gedge, the commanding officer of 809 Naval Air Squadron during the Conflict, that the Sea Harrier dropped three times the number of weapons of the Harrier GR3 force.[97] As shown in Figure 7.2, both the Sea Harrier and Harrier GR3 each delivered three times the number of weapons of the Vulcan.

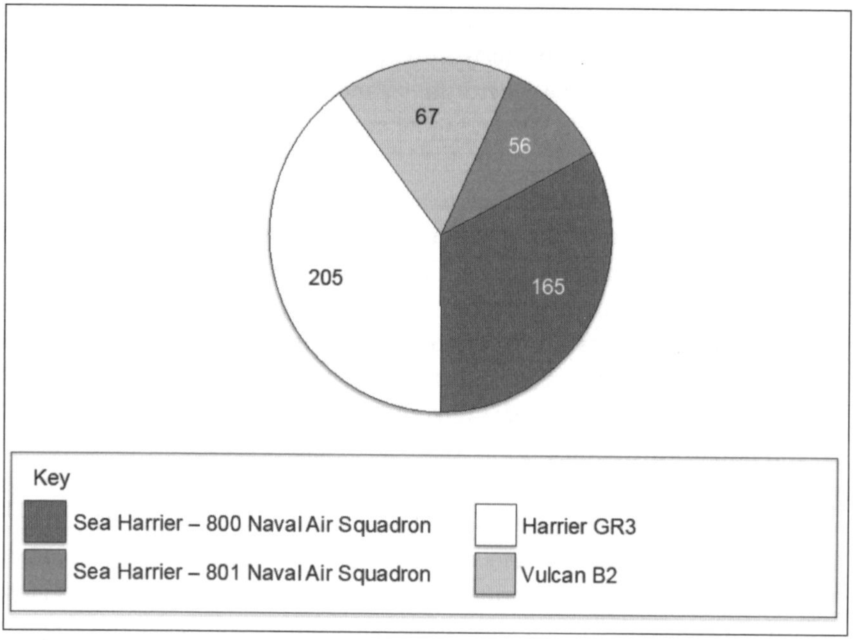

Figure 7.2 – British Attack Weapons Usage by Platform.

Nevertheless, what outcomes did the Vulcan achieve? During the Conflict, the Vulcan employed sixty-seven weapons. While the Vulcan's output is significantly less than that of the Sea Harrier and Harrier GR3 communities, and as validated in the Scientific Evaluation Team's post-Conflict analysis, the Vulcan was the only aircraft that was to deliver a weapon that penetrated the runway at Stanley.[98] Although the result delivered by the Vulcan was more significant than that produced by the combined efforts of the Harrier and Sea Harrier force, the joint British combat air tactical efforts failed to deliver the required operational outcome – impeding the use of Stanley airport.

The third point to note, and despite the numerical advantage in terms of outputs, is that the results of many attack missions have been challenging to identify. Notwithstanding the debate regarding the Vulcan's utility, there is little analysis on the conduct of the broader British attack missions. The lack of understanding of the effects produced by the British attacks reflects the limited battle-damage assessment conducted. The point was reiterated to the Chief of the Air Staff by Harrier GR3 pilots who flew during the Conflict when they stated that 'weapon effects were difficult to judge.'[99] With limited, timely feedback from British ground forces and a lack of on board sensors to record the results of their attacks, the British were unable to assure themselves that their attacks achieved the mission aims. As a result of inadequate battle damage assessment, targets were often reattacked. A lack of investment and understanding of the broader and more nuanced air power roles meant the inefficient, repetitive, and high-risk usage of finite resources.

The fourth point to broach is the significant effort put into conducting medium-level bombing of Stanley airport by the Sea Harrier force during transits to its combat air patrols. From 14 May, and as highlighted in Annex K, Sea Harriers dropped at least thirty-one bombs against the airfield during their over-flights. However, the intended target of these missions was not the runway but the wider airfield operating area – a pragmatic reflection on the limitations of medium-level bombing by the deployed British combat air assets. Consequently, the effect was not to destroy the airfield but to merely apply pressure onto the manpower, infrastructure, and equipment located at the airfield by causing 'damage and demoralisation in and around military installations and troop emplacements.'[100] As a result, the bombs used the airburst fuse rather than the 'Direct Action' fuse required for runway penetration.[101] As Ward suggested, the value of the raids was limited to 'damage [to] thin-skinned targets and keeping the enemy awake.'[102] In essence, the attacks impacted the morale of those located in and around the airport. However, measuring the effects achieved was recognised as a difficult proposition. As stated in the Scientific Evaluation Team Report, 'it is not possible to quantify secondary psychological or harassment effects on the enemy.'[103] However, perhaps a more astute move would have been to disrupt those critical Argentine soldiers and marines on the hilltops to the west of Stanley and, importantly, identified as a critical vulnerability in Table 7A.

The fifth deduction is that the lack of precision achieved from medium-level attacks meant that low-level attacks were required to deliver the necessary accuracy. Moreover, operating within range of enemy ground-based air defences increased the risk to the attacking aircraft. As a result, the attacking force needed to be able to detect, identify, and counter any emerging ground-based air defence system. However, the Sea Harrier and Harrier GR3 lacked the fleet-wide embodiment of radar-warning receivers, chaff and flares, and jamming pods.[104] Consequently, and as with the Sea Harrier's control of the air ability, there were deficits in the British attack capability that could be linked back to the triumvirate of platform, sensor, and weapon. As a result, low-level attacks had to be supported by dedicated aircraft tasked to suppress enemy air defences. Therefore, the need to toss airburst weapons against enemy defences diverted precious attack resources from their primary mission. For example, four of the nine Sea Harriers that conducted the initial raid against Stanley airport on 1 May flew suppression missions rather than attack missions. As a result, twelve of the twenty-seven bombs dropped were not employed directly against the airfield infrastructure. Moreover, as the vast majority of the British suppression weapons were area, rather than precision weapons, there was no guarantee that the suppression mission would achieve a 'soft,' never mind a 'hard,' kill. Additionally, there is little evidence to suggest that suppression aircraft attacked the stipulated critical vulnerabilities effectively. Even the Vulcan armed with its precision AGM-45A Shrike weapons was of limited value. As Curtiss suggested, 'these Vulcan sorties were not spectacularly successful, as the enemy operators were quick to switch off their radars.'[105] The demand for precision attack despite being limited to non-precision weapons came with the burden of suppression that generated a heavy weapons bill from a precious resource.

The last, and key, issue, to review is the weight of effort placed by British planners and attack aircraft against Stanley airport. As shown in Table 7A, the airport at Stanley was a critical vulnerability and supported the Argentine operational centre of gravity. However, the locations of the vast majority of the identified critical vulnerabilities are beyond the heavily defended Stanley airport. Therefore, the British focus on attacking the airfield throughout the campaign is perhaps surprising. As demonstrated in Figure 7.3, the majority of British attack weapons were targeted against the airport infrastructure – accounting for 249 or 51 per cent of British attack weapons. The inclusion of counter-air attacks beyond Stanley airport increases the figure to 67 per cent of the total weapons. Doctrine and good practice both establish the need to deliver an assured level of control of the air to provide the other environments with their required freedoms.[106] However, the British failed to achieve the required outcome. Consequently, the Argentines contested control of the air throughout the campaign; neither side had assured access to the air environment; it was at best fleeting and localised. Nevertheless, the British were relentless in the pursuit of denying Stanley airport. As a result, British air power planners could be accused of planning and executing a parochial counter-air programme to the detriment of a more balanced and effective air campaign that was coherent with the broader joint campaign requirements.

The relatively low importance paid to British air attacks against the Argentine troops dug-in to the hills surrounding Stanley is a significant oversight. As shown in Figure 7.3, the counter-land campaign accounted for only 28 per cent of British attack weapons. While the emphasis on the attack role grew as the British troops closed towards the defended mountains surrounding Stanley, the campaign needed the integration of a counter-land attack plan from its outset. Although the British attacked elements of the Argentine centre of gravity, it failed to target the Argentine force's fighting strength. Bicheno suggests that as of 30 May, the Argentine force in and around Stanley was in the order of 10,000 military personnel.[107] The Argentine force disposition showed an extensive defensive outer perimeter of combat arms protecting a much smaller inner ring in Stanley containing the various headquarters and their enabling functions, including communications, logistics, and engineering support.[108] Although British forces attacked elements of the inner ring, the bulk of Argentine military fighting strength ensconced in the hills surrounding Stanley was left unscathed until the latter stages of the campaign.

The prosecution of the Argentine operational centre of gravity was not solely the responsibility of air power; the British also used naval bombardment and artillery. Indeed, the Scientific Evaluation Team post-Conflict report informed that 'General Menendez is reported to have stated that the concentration persistence and accuracy of the 105mm Light Gun artillery fire and naval gunfire support constituted the principal cause of the break down of his troops' morale and will to fight.'[109] Indeed on 12 June, 'returning Sea Harrier pilots tell of the impressive sight to be seen over Port Stanley where star shells, naval bombardment and artillery are criss-crossing the sky.'[110]

Naval gunfire support was used throughout the campaign and fired an impressive 7,916 rounds of ammunition.[111] However, and in a similar vein to the air environment, its initial focus was on the airfield at Stanley. The first naval bombardment against Argentine forces protecting Stanley's western approaches came on the night of 27/28 May. HMS *Glamorgan*, *Alacrity* and *Avenger* engaged enemy positions at Mount Harriet, Tumbledown and Wireless Ridge with 259 high explosive shells, eleven star shells and two Sea Slug surface-to-air missiles used in the surface-to-surface mode.[112] As with the air attack campaign, the focus of naval bombardment switched belatedly to support the land campaign with the second naval gunfire support task against the hilltops occurring four nights later.[113]

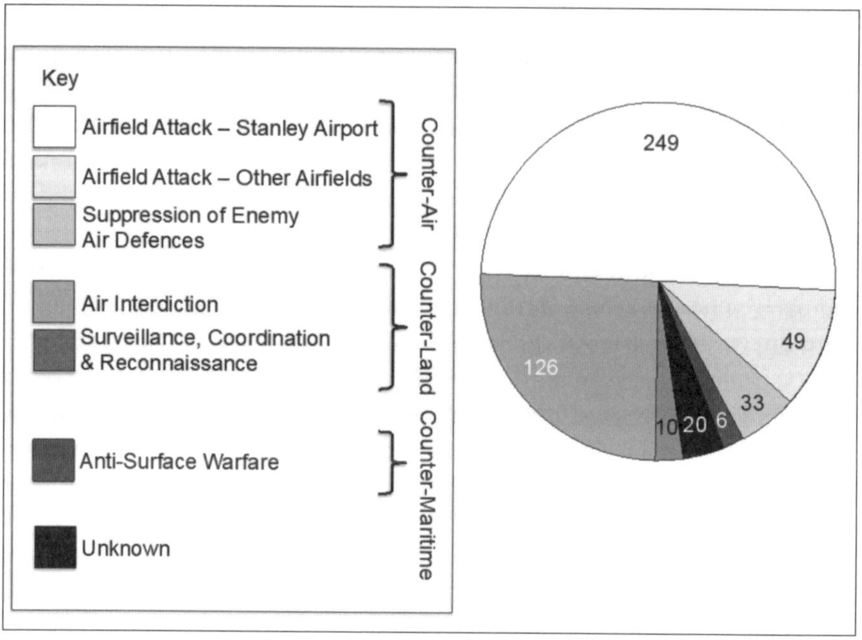

Figure 7.3 – British Attack Weapons Usage by Target.[114]

From a British land perspective, the army deployed thirty 105mm Light Guns during the Conflict and fired approximately 17,600 rounds of ammunition – over twice the number of rounds of its naval counterparts.[115] However, due to the limited range of the British artillery, as well as the problem of moving and supporting the guns, their campaign utility was of limited benefit. The 105mm Light Gun had a maximum range of twenty kilometres. As a result, the weapon had to be flown into position once ground forces secured the intended firing position.[116] To support such a move, Thompson suggested that it would take '60 - 70 Sea Kings to move one battery of artillery [six guns] plus all its ammunition' from San Carlos forward to the Mount Kent area.[117] Complicating the issue even further was the poor weather that delayed the forward deployment of some of the 105mm Light Guns until 3 June.[118] As a result of range, logistics, weather, and timing constraints, the British artillery employed their 105mm Light Guns against Argentine land forces during the latter, but critical, stages of the Conflict.

The combat air events were significantly fewer in number than their land and maritime counterparts. However, combat air had the advantage of being able to deliver effect throughout the campaign at a time and a place of the attackers choosing; air power could mitigate the inherent disadvantages of the other two environments. As a result, air power's advantages of speed, reach, and lethality could have been exploited earlier by the British. Moreover, from the outset of Operation Corporate, the British could have pressurised all of the elements that constituted the Argentine operational centre of gravity. While the focus on the counter-air war applied pressure on the Argentines, it was a slower and less direct route to undermining the Argentine operational centre of gravity. While this indirect approach certainly agreed with Liddell Hart's views on warfare, the strategy needs to balance the directness of the approach versus the time available to deliver the required outcome.[119] A more direct, joint, and collegiate approach may have been a more efficient and effective way of achieving the British end-state. If British planners understood the utility and effects that its air power could deliver, then a more equitable balance towards the counter-land role would have been a more appropriate and effective strategy. By directly targeting the Argentine troops, weapons, and positions on the hilltops to the west of Stanley earlier, and more aggressively, it may have offered a path to a quicker British victory and put greater strain on Menendez's fielded forces. Additionally, a change in air power focus may have provided an opportunity to reduce the amount of British blood and treasure expended during the battles on Mount Harriet, Tumbledown, Mount Longdon, Two Sisters, and Wireless Ridge. However, and discussed later in the book, the deficits in planning, personality, and process all hindered the effective and efficient use of the attack air power role.

During pre-Conflict planning, British air planners suggested that the Harrier GR3s 'should be used as early as possible on reconnaissance/ground attacks.'[120] The paper also recognised the diverse capabilities of the Sea Harrier but stated that 'air superiority over the task force must not be prejudiced by other tasking.'[121] Consequently, in the pre-landing phase Harrier GR3 and Sea Harrier, if available, would be tasked to conduct reconnaissance sorties to determine concentrations of enemy forces and influence attack planning during the post-landing phase.[122] Although the plan was robust and prioritised tasks by platform and time, the British never implemented it. The Scientific Evaluation Team report is stark, 'there was no co-ordinated pre-planned programme in support of land operations.'[123] Squadron Leader Peter Harris' paper captures the reality of the situation, '*Operation Corporate – A Worm's Eye View*.' Harris, a Harrier GR3 pilot during the Conflict, suggested that 'very few reconnaissance sorties were tasked.'[124] Harris continued by informing that 'had more air reconnaissance sorties been flown earlier in the conflict, numerous high-value targets would undoubtedly have been found which could have been subsequently tasked for air attack, artillery bombardment or naval gunfire support. The lack of understanding of the value of air reconnaissance could have had disastrous consequences had the Argentinian will to fight been stronger.'[125] The disparity between the theoretical plan and the reality in the South Atlantic is apparent, but what were the causal factors for the failure to implement the plan?

In Curtiss' own report on the Conflict, he highlighted several command and control problems that influenced campaign execution. Contrary to its actual role during the Conflict, Curtiss suggested that 'HMS *Hermes* was not established or equipped as an attack carrier.'[126] This position is not a reflection of the ship's magazine's capacity but a statement on the personnel and equipment available to conduct the air planning task. It was clear to the Harrier GR3 pilots that 'aboard ship, there was no adequate system for tasking sorties or monitoring missions.'[127] Curtiss also noted that HMS *Hermes* only had a single air tasking officer who was responsible for planning combat air missions and was also responsible for helicopter and replenishment at sea tasking.[128] As a result, mistakes occurred. Squire informed 'that on occasions we responded to air requests rather than air tasks.'[129] Moreover, Harris highlighted an example of the inefficient process in place. 'On 26 May, Brigade Staff asked for low level photographic cover of the Argentine defensive positions west of Port Stanley, an area of approximately seventy square kilometres. The task reached the Squadron during the afternoon of 9 June and required the photographs to be at the front line army units by the morning of 11 June.'[130] The manpower issue was further complicated by the lack of Intelligence Officer or Ground Liaison Officer to support the understandably parsimonious 1 (Fighter) Squadron deployment.[131] Moreover, inadequate communications between the key agencies and the dislocation of the intelligence cell from the squadron complicated matters further.[132] Ultimately, the lack of trained manpower was compromising the process and utility of the embarked attack assets.

Compounded by the late arrival of the land component commander, the slow build-up, and break out from San Carlos and the release of the land scheme of manoeuvre, the British lacked a definitive plan to support the land component. Consequently, in the post-Operation Sutton hiatus, British attack missions were predominantly retained in the offensive counter-air role. Although counter-land attack missions started on 19 May, it was not until ten days later that the first raids against the Argentine forces on the hills surrounding Stanley took place. Although a higher number of counter-land missions took place over the remainder of the campaign, the planning and intelligence associated with these raids led to significant frustration. The lack of attack missions planned and executed against the Argentine ground forces was, arguably, a missed opportunity. Consequently, British air power, and contrary to contemporary doctrine, was unable to coerce its adversary into changing or maintaining its behaviour to the benefit of the attacking force.[133] Even when the British eventually attacked the Argentine hilltop forces, it was in a near-term, reactive manner. The results were poor. As highlighted by Squire in his Operation Corporate report, 'many of the targets were … well dug in and camouflaged, thus difficult if not impossible to see at weapon release ranges ... there is no doubt, as proved by the few recce [reconnaissance] sorties flown, there were many lucrative targets in the Stanley area and the use of pure recce would not only have identified them but given the pilots much more acquisition data.'[134] Wing Commander Trowern's signal to the Air Officer Commander in Chief on the subject highlighted the frustration within the Harrier GR3 community, 'in the heat of battle our limited assets must be firmly husbanded; if not they will be squandered against low value and difficult to acquire targets.'[135] Although armed reconnaissance missions were tasked and flown by both Sea Harrier and the Harrier GR3, they had limited utility compared to dedicated and focussed reconnaissance missions that the Harrier GR3 community desired. The Scientific Evaluation Team's report suggested that armed reconnaissance was 'over emphasised' and 'does not produce detailed intelligence and it is wasteful to employ expensive aircraft against targets of opportunity which are often of questionable value in any event.'[136]

A more prudent method would have been to use British combat air assets in a coordinated, pre-emptive manner that exploited air power's strengths and allowed the shaping of the land battle to the advantage of the attacking force. Noting that the vast majority of land battles happened at night, the Harrier GR3 had an added disadvantage as it had no night attack capability.[137] To maximise its utility, the Harrier GR3 needed pre-emptive reconnaissance and sufficient time during daylight to prosecute Argentine fielded forces. Due to its misuse, British attack sorties became an equal partner alongside naval bombardment and artillery. Moreover, by delaying its use in the land battle, it could be argued that the benefit of the Harrier GR3 was, in fact, severely hampered and subject to increased risk. A 38 Group post-Conflict report reflects the limited exploitation of the Harrier GR3 during the Conflict. 'It is remarkable that [Number] 1 Squadron achieved any success at all.'[138]

The exasperated Harrier GR3 pilots felt that their attack and reconnaissance capabilities were neither understood nor exploited.[139] In addition to the lack of understanding across the embarked joint air wing, there were also issues regarding the command and control of the embarked Harriers. The designated Air Commander for Operation Corporate was Curtiss. However, he remained in the United Kingdom for most of the campaign, although he did venture as far south as Ascension Island. However, Curtiss delegated operational command of the Harrier GR3s to Woodward as the Carrier Task Group commander with operational control allocated to the Captain of HMS *Hermes*.[140] As a result, the de facto Air Commander in the South Atlantic was Captain Linley Middleton. In his post-Conflict report, Peter Squire suggested that 'in [HMS] *Hermes*, the Captain himself exercised a very tight control on flying operations and the Squadrons' programme was totally dictated by the ship.'[141] Moore's RAF liaison officer also commented in his post-Conflict analysis that tasking of sorties, 'differed from the RAF/NATO system by depending more on the intuitive wishes of the Admiral and the Captain.'[142] Due to Middleton's authoritarian command style, once he made a decision, it was difficult to rescind it. Pook highlighted the implications of one of the command's decisions by suggesting that 'several times we found ourselves attacking targets with unsuitable weapons which were wrongly fused.'[143] Middleton's directives were not just limited to the junior Service. Much to Ward's vexation, the Sea Harriers of 801 Naval Air Squadron were also subject to Middleton's robust, tactically focussed leadership style.[144] In an endeavour to rectify the issue, the Central Tactics and Trials Organisation's report into the Conflict suggested that 'specialist advisors with adequate authority should be deployed with RAF assets, if operational control is to be exercised by another Service, to ensure effective operational employment.'[145]

British air planners were guilty of fighting a parochial counter-air war to the detriment of the wider joint campaign. Although the British conducted attack missions, they were ineffective. They failed to strike the critical vulnerabilities efficiently, embarked capabilities and requirements were not understood, mission command was not employed, and the lack of planning staff compromised attack missions. As a result, British attack missions were inefficient and often less than decisive. With the British air power unable to undermine the Argentine operational centre of gravity, what could the Argentines do to defend their military strength?

Defending the Argentine Operational Centre of Gravity

With no maritime force air defence capability operating in and around the Falkland Islands as well as no dedicated manned fighters conducting defensive counter-air missions, only Argentine ground-based air defences could defend their operational centre of gravity. However, with no area air defence system, the Argentines were limited to localised, point-defence of the populated areas: Stanley, Goose Green, and Port Howard. Consequently, and as shown in Annex K, it is unsurprising that the vast majority of British attack missions reached their intended target areas with little enemy interference. As a result, and like their Argentine counterparts, the key reasons for British aircraft failing to reach the target area were infrequent aircraft failures and poor weather rather than Argentine intervention.

On arrival at the target area, British attack assets lacked a precision stand-off attack capability. Therefore, to ensure positive target identification and accurate weapon delivery, British attack assets needed to penetrate the Argentine umbrella of ground-based air defences. As a result, the Harrier GR3s and Sea Harriers faced an eclectic array of co-located ground-based air defence systems operated by several different organisations. For the Argentines, as with the British, the difficulty of coordinating the pan-Service assets would soon become apparent.

The provision of Argentine ground-based air defence was a joint affair and focused on the protection of Stanley. *Grupo de Artillería de Defensa Aérea 601* was the main anti-aircraft artillery unit. The Argentine Army unit operated a single Roland 2 surface-to-air missile fire unit, a dozen Oerlikon twin 35mm anti-aircraft guns, three Oerlikon twin 20mm anti-aircraft guns and three Tigercat surface-to-air missile launchers.[146] Although the majority of the fire units protected Stanley, a 35mm anti-aircraft gun defended Goose Green.[147] A second, smaller army unit also conducted ground-based air defence. *Grupo de Artillería de Defensa Aérea 101*, armed with eight Hispano HS-831 30mm cannons, operated solely in the vicinity of Stanley.[148]

Supporting its Army colleagues, *Grupo 1 de Artillería Antiaérea* from the *Fuerza Aérea Argentina* operated nine Rheinmetall twin 20mm anti-aircraft guns and four Oerlikon twin 35mm anti-aircraft guns.[149] In contrast to its land counterparts who operated the Skyguard fire control radar, the *Fuerza Aérea Argentina* used the Superfledermaus fire control radar to cue its guns.[150] As with *Grupo de Artillería de Defensa Aérea 601*, the focus of the *Fuerza Aérea Argentina* unit's efforts was the protection of Stanley, but six of the Rheinmetall 20mm anti-aircraft guns defended Goose Green.[151] Number 1 Marine Air Defence Battalion provided the naval contribution to the protection of Argentine key positions. The unit operated three Tigercat launchers and twelve Hispano HS-831 30mm cannons in and around Stanley. Lastly, the smaller and more difficult to reach locations of interest, such as Port Howard and the hills surrounding Stanley were protected by man-portable air defence systems such as the British-provided Blowpipe and the Soviet SA-7 'Grail' recently acquired via Peruvian sources.[152]

Consequently, the British faced a broad range of Argentine ground-based air defence systems. The most modern and effective weapon system operated by the Argentines was the Franco-German Roland 2 surface-to-air missile system. After initial confusion regarding whether or not the Roland 2 system was on the Falkland Islands, the British needed to answer a second and more fundamental question – what was the system's maximum operating height?[153] The Roland 2 system was almost unknown to British operators, who found it 'difficult to obtain a definitive assessment of the engagement envelope of this missile.'[154] Consequently, the British underestimated the Roland 2 capability.[155] In late April and early May, British assessments of Roland 2's maximum operating altitude varied from 11,500 feet to 17,600 feet.[156] This ambiguity regarding the Roland 2's true capability would percolate south to the task force, and the various combat air units worked with different Roland 2 engagement envelopes. Consequently, the needless disparity in figures would lead to the loss of a precious combat aircraft.

If the Argentines were to maximise the attrition of British attack aircraft, they had to ensure the utility and coordination of their various weapon suites. However, Moro admitted that joint action was not one of the Argentine armed forces' 'greater virtues.'[157] Despite their ad hoc arrangement, and as shown in Table 7B, Argentine ground-based air defences caused several losses to British combat air platforms throughout the campaign.

Three considerations drove the causal factors behind the loss of the five British aircraft. First, the lack of a comprehensive suite of defensive aids to detect and counter ground threats caused the loss of the first Sea Harrier. Lieutenant Nick Taylor's aircraft was originally a development aircraft for the Sea Eagle missile. As a result, the Sea Eagle weapons control panel replaced the radar-warning receiver.[158] Without the radar-warning receiver, Taylor was 'blind' to the threat posed by the Goose Green radar-laid guns, and he paid with his life before reaching his intended target.

<table>
<tr><th>Date</th><th>Aircraft</th><th>Unit</th><th>Pilot</th><th>Location</th><th>Air Defence</th></tr>
<tr><td>4 May</td><td>Sea Harrier</td><td>800 NAS</td><td>Lt Nick Taylor</td><td>Goose Green</td><td>35mm Cannon</td></tr>
<tr><td>21 May</td><td rowspan="3">Harrier GR3</td><td rowspan="3">1(F) Sqn</td><td>Flt Lt Jeff Glover</td><td>Port Howard</td><td>Blowpipe Missile</td></tr>
<tr><td>27 May</td><td>Sqn Ldr Bob Iveson</td><td>Goose Green</td><td>35mm Cannon</td></tr>
<tr><td>30 May</td><td>Sqn Ldr Jerry Pook</td><td>Stanley</td><td>Small Arms</td></tr>
<tr><td>1 June</td><td>Sea Harrier</td><td>801 NAS</td><td>Flt Lt Ian Mortimer</td><td>Stanley</td><td>Roland Missile</td></tr>
</table>

Table 7B – British Combat Aircraft Losses to Argentine Air Defences.[159]

HMS *Invincible* returns to Portsmouth post-Conflict. The British aircraft carriers have long been considered as critical to the success of the British enterprise. (Defence Images)

An Argentine Dagger is visible between the masts of the amphibious assault ship, HMS *Fearless* on 24 May 1982 during Operation Sutton, the British landings at San Carlos. (IWM)

Above left: 45 Royal Marine Commando marches towards Stanley. Marine Peter Robinson carries the Union Flag on his pack. The land force was the only force that could reclaim the campaign's vital ground of Stanley. (IWM)

Above right: The Vulcan first flew on 30 August 1952 and was the backbone of the UK's nuclear deterrent during much of the Cold War. However, its first kinetic operation, Operation Black Buck 1, occurred nearly three decades later. (Defence Images)

An AIM-9L Sidewinder-armed Sea Harrier of 800 Naval Air Squadron, piloted by Lt Simon Hargreaves lands on the flight deck of the amphibious assault ship, HMS *Intrepid*. (IWM)

Right: Harrier GR3s of 1 (Fighter) Squadron parked alongside Sea Harriers of 800 Naval Air Squadron and a Sea King helicopter on the flight deck of HMS *Hermes*. Note the near Harrier GR3 is armed with laser-guided bombs. (Defence Images)

Below: A Sea Harrier pilot of 801 Naval Air Squadron in his cockpit on the Flight Deck of HMS *Invincible*. The Sea Harrier pilots flew considerably more missions than their Argentine counterparts. (IWM)

A Rapier surface-to-air missile launcher set up to defend Royal Navy ships moored in San Carlos Water, June 1982. Post-Conflict analysis shows that the initial perception of Rapier's success was incorrect. (IWM)

Blowpipe missile operators of 5 Infantry Brigade train on board Cunard's *Queen Elizabeth II* during the voyage south. As with the maritime-based air defence weapons, Blowpipe's performance was disappointing. (IWM)

A Harrier GR3 of No 1 (Fighter) Squadron RAF is prepared for a sortie on the flight deck of HMS *Hermes*. (IWM)

On the afternoon of 1 May 1982, a 500lb Mk82 'Snakeye' is branded with its intended target prior to being uploaded to an A-4Q Skyhawk on board the Argentine aircraft carrier, ARA *25 de Mayo*. (Santiago Rivas Collection)

A Matra R550 Magic 1-armed Mirage 3 awaits instructions at its Rio Gallegos base in Southern Argentina. (Santiago Rivas Collection)

A bomb-laden Canberra from *II Brigada Aerea* taxies at Trelew, its base during the Conflict. After an inauspicious start to the Conflict, the Canberras and Mirage 3s were temporarily withdrawn from operations. (Santiago Rivas Collection)

Left: Taken at San Julian in May 1982, Capitan Dimeglio, Primer Teniente Roman, Primer Teniente Callejo and Teniente Aguirre Faget stand in front of a Dagger. All four pilots and the aircraft would survive the conflict. (Claudio Meunier Collection)

Below: Carrying three BRP bombs, an A-4C Skyhawk of *IV Brigada Aerea* conducts air-to-air refueling from a KC-130H Hercules. (Santiago Rivas Collection)

The British Task Force under Argentine air attack. The area would become known as 'Bomb Alley.' (IWM)

Two Argentine A4-B Skyhawks (flown by Pablo Carballo and Carlos Rinke) attack HMS *Broadsword*. During the attack, a bomb struck the ship's stern without exploding, but destroyed the embarked Lynx helicopter. (IWM)

A Sea Harrier piloted by Lieutenant Commander Tim Gedge, approaches MV *Atlantic Conveyor*. After disembarking its Sea Harriers and Harrier GR3s, the ship would be lost to an Exocet missile attack on 25 May 1982. (IWM)

A4-B Skyhawk from *V Brigada Aerea* armed with three BRP bombs on its centreline refuels from a KC-130H Hercules. (Santiago Rivas Collection)

With four A-4C Skyhawks waiting, a Super Etendard refuels while carrying the last AM-39 Exocet. The controversial 30 May 1982 mission failed to attack HMS *Invincible*; two Skyhawks and their pilots were also lost. (Santiago Rivas Collection)

The next two losses fell to the Harrier GR3 force. Operating in the low-level, high-speed environment without sensors, the Harrier GR3 pilots found it difficult to detect and strike their often concealed targets on their first pass. Forced to reattack the target, sometimes on multiple occasions, the Harrier GR3s were increasingly exposed to enemy ground fire. Iveson and Glover both fell prey to ground fire during reattacks, although both survived the ordeal. The Harrier GR3 reattack tactic was controversial both outside and within the Squadron. Indeed. Pook faced criticism from his wingman on 26 May following multiple passes over the same target in the Mount Kent area.[160] Commodore Mike Clapp, himself an experienced naval aviator, suggested that 'second passes over enemy positions were inviting disaster.'[161] The culture evident amongst the Harrier pilots was that achieving the task was important. At times, this perception was contrary to accepted good practice and at odds with the Argentine approach to their attack sorties. As evidenced in the previous chapters, the Argentines tended to favour only attacking when it was advantageous. Consequently, and unlike the British, the Argentines managed to preserve their force to the detriment of achieving the goal.

There is a dispute over the causal factor for the loss of the Harrier GR3 on 30 May. Due to the lack of warning, tracer, or smoke trail of a surface-to-air missile, Pook assumed that it was a small calibre weapon that brought down his aircraft.[162] Others suggest that radar-laid anti-aircraft artillery was responsible for downing the Harrier GR3.[163] Irrespective of which weapon system was accountable for bringing down Pook's Harrier, operating in the low-level and high-threat environment was a high-risk proposition. As a result, the British tolerated the risks and accepted that losses were inevitable. Therefore, the British maintained their high-risk strategy throughout the campaign. In contrast, the Argentine risk appetite ebbed and flowed throughout the campaign.

The last British combat air asset loss highlighted the different operating procedures across the community. Despite a recently imposed 20,000 feet minimum altitude for combat air patrols, Flight Lieutenant Ian Mortimer was flying at around 15,000 feet in the vicinity of Stanley when a Roland surface-to-air missile shot him down.[164] Although Mortimer was aware of the missile launch, he believed, along with his fellow aviators on board HMS *Invincible*, that he was flying above the maximum height of the missile system.[165] However, Morgan inferred that Mortimer was flying as low as 10,000 feet when he was engaged.[166] If true, Mortimer was flying below the 13,000 feet safe height previously used by his squadron and significantly below the more restrictive minimum altitude of 18,000 feet formerly used by the Sea Harriers on board HMS *Hermes*.[167] Of note, Mortimer's operating altitude reflected the Vulcan force's belief that they 'should be safe from the triple A [anti-aircraft artillery] and Roland as long as they remained above 10,000 feet.'[168] The Cold War focus on countering Soviet threats meant that British forces did not understand the capabilities of a Franco-German produced weapons system. Moreover, and as they rapidly adapted to the new threat, the lack of communication and coordination between both aircraft carriers and Ascension Island-based assets led to the needless loss of a valuable Sea Harrier.

In addition to the aircraft lost to Argentine ground-based air defences, numerous British aircraft suffered damage due to ground fire. In particular, the Harrier GR3 force was particularly affected as its low altitude attack profiles left them vulnerable to ground fire. At one point, the situation was so extreme that 1 (Fighter) Squadron only had one serviceable aircraft. Consequently, a combined Sea Harrier and Harrier GR3 formation flew on 1 June to maximise the combat air output as well as provide the minimum level of mutual support between the aircraft.[169] Effective battle damage repair quickly remedied the situation of the wounded Harrier GR3s. Indeed, Squire suggested that 'no aircraft spent longer than forty-eight hours in the hangar before it was flying again.'[170] Moreover, the arrival of replacement aircraft, flown directly from Ascension Island on 1 and 8 June, also alleviated the pressure on the Harrier GR3 force.[171]

However, the Argentine ground-based air defences believed they were even more successful. In claims that reflected the initial optimism of British ground-based air defences, the Argentines tended to exaggerate their ground-based air defence performance. For example, during the initial Sea Harrier Stanley airport attack on 1 May, the Argentines claimed four kills and a further two aircraft damaged.[172] However, this is at odds with the reality, expressed in BBC reporter Brian Hanrahan's famous phrase, 'I counted them all out and I counted them all back.'[173]

In addition to over-estimating the number of kills achieved, the Argentine ground-based air defences were involved in two fratricide incidents. The first event occurred on 1 May, when a battle-damaged or fuel-starved, accounts differ, Mirage III was attempting to make an emergency landing at Stanley. The aircraft was shot down by Argentine ground fire as it approached the airport.[174] Poor command and control of the eclectic mix and organisations of Argentine ground-based air defences led to the needless loss of one of their own assets. However, this was not the only

Argentine fratricide incident. Eleven days later, Argentine ground-based air defences shot down an A-4B Skyhawk as it overflew Goose Green while returning to the Argentine mainland after an effective attack against HMS *Glasgow*.[175] On both occasions, the Argentines lost the pilots and aircraft. However, poor communication and inability to identify friendly assets were not the sole preserve of Argentine forces. The Scots Guards were involved in an incident at Tumbledown when they endeavoured to engage a bomb-dropping Harrier GR3.[176] It is clear that the 'fog of war' pervaded both sides during the Conflict.

Just as the Argentines had a fascination with attacking the British aircraft carriers, Stanley airport beguiled the British. Consequently, the inter-Service bickering regarding the utility and success of the various platforms attacking the Stanley airport throughout the campaign is, in reality, a smoke screen that masks the real issue. Rather than focussing on a counter-air campaign, the British should have been concentrating on the counter-land campaign, particularly in the period immediately after Operation Sutton.

With the lack of a coherent joint campaign plan and a late insight into the land scheme of manoeuvre, it is easy to see why air planners planned and fought an independent, if not incoherent, air campaign. The result was a series of tactical bespoke set pieces that had few opportunities to blend into the operational campaign. From an operational and joint perspective, the air planners appear to have been mesmerised by what they could achieve rather than focus on the more essential aspects of what they must achieve.

Chapter 8

The Operational Level Lessons of the Falklands Air Campaign

'What is it today that I will wish tomorrow that I had done yesterday?'

Admiral 'Sandy' Woodward,
Carrier Task Force Commander[1]

Woodward's comment is an apposite reminder that commanders must continually reflect and critically analyse decisions made, outputs produced, and progress achieved towards delivering the required campaign outcomes. The process of continuous campaign reflection is necessary to ensure that the lessons are captured, learned, and not repeated. Indeed, both participants captured many lessons from the Conflict ranging from the grand strategic lessons of the Franks Report and the *Informe Rattenbach* to the tactical lessons of individual units. However, the rushed production of many of the documents meant that they contained several inaccuracies. Other campaign reflections took a more parochial approach, highlighting a national, Service, or individual bias and agenda. Additionally, other reports lacked an appropriate balance by focusing on the tactical level rather than a broader air environment viewpoint or the joint and operational level of warfighting.[2] Nevertheless, many of the lessons produced in the immediate aftermath of the Conflict were used to reinforce the validity of the existing and funded UK Defence procurement projects such as the JP233 runway denial weapon.[3]

Although it would be overly simplistic to compare the Falklands Conflict narrative with Deighton's views of the Battle of Britain chronicle, some elements do indeed resonate. Deighton argued that 'it became clear that the egos of the victors had started to obscure historical fact. It was time to untwist the record.'[4] While Deighton focused on the victors, and to deliver a balanced account, it is essential that the narrative for the Falklands Conflict also includes the vanquished. Therefore, this chapter aims to review the operational air power lessons.

However, the intent is not to limit these lessons to the British air campaign – Deighton's victors. As a result, this chapter will review the common operational level themes that affected both the British and Argentine air campaign.

As shown in Table 8A, several common operational level air power lessons apply to both sides during their planning and execution of their respective air campaigns. This chapter analyses the themes and looks at the contemporary relevance and the ramifications of each of the lessons.

Lesson 1	Generate and Distribute a Coherent Joint Air Campaign Plan
Lesson 2	Understand the Theatre
Lesson 3	Understand the Capabilities
Lesson 4	Deliver Outcomes, not Outputs

Table 8A – The Operational Level Lessons of the Falklands Air Campaign.

Lesson 1 – Generate and Distribute a Coherent Joint Air Campaign Plan. To produce and deliver an effective air campaign there is a need for a clear understanding of who is responsible for the planning, execution, and assessment of the plan. Therefore, the establishment of a logical and straightforward command and control structure is key. Ideally, a structure honed and exercised in peacetime. Although the focus of the book is on air power, it has to be set in a joint context to understand its true utility. Consequently, 'Joint Action' needs air power, and air power needs 'Joint Action.'[5] Contemporary United Kingdom defence doctrine would offer the concept of Joint Action as the exemplar model for delivering the required effects during joint operations. To provide Joint Action, and as shown in Figure 8.1, a single Joint Task Force Commander is accountable for each of the five subordinate components that sit below the commander. However, both participants in the 1982 Falklands Conflict adopted very different command and control arrangements. Consequently, the products and outcomes achieved by both sides were far from ideal.

From an Argentine viewpoint, the military *Junta* separated its subordinate units under geographic and Service lines. As a result, even before the Conflict started, the utility of Argentine air power was compromised as it was unable to mass its collected firepower efficiently. Before the Conflict, the *Fuerza Aérea Argentina* comprised of a staff headquarters and five commands – air defence, air operations, training, material, and air regions command through four geographical areas.[6] However, and to meet the demands of the emerging situation in the days leading up to the Falklands Conflict, the Argentine military changed its command structure, as shown in Figure 8.2.

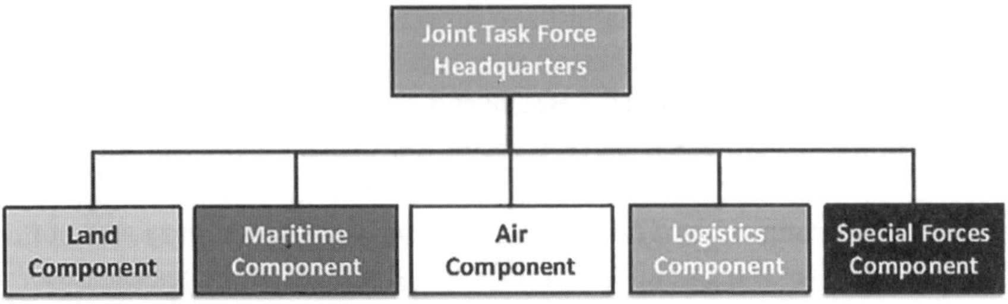

Figure 8.1 – Contemporary United Kingdom Joint Command and Control.[7]

Although Air Defence Command, *Comando Aereo de Defensa*, led by Brigadier Hughes, 'simply expanded its area of activity' to cover the Falkland Islands remit, the Argentines created a new command in early April.[8] Strategic Air Command, *Comando Aereo Estrategico,* was created to take responsibility for 'planning their reaction to the British Task Force, monitoring the size and progress of the fleet as it sailed south, assessing British preparations for war and the creation of the *Fuerza Aérea Argentina's* own battle plans.'[9] However, the relationship between the strategic coordination staffs, such as the *Estado Mayor de Coordination*, and their subordinate, deployed headquarters was troubled.[10] The challenge appeared not to be one of integrating new organisations under demanding timescales but one of authority. It seemed that the subordinate units believed that the plans generated by the coordination staffs were of limited utility and created by individuals who lacked credibility. Perhaps more surprisingly, on 30 April, the *Comando Aereo Estrategico,* 'was stood down, its task completed.'[11] So, on the eve of battle, the *Fuerza Aérea Argentina* elected to devolve all responsibility for planning and execution of its air war to the subordinate, operational level headquarters, *Comando de la Fuerza Aérea Sur*.

For day-to-day operational control of the air battle across the *Teatro de Operaciones Atlantico Sur*, both the *Comando de Aviación Naval* and the *Fuerza Aérea Argentina* had individual deployed headquarters located in southern Argentina. However, the deployed headquarters were geographically divorced from each other by several hundred miles. At Comodoro Rivadavia, the *Fuerza Aérea Argentina* adapted its existing regional air force headquarters, *Comando de Fuerza Aérea Sur*. Although the organisation existed before the Conflict, it consisted of only five personnel in early April and lacked plans, communications, and in-depth knowledge of the situation.[12] However, the Argentines bolstered the headquarters to 'be entrusted with the implementation of tactical missions'

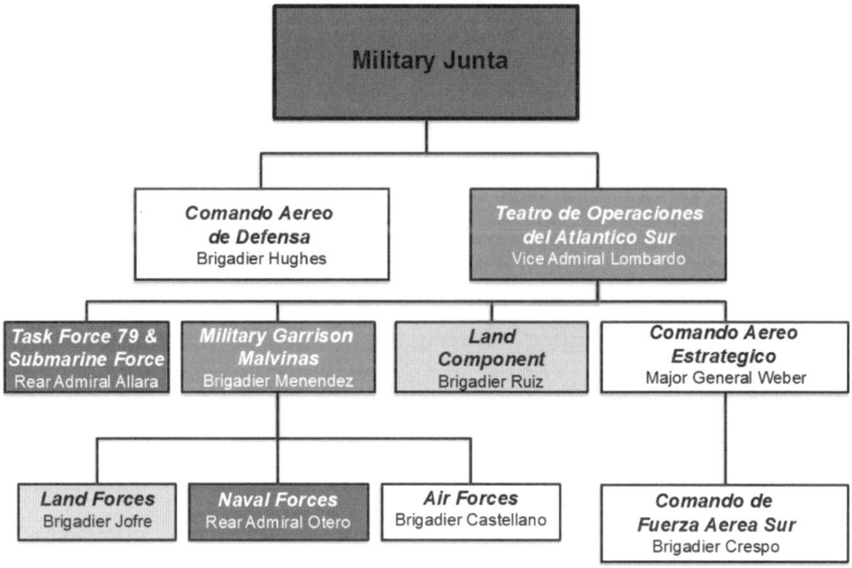

Figure 8.2 – Argentine Operational Command and Control.[14]

under the charge of Brigadier Ernesto Crespo, the *IV Brigada Aérea* commander.[13] As a result, the A-4C Skyhawk unit was devoid of its most senior leader; the decision did not aid the unit who were demonstrably the least successful Argentine combat air unit during the Conflict. Moreover, the *Comando de Fuerza Aérea Sur* had neither command nor control over the usage of *Fuerza Aérea Argentina* assets based on the Falkland Islands. Under the leadership of the Garrison Commander and Military Governor, the Falkland Islands-based aircraft contingent came under the control of Brigadier Castellana, who operated from the joint headquarters in Stanley. The net result was that command and control of *Fuerza Aérea Argentina* air power was not unified but divided across several ad hoc or modified organisations that were neither trained nor equipped for the task at hand. Consequently, the synchronization and focus of *Fuerza Aérea Argentina*'s assets during the Conflict were compromised at the outset of the campaign by a convoluted command and control structure.

In contrast and over 500 miles further south at Rio Grande, the *Comando de Aviación Naval* air command and control function was similar to its typical peacetime structures. The *Comando de Aviación Naval* headquarters and its aircraft benefitted from co-location, under the auspices of *Fuerza de Tareas 80*.[15] Although there were attempts in early May to marry up certain elements of the *Comando de Aviación Naval* under *Fuerza Aérea*

Argentina command and control, this aspiration never materialised.[16] As a result, both the *Comando de Aviación Naval* and *Fuerza Aérea Argentina* headquarters issued their own set of targeting priorities and attack plans, which, as described previously, differed significantly from each other. Consequently, the two services never aligned their conceptual thinking during the Conflict. The long-standing mutual distrust between the two Services meant that the physical interaction between the two Argentine air arms was also restricted. Although there was evidence of some inter-Service training before the Conflict, the benefits garnered from these events were, at best, limited.[17] During the Conflict itself, the two air arms only collaborated on one combat air mission, the combined Super Etendard and *Fuerza Aérea Argentina* A-4C Skyhawk attack mission conducted on 30 May. The limited interaction in the conceptual and physical environments caused Argentine air power to prosecute what, in effect, were two separate air campaigns managed along Service lines of interest. Ultimately, the Argentine air campaign lacked unity of effort. As a result, the Argentine's squandered their operational advantage of a larger force size through its inefficient employment.

However, as shown in Figure 8.3, the British ways of employing air command and control were equally disjointed. Although the British appointed an Air Commander, his remit did not encompass the totality of the British air power. Air Marshal Curtiss had responsibility for United Kingdom and Ascension Island-based activities, including launching Vulcan attack missions, Victor air-to-air refuelling sorties, C-130 Hercules airdrops and Nimrod maritime reconnaissance flights into the South Atlantic. However, the tasks required expertise beyond those that existed within his current peacetime 18 Group Headquarters construct. Curtiss stated, 'obviously my staff, which in normal times deals almost exclusively with maritime patrol aircraft and SAR [Search and Rescue] helicopter squadrons, had to be augmented with role specialists as different types of aircraft were drawn into the air order of battle.'[18]

In contrast, the British devolved responsibility for the embarked air power on board the two British aircraft carriers to the Carrier Battle Group Commander. In turn, Woodward empowered the commanding officer of HMS *Hermes*, Captain Linley Middleton, to act as the in-theatre Air Commander. However, on board HMS *Hermes*, the air planning staff was woefully undermanned. As a result, the product was underwhelming. The British planning effort was reactive, rushed, and failed to exploit its inherent deployed air power capability fully.

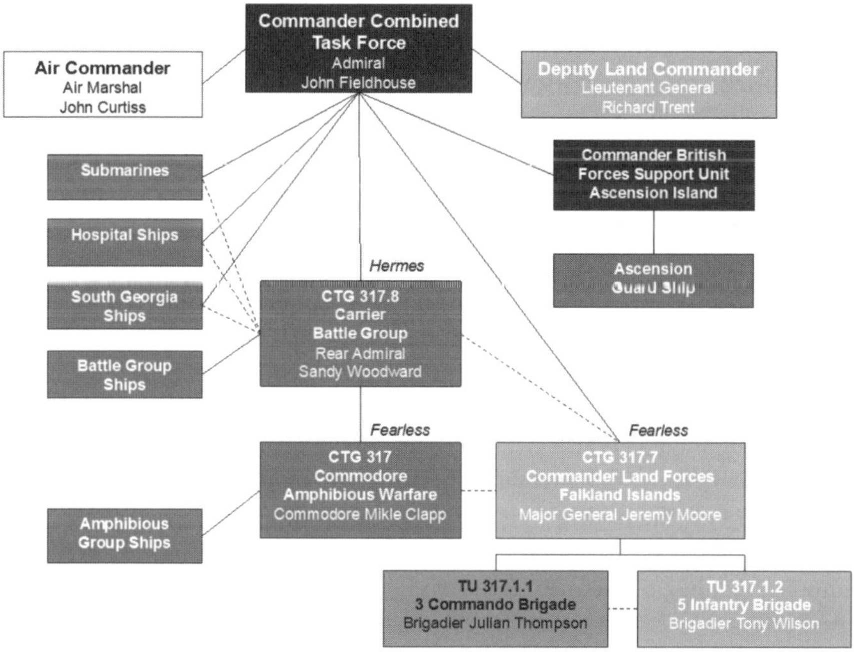

Figure 8.3 – British Operation Corporate Command and Control.[19]

Consequently, due to the ad hoc nature of many of the air planning requests, Middleton himself had to quickly assimilate, prioritise, and decide how to execute the tasks. Nevertheless, Middleton's management style was divisive. Squire felt that Middleton 'held a distorted view of the RAF.'[20] Consequently, Squire described his relationship with Middleton as 'antagonistic,' he was also warned by a senior Royal Navy officer that Middleton would 'go out of his way to make his life difficult.'[21] Uncharacteristically, Squire did not hold back on his views on Middleton when he suggested that 'he was a bully.'[22] Moreover, Middleton's wrath was not limited to the junior Service. Due to his autocratic management style, Middleton's decisions led to a set of disgruntled tactical operators, across both RAF and Fleet Air Arm aircrews, who justifiably felt that they were unable to exploit their tactical expertise and utility. Despite the 'good relationship' between the operators at the tactical level, poor execution of air command and control compromised both British combat air outputs and outcomes.[23]

The net result was that the British had two Air Commanders, but instead of splitting the assets along single Service lines, the distinction was geographic. While the Argentine air arms also had a geographic separation of their command and control teams measuring hundreds of miles, thousands of miles separated the British leadership.

So far, we have reviewed air command and control has been within the confines of the air campaign. However, that air effort is an integral part of the wider joint effort. Both participants could be critiqued for planning and executing independent air campaigns that rarely synchronised with the joint campaign. The evidence shows that the Argentine air campaigns began to run out of impetus before the critical land battles on the hills surrounding Stanley due to the ambivalent approach of the Argentine land and maritime components. From a British perspective, after a robust joint amphibious operation, the British had to wait for the arrival of the land commander and 5 Infantry Brigade. The delay meant that British air power failed to exploit the time available between the landings at San Carlos and the assaults on the high ground to the west of the capital. Air power was used ineffectively and reactively rather than in a planned, deliberate, pre-emptive manner that could shape and enable the joint battle space. The frustration was evident and highlighted by Wing Commander Trowern, the RAF liaison officer to the land commander, in his post-Conflict report when he suggested that 'military folk still look on our ac [aircraft] as airborne arty [artillery].'[24]

The lesson, therefore, is that to remain coherent and relevant, the co-location of the various component commanders must be seen as the exemplar to strive for as it enables collective understanding, ease of communication, and synchronised, coherent planning. If the co-location of the command team is unachievable, then empowered, knowledgeable, and embedded liaison staff in sufficient numbers can mitigate the absence of senior leadership. As a tertiary way of operating, secure communication systems and regular updates are essential to offset any face-to-face communication deficits. From both a British and an Argentine perspective, not one of these three proposed ways of working was in place during the Conflict.

Both protagonists suffered due to convoluted and inefficient joint and, in turn, air command and control processes. Geography, inter-Service rivalry, rushed implementation, inadequate infrastructure, and lack of credible staff all conspired to generate a distinct lack of unity of effort from both participants. However, could each side adapt their command and control flaws and build sufficient situational awareness to prosecute the conflict successfully?

Lesson 2 – Understand the Theatre. Critical to any campaign plan is the need to understand the operating environment, the enemy's capability, and its intent. In contemporary British doctrine, 'Understand' is defined as 'the perception and interpretation of a particular situation to provide the context, insight and foresight required for effective decision-making.'[25] In 1982, the Cold War was the focus of Britain's military effort. Despite significant and accurate reporting by the British Embassy in Buenos Aires on military affairs over the years, little tangible knowledge about the Argentine military capability, nor its intent, appears to have percolated down to the British units as they rapidly deployed to the South Atlantic. From an Argentine viewpoint, they faced strategic shock as they failed to predict the British reaction to the Argentine invasion of the Islands. Consequently, both participants needed to rapidly assimilate an understanding of what enemy force they faced and ensure they identified their opponents, as well as their own, strengths and weaknesses. In essence, before decisive operations could take place, each protagonist endeavoured to understand and control the land, sea, and air environments. From a British doctrinal perspective, the need to control the environments to generate the necessary freedoms of initiative and manoeuvre was well understood. Moreover, from an amphibious operations viewpoint, history has shown that the success of amphibious operations requires effective sea control and control of the air before and during the amphibious assault. So, how effective was each participant in controlling the environments?

Although the Argentines lacked an airborne early warning capability, they had deployed a long-range surveillance radar and associated control organisation to support air operations in and around the Islands. The *Centro de Informacion y Control* (CIC) unit based at Stanley used the Westinghouse AN/TPS-43F radar of *Escuadron del Grupo 2 de Vigilancia y Control Aereo*, to successfully warn Argentine aircraft approaching the Islands of the presence of Sea Harrier combat air patrols.[26] As a consequence, and without the benefit of sweep and escort aircraft to protect them, several Argentine formations aborted their intended attacks based upon the information provided to them by their controllers. Nevertheless, the British made concerted efforts to negate the Argentine early warning capability. Despite several dedicated armed reconnaissance and suppression of enemy air defence missions to find and destroy the Argentine radars, the damage was minimal, and the Argentine radar capability remained operational throughout the campaign.

Beyond the air environment, the Argentines struggled to dominate the other environments. There is little evidence suggesting that Argentine land forces adopted anything other than a static defensive position with localised surveillance. However, the limited reconnaissance effort was not without success. Argentine forces conducting observation duties on Pebble Island and to the north of Fitzroy led to the attacks against HMS *Coventry* on 25 May and the RFAs *Sir Tristram* and *Sir Galahad* on 8 June.[27] Nevertheless, the Argentine ability to understand and influence the maritime environment was limited by a lack of appetite to commit their forces to battle following the sinking of the ARA *General Belgrano* on 2 May. As a result, the British were able to approach the Falkland Islands unmolested throughout Operation Corporate.

The lack of British airborne early warning is a well-documented lesson from Operation Corporate.[28] Although the British made valiant efforts to mitigate the capability gap, these were of limited success. The Sea King airborne early warning helicopters were modified, tested, and deployed in an impressive timeframe, but they did not arrive in the South Atlantic until the Conflict was over. Consequently, the British employed several joint capabilities in an attempt to offset the critical gaps in capability. However, these endeavours came at a cost. The lack of a British airborne early warning capability meant that the Type 42 destroyers were placed up threat in an attempt to provide early warning of air attacks. As a result, attribution for the loss of two of the Type 42 destroyers links directly to the lack of airborne early warning assets. The insertion of special forces onto the South American mainland, the use of British-provisioned and manned radars in Chile, as well as submarines poised off the Argentine shore, all provided valuable early warning to the Task Force and the timely launch of Sea Harrier combat air patrols. However, the British failed to grasp the scale and complexity of Argentine air operations. For example, during the landings of 21 May, the Ministry of Defence believed, driven by overly optimistic kill assessments, that the Argentine mainland attack force had dwindled to twenty-six aircraft and was only able to generate thirty-five missions.[29] The reality was the force comprised seventy-three aircraft and was able to fly seventy-four missions. The British significantly under-estimated the size of the Argentine combat air force. However, the over-estimation of the Argentine air arms' ability to turn their force size into outputs mitigated this oversight somewhat.[30] Nevertheless, the British understanding of the Argentine combat air capability was far from perfect, and it is no surprise that the British subsequently skewed their claims.

With the Argentine surface fleet constrained to Argentine littoral waters for the vast majority of the Conflict, the battle for sea control rapidly became an anti-submarine warfare task. The Cold War era Royal Navy was very familiar and well equipped to deal with the anti-submarine task. Even so, the embarked anti-submarine Sea King force had to expend significant effort to deliver assurance and minimise the threat. Despite its considerable commitment to the task, the Sea King force could not guarantee sea control. As a result, the Task Force had to respect the Argentine submarine threat throughout the campaign, even though the Argentine submarine force 'had defects and could not get to the TEZ [Total Exclusion Zone.]'[31] Consequently, the Operation Sutton plan was 'to confuse enemy submarines and reconnaissance aircraft, the amphibious group will use evasive routing with a superimposed zig zag.'[32]

Although the British force was dominant in the maritime environment, the British struggled to understand the Argentine land environment in terms of its scale, location, capability, and intent. Even though British special forces had been inserted onto the Islands as early as 1 May and were able to provide a persistent presence, limiting their reconnaissance capability was their line of sight, distance from the target, and the hostile environment.[33] Consequently, the British estimate of the size of the Argentine garrison was inaccurate. For example, their initial evaluation of the size of the Goose Green garrison was 300 when, in fact, it was closer to 1000.[34] If the embarked command team tasked the Harrier force to conduct dedicated reconnaissance missions, as requested by its operators, then the command team would have additional information that could have been blended with other intelligence sources to provide a more accurate picture of what was actually occurring on the ground. However, the operational command team appeared to neglect this opportunity. As a result, British attack missions lacked focus, were poorly planned and operated in highly defended areas with limited preparation and awareness. In contrast, the strategic command team understood the utility of intelligence assets to gather information. Although many of the files remain redacted, several RAF transport and reconnaissance squadrons participated in Operations Folklore and Acme during the Conflict.[35] Once The National Archives have released these files, they may shed further light on intelligence gathering activities based in Chile and their contribution to the Falklands Conflict.

Ultimately, neither side was able to control the operating environments throughout the Conflict. This situation would have long-lasting consequences. As neither party achieved full situational awareness, the narrative becomes contested and a fertile ground for the myths to be nurtured and left to grow unabated. The next lesson aims to analyse the fielded capabilities of both sides and looks at the operational level implications of fielding flawed systems.

Lesson 3 – Understand the Capabilities.

> 'Bravery was no substitute for training, skill and experience.'[36]

Deighton's comment regarding the Battle of Britain hinted at the broader needs to ensure victory. Bravery alone would not guarantee success; it had to be supported by a more comprehensive series of attributes. However, training is only one element that defines military capability. In turn, military capability, articulated via Defence Lines of Development, is one element of the physical component of fighting power. Moreover, the physical component cannot work in isolation and must integrate with the moral and conceptual components, as shown in Figure 8.4.

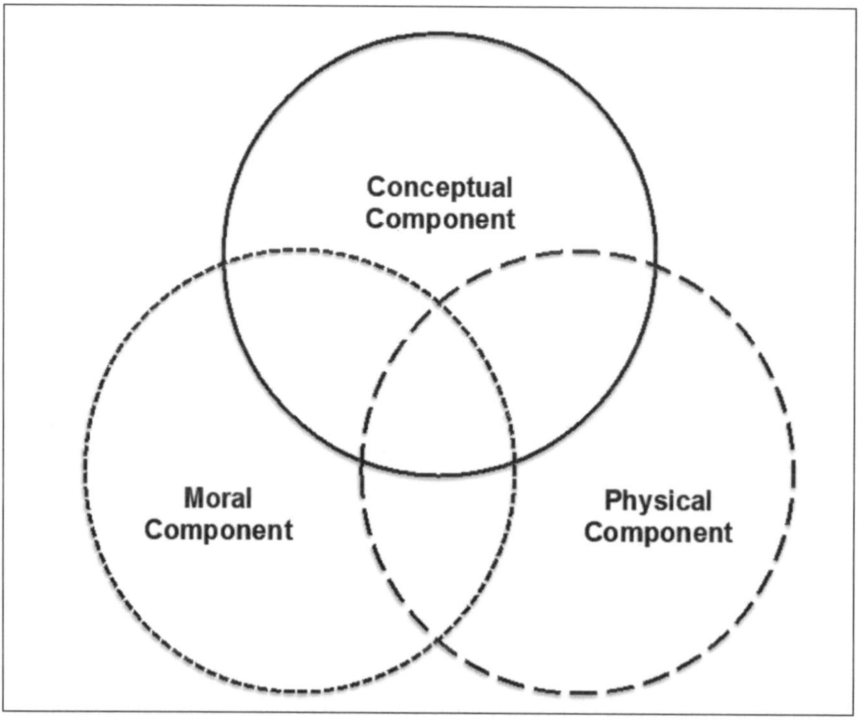

Figure 8.4 – The Components of Fighting Power.[37]

Current British doctrine states that 'the moral component is generally viewed as constant, but when we are fiscally constrained, we must grow the conceptual component (how we fight) to compensate for shortfalls in the physical component (what we fight with).'[38] During the Conflict, deficits in the physical and conceptual components degraded the moral component of at least one of the participants. Lesson 3 will focus on the physical component and the implications for the moral component, whereas Lesson 4 will address the conceptual component of fighting power.

The Physical Component. The conundrum of quality versus quantity is a constant challenge for military planners. With finite financial resource available, the desire to field and use capable forces on a sufficient scale is an enduring challenge. In contrast to the Argentine position, there is considerable documentation concerning the strength and weaknesses of the British fielded capability. Consequently, this short physical component assessment will focus on the Argentine situation. However, many of the issues faced by the Argentines resonated with the British deployed force.

The *Fuerza Aérea Argentina* official history documents several equipment and logistic deficits that impacted its operations during the Conflict. The limited number of Omega navigation systems and Canberra radars, the scarcity of electronic countermeasure systems, as well as fuel tanks all constrained *Fuerza Aérea Argentina* air operations.[39] Additionally, there were several weapons issues, including type, numbers, and locations.[40] With a variety of aircraft and weapons scattered over a number of austere airfields in southern Argentina, there was a distinct lack of weapons support equipment to meet the operational tempo.[41] This issue may explain why the *Comando de Aviación Naval* gave its air force counterparts access to its Mk 82 bomb stockpile.[42] However, there is no documented evidence of the *Fuerza Aérea Argentina* exploiting this opportunity. Nevertheless, the *Fuerza Aérea Argentina* took advantage of their naval colleagues' offer to mitigate its lack of sea survival equipment and salt corrosion procedures.[43]

Although there was evidence of localised and tactical assistance, the support at the operational level was more limited. As discussed previously, Argentine doctrine denied the *Fuerza Aérea Argentina* from conducting anti-maritime operations before the Conflict. Consequently, the doctrinal oversight denuded the Argentine air power of a significant capability. As a result, there were attempts by the *Comando de Aviación Naval* to rapidly adopt a more joint and collegiate approach with the *Fuerza Aérea Argentina*. During the early stages of the Conflict, the Argentines made attempts to train and organise their airmen in a more integrated fashion. However, few of the concepts materialised, either driven by ambivalence or lack of time and resources. Nevertheless, there were a few examples of a joint ethos. For example, a team of four naval aviators joined the *Fuerza Aérea Argentina* planning team at Comodoro Rivadavia in order to develop joint operations.[44] In particular, the *Comando de Aviación Naval* advisors discussed techniques and tactics for anti-surface warfare.[45] Moreover, this discussion materialised into several joint training sorties. However, the success of the training missions was questionable due to *Fuerza Aérea Argentina* aircraft serviceability.[46] Subsequently, the *Comando de Aviación Naval* tended to conduct bespoke and effective mission rehearsals in isolation.[47] Nevertheless, during the Conflict itself, the Rio Grande-based Dagger pilots shared information and their experiences with their co-located *Comando de Aviación Naval* pilots.[48] However, this sharing of corporate knowledge was a localised phenomenon, and not one that was widespread practice across both air arms.

Despite aircraft frailties during its rapid work-up period, the *Fuerza Aérea Argentina* continued to make requests to take command and control of the *Comando de Aviación Naval* combat air assets.[49] Argentine air arm integration may have resolved several issues. For example, the A-4Q Skyhawk's initial response to Operation Sutton may have been more successful if it had adopted *Fuerza Area Argentina* pathfinder practices rather than rely on its own recently introduced Omega navigation system. However, only two aircraft had the new navigation system installed.[50] The inability to understand, use and exploit the new navigation equipment meant that the first wave of *Comando de Aviación Naval* A-4Q Skyhawks was unable to find and attack the British amphibious force when it was at its most vulnerable.

However, capability is about more than merely looking across the Defence Lines of Development; scale plays a significant role. There is no point in having a highly advanced and expensive capability if it cannot sustain the required campaign effects throughout the campaign. The Argentine Super Etendard force is an excellent example of this dilemma; once the Argentines had expended their limited Exocet stockpile, the Super Etendards became an ineffective force and retired from the battle two weeks prior to the culmination of the campaign. The Sea Harrier also deployed in limited numbers. However, the Sea Harrier force, despite losses early in the campaign and a high tempo of operations, had sufficient resilience to sustain its outputs throughout the campaign. Moreover, the Harrier

GR3 force also had enough resilience to add additional aircraft and new capabilities throughout the Conflict. Argentine air power also increased the number of its deployed assets throughout the early stages of the campaign as aircraft that were unserviceable at the start of the campaign were rectified and subsequently implemented into the fight. However, once the reserve forces deployed south, there was no further pool of resources to call upon. Consequently, the deployed fleet size began to diminish irreversibly due to combat attrition.

Despite its highlighted capability deficiencies, the *Fuerza Aérea Argentina* still believed that the 'performance of maintenance personnel and the performance of the aircraft was optimised.'[51] Is this statement a true reflection of Argentine air power or merely an endeavour to protect the reputation and morale of a brave force operating under significant losses for a limited reward? However, the British were not immune to the pressures of the campaign. Several incidents within the British cadre of pilots demonstrate that fatigue was creeping into the deployed force. For example, Lieutenant Commander Neill Thomas, an experienced naval aviator embedded with 800 Naval Air Squadron on board HMS *Hermes,* recalled how fatigue caused him to become distracted while making a cockpit switch selection that resulted in a rapid descent from 300 feet down to 150 feet.[52] Dowding's worst fear during the Battle of Britain was 'the loss of quality that fatigue would bring.'[53] So, how robust was the morale of each participant? Moreover, would history repeat itself in the South Atlantic in 1982?

The Moral Component. The British were keen to have a quick and decisive air battle before the amphibious assault. Not only would control of the air allow the British to have the necessary freedoms to exploit the landing, but also, as Clausewitz observed, it would reinforce that the battle was 'rather a killing of the enemy's spirit than of his men.'[54] However, the Argentine air arms preserved their forces for the campaign's critical move, Operation Sutton. Nevertheless, once the Argentines committed their air arms, the air battle quickly became one of attrition that the Argentines were steadily losing. Once Argentine air power resilience began to unravel, its sortie rates and willingness to prosecute its targets fell rapidly as the moral component began to erode. Moro rejects the claim that Argentine morale was diminishing. However, the *Fuerza Aérea Argentina* official history highlighted two cases of Argentine attack pilots returned to their units during the Conflict; one during Operation Sutton and another in the final days of the Conflict.[55] Indeed, the commander at San Julian informed the official history that his work to maintain his subordinates' morale was very difficult.[56] The latter situation may well reflect the incident where an A-4C Skyhawk pilot who, on 24 May, ordered his wingmen to jettison their weapons and return to base.[57] However, his wingmen questioned the order both in the air and, subsequently, on the ground. The issue was not an isolated event, and five other officers were also subject to an inconclusive post-Conflict military inquiry. Nevertheless, the shadow cast by the incident precluded the individual from attaining promotion to Brigadier several years later.[58]

The Argentines were under no illusion regarding the difficulty of the task that faced them during Operation Sutton. The anticipated attrition rates were daunting. During the pre-campaign training missions, the *Comando de Aviación Naval* advised its *Fuerza Aérea Argentina* counterparts that during anti-ship attacks against a modern British fleet, they could expect 90 per cent losses.[59] In contrast, the more experienced *Comando de Aviación Naval* faced no less of a task, they would expect to launch four aircraft, from a fleet of six, and lose two aircraft during the attack.[60] Neither force expected to survive a long campaign. Indeed, the *Fuerza Aérea Argentina* expected to lose 50 per cent of its attack aircraft on the first raid; the second, and last, attack would account for the remainder of the force.[61] Ultimately, from the start of operations, the outlook was bleak for the Argentine air arms, and it is no surprise that their fighting spirit collapsed during the latter stages of the Conflict.

The moral component of the British pilots was also under pressure. During the first phase of the campaign, the small cadre of Sea Harrier pilots was reduced by four following the loss of three aircraft and the removal of a pilot who struggled to come to terms with the events he had witnessed on the first day of fighting.[62] With no respite in their tasking, the burden placed upon the remaining Sea Harrier pilots was significant. Moreover, some raised concerns that the subsequent tasking was far from equitable, applying additional strain on individuals and generating further friction between the two aircraft carriers.[63] Additionally, some British operators viewed the apportionment of risk as a differentiator between the Sea Harrier and Harrier GR3 cadres. Pook critiqued his Sea Harrier compatriots when he suggested that they had a 'cushy job' conducting air defence duties in contrast to the high risk, low altitude roles of the Harrier GR3 force.[64] Despite the increased pressure, the British combat air pilots were a resilient group and, no doubt, bolstered by their successes, belief in their ability, equipment, and cause as well as the news that additional aircraft and pilots would join them throughout the campaign.

Lesson 4 – Deliver Outcomes, not Outputs.

'Göring found it convenient to stick to von Richtofen's simplistic dictum that shooting down enemy planes was "the only important thing" and that "everything else is nonsense"'[65]

Even with deficits in both the physical and moral components, defeat is not inevitable. Exploiting the conceptual component can mitigate shortcomings in the other components of national power and achieve campaign goals. Therefore, airpower must focus on attacking enemy critical vulnerabilities while protecting its own. Consequently, Göring's philosophy during the Battle of Britain, where he overly focused on outputs rather than the broader outcomes and effects that were needed to ensure victory, chimed with the 1982 philosophy in the South Atlantic.

After the initial air battles of 1 May, the Argentine strategy of preserving their force was a prudent measure. It reflected the views of the former Minister for the Co-ordination of Defence, Sir Thomas Inskip, that during the Battle of Britain that, 'the role of our Air Force is not an early knock-out blow … but to prevent the Germans from knocking us out.'[66] However, when committed to the battle, it was evident that the Argentines were unable to focus their air power on the critical components of British military capability. Although the Argentine operational order specified the correct targeting priorities to counter an amphibious assault, the Argentine tacticians failed to implement the cogent targeting policy. Analysis of Annexes F and G show that during Operation Sutton, the Argentines were unable to breach the inner ring of British defences during the early stages of the amphibious assault. As a result, there were no attacks against British transport ship or associated critical vulnerability until 24 May. Also, the only British transport ship to be sunk during Operation Sutton, MV *Atlantic Conveyor*, was struck during the latter, and less critical, stages of the operation. The sole focus of the Argentine attacks during Operation Sutton should have been the transport ships and the troops ashore around San Carlos. However, the Argentines attacked several irrelevant targets during the period of the landings. As shown in Annex G, the targets included non-existent radar sites, supposed troop concentrations, and targets on West Falkland; the attacks were both unnecessary and unsuccessful. More importantly, the attacks dragged precious resources away from the critical fighting area.

Nevertheless, and despite the poor execution of the Argentine operational plan, there were several successes for Argentine air power during Operation

Sutton – notably, the sinking of HMS *Ardent*, *Antelope* and *Coventry,* as well as MV *Atlantic Conveyor*. Indeed, the *Comando de Aviación Naval* official history of the Conflict stated that two out of three sorties hit an enemy target.[67] Consequently, the *Comando de Aviación Naval* would claim that for every aircraft its air arm lost would result in the sinking of 4,250 tonnes of British shipping during the campaign.[68] However, this Argentine view assumes that each tonne of British shipping is equally important. The Argentine assessment is an output-based analysis of the campaign rather than the more astute effect-based result. Consequently, the Argentine report is overly optimistic. A more appropriate measure of effect would be to base the analysis on the tonnage of transport ships lost during 21 May or throughout Operation Sutton. If the *Comando de Aviación Naval* analysis was to reflect its total losses during the Conflict and compared to the loss of British transport shipping on 21 May and for the period of Operation Sutton, the results would be zero and 1,900 tonnes per aircraft respectively.[69]

From a *Fuerza Aérea Argentina* viewpoint, despite a set of valid targeting priorities, and being cognisant of the limited prospects for survival, they felt that sinking a single frigate would be sufficient reward for its endeavours.[70] The *Fuerza Aérea Argentina* was simply after a heroic reward for its efforts and not necessarily one that matched with its higher headquarters intent or prudent operational level planning.

In a similar vein to the Argentine issues, the success of the Sea Harrier against its Argentine counterparts dominates the British narrative. The twenty-one Sea Harrier air-to-air kills during the campaign for no loss is an impressive feat. However, this is another output-based parameter. Few commentators articulated the overall effect that the control of the air battle achieved. Indeed, British narratives use almost every conceivable doctrinal term to describe the level of control of the air attained by the British during the Conflict. While this book does not aim to provide another answer to that question, it is evident that throughout the Conflict, Argentine air power was capable of penetrating the British defences on a regular basis.

From the perspective of British attack operations, it would appear that they were inefficient in the prosecution of the Argentine operational centre of gravity. In addition to the fascination with Stanley airport, several attacks were of questionable value, either from a location or preparation perspective. Consequently, the utility of attacks on the grass airstrip at Dunnose Head on West Falkland by four Harrier GR3s on 23 May, or the reactive nature of many missions in the latter stages of the campaign, is of questionable benefit.[71] As a result, it is difficult to quantify the utility of the Harrier GR3 during the Conflict other than to measure the outputs of hours and missions flown and weapons employed. This statement is not to decry the Harrier GR3 activities. It is a reflection of how the platform employment appears to be a series of tactical, component level attacks rather than a fully integrated joint operation.

This chapter has looked at the campaign through five simple, straightforward, and apparently obvious questions. In essence, the questions posed are: Who is in charge? What is the plan? What is the current situation? What resources do we have? And what do we need to achieve? Despite their uncomplicated nature, analysis of the five questions demonstrates that neither side provided a clear set of answers. Moreover, these questions are as relevant today as they were in 1982. Consequently, contemporary military planners must understand the shortfalls and mitigate accordingly. The United Kingdom's approach to joint operations has developed significantly since their experiences in the South Atlantic. As a result, the introduction of the Permanent Joint Headquarters at Northwood in the late 1990s largely mitigates the complex and dislocated command and control arrangements. However, no matter how much process and joint doctrine is in place, the role of personality remains an enduring variable. Nevertheless, with greater dialogue, training, exposure, and trust between single Service and joint units, individuals will have a better understanding of the needs, concerns, and advantages of their own and other Services. Culture and ethos can take generations to change. The animosity of the early 1960s between the RAF and Royal Navy over the CVA01 aircraft carrier debacle was still evident and detrimental to the British campaign in the South Atlantic two decades later. As the United Kingdom looks to introduce new military capabilities into service, it is clear that a joint approach rather than a parochial single Service perspective is needed. By way of example, the *Queen Elizabeth*-class of aircraft carriers is a joint capability and one that requires the help and support of all three Services to fulfil its roles. The Single Statement of User Need specified that the Carrier Enabled Power Projection provided an 'integrated and sustainable joint capability, interoperable with NATO that enables the projection of UK Carrier Strike and Littoral Manoeuvre power, as well as delivering Humanitarian assistance and Defence Diplomacy, enabling joint effect across the maritime, land and air environments at a time and a place of political choosing.'[72] To continue to deliver against national ambition, new military capabilities will need to embrace and teach the lessons of the Falklands Conflict if it is to realise their true potential.

Chapter 9

Conclusion

'War is mainly a catalogue of blunders.'

The Right Honourable Winston Churchill MP,
British Prime Minister.[1]

The premise behind this book reflected Deighton's views on the Battle of Britain:

> 'There was a time when I believed that History was self-rectifying. I believed that no matter how distorted the accounts of news and current events, in the course of time a more truthful and useful consensus would emerge. Now I know better. In fact, it is the myths and fabrications that endure and become each nation's historical reference.'[2]

From the perspective of the Falklands Conflict, several competing narratives are, frequently, at odds with each other. The inability or reluctance to moderate the tales has resulted in a variety of stakeholders adopting their own perspective of the Conflict.

Churchill's quote above is an excellent reminder that the combatant that makes fewer mistakes tends to be the victor. Nevertheless, it is important that the victor and the vanquished both learn from their hard-earned errors. However, some commentators have suggested that there is little to learn from the Conflict. In their eyes, the 1982 campaign was a Cold War aberration. The Argentines simply misinterpreted the British desire to fight for a set of desolate islands thousands of miles away from their 'mother' country. Despite the strategic mismanagement of the Falkland Islands during the prelude to the Conflict, the British had to rapidly adapt from their steady-state configuration and focus on their NATO commitments in north-west Europe and the North Atlantic sea lanes.

Nevertheless, the battle was not only a physical contest, but as Nye suggested, 'victory may sometimes depend not on whose Army wins, but on whose story wins.'[3] Although Nye specifically talks about the Army, the lessons are equally relevant to the other environments. Consequently, the Conflict raised a significant number of air power lessons that remain relevant today.

The British and Argentine Operational Centres of Gravity

The first research question opened by looking at the current perception of the British operational centre of gravity during Operation Corporate. Contemporary British doctrine suggests that, due to their embarked control of the air capability, the two aircraft carriers were the British operational centre of gravity. As control of the air was an enduring campaign requirement, particularly during the lead-up and execution of the amphibious assault, the aircraft carriers were undoubtedly crucial to British success. However, this book suggests that control of the air is an enabling and enduring function but not an end in itself. The British could have achieved complete control of the air, but they could not assure the military end-state's delivery. If, as decreed, the initial British operational aim was to 'repossess the Falkland Islands as quickly as possible,' the aircraft carriers and their embarked Sea Harriers delivering control of the air could not produce that requirement in isolation.[4] Moreover, it is apparent that there were differing perspectives from the senior British commanders. Despite operating in the same command chain, albeit at different locations and levels of warfare, Woodward, Fieldhouse, and Leach had different risk appetites regarding losses to personnel and equipment at various stages of the Conflict. It is now evident that the communication of the risk appetite between the multiple levels was poor.

The contemporary and retrospective view of the British operational centre of gravity is flawed. As a result, this book suggests that control of the air is, predominantly, a critical vulnerability and not an enduring centre of gravity. The only force that could deliver the required end-state before the rapidly approaching austral winter was a ground force. Therefore, the British operational centre of gravity was ultimately the British fielded land force that was able to seize and hold land, specifically Stanley. However, the British land force had to mount, deploy, and project ashore before it could capture Stanley. As a result, it is the contention of this book that there were three British operational centres of gravity that ran sequentially. The British centres of gravity are the aircraft carriers, the amphibious force, and the land forces on the Falkland Islands.

The initial British maritime force to arrive in the South Atlantic was devoid of a large enough embarked land force to achieve the end-state. As a result, and despite Argentine rhetoric to the contrary, this force neither planned to, nor was capable of, conducting an amphibious assault against the Falkland Islands. Nevertheless, the initial maritime force, including the two aircraft carriers, was sufficient to prepare for the arrival of the amphibious force. The British planners were acutely aware that 'history has repeatedly shown the folly of operating with inadequate air support.'[5] Consequently, and enshrined in contemporary British amphibious warfare doctrine, the British command team knew that control of the air was critical to the success of the amphibious operations. Therefore, the British planning staffs stated that 'their objective will be to achieve complete air and sea control of the area, thereby isolating the Argentine garrison and reducing its will and capacity to resist a determined amphibious assault.'[6] So, over the period 1 – 19 May, and before the arrival of the amphibious assault force, the British gambit was to entice the Argentine air and maritime forces from the shelter of the Argentine mainland for a decisive air and naval battle. Chapter 3 of this book proposes that the aircraft carriers, with their embarked Sea Harriers and Sea Kings, constituted the British operational centre of gravity during this initial phase and were critical to preparing the battle space before the amphibious assault.

To project British land forces ashore on a sufficient scale, the most efficient mechanism was via an amphibious assault. Led by Commodore Mike Clapp, the British generated an initial amphibious assault force of twelve ships encompassing the two Land Platform Docks, HMS *Fearless* and *Intrepid*, seven Royal Fleet Auxiliary ships and three ships taken up from trade. On board the vessels were the troops of 3 Commando Brigade, Royal Marines supported by two battalions from the Parachute Regiment, and the various key enablers to secure the beachhead. Consequently, Chapter 4 of this book suggests that during the period of the amphibious assault, the British operational centre of gravity transferred from the aircraft carriers to the amphibious assault force. The amphibious assault was activated on the morning of 20 May as the ships commenced their transit from the edge of the Total Exclusion Zone and culminated on 26 May when 2 PARA left its positions on the Sussex Mountains to attack Goose Green. Protecting the British operational centre of gravity was the responsibility of the Sea Harrier force as well as the seven frigates and destroyers that escorted the amphibious assault force during the transit from the edge of the Total Exclusion Zone to San Carlos. Moreover, the escorts also provided a layer of protection to the twelve assault ships as they disembarked their troops and equipment onto the beaches at San Carlos. However, if the Argentines could bypass the Sea Harriers and the escort ships to strike the British amphibious assault force, they would have either bought themselves more valuable time or even achieved a decisive victory.

During the last phase of the Conflict, which spanned the period 27 May to 14 June, the British operational centre of gravity would transfer from the amphibious assault force to the British fielded land forces. The new centre of gravity was the only military capability that was able to achieve the end state of recovering and holding Stanley. With the beachhead at San Carlos now secured, the various elements of 3 Commando Brigade were waiting for the arrival of 5 Infantry Brigade to strengthen the breakout from San Carlos and participate in the investment of Stanley. Due to the size of the Argentine garrison, and from the outset of their campaign, British planners recognised the need for 5 Infantry Brigade to support 3 Commando Brigade during the land campaign. Nevertheless, if the Argentine air force could find and strike the British force as it moved from the beachhead to Stanley, the British centre of gravity could, once again, be compromised.

The Argentine operational centre of gravity is the last position considered. In contrast to the British operational centre of gravity that changed as the emphasis of the campaign developed, the Argentine operational centre of gravity throughout the campaign was a constant – the Argentine fielded land forces. Just as the last of the British operational centres of gravity was capable of seizing and holding the vital ground of Stanley, it was the same effect that meant that the Argentine operational centre of gravity rested with the Argentine troops located in and around Stanley. Although the Argentine garrison also had outposts at Goose Green and across West Falkland, the location of the majority of the Argentine force was in and around Stanley. Notwithstanding that the Argentines outnumbered their opposition; the Argentine land force adopted a strategy that saw the majority of its land force remaining static on the high ground that protected the western approaches to Stanley. The town itself contained a sizeable headquarters element that delivered the command and control function to all three Services garrisoned on the Islands. At Stanley airport, situated several miles east of the town, an eclectic force of ground-based air defence assets protected the aviation and air assets from all three services located at the small airfield. The British faced a dispersed enemy force that had the luxury of time and geography to plan and prepare for its defence of Stanley. With each of the operational centres of gravity now articulated, the next section will look at how effectively each centre of gravity was attacked and defended.

Defending and Attacking the Operational Centres of Gravity

The second research question addresses the utilisation of British and Argentine air power during Operation Corporate. As part of their work, several commentators identified the number of sorties flown by a specific platform or the amount of aircraft that arrived in the target area.[7] However, there is no single narrative that maps all of the planned sorties to the effect that they managed to achieve against the designated operational centre of gravity. This book provides that single source of data. To achieve that goal, the question clarified the types of aircraft involved, the weapon load carried by each aircraft, and how each weapon was employed. Adopting this methodology develops a transparent and auditable trail that is open to further scrutiny if required. Additionally, this approach allows the identification and further analysis of the causal factors for any notable failings. So, what state was the Argentine military in before the start of the Conflict?

The friction between the various Argentine Services was well documented by the British. During their early planning, British military planners noted that 'each of the armed forces is autonomous and little if any experience of joint operations is available to them. Control of exercises is vested in the individual arm's Commanders in Chief and there has been no apparent co-operation and co-ordination.'[8] In contrast, the British forces were more used to working as part of a collegiate NATO Cold War construct. Consequently, although notionally more inclusive in their approach, the British had to adapt quickly to a crisis thousands of miles from home. So, how effective were both sides in the prosecution of their air campaigns?

The British air campaign to repossess the Falkland Islands commenced on 1 May. In response to the Vulcan and Sea Harrier attacks on Stanley airport, the Argentine air arms endeavoured to respond in kind. However, the Argentine counterattack was ineffective; they lost four aircraft to the Sea Harrier and AIM-9L Sidewinder combination for no substantial gains. After a disappointing start, Argentine air power flew a limited number of missions during the Conflict's opening phase. The Argentine strategy was a prudent move to preserve its force until the inevitable British amphibious assault took place. Nevertheless, there were notable Argentine successes during this period. Most conspicuously, on 4 May, the first successful Super Etendard attack took place that resulted in the loss of HMS *Sheffield*. Eight days later, HMS *Glasgow* was attacked and damaged to such an extent that the Royal Navy withdrew it from battle. Through luck rather than judgement the Argentines had negated two of the three Type 42 destroyers – key air defence ships that were needed to offset the lack of deployed airborne early warning within the British fleet. However, the Argentine successes were themselves offset by the loss of seven aircraft during the initial phase. Nevertheless, the Argentines replaced its losses, and the *Fuerza Aérea Argentina* would start Operation Sutton with more aircraft than they had at the outset of its campaign. Chapter 3 identifies that of the 206 planned Argentine weapons during the pre-amphibious assault phase, the Argentines only dropped fifteen. Additionally, only two Argentine bombs hit their intended target, but critically none were targeted against the British operational centre of gravity. However, did the surge in Argentine air activity during the amphibious assault produce more effective results?

With the Argentine maritime surface fleet confined to port and the land component fixed in situ in the hills surrounding Stanley, the burden of responsibility for attacking the British operational centres of gravity fell to Argentine air power. However, the relationship between the two Argentine air arms was problematic, with limited interaction between them throughout the Conflict. Chapter 4 identified that the Argentine air arms surged their aircraft flying rates to counter the threat of the amphibious assault. Consequently, the Argentines planned to use 390 weapons throughout Operation Sutton. Of those, only eight weapons detonated against the British ships. During the amphibious assault, the British lost four British ships, including one destroyer, two frigates, and a merchant ship. The British escort ships acted as an outer layer of protection for the amphibious force and faced the brunt of the Argentine air attacks. Consequently, few Argentine aircraft and weapons penetrated the inner sanctum of the British amphibious assault force. Indeed, only four weapons struck at elements that constituted the British operational centre of gravity. Of those four weapons, three hit and damaged Royal Fleet Auxiliary ships on 24 May – four days after the start of Operation Sutton. The remaining weapon struck and sank MV *Atlantic Conveyor* on 25 May, along with its precious cargo of helicopters, weapons, airfield matting, and tents. Although the supply ship was not the intended target, the attack constituted the biggest drawback to the British operation to retake the Falkland

Islands. Nevertheless, and despite a cogent Argentine operational plan that identified the correct target set to negate an amphibious assault, the Argentines missed the fleeting opportunity to strike the British operational centre of gravity when it was in its most concentrated and vulnerable state. During Operation Sutton, the Argentine air attacks were also costly; they had lost twenty-six aircraft and twenty-one aircrew since the start of the Conflict. Although disputed by some commentators, the implications on the moral component were clear.

With British ground forces dispersing from the concentrated beachhead to their ultimate goal of Stanley, the task facing the Argentine air arms during the last phase of the Conflict was daunting. Nevertheless, this period accounted for nearly half of the Argentine weapons used during the Conflict. However, the Argentines now faced weapon employment against a much broader set of targets residing in both the land and maritime environment. Of note, Argentine weapon usage was biased towards the land environment, but Argentine air power achieved little in terms of targeting the British fielded forces. Although the maritime environment was not the focus of operations during this period, it did provide the most lethal Argentine attack of the campaign when on 8 June, *Fuerza Aérea Argentina* A-4 Skyhawks attacked the RFAs *Sir Tristram* and *Sir Galahad* with the loss of fifty-four lives. While the attack reduced the fighting capability of the First Battalion of the Welsh Guards, the attack forced the British to delay the campaign by no more than two days. The pause allowed two companies of 40 Commando, the operational reserve, to bolster the Welsh Guards. Notwithstanding the success of 8 June, Argentine air power again failed to strike the key British targets with the necessary weight to make a considerable difference. As shown in Chapter 5, of the 550 weapons planned for the phase, the Argentines only employed 178, with eighteen hitting targets. In the latter stages of the battle, Argentine air power was unable to sustain its outputs. As a result, sortie rates dwindled. Moreover, those aircraft that did make it to the Islands appeared increasingly reluctant to prosecute their targets. Consequently, Argentine air power was unable or unwilling to support the critical land battles. Ultimately, the moral component of Argentine air power capitulated before Argentine land forces at Stanley surrendered.

As shown in Figure 9.1, the Argentines planned to use 1,146 weapons against the British force throughout the Conflict. However, the scale and effectiveness of the weapon stockpile rapidly diminished as it closed on the enemy force. As a result, only thirty-nine of those weapons struck a target, and these targets were rarely part of the centre of gravity construct.

The majority of the burden and attention on protecting the British operational centres of gravity fell to the small fleet of twenty Sea Harriers that had initially deployed on board the two aircraft carriers. The Sea Harrier had a problematic gestation from the drawing board to its arrival on the front line. Indeed, during its development, even the Royal Navy perceived the Sea Harrier as 'a limited aircraft for a limited role.'[9] Even during its early tenure in service, some of the pilots were still coming to terms with the Sea Harrier's nuances. As a result, there was a disparity between the two front line squadrons regarding the utility of some of the aircraft's systems.[10] While some were ardent acolytes of the capability, others were less endearing. Indeed, Middleton suggested that the Sea Harrier was 'the Swiss watch of aircraft.'[11] In contrast, one assessment reported that 'the SHAR [Sea Harrier] lacked the range, speed, sufficient missiles and high speed dash and acceleration capability of a true AD [Air Defence] fighter.'[12] Nevertheless, and in collaboration with ground-based air defence systems as well as embarked maritime force air defence capabilities, the Sea Harrier was responsible for the defence of the British operational centre of gravity and its associated critical vulnerabilities. So, were the British air defence systems as effective as some have suggested?

The British defences throughout Operation Corporate, and particularly Operation Sutton, were claimed by many to be the salient factor in the Conflict's outcome. Indeed, after an impressive showing in the first day of air battles, the Sea Harriers had rightly garnered a dominant reputation. The Sea Harrier and AIM-9L Sidewinder delivered exceptional levels of platform and weapon reliability. As a result, the Sea Harriers could, unlike their Argentine adversaries, sustain their outputs throughout the Conflict. Archival evidence suggested that during the campaign, there were 'fifteen fighter engagements over six days from a total of over 1,100 missions flown in fourteen days, but the deterrent value of the CAPs [combat air patrols] flown outweighed their cost.'[13] While the record of Sea Harrier outputs may be broadly accurate, the deterrent value ascribed to the Sea Harrier appears to be overly optimistic when compared with the data highlighted within this book. Ultimately, the Sea Harrier accounted for the destruction of twenty-one Argentine aircraft for no losses during air-to-air combat. However, this impressive feat underscores the lack of Argentine investment, understanding, and commitment in their control of the air capability rather than Sea Harrier dominance. Moreover, the one-sided kill ratio also masked the fact that the vast majority of Argentine aircraft were able to successfully breach the British defences on a routine basis throughout the Conflict.

As shown in Figure 9.1, of the 849 weapons that reached the Islands throughout the campaign, 648 (or 76 per cent of the weapons that reached the Islands) breached British defences. Of those weapons that were unable to breach the defences, Sea Harrier combat air patrols account for only eighty-seven Argentine weapons, or achieved a 'soft kill.' Of note, the number of 'soft kills' achieved peaked during the initial air battles of 1 May and the latter stages of the Conflict. However, some commentators still dispute the effectiveness and limitations of the Sea Harrier. For example, there is a significant discrepancy between the data laid out in Figure 9.1 and Ward's assertion that 'all Argentinian missions that were confronted by a Sea Harrier CAP [Combat Air Patrol] station were instructed to ditch their weapons and return home. They further stated that approximately 450 such missions were aborted when the attackers found Sea Harriers "in the way" – and approximately 1,800 bombs destined for use against our ships and landing forces were thrown away (these are Argentine figures).'[14] In contrast to the 1,146 planned Argentine weapons that this book identified, it is clear that Ward's figures of 1,800 jettisoned weapons exaggerated the scale of Argentine air operations. This apparent oversight is to the benefit of the positive post-Conflict reputation of the Sea Harrier. To reiterate, this book, based on British and Argentine primary and secondary source material, suggests that Sea Harrier 'soft kill' capability accounted for eighty-seven weapons throughout the Conflict, not 1,800.

Although the Sea Harrier was the most successful of the three British contributors to the control of the air function, the platform suffered from several limitations. The Sea Harrier struggled with restrictive persistence, a limited fleet size as well as a small payload to be genuinely useful and secure control of the air during Operation Corporate. Moreover, the Blue Fox radar, which was sub-optimal for the preferred Argentine low-level overland ingress routes, limited Sea Harrier operations. As a result, neither the Sea Harrier nor its associated radar could fully exploit the advantages offered by the new generation of Sidewinder weapons. Ground and maritime surface-to-air missile employment around San Carlos also suffered due to sensor limitations. At the capability level, irrespective of the platform, is land, sea, or air-based, there is a need to create an equitable balance between the triumvirate of the sensor, platform, and weapon. This book has shown that a weakness in one attribute can have a detrimental impact on the total capability.

In contrast to their Sea Harrier counterparts, the initial perceptions of ground-based and maritime force air defence performance were overly

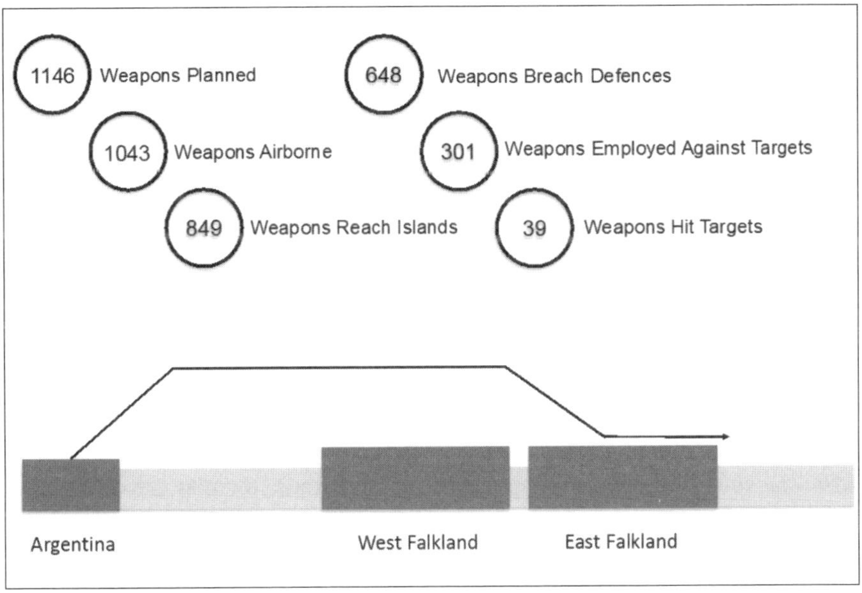

Figure 9.1 – The Utility of Argentine Weapons during Operation Corporate.

optimistic. In reality, the output of the various surface-to-air missile capabilities had a limited impact on the outcome of Operation Corporate.

The British prosecution of the Argentine operational centre of gravity is a tale of inter-Service rivalry and a fascination regarding Stanley airport. The use and utility of the Vulcan raids against Stanley airport will always stimulate debate over whether it achieved its intended aim. Of the sixty-three bombs dropped by the Vulcan, only one weapon cratered the runway. It was also the only weapon to crater the runway even though Sea Harriers and Harrier GR3s collectively dropped more weapons against the airport. Nevertheless, the runway at Stanley remained operational throughout the campaign. However, the broader question was why the British spent so much effort on a target that was only one of the many Argentine critical vulnerabilities.

Although attacking the critical vulnerabilities is a prudent and indirect approach to the centre of gravity, it will take time to achieve the desired outcome. Time was one thing that the British forces did not have in abundance – the approaching austral winter and a task force at the end of an 8,000-mile logistics chain demanded a rapid campaign. So, why was Stanley airport the focus of the air campaign? One of the key advantages of attacking Stanley airport was that it was easy to identify using an aircraft's on-board radar system. Therefore, both the Sea Harrier and the Vulcan could strike the airport in inclement weather conditions and at night. Moreover, the airport was geographically separated from the town and thereby minimised the risk of collateral damage. However, the Argentine fielded forces protecting the approaches to Stanley from the west were mostly untouched by air power until the period directly leading up to the land battles. A lack of foresight, understanding, and influence meant that any opportunities to exploit the unique attributes of their air power were squandered by the British. As a result of command and control frailties and limited investment in reconnaissance missions led to ineffective and belated attack missions. Instead, the British used air power in a reactive, short-notice, and inefficient manner. If used more appropriately, British air power could have weakened the Argentine operational centre of gravity from the start of the campaign and could have made the capture of the high ground surrounding Stanley a more straightforward proposition.

From an Argentine perspective, the inability to conduct air-to-air refuelling limited the mainland-based Mirage III fighters ability to deliver its manned fighter control of the air capability. As a result, the Mirage IIIs had minimal persistence over the Falkland Islands and consequently, the Argentine defence of their operational centre of gravity was limited to their ground-based air defence capabilities. Nevertheless, the Argentines deployed a broad mix of units and equipment from across all three Services to conduct the role. The Argentine ground-based air defence capability was co-located with each of the main military units but focussed on Stanley airport. During the campaign, the units had several successes but also suffered from a notable number of damaging fratricides. In addition to improving efforts to contest control of the air, clear command and control, effective rules of engagement, and joint training opportunities would have assisted in the defence of the Argentine operational centre of gravity.

Analysing the Factors Affecting the Prosecution of the Air Campaign

Building on the information generated from the previous research question, the third, and last, research question analysed the causes, and the relative importance, of Argentine weapons that failed to strike their intended targets. As shown in Table 9A, and contrary to popular belief, the top four factors are all influenced by Argentine activities rather than those imposed by the British. The most influential British factor is the Sea Harrier's 'soft kill' capability in fifth position. Even if all the British air defence capabilities were combined, the British ability to influence the weapons' journey would only be the fourth most influential factor. So, what stopped the Argentines from becoming a more efficient attacking force?

Ranking	Causal Factor	Scale (out of 1146)	Percentage
1	Weapons not Dropped	291	25
2	Weapon Employment – Missed Target	272	24
3	Serviceability – Air Abort	162	14
4	Mission Cancelled	131	11
5	**Sea Harrier – Soft Kill**	**87**	**8**
6	Serviceability – Ground Abort	37	3
7	Serviceability – Weapon Employment	33	3
8	**Maritime Force Air Defence – Soft Kill**	**32**	**3**
9	Navigation Errors	21	**2**
10	Weapon Employment – Hit and Detonates	20	2
=11	Weapon Employment – Unexploded Bomb	19	2
=11	**Sea Harrier – Hard Kill**	**19**	**2**
13	**Maritime Force Air Defence – Hard Kill**	**8**	**<1**
14	**Ground-based Air Defence – Soft Kill**	**7**	**<1**
15	Aircraft Crashed before Dropping Weapon	2	<1
16	Target Mis-Identified	5	<1
	Total	**1146**	**100**

Table 9A – Causal Factors for Failure to Deliver Weapons during Operation Corporate.

Argentina's *Muerte Negra – Black Death* – was not the Sea Harrier, as portrayed by some analysts, but a self-inflicted fatal potion of failure concocted of cancelled missions, weapons that missed their targets, poor aircraft serviceability and an inability to drop weapons. Also, just as the British suffered from the lack of an airborne early warning capability, the Argentines suffered from a shortage of enabling functions. In particular, the Argentines suffered from a lack of credible intelligence, surveillance, and reconnaissance assets. As a result, the Argentines were unable to find, never mind strike, the vital British force during its most vulnerable periods.

Despite a valid operational level concept of priority targets, the Argentine air arms were unable to turn this theory into a realistic tactical targeting plan. Complicating the picture further was the lack of coordination and cooperation between the *Fuerza Aérea Argentina* and the *Comando de Aviación Naval*. The net result was that the Argentines instantly squandered the numerical superiority that they had over their British counterparts. Additionally, doctrinal limitations and enforced limitations on what the *Fuerza Aérea Argentina* were allowed to train for during peacetime operations also constrained what it could achieve in wartime.

The ad hoc nature of mainland basing of Argentine combat air assets is also worthy of comment. When coupled with the fact that Argentine air power was struggling to maintain its beleaguered force due to several arms embargos, Argentine air power was unable to produce the anticipated sortie rates. Therefore, with a distinct lack of operational sovereignty over their air power, it is perhaps surprising that Argentina elected to divide their aircraft and limited spares pool over numerous bases in southern Argentina. Argentine air power also lacked precision, both in terms of delivering its weapons and in its ability to accurately navigate to the target area or rendezvous with enabling aircraft, such as air-to-air refuelling aircraft or pathfinders, particularly in poor weather conditions. As a consequence of their actions, the Argentine air arms were unable to exploit their numerical advantage and concentrate their mass against the enemy.

Many of the lessons identified above are pertinent to the United Kingdom today and in the future. To achieve success in future operations, the United Kingdom must deploy a balanced capability that embraces all of the Defence Lines of Development in sufficient strength. Moreover, the force must be inherently joint in its outlook as well as being capable of working and communicating at the strategic, operational, and tactical levels of warfare. It is easily said, difficult to fund in austere times, and will take time to train, educate, and inculcate the correct ways of working into the future generation of war fighters. However, if the United Kingdom fails to implement these attributes, the lessons of the 1982 Conflict will have to be learned once again.

One of the notable omissions from the top five most influential factors was the perceived influence of the unexploded bomb. Several narratives cite unexploded Argentine bombs as one of the crucial elements of the Conflict. However, as shown in Table 9A, it only resided in joint eleventh place and equated to only 2 per cent of the planned weapons. Consequently, the relevance of the Argentine unexploded bomb is one of the many enduring myths of the Falklands Conflict. As will be demonstrated, the basis for most of these myths are partial truths; others are simply false. Some of the myths ebbed and flowed throughout the Conflict; other myths make a fleeting appearance, but as will be discovered, none of the myths are valid throughout the entirety of the Conflict.

Myth 1 – The Sea Harrier was decisive. The Sea Harrier had an impressive first day on operations. After successful raids on Stanley airport and Goose Green airstrip, the aircraft showed its multi-role prowess by rapidly adapting to its primary role of control of the air. The subsequent air battle cost the Argentines four aircraft for no losses to the British in the air or on the sea. As a result, the Sea Harrier was blooded in battle and acquired a strong reputation that would endure beyond the Conflict. Strengthening the case for the Sea Harrier's performance was its consistent 'hard kill' capabilities during all three phases of the Conflict as well as achieving an undefeated record in air-to-air combat. However, the Sea Harrier's overall 'hard kill' performance only accounted for the negation of 2 per cent of the total Argentine weapons. Furthermore, the Sea Harrier's 'soft kill' capability was more erratic. After a strong performance on 1 May that accounted for 34 per cent of the planned Argentine weapons, the 'soft kill' performance dropped to 16 per cent when averaged across the first phase of the Conflict. Furthermore, the 'soft kill' performance bottomed out at 3 per cent during Operation Sutton before recovering to 8 per cent during the final phase of the campaign and for the overall Conflict. The inconsistent nature of the 'soft kills' is not a reflection on Sea Harrier tactics and procedures, but a manifestation of the Argentine pilots' risk appetite. At the start of the campaign, Argentine risk appetite was low to preserve the force. However, the Argentine's adopted a high-risk approach during Operation Sutton to make a campaign-winning impact. Nevertheless, the risk appetite reverted to low risk during the closing phase when there was an inevitability regarding the campaign's outcome. While the Sea Harrier may have had flaws as a thoroughbred air defence aircraft, with relatively few in number for the task in hand, it did have one key attribute; it was available and deployable. As a result, the threat that it posed had to be respected by the opposition. Consequently, it may have been a shrewd propaganda strategy by the Sea Harrier pilots to overstate their nascent capabilities. However, the Sea Harrier was not as decisive as some have suggested.

Myth 2 – The Sidewinder tipped the balance. Linked to the previous myth, many have suggested that the rapidly introduced and dispatched AIM-9L Sidewinder air-to-air missile provided an unparalleled level of superiority over its opposition. As shown in Chapter 6, the vast majority of the Sea Harrier Sidewinder firings were from the rear hemisphere of the target, akin to the performance of the previous generation of Sidewinders. However, to take advantage of the full AIM-9L Sidewinder capability, the Sea Harrier had to find, identify, acquire, and employ the weapon against the target. In a dynamic head-on engagement, this is difficult to achieve without using an on-board radar. However, and through necessity, the Sea Harrier's Blue Fox radar was a cheap, low-risk option that had a limited performance in high clutter or look down situations. Consequently, the Argentines, having learned the lessons from their unsuccessful tactics on 1 May, opted to attack in the low altitude, high clutter environment that rendered the Blue Fox radar almost useless. As a result, most intercepts occurred when the Argentine aircraft were visually acquired, which had a natural tendency to drag the Sea Harrier into the stern of the target aircraft. Although the AIM-9L Sidewinder did not tip the balance as some have claimed, air-to-air missiles did provide the British with an asymmetric advantage as Argentine lacked fighters to act as escorts for the attack aircraft, who, in turn, did not carry air-to-air missiles for self-defence purposes. As a result, during a fighter engagement, the Argentines were immediately put onto the defensive. The failure to contest the control of the air battle is another example of an Argentine self-inflicted wound – the former *Fuerza Aérea Argentina* mentor, Adolf Galland, would have been unimpressed.

Myth 3 – Mirages diverted to defend Buenos Aires from potential Vulcan raids. The British considered the utility of the Vulcan raids as a strategic option to strike mainland targets during the early stages of the campaign. However, the British quickly discarded the possibility due to the need to keep the Conflict limited in nature to maintain global consensus. However, the decision not to strike Argentina was never publicly denounced. Nevertheless, and from the campaign's outset, the Argentines kept a small force of Mirage IIIs and Daggers at their home bases in and around Buenos Aires to conduct alert duties. However, two activities may have generated the myth. First, on 29 April, the Argentine radars located at San Julian detected what they suspected was a British air attack on southern Argentina. As a result, several aircraft were quickly launched from the threatened airfield and landed at the safer Comodoro Rivadavia, but still located in southern Argentina.

After realising that the alert was a false alarm, the aircraft recovered to their original airfields. Second, throughout the campaign, there was a steady flow of Argentine replacement and battle-damaged aircraft between their deployed operating bases in southern Argentina and their home bases, most clustered near Buenos Aires. Ultimately, there is no evidence to suggest that the Argentines redeployed the Mirage fighters from southern Argentina to protect Buenos Aires.

Myth 4 – Argentine pilots were brave until the end. The Argentine pilots received great credit for pressing home their attacks from an ultra-low level, particularly during the period of Operation Sutton. They achieved several successes as well as generating angst amongst British commanders and troops alike throughout the campaign. Consequently, an inexperienced force, flying infrequently, and in basic and aged aircraft delivered beyond expectations. However, the *Fuerza Aérea Argentina's* practical knowledge and understanding of higher command's intent, operating procedures, local topography, and the enemy's capabilities were minimal. As a result, the tactical execution of the operational plan was flawed. It would appear that aircraft attacked the first ship they saw rather than focus on the key targets. As a result, during Operation Sutton, the critical amphibious assault ships were struck belatedly and without sufficient weight. Moreover, the Argentines were losing a significant number of aircraft and aircrew from a limited resource of manpower and equipment. Ultimately, the Argentine air arms were losing the battle of attrition; their outputs reduced as the campaign progressed and, in some cases, stopped before the key land battles. During the few Argentine missions conducted over the Falkland Islands during the last days of the Conflict, the number of mission aborts increased significantly due to the presence of Sea Harriers. It is clear that, as with capability, bravery is a finite resource. Once the physical component is compromised, the moral component also diminishes. The Argentine position reflected Peter Lee's view of the wider combat air fraternity when he described them as 'Brave – yes. Fearless – no.'[15]

Understanding the Source of the Myths

Did either participant deliberately create the Conflict's myths to deceive their counterparts into believing that the tide in the South Atlantic was turning against them? Alternatively, was the target audience and the narratives orientated towards a different market more associated with the internal post-Conflict attempts to preserve reputations? The issue will be viewed from two angles: during the Conflict and the post-campaign period.

This book would suggest that during the Conflict, the British and the Argentines were guilty of no more than believing the raw, unprocessed data that they had generated in the heat of the battle. Both participants understood that there was a need and an appetite to inform their nations about the battle's progress. Of note, there was the odd, blunt, and ineffective attempt to use propaganda during the Conflict to convey artificially escalated campaign progress and success. The most notorious example was the Argentine press showing a manipulated picture of a burning British aircraft carrier. From a British perspective, the *Muerte Negra* nickname allegedly attributed to the Sea Harrier force by the Argentine pilots was used in a similar manner; it reassured the British public but their Argentine counterparts refuted the claim. Neither side was able to compete effectively for the battle of the narrative. Both sides suffered from a lack of intelligence, surveillance, and reconnaissance capabilities, as well as ineffective command and control. As a result, neither party had a full understanding of its opponent's capabilities, outputs, and levels of commitment to the battle. Therefore, neither participant was able to understand or control the air environment. Consequently, there was insufficient evidence during or post the Conflict to refute the opponent's claims.

In very simple terms, both participants failed to think and do. Both sides failed to implement an operational level plan effectively. The failure to conceptualise the war in the South Atlantic is perhaps not surprising given the Argentine's lack of warfighting experience and the British focus on the Cold War. Nevertheless, the lack of operational level planning is quite stark. Planners must understand what constitutes both the friendly and enemy centres of gravity. Consequently, planners must be capable of apportioning their limited resources to ruthlessly attack the various critical vulnerabilities associated with the enemy centre of gravity. Participants must conduct this activity at the earliest opportunity and by utilising all its available energy before either the fleeting chance disappears, or the potential energy dissipates. In parallel, an actor must defend its own centre of gravity and associated critical vulnerabilities. Both participants focused on their deployed and flawed physical components to the detriment of the conceptual component and, as a result, were unable to maximise the utility and effectiveness of their forces. Both sets of forces had insufficient agility to adapt to the scenario before them. From a British perspective, their Cold

War focus constrained their training and lack of conceptual thinking to deal with alternative threats. The Argentines were simply stepping into the unknown. While understanding what constitutes your military main effort is vital, military planners must have sufficient resilience and freedoms to cater for tasks that sit outside the bounds of the main effort. As a result, if military force is being used in a unique environment and in finite numbers, military forces must be focused on what is vital. As the Argentines found to their cost, if you only have one good punch, you must make it count.

During the Conflict, both sides needed to assure their outputs to enable their mandated outcome. However, both protagonists suffered from the lack of a balanced force. The Argentines had a breadth of combat air power, but it was limited in depth. As a result, the Argentines were unable to exploit their numerical advantage. The Argentine opportunity for victory was for a decisive, coordinated mass strike at the centre of gravity at its most vulnerable. Therefore, and realising that they were limited to one mighty blow, it was imperative that the Argentines understood and were able to strike their enemy's centres of gravity. However, Argentine air power was an uncoordinated force that failed to prosecute the centres of gravity successfully. Ultimately, the Argentines ran out of time, energy, and ideas.

In contrast to the Argentine position, British air power lacked the breadth to saturate the area of interest. Still, its depth of capability ensured that it could sustain its focus on, albeit limited, outputs. However, the limited outputs meant that the operational commander carried significant risk. The risks rapidly translated into tangible problems as Argentine aircraft penetrated British defences with ease. Arguably, Operation Sutton was a successful joint campaign in terms of planning and execution. However, once ashore jointery was less efficient with separate land, maritime and air campaigns becoming evident. Limited time, as well as poor coordination and communication, compromised the joint campaign. The British commanders failed to use air power efficiently to understand, influence, and shape the battle space. Air power expertise must be engaged in the planning process from the outset. Although RAF personnel were in situ with the campaign planners, they were insufficient in number and unable to influence the decision-makers. Consequently, there was a lack of understanding, a balanced capability, and an inability to use the force in a coordinated and focused manner. Moreover, most commentators largely overlook the errors in the use of air power during the Falklands Conflict. Why was this the case?

Baron Tedder, a former Chief of the Air Staff, commented that 'the most important thing is not to look back at the past but look to the future from the past.'[16] This proposition remains valid today. Some would suggest that the Falklands Conflict was merely a Cold War sideshow. However, this book has demonstrated that there were several operational level mistakes from both participants that a contemporary student of operational level planning would quickly identify as rudimentary and basic. Nevertheless, experienced individuals made errors. General Vernon Walters, part of Haig's shuttle diplomacy team in the prelude to the Conflict, suggested that the dispute was a 'conflict of machismos' and 'a silly war and a conflict of egos.'[17] While Walters' statement may have been contentious, it is, to a certain degree, based on reality. Consequently, the egos and the machismos will have a desire to maintain their honour and preserve their legacy. As a result, there can be poetic licence in how their version of the story is told, maintained, and preserved at a national, Service, unit, or individual perspective. In addition to the battle of reality, there is a second equally vicious battle: the battle for the narrative.

The battle for the narrative is as important as the real battle itself. The first individuals to write their perspectives on the Conflict set the benchmark. Automatically, the initial work becomes the comparator for all further works on the subject matter. Their story becomes all the more compelling if they were a credible and central actor at the vanguard of the battle. However, many of these stories tell the reader what happened rather than what should have happened. As a result, many of the narratives focus on tactical and individual success rather than the Conflict's operational level lessons.

In the post-Conflict timeframe, the battle of the narrative truly blossoms. Despite a significant lessons process within the United Kingdom, many of the lessons were self-fulfilling prophecies linked to the funded future equipment programme. As a result, the analysis was at times Service-focused and with few perspectives that looked across all three Services and embracing the joint and operational levels of warfare. As a result, different Services had different approaches to the task.

The Falklands Conflict provided the Royal Navy with an exploitable opportunity to right the perceived wrongs of previous Defence Reviews. However, the RAF was arguably less proactive and perhaps focused on the rapid return to the more familiar and pressing Cold War context. Indeed, Air Commodore Derek Bryant, the Senior Air Staff Officer at 38 Group during 1982, stated that 'virtue is its own reward.'[18] Bryant's comments reflected his Service's view that it did not need to shape its participation and outcome to the same extent as the Royal Navy. There is some validity in his comments; before the Conflict, the RAF had already secured significant funding to procure a large force of Tornado multi-role combat aircraft. Moreover, and as a direct consequence of the Conflict, the RAF benefitted from new investment in air-to-air refuelling, strategic transport, and air defence fleets. However, the RAF's ambivalent approach to the public narrative on the Falklands Conflict was approaching the same level of culpability as demonstrated by the Argentines' failure to contest the control of the air battle. By failing to challenge the narrative, the RAF may compromise longer-term outcomes. For example, reflecting on the Air Commander's post-Conflict comments suggests that the RAF misjudged the utility of fighting for an accurate narrative. Air Marshal John Curtiss critiqued the United States Secretary for the Navy, John Lehman, on his paper to the United States Congress on the Falklands Conflict lessons. In particular, Curtiss reacted to the comment on the disappointing results of the Vulcan raids, when he suggested that 'as long as politicians refuse to be objective, we will never get our force mix structure right.'[19] Ultimately, by failing to influence key stakeholders, in this case, key foreign partners, but the group could include politicians, journalists, the electorate, historians, and biographers, they may dispute the outcome that the Service desires.

The 1982 Falklands Conflict was many things. Brave people doing extraordinary deeds was evident on both sides throughout the Conflict. Nevertheless, the lack of an operational plan obscured campaign execution for both parties. Complicating issues further was the lack of balance across the air power roles and capabilities. While both participants contested the battle, it ended with a decisive victory for the British. While the contemporary mantra of being 'first with the truth' appears to have been absent, the battle for the narrative remains contested driven by personal, Service, and National agendas. As a result, many of the Falklands Conflict myths may well remain an active battle space for years to come. Nevertheless, the joint and operational level lessons from the 1982 Falklands Conflict must be instilled into any future Defence operating model if it is to deliver against its considerable potential and meet Curtiss' demand for the correct 'force mix structure.'

Annex A

Argentine Combat Air Sorties Flown During the Falklands Conflict[1]

May	1	2	3	4	5	6	7	8	9	10	11	12	13	14	15	16
A-4B Skyhawk	13	0	8	0	0	0	0	0	0	0	0	8	0	0	0	0
A-4C Skyhawk	14	0	7	0	0	0	0	0	9	0	0	0	0	0	0	0
Dagger	13	0	2	4	0	2	0	0	8	0	0	0	0	0	3	0
Canberra	6	4	2	0	0	0	0	0	0	0	0	0	0	0	0	0
Mirage III	10	0	0	0	0	0	0	0	0	0	0	0	0	0	0	0
A-4Q Skyhawk	2	8	0	0	0	0	0	0	0	0	0	0	0	0	0	0
Super Etendard	2	0	0	2	0	0	0	0	0	0	0	0	0	0	0	0
Weather[2] (G=Good, F=Fair and P=Poor)	Falkland Islands Weather															
AM	G	G	P	F	P	G	F	F	G	P	P	G	G	F	G	G
PM	G	F	P	G	F	F	P	G	F	P	P	F	F	G	F	G
	Argentine Airfield Weather															
AM	F	G	F	F	F	G	F	G	P	G	G	F	G	G	F	F
PM	F	P	F	G	G	F	F	P	P	G	G	F	G	G	F	G
TOTAL	***60***	***12***	***19***	***6***	***0***	***2***	***0***	***0***	***17***	***0***	***0***	***8***	***0***	***0***	***3***	***0***

May	17	18	19	20	21	22	23	24	25	26	27	28	29	30	31
A-4B Skyhawk	0	0	0	0	18	6	10	6	8	0	11	6	2	0	0
A-4C Skyhawk	0	0	0	0	11	4	5	8	4	0	6	6	0	4	0
Dagger	0	0	3	5	22	0	17	10	4	2	0	4	10	0	0

Canberra	0	0	0	0	3	0	0	0	0	3	2	0	2	0	4
Mirage III	0	0	0	0	6	5	5	2	1	2	2	0	4	0	0
A-4Q Skyhawk	0	0	0	0	12	0	4	0	0	4	2	2	0	0	0
Super Etendard	0	0	0	0	0	0	2	0	2	0	0	0	0	2	0
Weather	Falkland Islands Weather														
AM / PM	G / F	F / P	F / P	F	G	F	G				F	P / F	G		
	Argentine Airfield Weather														
AM / PM	G	F / G	G / F	F / G	G		G / F	G		G / F	G / F	G / F	F	P / F	F / P
TOTAL	***0***	***0***	***3***	***5***	***72***	***15***	***43***	***26***	***19***	***11***	***23***	***18***	***18***	***6***	***4***
June	**1**	**2**	**3**	**4**	**5**	**6**	**7**	**8**	**9**	**10**	**11**	**12**	**13**	**14**	***Total***
A-4B Skyhawk	0	0	0	0	4	0	8	14	3	0	0	8	8	0	**141**
A-4C Skyhawk	0	0	0	0	0	0	0	4	4	0	0	0	0	0	**86**
Dagger	0	0	0	4	8	0	3	12	3	2	0	0	12	0	**155**
Canberra	3	0	0	5	3	0	4	0	0	2	0	6	4	0	**53**
Mirage III	0	0	0	0	0	0	2	4	0	4	0	0	4	0	**51**
A-4Q Skyhawk	0	0	0	0	0	0	0	2	2	0	0	2	0	0	**40**
Super Etendard	0	0	0	0	0	0	0	0	0	0	0	0	0	0	**10**
Weather	Falkland Islands Weather														
AM / PM	G / F	G / P	P		P / F	P / F	G / F	G				P / G	G		
	Argentine Airfield Weather														
AM / PM	P / F	G	P		F	F / G	F	F / G	G	P / G	G	P / G	F	P	
TOTAL	***3***	***0***	***0***	***9***	***15***	***0***	***17***	***36***	***12***	***8***	***0***	***18***	***28***	***0***	***536***

Annex B

British Combat Air Sorties Flown During the Falklands Conflict

May	1	2	3	4	5	6	7	8	9	10	11	12	13	14	15	16
Sea Harrier - *Hermes*[1]	30	16	2	23	2	4	0	13	10	0	0	12	0	10	15	22
Sea Harrier - *Invincible*	20	19	3	24	5	3	2	8	14	0	0	0	0	13	9	14
Harrier GR3[2]	0	0	0	0	0	0	0	0	0	0	0	0	0	0	0	0
Vulcan[3]	1	0	0	1	0	0	0	0	0	0	0	0	0	0	0	0
Weather[4]	Falkland Islands Weather															
AM / PM	G / G	G / F	P / P	F / G	P / F	G / F	F / P	F / G	G / F	P / P	P / P	G / F	G / F	F / G	G / F	G / G
	Carrier Group Weather															
AM / PM	G / G	G / F	P / P	F / G	F / P	P / P	P / P	P / P	G / F	P / P	P / G	G / G	P / P	G / G	G / G	G / G
DAILY SORTIES	***51***	***35***	***5***	***48***	***7***	***7***	***2***	***21***	***24***	***0***	***0***	***12***	***0***	***23***	***24***	***36***

May	17	18	19	20	21	22	23	24	25	26	27	28	29	30	31
Sea Harrier - *Hermes*	14	12	22	12	26	36	24	30	28	32	16	8	18	26	20
Sea Harrier - *Invincible*	10	11	12	6	28	25	25	26	24	25	18	10	21	21	22
Harrier GR3	0	0	0	3	8	6	10	4	9	9	9	8	3	10	6
Vulcan	0	0	0	0	0	0	0	0	0	0	1	0	0	0	1

Weather		Falkland Islands Weather														
AM	PM	G F	P F	P	F	G	F	G				F	P F	G		
		Carrier Group Weather														
AM	PM	G	F G		F P	G				P G		P G	P	F G		
DAILY SORTIES		***24***	***33***	***34***	***21***	***62***	***67***	***59***	***60***	***61***	***66***	***44***	***54***	***42***	***57***	***49***
June		**1**	**2**	**3**	**4**	**5**	**6**	**7**	**8**	**9**	**10**	**11**	**12**	**13**	**14**	***Total***
Sea Harrier - *Hermes*		22	12	0	0	8	4	14	24	10	16	16	14	11	9	**737**
Sea Harrier - *Invincible*		22	4	0	0	9	5	12	20	8	20	19	25	16	20	**598**
Harrier GR3		1	2	0	0	8	2	5	4	8	10	12	6	4	4	**151**
Vulcan		0	0	1	0	0	0	0	0	0	0	0	1	0	0	**6**
Weather		Falkland Islands Weather														
AM	PM	G F	G P			F	P F	G F	G				P G			
		Carrier Group Weather														
AM	PM	G	F P				G	F G						F G		
DAILY SORTIES		***45***	***18***	***1***	***0***	***25***	***11***	***31***	***48***	***26***	***46***	***47***	***46***	***31***	***33***	***1492***

Annex C

Argentine Attack Missions on 1 May

<table>
<tr><th rowspan="2">FragO& Callsign</th><th rowspan="2">Type</th><th rowspan="2">Take Off</th><th rowspan="2">Weapons Carried</th><th rowspan="2">Aircraft</th><th colspan="4">Weapons</th><th rowspan="2">Target</th><th colspan="2">Weapons</th></tr>
<tr><th>Planned</th><th>Airborne</th><th>Reached Island</th><th>Breached Defences</th><th>Dropped</th><th>Hits</th></tr>
<tr><td>OF.1092 Topo</td><td>A-4B Skyhawk</td><td>1130</td><td>3 x Expal</td><td>4</td><td>12</td><td>12</td><td>12</td><td>0[1]</td><td>N/A</td><td rowspan="2">0</td><td rowspan="5">0</td></tr>
<tr><td>OF.1095 Oso[2]</td><td>A-4C Skyhawk</td><td>1400</td><td>2 x BRP</td><td>4</td><td>8</td><td>8</td><td>8</td><td>8</td><td>Unable to find targets</td></tr>
<tr><td>OF.1105 Torno</td><td>Dagger</td><td>1845</td><td>2 x BRP[3]</td><td>3</td><td>6</td><td>6</td><td>6</td><td>6</td><td>HMS Alacrity, Glamorgan & Arrow</td><td>6[4]</td></tr>
<tr><td>OF.1110 Trueno</td><td>A-4B Skyhawk</td><td>1900</td><td>3 x Expal</td><td>4</td><td>12</td><td>12</td><td>9[5]</td><td>9</td><td>Unable to find targets</td><td>2[6]</td></tr>
<tr><td>OF.1111 Ruta</td><td>Canberra</td><td>1905</td><td>4 x Mk 17</td><td>3</td><td>12</td><td>12</td><td>12</td><td>0[7]</td><td>HMS Brilliant & Yarmouth</td><td>0</td></tr>
</table>

OF.1117 Rifle	Canberra	1920	4 x Mk 17	3	12	12	12	0[8]	N/A	0	0
OF.1112 Foca	A-4B Skyhawk	1929	3 x Expal	2	6	6	6	0[9]	N/A		
OF.1113 Rubio	A-4B Skyhawk	1930	3 x Expal	3	9	9	6[10]	0[11]	N/A		
OF.1114 Lana	A-4C Skyhawk	1930	3 x BRP	4	12	12	12	0[12]	N/A		
TBC TBC	Super Etendard	1938	1 x Exocet	2	2	2	0[13]	0	N/A		
TBC TBC	Super Etendard	N/A	1 x Exocet	2	2	0[14]	0	0	N/A		
Totals				**34**	**93**	**91**	**83**	**23**		**6**	**0**

Annex D

Argentine Control of the Air Missions on 1 May

Frag Order	Callsign	Type	Weapons Carried	Planned	Airborne	Take-Off	Land	Results
OF.1090	Fiera	Mirage III	1 x R530 + 2 x Magic	2	2	0940	1138	No targets found and unable to make contact with the ground controller
OF.1101	Fierro[1]	Dagger	2 x Shafrir	2	1	1900	2140	Manoeuvred against Sea Harrier Combat Air Patrol but no intercept occurred
OF.1091	Toro[2]			2	2	1045	1245	Manoeuvred against Sea Harrier Combat Air Patrol, jettisoned underwing fuel tanks but no intercept occurred
OF.1093	Tablon[3]	Mirage III	1 x R530 + 2 x Magic	2	2	1159	1358	Manoeuvred against Sea Harrier Combat Air Patrol but no intercept occurred
OF.1099	Limon[4]	Dagger	2 x Shafrir	2	2	1300	1515	
OF.1098	Foco	Mirage III	1 x R530 + 2 x Magic	2	2	1323	1513	No targets found
OF.1100	Ciclon	Dagger	2 x Shafrir	2	2	1530	1730	Manoeuvred against Sea Harrier Combat Air Patrol but no intercept occurred
OF.1103	Pampa	A-4C Skyhawk		2	2	1620	1910	No targets found
TBC	TBC[5]			2	2	1700	1800	
OF.1106	Pampa			2	2	1820	2020	

TBC	TBC	A-4Q Skyhawk	2 x AIM-9B	2	2	1830	TBC	Intercepted a Canberra formation returning to base following an attack mission
OF.1109	Dardo	Mirage III	1 x R530 + 2 x Magic	2	2	1845	N/A	The Mirages jettison fuel tanks prior to engagement but only 3 of the 4 fuel tanks successfully leave the aircraft, leaving Perona with a limiting asymmetric configuration to deal with.[6] Engaged by Sea Harriers flown by Flt Lt Barton & Lt Thomas from 801 NAS.[7]
OF.1107	Fortin	Dagger	2 x Shafrir	2	2	1905	2140	Vectored to chase Sea Harriers that were pursuing Torno flight during their egress.[8]
OF.1113	Rubio			2[9]	1	1854	N/A	Ardiles jettisons both of his underwing fuel tanks prior to the engagement.[10]However, Ardiles is shot down and killed by an AIM-9L Sidewinder fired from a Sea Harrier flown by Flt Lt Penfold at 1941.[11]
OF.1108	Buitre	Mirage III	1 x R530 + 2 x Magic	2	2	1850	2050	No targets found
			Total	**30**	**28**			

Annex E

Argentine Air Power Prior to Operation Sutton: 2–19 May

FragO& Callsign	Type	Take Off	Weapons Carried	Aircraft	Weapons				Target	Weapons	
					Planned	Airborne	Reached Island	Breached Defences		Dropped	Hits
2 May 1982											
TBC[1] TBC	Canberra	AM	4 x BRP	4	16	16	16	16	Unable to find targets	0	0
3 May 1982											
OF.1159 Lince	Canberra	1940	4 x Mk 17	2	8	8	8	8	Unable to find targets	0	0
OF.1150 Fiera	A-4B Skyhawk	1953	3 x Expal[2]	4	12	12	0[3]	0			
OF.1151 Trueno				4	12	12					
OF.1152Oso	A-4C Skyhawk	2007	3 x BRP	4	12	12	12	12			
OF.1153 Dogo		2022		3	9	9	9	9			
4 May 1982											
Aries & Liebre	Super Etendard	1345	1 x Exocet	2	2	2	2	2	HMS *Sheffield*	2	1

FragO& Callsign	Type	Take Off	Weapons Carried	Aircraft	Weapons				Target	Weapons	
					Planned	Airborne	Reached Island	Breached Defences		Dropped	Hits
9 May 1982											
OF.1175 Puma	Dagger	1700	2 x Expal	4	8	8	8	8	Unable to find targets	0	0
OF.1174 Trueno	A-4C Skyhawk	1600	1 x Mk 17[4]	4	4	4	2	0[5]	Unable to reach targets		
OF.1177 Condor		1815		3	3	3	3	3	Unable to find targets		
OF.1178 Fortin		1830		2	2	2	2	2			
OF.1176 Jaguar	Dagger	1900	2 x Expal	4	8	8	8	8		0	0
12 May 1982											
OF.1177 Cuna	A-4B Skyhawk	1620	1 x Mk 17[6]	4	4	4	4	3[7]	HMS *Glasgow*	3[8]	0
OF.1180 Oro		1630		4	4	4	4	4	HMS *Brilliant*	4	1[9]
15 May 1982											
TBC TBC	Dagger	2000	1 x Mk 17	3	3	3	3	3	Unable to find targets	0	0
19 May 1982											
TBC TBC	Dagger	1945	2 x Expal[10]	3	6	6	6	6	Unable to find targets	0	0
Totals				**54**[11]	**113**	**113**	**87**	**84**		**9**	**2**

Annex F

Argentine Air Power During Operation Sutton: 21 May

Callsign	Type	Weapons Carried	Number of Aircraft	Weapons				Target	Weapons			
				Planned	Airborne	Reached Islands	Breached Defences		Dropped	Hits	Detonated	Centre of Gravity
OF.1181 Nandu	Dagger	1 x Mk 17	3	3	3	3	2[1]	HMS *Argonaut* & *Broadsword*	2	0		
OF.1182 Perro[2]			3	3	3	3	3	HMS *Antrim*	3	1[3]		
OF.1183 Leon		2 x EXPAL	3	6	4[4]	4	4		4			
OF.1184 Zorro			3	6	6	6	6	HMS *Brilliant*	0[5]			
TBC TBC	A-4Q	4 x Mk 82	6	24	24	0[6]	0	N/A	0	0	0	0
OF.1187 Tero	A-4C	1 x Mk 17	2	2	2	1[7]	0[8]		0			
OF.1188 Pato			3	3	3	2[9]	0[10, 11]		0			
OF.1189 Mula	A-4B		4	4	4	2[12]	1[13]	HMS *Ardent*	1	0[14]		
OF.1190 Pico			4	4	4	3[15]	3	Unable to find targets	0	0		

OF.1191 Rondo	A-4C	1 x Mk 17	2	2	1[16]	1	0[17]	N/A	0	0	0	**0**
OF.1194 Libra	Dagger		2	2	2	1[18]	1	HMS *Ardent*	1			
OF.1196 Orion	A-4B		3	3	3	2[19]	2	HMS *Argonaut*	2			
OF.1197 Leo			3	3	3	3	3		3	2		
OF.1193 Cueca	Dagger		3	3	3	3	2[20]	HMS *Ardent*	2	2	1[21]	
OF.1198 Raton			3	3	3	3	0[22]	N/A	0	0	0	
OF.1199 Laucha			3	3	3	3	3	HMS *Brilliant*	2[23]			
TBC Tabano	A-4Q	4 x Mk 82	3	12	12	12	12	HMS *Ardent*	12	2	2[24]	
TBC TBC			3	12	12	12	12		12	1	1	
OF.1201 Raspon	A-4C	1 x Mk 17	3	3	2[25]	2	2	Unable to find targets	0	0	0	
OF.1202 Choclo			3	3	3	3	3					
OF.1203 Mate	A-4B		4	4	4	4	4					
TBC TBC	Canberra	8 x Mk 17	8	64	24	0[26]	0	N/A				
Totals			**74**	**172**	**128**	**73**	**63**		**44**	**8**	**4**	

Annex G

Argentine Air Power during Operation Sutton: 20–26 May

FragO& Callsign	Type	Weapons Carried	Number of Aircraft	Weapons				Target	Weapons			
				Planned	Airborne	Reached Islands	Breached Defences		Dropped	Hits	Detonated	Centre of Gravity
20 May 1982[1]												
OF. TBC[2]	Dagger	2 x EXPAL	3	6	6	6	6	Armed Recce	0	0	0	0
OF. TBC[3]			2	4	4	4	4					
22 May 1982												
OF.1204 Leon	A-4C Skyhawk	1 x Mk 17[4]	3	3	3	3	3	Sussex Bay	0[5]	0	0	0
OF.1207 Chispa	A-4B Skyhawk	3 x EXPAL	6	18	18	6[6]	6	Sussex Harbour	6[7]			
23 May 1982												
OF.1216 Coral	Dagger	2 x EXPAL	3	6	6	6	6	San Carlos	6[8]	0	0	0
OF.1205 Puma		1 x Mk17	3	3	3	3	0[9]	N/A	0			
OF.1206 Potro			3	3	3	3						

OF.1207 Lanza[10]	A-4B Skyhawk	1 x Mk17	3	3	3	4[11]	2	Unable to find targets	0	0	0	0
OF.1208 Tejo			3	3	3		2					
OF.1212 Plata	A-4C Skyhawk	3 x BRP	3	9	9	0[12]	0	N/A				
OF.1213 Oro			3	9	6[13]		0					
OF.1210 Trueno	A-4B Skyhawk	1 x Mk 17	3	3	2[14]	2	2	HMS *Antelope* & *Broadsword*	2	0[15]		
OF.1211 Nene			3	3	2[16]	2	2	HMS *Antelope*	1[17]	1		
TBC TBC	A-4Q Skyhawk	4 x Mk 82	4	16	16	12[18]	12	HMS *Antelope* & *Intrepid*	7[19]	1[20]		
OF.1214 Daga	Dagger	1 x Mk 17	3	3	3	2[21]	2	Unable to find targets	0	0		
OF.1215 Punal			3	3	2[22]	2	2		0[23]			
TBC TBC	Super Etendard	1 x Exocet	2	2	2	2	2		0[24]			

FragO& Callsign	Type	Weapons Carried	Number of Aircraft	Weapons				Target	Weapons			
				Planned	Airborne	Reached Islands	Breached Defences		Dropped	Hits	Detonated	Centre of Gravity
24 May 1982												
OF.1223 Chispa	A-4B Skyhawk	1 x Mk 17	3	3	3	2[25]	2	RFA *Sir Lancelot Sir Bedivere Sir Galahad*	2	3	0	3[26]
OF.1224 Nene			3	3	3	3	3		3			
OF.1228 Halcon	A-4C Skyhawk	3 x BRP	3	9	9	9	0[27]	N/A	0	0	0	0
OF.1229 TBC			2	6	6	6	6[28]					
OF.1230 Jaguar			3	9	9	9	9	RFA *Fort Austin Resource & Stromness*	9[29]			
OF.1225 Azul	Dagger	1 x Mk 17	4	4	4	4	4	RFA *Sir Lancelot*	3[30]	1[31]		1
OF.1227 Plata		2 x EXPAL	3	6	6	6	6	Fuel Tanks	5[32]	0		0
OF.1228 Oro			3	6	6	6	0[33]	N/A	0			
25 May 1982												
OF.1232 Marte	A-4B Skyhawk	1 x Mk 17	4	4	4	2[34]	0[35]	N/A	0	0	0	0
OF.1235 Toro	A-4C Skyhawk	2 x EXPAL	4	8	8	8	8	HMS *Plymouth & Arrow*	4[36]			

OF.1236 Vulcano	A-4B Skyhawk	3 x Mk 17[37]	3	9	6[38]	6	6	HMS *Broadsword*	6	1[39]	0	0
OF.1237 Zeus		3 x Mk 17	3	9	9	6[40]	6	HMS *Coventry*	3[41]	3	3	0
Tito and Leo[42]	Super Etendard	1 x Exocet	2	2	2	2	2	MV *Atlantic Conveyor*	2	1	1	1
OF.1233 Rango	Dagger	1 x Mk 17[43]	2	2	2	2	2	Beauchene Radar Site	0	0	0	0
OF.1234 Bingo			2	2	2	2	2	Troops at southern point of West Falkland				
OF.1238 Puma			3	1	3	0[44]	0	TBC	0	0	0	0
26 May 1982												
OF.1240 Odin	Canberra	4 x Mk 17[45]	3	12	12	12	0[46]	San Carlos	0	0	0	0
OF.1241 Pocker	Dagger	4 x EXPAL	2	8	8	8	8		4[47]			
TBC TBC	A-4Q Skyhawk	4 x Mk 82[48]	2	8	8	8	8[49]	Armed Recce	0			
TBC TBC			2	8	8	0[50]	0	Lively Island				
Totals			**104**	**218**	**205**	**164**	**117**		**64**	**11**	**4**	**5**

Annex H

Argentine Air Power Post-Operation Sutton: 27 May – 14 June

<table>
<tr><th rowspan="2">FragO& Callsign</th><th rowspan="2">Type</th><th rowspan="2">Take Off</th><th rowspan="2">Weapons Carried</th><th rowspan="2">Aircraft</th><th colspan="4">Weapons</th><th rowspan="2">Target</th><th colspan="2">Weapons</th></tr>
<tr><th>Planned</th><th>Airborne</th><th>Reached Island</th><th>Breached Defences</th><th>Dropped</th><th>Hits</th></tr>
<tr><td colspan="12">27 May 1982</td></tr>
<tr><td>OF.1240 Odin</td><td>Canberra</td><td>0720</td><td>4 x BRP + 2 Mk 17s</td><td>2</td><td>12</td><td>12</td><td>12</td><td>12</td><td>Ajax Bay</td><td>12</td><td>0[1]</td></tr>
<tr><td>TBC TBC</td><td>A-4Q Skyhawk</td><td>1327</td><td>4 x Mk 82[2]</td><td>2</td><td>8</td><td>8</td><td>8</td><td>8</td><td>Unable to find target</td><td rowspan="5">0</td><td rowspan="5">0</td></tr>
<tr><td>OF.1248 Toro</td><td rowspan="2">A-4B Skyhawk</td><td>1330</td><td rowspan="2">1 x Mk 17[3]</td><td>3</td><td>3</td><td>3</td><td rowspan="2">0[4]</td><td rowspan="2">0</td><td rowspan="2">Unable to confirm target</td></tr>
<tr><td>OF.1245 Trueno</td><td>1400</td><td>3</td><td>3</td><td>3</td></tr>
<tr><td>OF.1246 Tigre</td><td rowspan="2">A-4C Skyhawk</td><td rowspan="2">1400</td><td rowspan="2">3 x BRP[5]</td><td>3</td><td>9</td><td>9</td><td>6[6]</td><td>6</td><td rowspan="2">Unable to find targets</td></tr>
<tr><td>OF.1249 Tanque</td><td>3</td><td>9</td><td>9</td><td>6[7]</td><td>6</td></tr>
<tr><td>OF.1244 Pocker</td><td rowspan="2">A-4B Skyhawk</td><td>1900</td><td rowspan="2">4 x BRP</td><td>3</td><td>12</td><td>12</td><td>8[8]</td><td>8</td><td rowspan="2">Ajax Bay</td><td>8</td><td rowspan="2">7[9, 10]</td></tr>
<tr><td>OF.1247 Truco</td><td>1930</td><td>3</td><td>12</td><td>8[11]</td><td>8</td><td>8</td><td>8</td></tr>
</table>

28 May 1982											
OF.1256 Pocker	Dagger	1400	2 x BRP[12]	4	8	8	8	8	Unable to find target	0	0
OF.1254 Cuna	A-4B Skyhawk	1530	3 x BRP[13]	3	9	9	6[14]	6			
OF.1258 Nene		1530		3	9	9	6[15]	6			
OF.1259 Chispa	A-4C Skyhawk	1700	1 x Mk 17[16]	3	3	3	2[17]	2			
OF.1253 Toro		1710		3	3	3	3	3			
TBC TBC	A-4Q Skyhawk	TBC	4 x Mk 82[18]	2	8	8	8	8			
29 May 1982											
OF.1260 Charrua	Canberra	0500	4 x Mk 17	2	8	8	8	8	Troops at San Carlos	8	0[19]
OF.1267 Oro	A-4B Skyhawk	1200	3 x BRP	2	6	6	6	6	Unable to find targets	0	0
OF.1264 Patria	Dagger	1400	2 x BRP[20]	3	6	4[21]	4	0[22]	Unable to reach target		
OF.1266 Nandu		1530		2	4	4	4	4	Unable to find target[23]		
OF.1269 Puma		1630		3	6	6	6	0[24]	Unable to reach target		
OF.1270 Leon				2	4	4	4				

FragO& Callsign	Type	Take Off	Weapons Carried	Aircraft	Weapons				Target	Weapons	
					Planned	Airborne	Reached Island	Breached Defences		Dropped	Hits
30 May 1982											
OF.1268 Zonda	A-4C Skyhawk	1630	3 x BRP	4	12	12	12	6[25]	HMS *Avenger*[26]	6	0
TBC Ala	Super Etendard		1 x Exocet[27]	2	1	1	1	1		1	
31 May 1982											
OF.1269 Charrua	Canberra	0800[28]	4 x Mk 17	2	8	8	4[29]	4	San Carlos helicopter site	4	0[30]
OF.1279 Odin				2	8	8	8	8		8	
1 June 1982											
OF.1273 Huinca	Canberra	0759	3 x Mk 17	3[31]	9	9	6[32]	6	Mount Kent	6	0[33]
4 June 1982											
OF.1277 Pina	Dagger	1900	4 x BRP	4	16	16	16	16	Mount Kent	14[34]	0[35]
OF.1275 Lince	Canberra	2123	4 x BRP + 2 Mk 17s[36]	3	18	18	18	18		18	
OF.1276 Puma				2	12	12	12	12		12	

5 June 1982											
OF.1278 Pato	Canberra	0900	5 x Mk 17	2	10	10	10	0[37]	Unable to reach targets	0	0
OF.1279 Gaucho				2[38]	10	10	10				
OF.1281 Puno	A-4B Skyhawk	1730	3 x BRP	4	12	12	12	12	Unable to find targets		
OF.TBC TBC	Dagger	1730	2 x BRP[39]	3	6	6	6	6			
OF.1280 Fierro		1800	Nil	2	0	0	0	0			
OF.1283 Nene		1840	2 x BRP	3	6	6	6	6	King George Bay area	6	
7 June 1982											
OF.1286 Potro	A-4B Skyhawk	1230	3 x BRP[40]	3	9	9	9	9	Unable to find targets	0	0
OF.1282 Trueno		1330		4	12	12	12	12			
TBC TBC	Dagger	1845	2 x BRP[41]	3	6	6	6	6			

FragO& Callsign	Type	Take Off	Weapons Carried	Aircraft	Weapons Planned	Weapons Airborne	Weapons Reached Island	Weapons Breached Defences	Target	Weapons Dropped	Weapons Hits
8 June 1982											
TBC TBC	A-4Q Skyhawk	TBC	4 x Mk 82[42]	2	8	8	8	8	Building on Broken Island	5[43]	0
TBC TBC	Canberra	1530	2 x Mk 17	2	4	4	4	4	MV *Hercules*	2	
TBC TBC		1540		2	4	4	4	4		2	1[44]
OF.1289 Mastin	A-4B Skyhawk	1530	3 x BRP[45]	4	12	12	6[46]	6	RFA *Sir Tristram*	6	2[47]
OF.1290 Dogo				4	12	12	9[48]	9	RFA *Sir Galahad*	6[49]	3[50]
OF.1291 Perro	Dagger		2 x BRP	3	6	6	6	6	HMS *Plymouth*	5[51]	4[52]
OF.1292 Gato				3	6	4[53]	4	4		4	
OF.1293 Carta	Dagger	1720	Nil	3	0	0	0	0	Diversionary mission	0	0
OF.1294 Sobre				3							

OF.1296 Mazo	A-4B Skyhawk	1900	3 x BRP	3	9	9	6[54]	6	LCU F4 from HMS *Fearless*	6	1[55]
OF.1297 Martillo				3	9	9	6[56]	6		0	
OF.1298 Yunque	A-4C Skyhawk	1936		4	12	12	12	12	British troops at Fitzroy	5[57]	0
9 June 1982											
OF.1303 Cobra	A-4C Skyhawk	1800	3 x BRP[58]	4	12	6[59]	6	6	Unable to find targets	0	0
OF.1302 Piton	A-4B Skyhawk	1800		3	9	9	9	9			
TBC TBC	A-4Q Skyhawk	TBC	4 x Mk 82[60]	2	8	8	8	0[61]	Unable to reach targets	0	0
OF.1304 Coral	Dagger	1845	2 x BRP[62]	3	6	6	6	6	Unable to find targets		
10 June 1982											
TBC TBC	Dagger	1800	2 x BRP[63]	2	4	4	4	4	Unable to find targets	0	0
OF.1308 Tigre	Canberra	0040	5 x Mk 17	2	10	5[64]	5	0[65]	Unable to reach targets		
OF.1309 Leon			2 x Mk 17[66]	2	4	2	2				

FragO& Callsign	Type	Take Off	Weapons Carried	Aircraft	Weapons				Target	Weapons	
					Planned	Airborne	Reached Island	Breached Defences		Dropped	Hits
12 June 1982											
OF.1310 Tauro	Canberra	0130	4 x Mk 17	2	8	8[67]	0	0	Unable to reach target	0	0
OF.1311 Acuario		0420	2 x Mk 17	2	4	4	2[68]	2	Bluff Cove	2	0[69]
OF.1312 Alfa	A-4B Skyhawk	TBC	3 x BRP	4	12	6[70]	6	0[71]	Unable to reach targets	0	0
OF.1314 Paris		1920	3 x BRP	4	12	3[72]	3	3	Unable to find targets	0	0
TBC TBC	A-4Q Skyhawk	TBC	4 x Mk 82[73]	2	8	8	8	0[74]	Unable to reach targets	0	0
OF.1315 Roma	Canberra	2301	4 x Mk 17	2	8	8	8	0[75]	Unable to reach target		
13 June 1982											
OF.1316 Berlin	Canberra	0300	4 x Mk 17	2	8	8	4[76]	4	Mt Kent area	4	0[77]
OF.1317 TBC[78]	Dagger	1300	2 x BRP[79]	3	6	4[80]	4	0[81]	Unable to reach targets	0	0
OF.1318 Gaucho		1310		3	6	4[82]	4	4[83]			

OF.1319 Nene	A-4B Skyhawk	1441[84]	3 x BRP	4	12	12	9[85]	9	Mt Kent area	9	0[86]
OF.1320 Chispa				4	12	12	12	12		12	0[87]
OF.1323 Zeus	Dagger	1845	2 x BRP[88]	3	6	4[89]	4	4	Unable to find targets	0	0
OF.1324 Vulcano				3	6	4[90]	2[91]	2			
OF.1326 Baco	Canberra	0130	5 x Mk 17	2	10	10	10	10	7 kms west of Stanley	10[92]	0[93]
Totals				**195**	**550**	**506**	**442**	**361**		**178**	**18**

Annex I

The Reduction in Argentine Combat Air Capability during the Falklands Conflict[1]

		Assets Used During Conflict	May					June													
			1	21	26	30	31	1	2	3	4	5	6	7	8	9	10	11	12	13	14
Canberra	Aircrew	39	37	37	37	37	37	37	37	37	37	37	37	37	37	37	37	37	37	36	
	Aircraft & Weapons	9	8	8	8	7	8	8	8	8	8	8	8	8	8	8	8	8	8	7	
Dagger (San Julian)	Pilots	19	19	19	18	18	18	18	18	18	18	18	18	18	18	18	18	18	18	18	
	Aircraft & Weapons	15	15	12	9	9	9	9	9	9	9	9	9	9	9	9	9	9	9	9	
Dagger (Rio Grande)	Pilots	16	15	14	13	12	12	12	12	12	12	12	12	12	12	12	12	12	12	12	
	Aircraft & Weapons	11[2]	10	8	7	6	6	6	6	6	6	6	6	6	6	6	6	6	6	6	
A-4B Skyhawk	Pilots	36	36	32	30	29	29	29	29	29	29	29	29	29	26	26	26	26	26	26	
	Aircraft & Weapons	28	28	24	22	21	21	21	21	21	21	21	21	21	18	18	18	18	18	18	
A-4C Skyhawk	Pilots	22	22	18	14	12	12	12	12	12	12	12	12	12	12	12					
	Aircraft & Weapons	17	17	13	10	8	8	8	8	8	8	8	8	8	8	8					

A-4Q Skyhawk	Pilots	12	12	11	10	10	10	10	10	10	10	10	10	10	10	10	10	10	10		
	Aircraft & Weapons	8	8	5	5	5	5	5	5	5	5	5	5	5	5	5	5	5	5		
Super Etendard	Pilots	10	10	10	10	10															
	Aircraft & Weapons	4[3]	4	4	4	4															

Key	100%	>100-<75%	>75-<50%	>50%
Aircrew/Pilots				
Aircraft & Weapons				

Annex J

Sea Harrier/AIM-9L Sidewinder Employment During Operation Corporate

Serial	Date	Time	Sea Harrier Pilot/Sqn	Launch Height (Feet)	Target Aircraft & Serial Number	Argentine Pilot	Target Height (Feet)	Aspect	Range (Nautical Miles)	Target Reaction	Result	Comments and References.
1	1 May	1928	Flt Lt Barton 801 NAS	12k'	Mirage III I-015	Primer Teniente Perona	13k'[1]	20°off Tail[2]	1	Gentle left turn	Kill	Perona ejected but survived, missile flight time 4 seconds.[3]
2			Lt Thomas 801 NAS	10k'	Mirage III I-019	Captain Cuerva	Lower	20°off Tail	1	Descending rapidly towards cloud[4]	Hit	The damaged Mirage diverted to Stanley but was shot down by Argentine defences killing Cuerva.[5]
3		1941	Flt Lt Penfold 800 NAS	20k'	Dagger C-433	Primer Teniente Ardiles	35k'	20°off Tail[6]	3	Nil	Kill	Ardilles killed in action.[7]
4		2047	Lt Curtis 801 NAS	100'	Canberra B-110	Teniente Ibanez & Primer Teniente Gonzales	50'	10°off Tail[8]	1	Nil	Kill	Crew ejected but killed in action.[9]

5	1 May	2047	Lt Curtis 801 NAS	100'	Canberra B-110	Teniente Ibanez & Primer Teniente Gonzales	50'	10°off Tail	1	Nil	Hit	Same target as above, first missile impacted, and crew ejected as the second missile intercepted target.[10]
6	1 May	2047	Lt Cdr Broadwater 801 NAS	100'	Canberra B-102 or 104	Captains Rodino & Dubroca or Captain Lozano & Teniente Cooke	50'	10°off Tail	2[11]	Nil	Miss	Undetermined Canberra. Fired at 2 nautical miles, out of range.[12]
7	1 May	2047	Lt Cdr Broadwater 801 NAS	Low Level	Canberra B-102 or 104	Captains Rodino & Dubroca or Captain Lozano & Teniente Cooke	Low Level	10°off Tail	2	Nil	Miss	Same target as above.[13]
8	21 May	1340	Lt Hale 800 NAS	Low Level	Dagger C-437/ 418/ 435	Captain Moreno, Teniente Volponi or Major Martinez	Low Level	Tail	Unknown	Nil	Miss	Speculative shot against an egressing formation (Callsign Perro) that was opening in range.[14]
9	21 May	1605	Lt Cdr Thomas 800 NAS	500'	A-4C C-309	Teniente Lopez	200-700'	Tail	1[15]	Nil	Kill	Lopez killed in action.[16]
10	21 May	1605	Lt Cdr Blissett 800 NAS	300'	A-4C C-325	Primer Teniente Manzotti	200'	Tail	800 yards	Nil	Kill	Missile flight time was 5 seconds. Manzotti ejected but killed in action.[17]

Serial	Date	Time	Sea Harrier Pilot/Sqn	Launch Height (Feet)	Target Aircraft & Serial Number	Argentine Pilot	Target Height (Feet)	Aspect	Range (Nautical Miles)	Target Reaction	Result	Comments and References.
11	21 May	1735	Lt Cdr Frederiksen 800 NAS	250’	Dagger C-409	Primer Teniente Luna	250’	Tail	Unknown	Nil	Kill	Luna ejected and survived.[18]
12		1750	Lt Thomas 801 NAS	250’	Dagger C-404	Major Piuma	100’	Tail	1000 yards[19]	Nil	Kill	Piuma ejected and survived.[20]
13				500’	Dagger C-403	Captain Donadille	Low Level	20°off Tail	1500-2000 yards[21]	Climbing right turn towards cloud	Kill	Donadille ejected and survived.[22]
14			Lt Cdr Ward 801 NAS	200’	Dagger C-407	Primer Teniente Senn	50’	10°off Tail	Unknown	Nil	Kill	Senn ejected and survived.[23]
15		1810	Lt Morrell 800 NAS	150’	A-4Q 3-A-307	Capitan de Corbeta Philippi	75’	Tail	800-1000 yards[24]	Nil	Kill	Philippi ejected and survived[25]
16				150’	A-4Q 3-A-312	Teniente de Navio Arca	75’	Tail	800-1000 yards[26]	Nil	Miss	Missile initially hangs up then fires but missed target. Arca’s damaged aircraft diverted to Stanley where he ejected and survived.[27]
17	23 May	1900	Lt Hale 800 NAS	100’	Dagger C-437	Teniente Volponi	50’	Tail	0.5	Nil	Kill	Volponi killed in action.[28]

18	24 May	1415	Lt Cdr Auld 800 NAS	300’	Dagger C-419	Teniente Castillo	50-100’	10°off Tail	1[29]	Nil	Kill	Castillo killed in action.[30]
19				300’	Dagger C-410	Major Puga	50-100’	10°off Tail	1[31]	Nil	Kill	Puga ejected and survived.[32]
20			Lt Smith 800 NAS	300’	Dagger C-430	Captain Diaz	200’	50°off Tail	Unknown	Turning hard right towards beam[33]	Kill	Diaz ejected and survived.[34]
21	29 May	AM	Lt Cdr Ward 801 NAS	Medium Level	N/A	N/A	N/A	N/A	N/A	N/A	Miss	Inadvertent firing.[35]
22	1 June	1346		800’	C-130 TC-63	Captain Martel	300-200’	10°off Tail	2[36]	Nil	Miss	Running short of fuel so fired early.[37]
23								Tail	1.25[38]	Nil	Hit	Damaged, kill completed using Aden Cannon, 7 killed in action.
24	8 June	1945	Flt Lt Morgan 800 NAS	200’	A-4B C-226	Teniente Arraras	100’	Tail	1000 yards[39]	Nil	Kill	Arraras ejected but is killed.[40]
25				150’	A-4B C-228	Teniente Vazquez	100’	Tail to Beam[41]	1200 yards[42]	Reversed turn, Angle off is 60-70 degrees at impact[43]	Kill	Vazquez killed in action.[44]
26			Lt Smith 800 NAS	150’	A-4B C-204	Primer Teniente Bolzan	50’	Tail	2-3[45]	Nil	Kill	‘after some seven seconds of flight there was a brilliant white flash’[46]

Annex K

Employment of British Attack Weapons during Operation Corporate

Take Off	Aircraft			Weapons							Mission		
	Unit	Type	Number	Load	Planned	Airborne	Reaching Target	Breaching Defences	Dropped	Hit	Counter	Task	Target
1 May 1982													
2350*	44 Sqn	Vulcan	1	1000lb	21	21	21	21	21	1[1]	Air	Airfield Attack	Stanley Airport
1048	800 NAS	Sea Harrier	5	Mixed[2]	3	15	15	15	15	2[3]	Air	Airfield Attack	Stanley Airport
			4	1000lb	3	12	12	12	12	?[4]	Air	Suppression	Stanley Airport
1058	800 NAS	Sea Harrier	3	Mixed[5]	3	9	9	9	9	9[6]	Air	Airfield Attack	Goose Green Airstrip
3 May 1982													
0500	815 NAS	Lynx HAS2	2	Sea Skua	2	4	4	4	4	4[7]	Sea	Anti-Surface Warfare	*Alferez Sobral*
4 May 1982													
2345*	44 Sqn	Vulcan	1	1000lb	21	21	21	21	21	0[8]	Air	Airfield Attack	Stanley Airport
1530	800 NAS	Sea Harrier	3	Mixed[9]	3	9	9	9	6[10]	6[11]	Air	Airfield Attack	Goose Green Airstrip
9 May 1982													
1119	800 NAS	Sea Harrier	2	1000lb	1	2	2	2	2	1[12]	Sea	Anti-Surface Warfare	*Narwhal*

12 May 1982													
1155	800 NAS	Sea Harrier	2	1000lb	1	2	2	2	2	0[13]	Air	Airfield Attack	Stanley Airport
1545			2		1	2	2	2	2	1[14]			
1640			2		2	4	4	4	0[15]	0			
15 May 1982													
TBC	801 NAS	Sea Harrier	5	1000lb	1	5	5	5	5	?[16]	Land	Air Interdiction	Troops North West of Stanley
16 May 1982													
N/A	44 Sqn	Vulcan	1	1000lb	21	21	0[17]	0	0	0	Air	Airfield Attack	Stanley Airport
1603	800 NAS	Sea Harrier	2		2	4	4	4	4	0[18]	Sea	Anti-Surface Warfare	*Rio Caracana*
1646			2		2	4	4	4	0[19]	0			*Bahia Buen Suceso*
19 May 1982													
1215	801 NAS	Sea Harrier	4	1000lb	2	8	8	8	8	0[20]	Land	Air Interdiction	Helicopters at Mt Kent
20 May 1982													
1430	1(F) Sqn	Harrier GR3	3	BL755	3[21]	9	9	9	9	9[22]	Land	Air Interdiction	Fuel dump at Fox Bay
21 May 1982													
1100	1(F) Sqn	Harrier GR3	2	BL755	2	4	4	4	2[23]	0	Land	Air Interdiction	Helicopters at Mt Kent
1156			2		2[24]	4	4	2[25]	0	0[26]		SCAR[27]	Port Howard
1345			2		2	4	4	4	0	0[28]			San Carlos/ Dunnose Head
1900			2		2[29]	4	4	4	0	0[30]			Dunnose Head

Take Off	Aircraft			Weapons							Mission		
	Unit	Type	Number	Load	Planned	Airborne	Reaching Target	Breaching Defences	Dropped	Hit	Counter	Task	Target
22 May 1982													
1701	1(F) Sqn	Harrier GR3	4	BL755	2	8	8	8	6	6[31]	Air	Airfield Attack	Goose Green Airstrip
1942			2		2	4	4	4	0	0[32]	Land	SCAR	Weddell Island/ Dunnose Head
23 May 1982													
1216	1(F) Sqn	Harrier GR3	4	Mixed[33]	2 or 3	10	10	10	10	10[34]	Air	Airfield Attack	Dunnose Head Airstrip
1530			2	BL755	2	4	4	4	0	0[35]	Land	SCAR	Chartres/Port Howard
1600	815 NAS	Lynx HAS2	2	Sea Skua	2	4	4	4	2	2[36]	Sea	Anti-Surface Warfare	*Rio Carcarana*
1854	1(F) Sqn	Harrier GR3	2	BL755[37]	2	4	4	4	4	4	Air	Airfield Attack	Pebble Island Airstrip
			2	1000lb	3	6	6	3[38]	3[39]	0			
2250	800 NAS	Sea Harrier	4		3	12	12	6[40]	6	0[41]			Stanley Airport
24 May 1982													
1203	1(F) Sqn	Harrier GR3	4	1000lb	3	12	12	12	12	3[42]	Air	Airfield Attack	Stanley Airport
	800 NAS	Sea Harrier	2		3	6	6	6	5	0[43]		Suppression	
2045			2		3	6	6	6	6	0[44]		Airfield Attack	

25 May 1982													
1415	800 NAS	Sea Harrier	2	1000lb	3	6	6	6	6	0[45]	Air	Airfield Attack	Stanley Airport
1420	1(F) Sqn	Harrier GR3	4		3	12	12	12	12				
1631			2	BL755	2	4	4	4	0	0[46]	Land	SCAR	Not stipulated
1728			2	1000lb	3	6	6	6	6	0[47]	Air	Airfield Attack	Stanley Airport
1927			1		3	3	3	3	3	0[48]			
	800 NAS	Sea Harrier	2		3	6	6	6	6	0[49]			
2155			3		3	9	9	9	9	?[50]			
26 May 1982													
1233	1(F) Sqn	Harrier GR3	2	BL755	2	4	4	0[51]	0	0	Land	SCAR	Stanley
1240			2	BL755	2	4	4	4	4	4[52]		Air Interdiction	Port Howard
1659			1	1000lb	3	3	3	3	2	0[53]	Air	Airfield Attack	Stanley Airport
1756			2	BL755	2	4	4	4	2	2[54]	Land	SCAR	Teal Inlet/ Stanley
27 May 1982													
1420[55]	1(F) Sqn	Harrier GR3	2	1000lb	3	6	6	6	6	0[56]	Air	Airfield Attack	Stanley Airport
1400			2	BL755	2	4	4	4	4	2[57]	Land	Air Interdiction	Goose Green
1545			2		2	4	4	4	0	0[58]			
1612			2		2	4	4	4	4	0[59]			
1902			1		2	2	2	2	0[60]	0			

Take Off	Aircraft			Weapons							Mission		
	Unit	Type	Number	Load	Planned	Airborne	Reaching Target	Breaching Defences	Dropped	Hit	Counter	Task	Target
28 May 1982													
1330	1(F) Sqn	Harrier GR3	3	Rockets	2	6	6	6	4	4[61]	Land	Air Interdiction	Ammo dump, Mt Kent
1600			2	BL755	2	4	4	4	0	0[62]		SCAR	Armed Recce
1905			3	Mixed[63]	2	6	6	6	6	6[64]		Close Air Support	Goose Green
<2359	101 Sqn	Vulcan	1	Shrike	2	2	2	0[65]	0	0	Air	Suppression	Stanley Airport Radars
29 May 1982													
1208	800 NAS	Sea Harrier	2	1000lb	3	6	6	6	24	14[66,67]	Air	Airfield Attack	Stanley Airport
1430			2		3	6	6	6					
1555			2		3	6	6	6					
TBC	801 NAS		2		3	6	6	6					
1238	800 NAS		2		3	6	6	6	12	1[68]			Pebble Island
1737			2		3	6	6	6					
1545	1(F) Sqn	Harrier GR3	2	Rockets	2	4	4	4	4	0[69]	Land	Close Air Support	Mount Kent
1700			2	BL755	2	4	2	2	0	0[70]	Land	SCAR	Stanley Radars
30 May 1982													
1130	1(F) Sqn	Harrier GR3	2	1000lb	3	6	6	6	6	?[71]	Land	SCAR	Mount Kent
1150			2	Rockets	2	4	4	4	4	?[72]			
1435			2	Mixed[73]	2	4	4	4	4	?[74]	Air	Airfield Attack	Stanley Airport
			2	Rockets	2	4	4	4	4	4[75]	Land	Air Interdiction	Mount Wall

1717	800 NAS	Sea Harrier	2	1000lb	3	6	6	6	6	0[76]	Air	Airfield Attack	Stanley Airport
1750	1(F) Sqn	Harrier GR3	2	Rockets	2	4	4	4	4	?[77]	Land	Air Interdiction	Mount Kent
31 May 1982													
<2359	101 Sqn	Vulcan	1	Shrike	4	4	4	4	2	1[78]	Air	Suppression	Stanley Airport Radars
0720[79]	801 NAS	Sea Harrier	1	1000lb[80]	3	3	3	3	3	0			
0810			1		3	3	3	3	3	0			
1130	1(F) Sqn	Harrier GR3	3	Mixed[81]	2	6	6	6	4	0[82]		Airfield Attack	Stanley Airport
1452			2	Rockets	2	4	4	4	4	?[83]			
	800 NAS	Sea Harrier	2	1000lb	3	6	6	6	6			Suppression	
1647			1	Paveway	2	2	2	2	2	0[84]		Airfield Attack	
			2	1000lb	2	4	4	4	4				
	1(F) Sqn	Harrier GR3	1	Rockets	2	2	2	2	2	?[85]	Land	Air Interdiction	Hills West of Stanley
1 June 1982													
1700	1(F) Sqn	Harrier GR3	1	Rockets	2	2	2	2	2[86]	?	Land	SCAR	Bluff Cove/ Goose Green
	800 NAS	Sea Harrier	1	1000lb	2	2	2	2	2[87]				
2 June 1982													
AM	1(F) Sqn	Harrier GR3	2	Rockets	2	4	4	4	0	0[88]	Air	Suppression	North of East Falkland
3 June 1982													
2359*	101 Sqn	Vulcan	1	Shrike	4	4	4	4	2	1[89]	Air	Suppression	Stanley Airport Radars

Take Off	Aircraft			Weapons							Mission		
	Unit	Type	Number	Load	Planned	Airborne	Reaching Target	Breaching Defences	Dropped	Hit	Counter	Task	Target
5 June 1982													
1530	1(F) Sqn	Harrier GR3	2	Rockets	2	4	4	4	4	?[90]	Land	Air Interdiction	Two Sisters
1850			2		2	4	4	4	4	4[91]		SCAR	South West of Stanley[92]
	800 NAS	Sea Harrier	2	1000lb	2	4	4	4	0	0[93]			
6 June 1982													
1310	1(F) Sqn	Harrier GR3	2	BL755	2	4	4	4	2	?[94]	Land	SCAR	Stanley
7 June 1982													
1200	1(F) Sqn	Harrier GR3	4	Rockets	2	8	4	4	4	0[95]	Land	Air Interdiction	Sapper Hill
9 June 1982													
1200	1(F) Sqn	Harrier GR3	2	Rockets	2	4	4	4	4	?[96]	Land	Air Interdiction	Mount Longdon
1340			2		2	4	4	4	4	?[97]			Sapper Hill
10 June 1982													
1300	1(F) Sqn	Harrier GR3	2	BL755	2	4	4	4	4	?[98]	Land	Air Interdiction	Mount Longdon
1631			2	Paveway	2	2	2	2	0	0[99]			Lafonia
			2	1000lb	2	4	4	4	0	0[100]			Port Howard
1854			2	BL755	2	4	4	4	4	2[101]			Mount Longdon
11 June 1982													
1058	800 NAS	Sea Harrier	4	1000lb	3	12	12	12	12	11[102]	Air	Airfield Attack	Stanley Airport

1100	848 NAS	Wessex HU5	1	AS-12	2	2	2	2	2	0[103]	Land	Air interdiction	Headquarters, Stanley
1122	1(F) Sqn	Harrier GR3	2	Paveway	2	2	2	2	2	?[104]			Wireless Ridge
1148			2	BL755	2	4	4	0[105]	0	0			Mount Harriet
1350			2	Rocket[106]	2	4	2	2	4	0[107]			Mount Longdon
1450			2	BL755	2	4	4	4	4	?[108]			Mount Harriet
1810			2		2	4	4	4	4	?[109]			Mount Longdon
1823			2	1000lb	2	4	4	4	4	0[110]			Moody Brook
12 June 1982													
<2359	44 Sqn	Vulcan	1	1000lb	21	21	21	21	21	0[111]	Air	Airfield Attack	Stanley Airport
1145	1(F) Sqn	Harrier GR3	2	BL755	2	4	4	4	4	?[112]	Land	Air Interdiction	Sapper Hill
1400			2		2	4	4	4	4	?[113]			
1405			2		2	4	4	4	4	?[114]		SCAR	Bluff Cove-Stanley
13 June 1982													
1430	1(F) Sqn	Harrier GR3	2	Paveway[115]	2	2	2	2	2	1[116]	Land	Air Interdiction	Tumbledown
1850			2		2	2	2	2	2	1[117]			Moody Brook
14 June 1982													
TBC	3CBAS & 656 Sqn	Scout AH1	1	SS-11	4	4	4	4	4	?[118]	Land	Air Interdiction	Sapper Hill
TBC			4		4	16	16	16	10	9[119]			Tumbledown
1500	1(F) Sqn	Harrier GR3	1	Paveway	2	2	2	2	0	0[120]			Sapper Hill
			1	BL755	2	2	2	2					
Combat Air Patrol Bombing from 14 May[121]													
N/A	801 NAS	Sea Harrier	31[122]	1000lb	1	31				??	Air	Airfield Attack	Stanley Airport

Bibliography

Primary Sources

Air Historical Branch. CTTO/26/2/Ops. CTTO Report on Tactical Lessons Learned from Operation Corporate.

Fleet Air Arm Archives. Record Book, 800 Naval Air Squadron.

Fleet Air Arm Archives. Fair Flying Log, May – June 1982, 800 Naval Air Squadron.

Fleet Air Arm Archives. Flight Authorisation Sheets, May – June 1982, 800 Naval Air Squadron.

Fleet Air Arm Archives. Record Book, 801 Naval Air Squadron.

Fleet Air Arm Archives. Flight Authorisation Sheets, May – June 1982, 801 Naval Air Squadron.

Fleet Air Arm Archives. Fair Flying Log, May – June 1982, 809 Naval Air Squadron.

Fleet Air Arm Archives. Flight Authorisation Sheets, May – June 1982, 809 Naval Air Squadron.

TNA. ADM 1/29055. Replacement of Sea Vixen Aircraft by F-4J Phantom II.

TNA. ADM 53/188786. HMS *Ardent* Ship's Log (Falklands Conflict), May 1982.

TNA. ADM 53/189227. HMS *Fearless* Ship's Log (Falklands Conflict), May 1982.

TNA. ADM 53/189351. HMS *Hermes* Ship's Log (Falklands Conflict), May 1982.

TNA. ADM 53/189396. HMS *Intrepid* Ship's Log. (Falklands Conflict), May 1982.

TNA. ADM 53/189408. HMS *Invincible* Ship's Log (Falklands Conflict), May 1982.

TNA. ADM 201/266. Logistics Situational Reports, 1982.

TNA. ADM 201/276. Falklands Conflict: report on proceedings of forces under the command of Major General J.J. Moore (commander of British land forces).

TNA. ADM 202/815/1. Headquarters 3 Commando Brigade, Royal Marines: Operation Corporate (Falklands Conflict), April – May 1982.

TNA. ADM 202/815/2. Headquarters 3 Commando Brigade, Royal Marines: Operation Corporate (Falklands Conflict), April – May 1982.

TNA. ADM 202/816/1. Headquarters 3 Commando Brigade, Royal Marines: Operation Corporate (Falklands Conflict), April – May 1982.

TNA. ADM 202/816/2. Headquarters 3 Commando Brigade, Royal Marines: Operation Corporate (Falklands Conflict), April – May 1982.

TNA. ADM 202/830. Commando Logistic Regiment, Royal Marines: Operation Corporate; Occurrences (Falklands Conflict), May – June 1982.

TNA. ADM 202/850. Commando Logistic Regiment, Royal Marines: Operation Corporate (Falklands Conflict), April – June 1982.

TNA. ADM 202/864. Commando Logistic Regiment, Royal Marines: Operation Corporate: Annex M - Commander's Policy/Plans (Falklands Conflict), May – June 1982.

TNA. ADM 202/875. Headquarters 3 Commando Brigade, Royal Marines: Operation Corporate; Report of Proceedings.

TNA. ADM 202/879. Operation Corporate: Landing Force Situation Reports (Falklands Conflict).

TNA. ADM 202/881. 3 Commando Brigade, Royal Marines: Operation Corporate (Falklands Conflict), April – October 1982.

TNA. ADM 202/892. Operation Corporate: Carrier Battle Group (CTG 317.8) (Falklands Conflict), March – May 1982.

TNA. ADM 202/938. Operation Corporate: Summary of Naval aircraft flying operations accidents and statistics.

TNA. AIR 2/17079. F-4 (Phantom) Aircraft: purchase from US Government.

TNA. AIR 2/17080. F-4 (Phantom) Aircraft: purchase from US Government.

TNA. AIR 2/17180. F-4 (Phantom): purchase agreements etc.

TNA. AIR 8/2629. The Harrier aircraft and the RAF Position on maritime VSTOL.

TNA. AIR 8/2631. The Harrier aircraft and the RAF Position on maritime VSTOL.

TNA. AIR 8/2633. The Harrier aircraft and the RAF Position on maritime VSTOL.

TNA. AIR 8/2665. Multi-Role Combat Aircraft (MRCA).

TNA. AIR 8/3109. Operation Corporate (Falklands Conflict): air intelligence and assessments.
TNA. AIR 8/3112. Operation Corporate (Falklands Conflict): scientific evaluation team.
TNA. AIR 20/13017. Operation Corporate (Falklands Conflict): lessons and presentations; Harrier aircraft operations; geographic support.
TNA. AIR 20/13030. Operation Corporate (Falklands Conflict): Argentine combat reports.
TNA. AIR 20/13031. Operation Corporate (Falklands Conflict): Argentine Army Official Report.
TNA. AIR 20/13044. Operation Corporate (Falklands Conflict): transcripts of interviews with personnel involved.
TNA. AIR 20/13046. Operation Corporate (Falklands Conflict): Vulcan aircraft operations, including Black Buck operations.
TNA. AIR 20/13047. Operation Corporate (Falklands Conflict): Vulcan aircraft operations, including Black Buck operations.
TNA. AIR 20/13048. Operation Corporate (Falklands Conflict): Vulcan aircraft operations, including Black Buck operations.
TNA. AIR 20/13049. Operation Corporate (Falklands Conflict): Vulcan aircraft operations, including Black Buck operations.
TNA. AIR 20/13050. Operation Corporate (Falklands Conflict): Vulcan aircraft operations, including Black Buck operations.
TNA. AIR 20/13054. Operation Corporate (Falklands Conflict): proposed official history of the campaign; Air Historical Branch article on the RAF's roles.
TNA. AIR 20/13058. Operation Corporate (Falklands Conflict): lessons learned; procurement issues.
TNA. AIR 20/13102. Operation Corporate (Falklands Conflict): Operation Fingent.
TNA. AIR 20/13103. Operation Corporate (Falklands Conflict): RAF operations; daily briefings.
TNA. AIR 20/13104. Operation Corporate (Falklands Conflict): air operations; deployments, detachments and reports.
TNA. AIR 20/13105. Operation Corporate (Falklands Conflict): summary of activities.
TNA. AIR 20/13109. Operation Corporate (Falklands Conflict): RAF involvement.
TNA. AIR 20/13113. Operation Corporate, Falklands Conflict: bombing raids on Port Stanley airfield.

TNA. AIR 20/13126. Operation Corporate (Falklands Conflict): reports and articles; Harrier aircraft operations.
TNA. AIR 20/13127. Operation Corporate (Falklands Conflict): Harrier aircraft matters.
TNA. AIR 20/13128. Operation Corporate (Falklands Conflict): Harrier aircraft policy.
TNA. AIR 20/13132. Operation Corporate (Falklands Conflict): RAF Regiment operations.
TNA. AIR 20/13190. Operation Corporate (Falklands Conflict): Harrier aircraft matters.
TNA. AIR 20/13191. Operation Corporate (Falklands Conflict): report and debriefs.
TNA. AIR 24/3298. HQ Strike Command (Falklands Conflict), May 1982.
TNA. AIR 24/3299. HQ Strike Command (Falklands Conflict), June 1982.
TNA. AIR 27/2799. No 83 Squadron: Operations Record Book. With appendices.
TNA. AIR 27/2807. No 101 Squadron: Operations Record Book.
TNA. AIR 27/3007. No 1 (F) Squadron: Operations Record Book.
TNA. AIR 27/3525. No 1 (Fighter) Squadron (Falklands Conflict).
TNA. AIR 27/3527. No 3 (Fighter) Squadron.
TNA. AIR 27/3528. No 4 Squadron.
TNA. AIR 27/3577. No 44 (Rhodesia) Squadron (Falklands Conflict).
TNA. AIR 27/3578. No 47 Squadron (Falklands Conflict).
TNA. AIR 27/3579. No 50 Squadron (Falklands Conflict).
TNA. AIR 27/3593. No 101 Squadron (Falklands Conflict).
TNA. AVIA 18/3473. Harrier GR Mk1: Sea Trials on HMS *Blake*.
TNA. AVIA 54/95. Design Branch Specification B35/46: Medium Range Bomber.
TNA. CAB 128/73/16. Cabinet Conclusion: Minutes and Papers, 6 April 1982.
TNA. CAB 128/75/4. Cabinet Conclusion: Minutes and Papers, 14 April 1982.
TNA. CAB 128/75/5. Cabinet Conclusion: Minutes and Papers, 22 April 1982.
TNA. CAB 128/73/19. Cabinet Conclusion: Minutes and Papers, 22 April 1982.
TNA. CAB 128/73/20. Cabinet Conclusion: Minutes and Papers, 28 April 1982.
TNA. CAB 128/75/6. Cabinet Conclusion: Minutes and Papers, 28 April 1982.
TNA. CAB 128/73/23. Cabinet Conclusion: Minutes and Papers, 5 May 1982.
TNA. CAB 128/73/24. Cabinet Conclusion: Minutes and Papers, 6 May 1982.
TNA. CAB 128/73/25. Cabinet Conclusion: Minutes and Papers, 11 May 1982.

TNA. CAB 128/73/27. Cabinet Conclusion: Minutes and Papers, 18 May 1982.
TNA. CAB 128/73/28. Cabinet Conclusion: Minutes and Papers, 20 May 1982.
TNA. CAB 128/73/29. Cabinet Conclusion: Minutes and Papers, 25 May 1982.
TNA. CAB 128/73/30. Cabinet Conclusion: Minutes and Papers, 27 May 1982.
TNA. CAB 128/74/1. Cabinet Conclusion: Minutes and Papers, 3 June 1982.
TNA. CAB 128/74/2. Cabinet Conclusion: Minutes and Papers, 9 June 1982.
TNA. CAB 128/74/3. Cabinet Conclusion: Minutes and Papers, 15 June 1982.
TNA. CAB 128/74/4. Cabinet Conclusion: Minutes and Papers, 17 June 1982.
TNA. CAB 129/124/33. Defence Review: The Statement on the Defence Estimates 1966, Part I.
TNA. DEFE 4/278/2. Chiefs of Staff Committee Meeting Minutes.
TNA. DEFE 4/279/8. Chiefs of Staff Committee Meeting Minutes.
TNA. DEFE 13/810. Sale of Harriers to Argentina.
TNA. DEFE 13/1066. Harrier development and financing (including Maritime Harrier).
TNA. DEFE 13/1121. Harrier (including Sea Harrier): Discussions of Operational Requirements and Development.
TNA. DEFE 13/1228. Sidewinder 9L Procurement.
TNA. DEFE 19/276. Operation Corporate (Falklands Conflict): weapon systems used in the Falklands Conflict; report of the Scientific Evaluation Team.
TNA. DEFE 24/1088. Proposed disclosure of classified military weaponry information to Argentina: SEADART and SEAWOLF.
TNA. DEFE 31/232: Operation Corporate (Falklands Conflict): missile engagements.
TNA. DEFE 48/1162. Reconstruction and analysis of the air war during Operation Corporate (Falklands Conflict).
TNA. DEFE 56/94. Harrier: Air Combat Evaluation.
TNA. DEFE 56/153. Report on Trial Tropical; joint RAF/United States Air Forces in Europe (USAFE) trials of Pave Way laser guided bomb and Pave Spike laser designator.
TNA. DEFE 58/212. An examination of Argentine air effort during the Falklands Campaign.
TNA. DEFE 58/258. HQ 11 Group: Operation Corporate (Falklands Conflict); operations / training aspects.
TNA. DEFE 58/259. HQ 18 Group: Operation Corporate (Falklands Conflict); lessons learned.
TNA. DEFE 58/260. HQ 18 Group: Operation Corporate (Falklands Conflict); lessons learned.

TNA. DEFE 58/261. HQ 18 Group: Operation Corporate (Falklands Conflict); lessons learned.

TNA. DEFE 58/262. HQ 18 Group: Operation Corporate (Falklands Conflict); lessons learned.

TNA. DEFE 58/268. HQ No. 1 Group: Operation Corporate (Falklands Conflict); operational orders.

TNA. DEFE 58/272. Strike Command Intelligence Branch: Operation Corporate (Falklands Conflict); Results of Actions Against Argentinian Forces; Argentine Air Losses, May 1982.

TNA. DEFE 58/273. Strike Command Intelligence Branch: Operation Corporate (Falklands Conflict): Results of Actions Against UK forces; Argentinian Air Defences, May 1982.

TNA. DEFE 58/274. Strike Command Intelligence Branch: Operation Corporate (Falklands Conflict): Historical Record; An Examination of Argentine Air Effort During the Falklands Campaign, May 1982.

TNA. DEFE 58/278. HQ 1 Group: Operation Corporate (Falklands Conflict); Vulcan operations.

TNA. DEFE 58/279. HQ 1 Group: Operation Corporate (Falklands Conflict); air matters - Vulcans.

TNA. DEFE 58/282. Operation Corporate (Falklands Conflict): Air Commander's Report; Report of Proceedings.

TNA. DEFE 58/311. Operation Corporate (Falklands Conflict): Vulcan bomber reports.

TNA. DEFE 58/323. Operation Corporate (Falklands Conflict): Vulcan bombers.

TNA. DEFE 67/124. Operation Corporate, Falklands Conflict: Harrier Aircraft Operations.

TNA. DEFE 67/125. Operation Corporate, Falklands Conflict: summary of Exocet attacks carried out against ships of Task Force (TF) 317.

TNA. DEFE 67/126. Operation Corporate, Falklands Conflict: Preliminary Overview.

TNA. DEFE 67/128. Operation Corporate, Falklands Conflict: Meteorological Records, October 1982.

TNA. DEFE 67/134. Operation Corporate, Falklands Conflict: Exocet attack on Carrier Vessel Battle Group (CVBG), 30 May 1982.

TNA. DEFE 67/135. Operation Corporate, Falklands Conflict: Reconstruction of the Anti-Air Warfare (AAW) Conflict, Volume 1, 1 May 1982.

TNA. DEFE 68/377. Potential sales of defence equipment to Argentina.

TNA. DEFE 68/457. Falklands Conflict: operational planning.

TNA. DEFE 68/473. Falklands Conflict: Argentine force capabilities.
TNA. DEFE 68/628. Falklands Conflict: post-operation analysis and research.
TNA. DEFE 68/669. Operation Corporate (Falklands Conflict): operational planning.
TNA. DEFE 69/338. Phantom aircraft procurement: size and purchase for Royal Navy and RAF.
TNA. DEFE 69/343. Templer Report on the Rationalisation of Air Power.
TNA. DEFE 69/441. Rationalisation between the Services.
TNA. DEFE 69/443. Study of intervention operations and amphibious capability (Byfleet study).
TNA. DEFE 69/481. Defence Review: 'The Navy without carriers' and related studies.
TNA. DEFE 69/622. Sea Harrier: Interception Capability Studies.
TNA. DEFE 69/624. Naval Staff Study: anti-air warfare.
TNA. DEFE 69/660. Maritime anti-air warfare equipment policy.
TNA. DEFE 69/676. Future war strategy and planning guidance.
TNA. DEFE 69/791. Operation Corporate, Falkland Islands: concept of operations and lessons learned.
TNA. DEFE 69/836. Operation Corporate, Falklands Conflict: 801 Naval Air Squadron, HMS *Invincible*; flight report.
TNA. DEFE 69/844. Operation Corporate, Falklands Conflict: HMS *Invincible*; campaign diary.
TNA. DEFE 69/850. Operation Corporate, Falklands Conflict: Commander Task Force 317; war diary, April 1982; section I, synopsis of policy, planning and principal events.
TNA. DEFE 69/852. Operation Corporate, Falklands Conflict: Commander Task Force 317; war diary, April 1982; section III, summary of losses.
TNA. DEFE 69/853. Operation Corporate, Falklands Conflict: Commander Task Force 317; war diary, April 1982; section IV, monthly summary of shipping movements.
TNA. DEFE 69/854. Operation Corporate, Falklands Conflict: Commander Task Force 317; war diary, April 1982; section V, standing orders issued in the fleet or on the station.
TNA. DEFE 69/855. Operation Corporate, Falklands Conflict: Commander Task Force 317; war diary, April 1982; section I, synopsis of policy, planning and principal events.
TNA. DEFE 69/856. Operation Corporate, Falklands Conflict: Commander Task Force 317; war diary, 1 May-15 June 1982; section II, day to-day record of events.

TNA. DEFE 69/857. Operation Corporate, Falklands Conflict: Commander Task Force 317; war diary, 1 May-15 June 1982; section III, summary of losses.

TNA. DEFE 69/858. Operation Corporate, Falklands Conflict: Commander Task Force 317; war diary, 1 May-15 June 1982; section IV, monthly summary of shipping movements.

TNA. DEFE 69/854. Operation Corporate, Falklands Conflict: Commander Task Force 317; war diary, April 1982; section V, standing orders issued in the fleet or on the station.

TNA. DEFE 69/856. Operation Corporate, Falklands Conflict: Commander Task Force 317; war diary, 1 May-15 June 1982; section II, day-to-day record of events.

TNA. DEFE 69/857. Operation Corporate, Falklands Conflict: Commander Task Force 317; war diary, 1 May-15 June 1982; section III, summary of losses.

TNA. DEFE 69/858. Operation Corporate, Falklands Conflict: Commander Task Force 317; war diary, 1 May-15 June 1982; section IV, monthly summary of shipping movements.

TNA. DEFE 69/868. Operation Corporate, Falklands Conflict: capabilities of Argentinian forces.

TNA. DEFE 69/988. Operation Corporate, Falklands Conflict: Argentinian forces.

TNA. DEFE 69/1009. Operation Corporate, Falklands Conflict: Rapier Reinforcements.

TNA. DEFE 69/1085. 801 Naval Air Squadron. Record of Proceedings.

TNA. DEFE 69/1112. Operation Corporate, Falklands Conflict: air matters.

TNA. DEFE 71/233. Sea Harrier training.

TNA. DEFE 71/126. Correspondence about Sea Harrier and about Advanced STOVL aircraft.

TNA. DEFE 72/257. Aircraft Specification No. 287 D&P: Sea Harrier; Fighter, Reconnaissance and Strike Aircraft.

TNA. DEFE 72/271. Operation Corporate (Falklands Conflict): includes intelligence summaries.

TNA. FCO 7/90. Sale of HMS *Hermes* to Argentina.

TNA. FCO 7/121. Annual reviews for 1966 and 1967.

TNA. FCO 7/1100. Defence Attaché's Annual Report on Argentine armed forces 1968.

TNA. FCO 7/1492. Sale of military aircraft to Argentina.

TNA. FCO 7/1878. Argentina: Annual Review for 1970.

TNA. FCO 7/1886. State of the armed forces in Argentina.
TNA. FCO 7/2193. Report on armed forces in Argentina.
TNA. FCO 7/2399. Annual report on the armed forces of Argentina.
TNA. FCO 7/2758. Argentine Armed Forces: Annual report for 1974.
TNA. FCO 7/3271. Annual defence report on Argentina for 1976.
TNA. FCO 7/3464. Armed Forces of Argentina.
TNA. FCO 7/3578. Armed Forces of Argentina.
TNA. FCO 7/3579. Arm Sales to Argentina: Policy.
TNA. FCO 7/3580. Sales of aircraft to Argentina.
TNA. FCO 7/3730. Arm Sales to Argentina: Policy.
TNA. FCO 7/3874. Arm Sales to Argentina: Policy.
TNA. FCO 7/4087. Armed forces of Argentina.
TNA. FCO 7/4088. Sales of defence equipment to Argentina.
TNA. FCO 7/4379. Admiral Fieldhouse's Official Despatch on the Falklands Operation.
TNA. FCO 7/4409. Argentine Air Force, Army and Navy.
TNA. FCO 7/4419. Falkland Islands: monitoring Argentine activity.
TNA. FCO 7/4423. Vulcan diversion to Brazil: Shrike Missile.
TNA. FCO 7/4424. Performance of British Military Equipment and Personnel in Falkland Islands Conflict: Lessons.
TNA. FCO 7/4425. Performance of British Military Equipment and Personnel in Falkland Islands Conflict: Lessons.
TNA. FCO 7/4426. Performance of British Military Equipment and Personnel in Falkland Islands Conflict: Lessons.
TNA. FCO 7/4432. Arms Supplies to Argentina: Exocet Missile.
TNA. FCO 7/4433. Arms Supplies to Argentina: Exocet Missile.
TNA. FCO 7/4434. Arms Sales to Argentina: British Policy.
TNA. FCO 7/4435. Arms Sales to Argentina by Other Countries.
TNA. FCO 7/4436. Arms Sales to Argentina by Other Countries.
TNA. FCO 7/4437. Arms Sales to Argentina by Other Countries.
TNA. FCO 7/4438. Arms Sales to Argentina by Other Countries.
TNA. FCO 7/4439. Arms Sales to Argentina by Other Countries.
TNA. FCO 7/4472. Falkland Islands Conflict: Minutes of Chiefs of Staff Meetings.
TNA. FCO 7/4473. Falkland Islands Conflict: Minutes of Chiefs of Staff Meetings.
TNA. FCO 7/4474. Falkland Islands Conflict: Minutes of Chiefs of Staff Meetings.
TNA. FCO 7/4475. Falkland Islands Conflict: Minutes of Chiefs of Staff Meetings.

TNA. FCO 7/4490. Argentine invasion of the Falkland Islands.
TNA. FCO 7/4499. Recapture of the Falkland Islands by British forces: military options.
TNA. FCO 7/4500. Recapture of the Falkland Islands by British forces: military options.
TNA. FCO 7/4506. The political costs of retaking the Falkland Island.
TNA. FCO 7/4547. Reactions in Argentina to the Falkland Islands conflict.
TNA. FCO 7/4561. Falkland Islands conflict: Chiefs of Staff meetings.
TNA. FCO 7/4562. Falkland Islands conflict: UK Task Force.
TNA. FCO 7/4564. Falkland Islands Conflict: Military Co-operation Between the UK and USA.
TNA. FCO 7/4565. Falkland Islands conflict: military planning.
TNA. FCO 7/4566. Falkland Islands conflict: military planning.
TNA. FCO 7/4609. Falkland Islands conflict: UK Task Force; military operations.
TNA. FCO 7/4610. Falkland Islands conflict: UK Task Force; military operations.
TNA. FCO 7/4612. Falkland Islands Conflict: Argentine Military Capability, 1982.
TNA. FCO 7/4615. Military activity on the Falkland Islands.
TNA. FCO 46/1075. Research and development of Maritime Harrier aircraft.
TNA. FCO 46/3245. UK Defence sales to Argentina.
TNA. FCO 46/3246. UK Defence sales to Argentina.
TNA. FO 371/81210. Report on the Argentine Air Force in 1949.
TNA. FO/371/97415. Report on the Argentine Air Force for 1951 by the Air Attaché.
TNA. FO 371/103202. Report on the Argentine Air Force for 1952.
TNA. FO 371/108816. Report on Argentine Air Force for 1953.
TNA. FO 371/114053. Supply of Canberra aircraft by UK to Argentine.
TNA. FO 371/155855. Air Force.
TNA. FO 371/119893. Air Force of Argentina.
TNA. FO 371/126185. Air Force of Argentina: USAF mission to Argentina.
TNA. FO 371/167879. Air Force.
TNA. FO 371/173756. Air Attaché's Annual Report.
TNA. FO 371/179247. Air Attaché's Annual Report.
TNA. FO 371/184660. Air Attaché's Annual Review; aircraft sales.
TNA. PREM 19/623. Relations with Argentina Position of the Falkland Islands – Part 12, 30 April – 2 May 1982.
TNA. PREM 19/624. Relations with Argentina Position of the Falkland Islands – Part 13, 3-5 May 1982.

TNA. PREM 19/627. Relations with Argentina Position of the Falkland Islands – Part 16, 11-13 May 1982.

TNA. PREM 19/629. Relations with Argentina Position of the Falkland Islands - Part 18, 18-21 May 1982.

TNA. PREM 19/630. Relations with Argentina Position of the Falkland Islands – Part 19, 22-24 May 1982.

TNA. PREM 19/631. Relations with Argentina Position of the Falkland Islands – Part 20, 25-27 May 1982.

TNA. PREM 19/647. The Handling of the Falklands Invasion – Part 5, 5-14 May 1982.

TNA. PREM 19/649. The Handling of the Falklands Crisis – Part 7, 21-31 May 1982.

TNA. T 225/3478. Requirements of surface-to-air guided missiles: development of Seawolf GWS-25 equipment.

TNA. WO 305/5600. Royal Artillery: Operation Corporate (Falklands Conflict).

Secondary Sources:

Books

Aitken, J., *Margaret Thatcher – Power and Personality*. London: Bloomsbury, 2013.

Anderson, D., *The Falklands War 1982*. Oxford: Osprey Publishing, 2002.

Armitage, M.J and Mason, R.A., *Air Power in the Nuclear Age – Theory and Practice.* Basingstoke: The Macmillan Press Ltd, 1985.

Arthur, M., *Above All, Courage*. London: Cassell, 2002.

Badsey, S., et al., *The Falklands Conflict Twenty Years On*. London: Frank Cass, 2005.

Beeny, S., *The Canberra Experience*. United States: edocPublish.com, 2016.

Benson, H., *Scram!* London: Preface, 2012.

Bicheno, H., *Razor's Edge*. London: Weidenfeld and Nicholson, 2006.

Bilton, M. and Kosminsky, P., *Speaking Out*. London: Andre Deutsch, 1989.

Blackman, T., *Vulcan Boys*. London: Grub Street, 2014.

Briasco, J.R. and Hafes, S.M., *Falklands – Witness of Battles*. Valencia: Federico Domenech, 1984.

Brookes, A., *Vulcan Units of the Cold War*. Oxford: Osprey, 2009.

Brown, D., *The Royal Navy and the Falklands War*. London: Leo Cooper, 1987.

Brown, J., *A South American War*. Brighton: Book Guild Publishing, 2013.
Burden, R.A et al. *Falklands – The Air War*. London: Arms and Armour Press, 1986.
Burns, J., *The Land That Lost Its Heroes*. London: Bloomsbury, 2002.
Campbell, J., *Margaret Thatcher, Volume Two: The Iron Lady*. London: Vintage Books, 2003.
Churchill, W.S., *The Second World War, Volume V: Closing the Ring*. London: Cassell & Co Ltd, 1952.
Clancy, T., *Every Man a Tiger*. London: Sidgwick and Jackson, 2000.
Clapp, M and Southby-Tailyour, E., *Amphibious Assault Falklands*. London: Leo Cooper, 1996.
Coates, T., *War in the Falklands, 1982*. London: The Stationary Office, 2001.
Cohen, E.A., *Gulf War Air Power Survey Volume 1 – Planning and Command and Control*. Washington D.C.: US Government Printing Office, 1993.
Cohen, E.A., *Gulf War Air Power Survey Volume 4 – Weapons, Tactics, and Training and Space Operations*. Washington D.C.: US Government Printing Office, 1993.
Cohen, E.A., *Gulf War Air Power Survey Summary Report*. Washington D.C.: US Government Printing Office, 1993.
Cordesman, A. and Wagner, A., *The Lessons of Modern War Volume 1*. Oxford: Westview Press, 1991.
Cordesman, A. and Wagner, A., *The Lessons of Modern War Volume 3*. Oxford: Westview Press, 1991.
Dabat, A. and Lorenzano, L., *Argentina – The Malvinas and the End of Military Rule*. London: Verso Editions, 1984.
Dale, I., *Memories of the Falklands*. London: Politico's Publishing, 2002.
Danchev, A., *International Perspectives on the Falklands Conflict*. New York: St Martin's Press, 1992.
Davis, R.G., *On Target*. Washington D.C.: Air Force History and Museums Program, 2002.
Deighton, L., *Fighter*. London: William Collins, 2014.
Delves, C., *Across An Angry Sea*. London: Hurst & Co, 2018.
Dildy, D.C. and Calcaterra, P., *Sea Harrier vs Mirage III/Dagger*. Oxford: Osprey Publishing, 2017.
Dingemans, P., *My Incredible Journey: From Cadet to Command*. Studley: Brewin Books, 2016.
Dyndal, G.L., *Land Based Air Power or Aircraft Carriers?: A Case Study of the British Debate about Maritime Air Power in the 1960s*. Farnham: Ashgate, 2012.

Edwards, S., *My Secret Falklands War*. Sussex: Book Guild Publishing, 2014.

Ethell, J. and Price, A., *Air War South Atlantic*. London: Sidgwick and Jackson, 1983.

Freedman, L., *Strategy*. Oxford: Oxford University Press, 2013.

Freedman, L., *The Official History of the Falklands Campaign, Volume 1*. New York: St Martin's Press, 1992.

Freedman, L., *The Official History of the Falklands Campaign, Volume 2*. New York: St Martin's Press, 1992.

Freedman, L. and Gamba-Stonehouse, V., *Signals of War*. London: Faber and Faber Limited, 1990.

Fursden, E., *Falklands Aftermath*. London: Leo Cooper, 1988.

Galland, A., *The First and the Last*. New York: Buccaneer, 1954.

Gamba, V., *The Falklands/Malvinas War*. Boston: Allen & Unwin, 1987.

Gardiner, I., *The Yompers*. Barnsley: Pen and Sword, 2016.

Gray, C., *The Air Power Advantage in Future Warfare: The Need for Strategy*. Alabama: Airpower Research Institute, 2007.

Gray, C., *Another Bloody Century*. London: Phoenix, 2005.

Grey, J., *The Last Word? Essays on Official History in the United States and British Commonwealth*. London: Praeger, 2003.

Gray, P., *Air Warfare – History, Theory and Practice*. London: Bloomsbury, 2016.

Gray, P.W., *British Air Power*. London: The Stationary Office, 2003.

Griffin, S., *Joint Operations: A Short History*. Shrivenham: Joint Doctrine and Concepts Centre, 2005.

Guevara y Moyano, I., *Latin American Fighters*. Houston: Harpia Publishing, 2009.

Hallion, R.P., *Control of the Air: The Enduring Requirement*. Washington DC: Air Force History and Museums Program, 1999.

Harris, K., *Thatcher*. London: Weidenfeld and Nicholson, 1988.

Hastings, M. and Jenkins, S., *The Battle for the Falklands*. London: Pan, 1997.

Hart-Dyke, D., *Four Weeks in May*. London: Atlantic Books, 2007.

Healey, D., *The Time of My Life*. London: Michael Joseph, 1989.

Higgitt, M., *Through Fire and Water*. Edinburgh: Mainstream, 2007.

Higham, R. and Harris, S.J., *Why Air Forces Fail – The Anatomy of Defeat*. Lexington: The University Press of Kentucky, 2006.

Hobbs, D., *The British Carrier Strike Fleet after 1945*. Barnsley: Seaforth Publishing, 2015.

Hobbs, D., *British Aircraft Carriers*. Barnsley: Seaforth Publishing, 2013.

Hobson, C., *Falklands Air War*. Hinkley: Midland, 2002.

Huertas S.M. and Briasco J.R., *Argentine Air Forces in the Falklands Conflict*. Poole: Arms and Armour Press, 1987.

Hutchings, R., *Special Forces Pilot*. Barnsley: Pen and Sword, 2008.

Inskip, I., *Ordeal by Exocet*. London: Frontline Books, 2002.

Jackson, R., *Sea Harrier and the AV-8B*. London: Blanford Press, 1989.

Jacobs, P., *Stay The Distance*. London: Frontline books, 2011.

Johnson-Allen, J., *They Couldn't Have Done It Without Us*. Woodbridge: Seafarer Books, 2011.

Lambert, A. and Williamson, A.C., *The Dynamics of Air Power*. Bracknell: Her Majesty's Stationary Office, 1996.

Leach, H., *Endure No Makeshifts*. Barnsley: Pen & Sword, 1993.

Lee, P., *Reaper Force*. London: John Blake, 2018.

Liddell-Hart, B.H., *Strategy*. London: Penguin, 1991.

Mahle, M., *The Lonesome Commander*. Munster: Edition Octopus, 2012.

Marston, B., *Harrier Boys – Volume One*. London: Grub Street, 2015.

Mason, F.K., *Harrier*. Wellingborough: Patrick Stevens Limited, 1986.

McManners, H., *Forgotten Voices of the Falklands*. London: Edbury Press, 2007.

Michel, M., *Clashes – Air Combat over North Vietnam*. Maryland: Naval Institute Press, 1997.

Middlebrook, M., *The Argentine Fight for the Falklands*. Barnsley: Pen and Sword, 2003.

Middlebrook, M., *The Falklands War 1982*. London: Penguin, 2001.

Middlemas, K. and Barnes, J., *Baldwin: A Biography*. London: Weidenfeld and Nicholson, 1969.

Moore, C., *Margaret Thatcher, The Authorized Biography: Volume One*. London: Penguin Books, 2013.

Morgan, D., *Hostile Skies*. London: Weidenfeld and Nicholson, 2006.

Moro, R.O., *The History of the South Atlantic Conflict*. New York: Praeger, 1989.

Mottino, H.R., *La Artillería Argentina en Malvinas*. Buenos Aires: Clio, 1984.

Murray, W and Sinnreich, R.H., *The Past as Prologue – The Importance of History to the Military Profession*. Cambridge: Cambridge University Press, 2006.

Norden, D.L., *Military Rebellion in Argentina*. Lincoln: University of Nebraska Press, 1996.

Nott, J., *Here Today Gone Tomorrow*. London: Politico's Publishing, 2002.
O'Connell, J.F., *The Effectiveness of Air Power in the 20th Century, Part 3 (1945-2000)*. Lincoln: iUniverse, 2006.
Olsen, J.A., *Airpower Reborn*. Annapolis: Naval Institute Press, 2015.
Olsen, J.A., *John Warden and the Renaissance of American Air Power*. Washington D.C., Potomac Books, 2007.
Olsen, J.A., *A History of Air Warfare*. Dulles: Potomac Books, 2010.
Orgill, A., *The Falklands War – Background, Conflict, Aftermath*. London: Mansell, 1993.
Parry, C., *Down South*. London: Penguin, 2012.
Pook, J., *RAF Harrier Ground Attack – Falklands*. Barnsley: Pen and Sword, 2007.
Privratsky, K.L., *Logistics in the Falklands War*. Barnsley: Pen and Sword, 2014.
Puddlefoot, G., *No Sea Too Rough*. London: Chatham Publishing, 2007.
Ramsey, G., *The Falklands War – Then and Now*. Old Harlow: Battle of Britain Publishing, 2009.
Rivas, S., *Wings of the Malvinas*. Buenos Aires: Hikoki Publications, 2010.
Rivas, S. and Cicalesi, J.C., *Latin American Mirages*. Houston: Harpia Publishing, 2010.
Rock, D., *Argentina 1516-1982*. London: I.B. Tauras and Company Limited, 1986.
Rock, D., *Argentina in the Twentieth Century*. London: Duckworth, 1975.
Ross, P.J., *HMS Invincible – The Falklands Deployment*. Portsmouth: Eyre & Spottiswoode, 1982.
Shaw, R., *Fighter Combat*. Maryland: United States Naval Institute, 1985.
Smith, R., *The Utility of Force*. London: Penguin Books, 2005.
Southby-Tailyour, E., *Exocet Falklands*. Barnsley: Pen and Sword Military, 2014.
Southby-Tailyour, E., *Reasons in Writing*. Barnsley: Pen and Sword, 2003.
Stewart, N.K., *Mates and Muchachos*. Washington DC: Brassey's (US), Inc., 1991.
Strange, J., *Centers of Gravity and Critical Vulnerabilities: Building on the Clausewitzian Foundation So That We Can All Speak The Same Language*. Quantico: Marine Corps University Foundation, 1996.
Thatcher, M., *The Downing Street Years*. London: Harper Collins Publishers, 1993.
Thompson, J., *3 Commando Brigade in the Falklands: No Picnic*. Barnsley: Pen and Sword, 1985.

Un-named Author, *The Falklands War – 25th Anniversary*. London: Marshall Cavendish, 2007.

Van der Bijl, N. and Aldea, D., *5th Infantry Brigade in the Falklands*. Barnsley: Pen and Sword, 2014.

Vaux, N., *March to the South Atlantic*. Barnsley: Pen and Sword, 2007.

Villar, R., *Merchant Ships at War.* London: Conway Maritime Press and Lloyd's of London Press, 1984.

Vine, A., *A Very Strange Way to go to War*. London: Aurum Press, 2012.

Von Clausewitz, C., *On War*. Princeton University Press: Princeton, 1976.

Ward, N., *Sea Harrier over the Falklands*. London: Cassell, 2005.

Warden, J., *The Air Campaign*. Washington: Pergamon: Brassey's, 1989.

Watson, B.W. and Dunn P.M., *Military Lessons of the Falklands War – Views from the United States*. London: Arms and Armour Press, 1984.

West, N., *The Secret War for the Falklands*. London: Sphere, 1997.

Westrum, R., *Sidewinder*. Annapolis: Naval Institute Press, 1999.

White, R., *Vulcan 607*. London: Bantam Press, 2006.

Winton, J., *Signals from the Falklands*. London: Leo Cooper, 1995.

Wood, D. and Dempster, D., *The Narrow Margin*. Barnsley: Pen and Sword Aviation, 2010.

Woodward, S., *One Hundred Days*. London: Harper Collins, 2003.

Yates, D., *Bomb Alley*. Barnsley: Pen & Sword, 2006.

Articles

Atilo, M., Celleto, V. and Mosquera, J., 'Argentina's "Heavies": Avro Lancaster, Lincoln and Lancastrian in Military Service: Part One.' *Air Enthusiast.* No. 95 (September/October 2001): 64–70.

Atilo, M., Celleto, V. and Mosquera, J., 'Argentina's "Heavies": Avro Lancaster, Lincoln and Lancastrian in Military Service: Part Two.' *Air Enthusiast.* No. 97 (January/February 2002): 36–43.

Autiero, V.L., 'The Attack on HMS *Argonaut*.' *Aerospacio*. Numero 468 (1989): 34–38.

Baldwin, N., 'The Post-QRA Era, 1969–1984.' *RAF Historical Society – The Vulcan*. (2014): 65–79.

Beaver, P., 'The Air Lessons Post Falklands.' *Navy International*. Volume 88, Number 4 (1983): 216–223.

Beaver, P., 'The Falklands – Lessons for Light Helicopters.' *Defence Helicopter World*. (June-August 1984): 76–78.

Braybook, R., 'New Power for Air Defence Guns.' *Pacific Defence Writer*. Volume 15 (1989): 41–44.

Braybook, R., 'Reassessing the Lessons of the Falklands War.' *Asia-Pacific Defence Reporter*. (April/May 1992): 41–42.

Brown, D., 'Nimrods in the Falklands.' *Maritime Patrol Aviation*. Volume 1, Number 3 (October 1989): 11–12.

Cicalesi, J. and Rivas, S., 'The Darkest Day.' *Air Forces Monthly*. (May 2007): 30–34.

Cicalesi, J. and Rivas, S., 'The Fight for "Las Malvinas".' *Aircraft Illustrated*. (May 2007): 29–34.

Colombo, J.L., 'Super Etendard Naval Aircraft Operations during the Malvinas War.' *Naval War College Review*. Volume 37, Number 3. (May/June 1984): 12–22.

Corum, J., 'Argentine Airpower in the Falklands War – An Operational View.' *Air and Space Power Journal*. Volume XVI, Number 3 (2002): 59–77.

Curtiss, J., 'The RAF Contribution to the Falklands Campaign.' *Naval Review*. Volume 71, Number 1 (June 1983): 24–32.

D'Odorico, J.C., 'The Surprising War of the Malvinas.' *Aerospace Historian*. (November/December 1983): 240–245.

Duffner, R.W., 'Conflict in the South Atlantic: The Impact of Air Power'. *Air University Review*. Volume 35, Number 3 (March/April 1984): 79–87.

Freedman, L., 'British Defence Policy after the Falklands.' *The World Today*. (September 1982): 331–339.

Freedman, L., "The War of the Falkland Islands, 1982." *Foreign Affairs*. (Fall 1982): 196–210.

Garden, T., 'Air Power, the Falklands and the Principles of War.' *Aerospace Historian*. 30(4). (December 1983): 246–253.

Hart-Dyke, D., 'HMS *Coventry* in the Falklands Conflict.' *Naval Review*. Volume 71, Number 1 (June 1983): 9–13.

Hewish, M., 'The Falklands Conflict – Part 3: Naval Operations.' *International Defence Review*. Number 10. (1982): 1340–1343.

Huertas, S., 'Pucara's Wrong War.' *Air International*. Volume 50, Number 4 (1996): 248–251.

Huertas, S., 'South American Mirages.' *Air Forces Monthly*. (November 1989): 26–29.

Huertas, S., 'Tabanos at War.' *Air Forces Monthly* (April 1989): 34–38.

Huertas, S., 'The Last Raid.' *Air Forces Monthly*. (June 1989): 44–47.

Huertas, S., 'San Carlos: Insights into an Intense Battle.' *Air Enthusiast*. (September/October 1988): 20–29.

Jackson, P., 'Strike Force South.' *Air International*. (April 1983): 163–171 and 202.

Jefford, J., 'The View from the Back – The Vulcan Nav/Attack System.' *RAF Historical Society – The Vulcan*. (2014): 51–64.

Jones, B., '820 Naval Air Squadron in Operation Corporate.' *The Navy Review*. Volume 77, Number 3 (1983): 179–181.

Layman, C., 'Duty in Bomb Alley.' *US Naval Institute Proceedings*. Volume 109 (1983): 35–40.

Litrenta, L., 'We Help to Attack HMS *Invincible*.' *Aerospacio*. Numero 456 (1987): 30–40.

Mason, R.A., 'Hay for the Horses: Reflections on the war in the South Atlantic 1982.' *Journal of the RUSI*. Volume 127, Number 4. (December 1982): 34–41.

Morgan, D., 'Sea Harrier at War.' *Aircraft Illustrated*. (May 2007): 35–38.

Murguizur, J.C., 'The South Atlantic Conflict: An Argentinian Point of View.' *International Defence Review*. Number 2. (1983): 135–140.

Nott, J., 'The Falklands Campaign.' *USNI Proceedings*. 109(5). (May 1983): 118–139.

Nye, J.S., 'The Information Revolution and Soft Power.' *Current History*. 113(759). (2014): 19–22.

Ogilvy, A., '801 Naval Air Squadron.' *The Navy Review*. Volume 71, Number 2. (April 1983): 120–123.

Pereyra, R., 'Clausewitz and the Falklands Air War.' *Air and Space Power Journal*. Volume XX Number 3 (2006): 111–119.

Philippi, A., 'Odyssey of a Skyhawk Pilot.' *USNI Proceedings*. 109(5). (May 1983), 111–113.

Piuma, G., 'A Fighter Pilot in Malvinas.' *Aerospacio*. Numero 480 (1991): 34–41.

Pook, J., 'Freestyle Mudmoving in the Falklands.' *Air Clues*. Volume 42, Number 6 (1998): 210–213.

Price, A., 'Black Buck to the Falklands.' *Air Power Review*. Volume 5, Number 2 (2002): 1–11.

Pugh, P., '"The Empire Strikes Back": The Falklands/Malvinas Campaign of 1982.' *The Mariner's Mirror*. Volume 93, Number 3 (2007): 307–324.

Rey, C., 'Lessons from the South Atlantic War.' *Aerospacio*. Numero 462 (1988): 30–41.

Ryan, J., 'Falklands Fallout.' *US Marine Corps Gazette*. Volume 67 (1983): 45–52.

Schiena, R., 'Argentinian Jointness in the Malvinas.' *Joint Forces Quarterly*. Number 5 (Summer 1994): 95–101.

Scheina, R., 'Super Etendard; Super Squadron.' *US Naval Institute Proceedings*. Volume 109 (1983): 135–137.

Sheffield, G. and Crang, J.A., 'From San Carlos to Stanley: The Falklands Land/Air Operations.' *International Relations*, Volume 20, Issue 3 (2006): 370–375.

Tallis, J., 'Black Buck Raid.' *Air Forces Monthly*. (May 1992): 48–53.

Teakle, I., 'Viewpoint.' *Air Power Review*. Volume 20, Number 2 (2018).

Thompson, J., 'Operation Corporate: 3 Commando Brigade Air Squadron.' *Army Air Corps Journal*. (1983): 11–25.

Train, H.D., 'An Analysis of the Falklands/Malvinas Islands Campaign.' *Naval War College Review*. Winter (1988): 33–50.

Whitmarsh, A., 'British Army Manoeuvres and the Development of Military Aviation, 1910–1913.' *War in History*. Volume 14, Number 3. (2007), 325–346.

Williamson, K., 'The Future of Air Power.' *RUSI Journal*. Volume 130, Number 1 (1985): 33–36.

Withers, M., 'The Vulcan Bomber in Action – Operation Black Buck.' *RAF Historical Society – The Vulcan* (2014). 102–116.

Wood, D. and Hewish, M., 'The Falklands Conflict – Part 1: The Air War.' *International Defence Review*. Number 8. (1982): 977–980.

Wood, D. and Hewish, M., 'The Falklands Conflict – Part 2: Missile Operations.' *International Defence Review*. Number 9. (1982): 1151–1154.

Wood, D. and Hewish, M., 'Rapier in the Falklands.' *International Defence Review*. Number 12. (1982): 1704.

Wrixon, T., 'Helicopter Experience in the Falklands Conflict.' *Janes Defence Weekly*. Volume 1, Number 13. (1984): 529–532.

Essays in Books

Freedman, L., 'Air Power in the Falklands, 1982.' In *A History of Air Warfare*, edited by John Andreas Olsen, 157–174. Washington DC: Dulles Books (2010).

Hampshire, E., 'The Battle for CVA01.' In *British Naval Aviation – The First 100 Years*. Farnham: Ashgate Publishing Limited (2011).

Norden, L., 'Battle for Malvinas: Falkland Islands Conflict, 1982.' In *Air Warfare in the Missile Age*. 191–206. Washington DC: Smithsonian Institution Press (2002).

Speller, I., 'Limited War and Crisis Management.' In *British Naval Aviation – The First 100 Years*. Farnham: Ashgate Publishing Limited (2011).

Dissertations

Dunn, R.C., 'Operation Corporate: Operational Artist's View of the Falkland Islands Conflict.' Naval War College (1993).

Green, G.V., 'Argentina's Tactical Aircraft Employment in the Falkland Islands War.' Air War College Research Report. Air University, United States Air Force, Maxwell Air Force Base (2005).

Hezsely, C.B., 'Argentine Air Power in the Falklands War.' Air War College Research Report. Air University, United States Air Force, Maxwell Air Force Base (1988).

Marr, J.E., 'War in the Falklands: Perspectives on British Strategy and Use of Air Power.' Air War College Research Report. Air University, United States Air Force, Maxwell Air Force Base (1988).

Puche, R.A., 'The Malvinas War from the Argentinian Viewpoint.' Air War College Research Report. Air University, United States Air Force, Maxwell Air Force Base (1988).

Reumkens, B.J., 'Sea-Based Air Power and Maritime Expeditionary Operations: UK Limited Naval Air Capability in the 1982 Falklands War.' Masters of Strategic Studies Thesis. Center for Military and Strategic Studies (2014).

Schepel, R., 'The Falklands/Malvinas 1982: Why Didn't Argentina Win the War?' Masters of Military Studies Thesis. United States Marine Corps, School of Advanced Warfighting, Marine Corps University (2009).

Shields, J., 'Future Air Power – The Need to Balance the Ends, Ways and Means.' Defence Research Paper. Joint Services Command and Staff College (2009).

Wilcox, M.A., 'Fleet Air Defense in the Falklands Conflict: A Failure in Operational Protection.' Naval War College (1999).

Online Material

Argentine Air Force Website. 'Air Operations 1 May 1982.' http://www.fuerzaaerea.mil.ar/conflicto/dias/may01.html (accessed 5 January 2015).

Argentine Air Force Website. 'Air Operations 20 May 1982.' http://www.fuerzaaerea.mil.ar/conflicto/dias/may20.html (accessed 5 January 2015).

Argentine Air Force Website. 'Air Operations 21 May 1982.' http://www.fuerzaaerea.mil.ar/conflicto/dias/may21.html (accessed 5 January 2015).

Argentine Air Force Website. 'Air Operations 22 May 1982.' http://www.fuerzaaerea.mil.ar/conflicto/dias/may22.html (accessed 5 January 2015).

Argentine Air Force Website. 'Air Operations 23 May 1982.' http://www.fuerzaaerea.mil.ar/conflicto/dias/may23.html (accessed 5 January 2015).

Argentine Air Force Website. 'Air Operations 24 May 1982.' http://www.fuerzaaerea.mil.ar/conflicto/dias/may24.html (accessed 5 January 2015).

Argentine Air Force Website. 'Air Operations 25 May 1982.' http://www.fuerzaaerea.mil.ar/conflicto/dias/may25.html (accessed 5 January 2015).

Argentine Air Force Website. 'Air Operations 26 May 1982.' http://www.fuerzaaerea.mil.ar/conflicto/dias/may26.html (accessed 8 January 2015).

Acquisition Operating Framework. 'Defence Lines of Development.' http://www.aof.mod.uk/aofcontent/strategic/guide/sg_dlod.html (accessed 11 February 2015).

British Broadcasting Corporation. 'On This Day.' http://news.bbc.co.uk/onthisday/hi/dates/stories/july/21/newsid_2515000/2515987.stm. (accessed 3 January 2016).

Casa Rosada. 'Informe Rattenbach.' http://www.casarosada.gob.ar/informacion/archivo/25773-informe-rattenbach (accessed 16 October 2016).

Clarin. '*Un aviador en tela de juicio*.' https://www.clarin.com/politica/aviador-tela-juicio_0_HJGj1AgRYg.html (accessed 8 August 2017).

Gray, C. 'Understanding Air Power: Bonfire of the Fallacies.' http://www.maxwell.af.mil/au/ssq/2008/Winter/gray.pdf (accessed 24 January 2015).

Hallion, R. 'Control of the Air: The Enduring Requirement.' http://www.af.mil/shared/media/document/AFD-060726–027.pdf (accessed 8 January 2015).

Imperial War Museum. 'Black, John Jeremy (Oral History).' https://www.iwm.org.uk/collections/item/object/80008797 (accessed 28 November 2018).

Imperial War Museum. 'Braithwaite, David (Oral History).' https://www.iwm.org.uk/collections/item/object/80032611 (accessed 29 November 2018).

Imperial War Museum. 'Curtiss, John Bagot (Oral History).' https://www.iwm.org.uk/collections/item/object/80017587 (accessed 3 December 2018).

Imperial War Museum. 'Gedge, Timothy John Henry (Oral History).' https://www.iwm.org.uk/collections/item/object/80016228 (accessed 30 November 2018).

Imperial War Museum. 'Leach, Henry Conyers (Oral History).' https://www.iwm.org.uk/collections/item/object/80024622 (accessed 29 November 2018)

Imperial War Museum. 'Middleton, Linley Eric (Oral History).' https://www.iwm.org.uk/collections/item/object/80032610 (accessed 29 November 2018).

Imperial War Museum. 'Moore, Jeremy (Oral History).' https://www.iwm.org.uk/collections/item/object/80010260 (accessed 2 December 2018).

Imperial War Museum. 'Morgan, David (Oral History)' https://www.iwm.org.uk/collections/item/object/80032738 (accessed 1 December 2018).

Imperial War Museum. 'Pook, Jeremy John (Oral History).' https://www.iwm.org.uk/collections/item/object/80030369 (accessed 1 December 2018).

Imperial War Museum. 'Squire, Peter (Oral History).' https://www.iwm.org.uk/collections/item/object/80025717 (accessed 29 November 2018).

Imperial War Museum. 'Thomas, Neill (Oral History).' https://www.iwm.org.uk/collections/item/object/80032984 (accessed 29 November 2018).

Imperial War Museum. 'Thompson, Julian Howard Atherton (Oral History).' https://www.iwm.org.uk/collections/item/object/80012160 (accessed 2 December 2018).

Imperial War Museum, 'Ward, Nigel David 'Sharkey' (Oral History).' https://www.iwm.org.uk/collections/item/object/80012551 (accessed 28 November 2018).

Land Warfare Centre. 'A Guide to the Tactical Appreciation.' https://www.army.gov.au/sites/g/files/net1846/f/a_guide_to_tactical_appreciation_1987_0.pdf (accessed 10 February 2019).

Margaret Thatcher Foundation. 'FCO to MOD (sale of Vulcans to Argentina).' http://www.margaretthatcher.org/document/118426 (accessed 15 January 2016).

Margaret Thatcher Foundation. 'Margaret Thatcher's Falklands Memoir.' http://www.margaretthatcher.org/archive/1982retpap2.asp (accessed 29 June 2015).

Margaret Thatcher Foundation. 'The Franks Report.' http://www.margaretthatcher.org/archive/displaydocument.asp?docid=109481 (accessed 16 October 2016).

Margaret Thatcher Foundation. 'The United Kingdom Defence Programme: The Way Forward.' http://www.margaretthatcher.org/document/121307 (accessed 14 January 2016).

Margaret Thatcher Foundation. 'UK Embassy Buenos Aires to FCO - Vulcan.' http://www.margaretthatcher.org/document/118427 (accessed 17 January 2016).

Meilinger, P. 'Ten Propositions Regarding Air Power.' http://www.airpower.maxwell.af.mil/airchronicles/cc/meil.html (accessed 8 January 2015).

RAF. '83 Squadron.' http://www.raf.mod.uk/history/83squadron.cfm (accessed 21 February 2016).

RAF. 'Attack.' http://www.raf.mod.uk/role/attack.cfm (accessed 13 October 2016).

RAF. 'Operation Black Buck.' http://www.raf.mod.uk/history/OperationBlackBuck.cfm (accessed 25 September 2016).

RAF. 'To South America by Vulcan and Comet.' https://www.raf.mod.uk/rafcms/mediafiles/E00B56CB_5056_A318_A8E56775B941EA8B.pdf (accessed 7 August 2017).

RAF Historical Society. 'Journal 11 – Air Force Policy in the 1950s and 1960s.' http://www.rafmuseum.org.uk/documents/Research/RAF-Historical-Society-Journals/Journal-11-Sir%20Frank-Cooper-on-Air-Force-Policy-in-the-1950s-1960s.pdf (accessed 17 January 2016).

RAF Historical Society. 'Journal 20 – Training in Peace for War.' http://www.rafmuseum.org.uk/documents/Research/RAF-Historical-Society-Journals/Journal-20-Seminar-Training-in-Peace-for-War.pdf (accessed 27 September 2016).

RAF Historical Society. 'Journal 27A – Birth of Tornado.' http://www.rafmuseum.org.uk/documents/Research/RAF-Historical-Society-Journals/Journal-27A-Seminar-Birth-of-Tornado.pdf (accessed 17 January 2016).

RAF Historical Society. 'Journal 30 – The Falklands Campaign.' http://www.rafmuseum.org.uk/documents/Research/RAF-Historical-Society-Journals/Journal-30-Seminar-The-Falklands-Campaign.pdf (accessed 20 November 2015).

RAF Historical Society. 'Journal 35A – The RAF Harrier Story.' http://www.rafmuseum.org.uk/documents/Research/RAF-Historical-Society-Journals/Journal-35A-Seminar-the-RAF-Harrier-Story.pdf (accessed 17 January 2016).

Radar Malvinas. 'Plan de Operaciones 2/82 – *Mantenimiento de la Soberania.*' http://www.radarmalvinas.com.ar/document_guerra/ABR07%2082%20plan%20cae.pdf (accessed 20 December 2016).

Radar Malvinas. 'Plan de Operaciones de la Fuerza de Tareas Aeronaval No 02/82.' http://www.radarmalvinas.com.ar/document_guerra/ABR15%2082%20plan%20ops%20aeronaval.pdf (accessed 23 December 2016).

Squire, P. 'Harrier goes to War.' http://www.raf.mod.uk/history/TheHarrierGoestoWar.cfm (accessed 8 January 2016).

Strange, J. and Iron, R. 'Understanding Centers of Gravity and Critical Vulnerabilities: Part 1 – What Clausewitz (Really) Meant by Centers of Gravity.' http://www.au.af.mil/au/awc/awcgate/usmc/cog1.pdf (accessed 5 January 2015).

Strange, J. and Iron, R. 'Understanding Centers of Gravity and Critical Vulnerabilities: Part 2 - Part 2: The CG-CC-CR-CV Construct: A Useful Tool to Understand and Analyze the Relationship between Centers of

Gravity and their Critical Vulnerabilities.' http://www.au.af.mil/au/awc/awcgate/usmc/cog2.pdf (accessed 5 January 2015).

UPI Archives. 'Argentine pilot shot down and captured over the Falkland Islands.' https://www.upi.com/Archives/1982/05/28/An-Argentine-pilot-shot-down-and-captured-over-the/4718391406400/ (accessed 29 January 2019).

Official Publications

Argentina. Armada Argentina. Historia de la Aviacion Naval Argentina (Conflicto Del Atlantico Sur.) (Buenos Aires: Departamento de Estudios Historicos Navales, 1992.)

Argentina. Fuerza Aérea Argentina. Historia de la Fuerza Aérea Argentina. Tomo VI, Volumen 1, 'La Fuerza Aérea en Malvinas' (Buenos Aires: Dirección de Estudios Históricos, 1998.)

Argentina. Fuerza Aérea Argentina. Historia de la Fuerza Aérea Argentina. Tomo VI, Volumen 2, 'La Fuerza Aérea en Malvinas' (Buenos Aires: Dirección de Estudios Históricos, 1998.)

United Kingdom. British Army. Army Doctrine Publication: Army Doctrine Primer. (Shrivenham: The Development, Concepts and Doctrine Centre, 2011).

United Kingdom. British Army. Army Doctrine Publication: Operations. (Shrivenham: The Development, Concepts and Doctrine Centre, 2010).

United Kingdom. Ministry of Defence. Allied Joint Publication 5–00: Allied Joint Doctrine for Operational-Level Planning. (Shrivenham: The Development, Concepts and Doctrine Centre, 2013).

United Kingdom. Ministry of Defence. Carrier Enabled Power Projection Concept of Employment, Issue 2. (London: Ministry of Defence, 2014).

United Kingdom. Ministry of Defence. Joint Concepts Note 3/12: Future Air and Space Operational Concept. (Shrivenham: The Development, Concepts and Doctrine Centre, 2012).

United Kingdom. Ministry of Defence. Joint Doctrine Publication 0–01: UK Defence Doctrine – 5*th* Edition. (Shrivenham: The Development, Concepts and Doctrine Centre, 2015).

United Kingdom. Ministry of Defence. Joint Doctrine Publication 0–10: British Maritime Doctrine. (Shrivenham: The Development, Concepts and Doctrine Centre, 2011).

United Kingdom. Ministry of Defence. Joint Doctrine Publication 0–30: UK Air and Space Doctrine. (Shrivenham: The Development, Concepts and Doctrine Centre, 2013).

United Kingdom. Ministry of Defence. Joint Doctrine Publication 0–30: UK Air and Space Doctrine, Second Edition. (Shrivenham: The Development, Concepts and Doctrine Centre, 2017).
United Kingdom. Ministry of Defence. Joint Doctrine Publication 04: Understanding. (Shrivenham: The Development, Concepts and Doctrine Centre, 2010).
United Kingdom. Ministry of Defence. Joint Doctrine Publication 3–00: Campaign Execution. (Shrivenham: The Development, Concepts and Doctrine Centre, 2009).
United Kingdom. Ministry of Defence. RAF Operations during the Falklands Conflict. (London: Air Historical Branch, 1988).
United Kingdom. Ministry of Defence. The Falklands Campaign: The Lessons. (London: Her Majesty's Stationery Office, 1982).
United Kingdom. RAF. Air Publication 3002: Air Warfare. (Waddington: Air Warfare Centre, 2016).
United Kingdom. Royal Navy. The United Kingdom Approach to Amphibious Operations. (Portsmouth: Maritime Warfare Centre, 1997).
United Kingdom. Royal Navy. BRd 4487 Volume 2.2 – Amphibious Warfare, First Edition. (Portsmouth: Maritime Warfare Centre, 2014).
United States of America. United States Army. Combat History Analysis Study Effort (CHASE): Progress Report (Washington DC: US Army Concepts Analysis Agency, August 1986).

Podcasts

Clarke, A. 'Sea Control 87A – Falklands Series 7.' *Amphibious Panel*. Podcast Audio, 27 July 2015. http://cimsec.org/sea-control-87a-falklands-series-7-amphibious-panel/17637.
Clarke, A. 'Sea Control 87B – Falklands Series 7.' *Amphibious Panel*. Podcast Audio, 27 July 2015. http://cimsec.org/sea-control-87b-falklands-series-7-amphibious-panel/17640.
Clarke, A. 'Sea Control 97.' *Falklands w/ Sharkey Ward*. Podcast Audio, 12 October 2015. http://cimsec.org/sea-control-97-falklands-w-sharkey-ward/19236.
Clarke, A. 'Sea Control 101 – Falklands 10.' *21 Days to take a Squadron to War.* Podcast Audio, 16 November 2015. http://cimsec.org/sea-control-101-falklands-10–21-days-to-take-a-squadron-to-war/19976.

Morgan, D. 'BBC World Service – Witness.' *The Harrier in the Falklands War*. Podcast Audio, 19 April 2016. http://www.bbc.co.uk/programmes/p03qr75s.

Willis, M. 'Xtended – Episode 70.' *Falklands Air War Part 1*. Podcast Audio, 15 June 2017. http://aviation-xtended.co.uk/ep-70-falklands-air-war-part-1/.

Willis, M. 'Xtended – Episode 71.' *Falklands Air War Part 2*. Podcast Audio, 15 June 2017. http://aviation-xtended.co.uk/ep-71-falklands-air-war-part-2/.

Willis, M. 'Xtended – Episode 75.' *Falklands Air War Part 3*. Podcast Audio, 21 October 2017. http://aviation-xtended.co.uk/ep-75-falklands-air-war-part-3/.

Willis, M. 'Xtended – Episode 77.' *Falklands Air War Part 4*. Podcast Audio, 9 December 2017. http://aviation-xtended.co.uk/ep-77-falklands-air-war-part-4/.

Endnotes

Pre-Amble

1. Based on data contained within S. Rivas, *Wings of the Malvinas of the Malvinas*. (Buenos Aires: Hikoki Publications, 2010).

Chapter 1 – Introduction

1. The National Archives (TNA), DEFE 69/836. Operation Corporate, Falklands Conflict: 801 Naval Air Squadron, HMS *Invincible*; flight report.
2. The actual name of the Conflict differs between the two participants. While the Argentines prefer the term 'Malvinas War,' the term used throughout this book will be the Falklands Conflict. The use of the British name is not meant to be divisive but provides a simpler narrative and a term that English-speaking readers will be more familiar with.
3. Unless otherwise stated, the dates shown within the book are 1982.
4. C. Hobson, *Falklands Air War.* (Hinkley: Midland Publishing, 2002), 94.
5. UPI Archives, 'Argentine pilot shot down and captured over the Falkland Islands.' https://www. upi. com/Archives/1982/05/28/An-Argentine-pilot-shot-down-and-captured-over-the/4718391406400/ (accessed 29 January 2019). Additionally, Lucero makes two further unusual comments in the article. During Lucero's third mission, conducted the day prior and in the same location, he aborted the mission due to intense ground fire. Therefore, his comment that 'I was immensely surprised on the fourth raid to find all kinds of missile and gunfire rising to meet me and my three fellow pilots,' appears out of context. Lastly, and a point that will be analysed later in the book, Lucero exaggerated the attrition he faced when he suggested that, 'half his squadron failed to return from missions against the British force over the past six days.'
6. Rivas, *Wings of the Malvinas*, 119, 120 and 123, R.A. Burden et al, *Falklands – The Air War* (London: Arms and Armour Press, 1986), 111 and 112 as well as Hobson, *Falklands Air War*, 50, 61 and 92.

7. M. Howard, 'Military History and the History of War.' In *The Past as Prologue – The Importance of History to the Military Profession* edited by W. Murray and R.H. Sinnreich (Cambridge: Cambridge University Press, 2006), 14.
8. W. Murray and R.H. Sinnreich, 'Introduction.' In *The Past as Prologue – The Importance of History to the Military Profession* edited by W. Murray and R. H. Sinnreich (Cambridge: Cambridge University Press, 2006), 2.
9. J.P. Kiszely, 'The Relevance of History to the Military Profession: A British View.' In *The Past as Prologue – The Importance of History to the Military Profession*. (Cambridge: Cambridge University Press, 2006), 26.
10. *Ibid.*, 24.
11. Murray, *Introduction*, 1.
12. Howard, *Military History*, 13.
13. TNA, CAB/128/73/30. Cabinet Conclusion: Minutes and Papers 27 May 1982.
14. *Ibid.*
15. H. Bicheno, *Razor's Edge.* (London: Weidenfeld and Nicholson, 2006), 132.
16. TNA, CAB/128/73/29. Cabinet Conclusion: Minutes and Papers 25 May 1982.
17. The Argentine military changed the name of the Operation in the prelude to its execution from *Azul* to *Rosario*. Bicheno, *Razor's Edge*, 56; R. Higham and S.J. Harris, *Why Air Forces Fail – The Anatomy of Defeat* (Lexington: The University Press of Kentucky, 2006), 237.
18. J.C. Murguizur, 'The South Atlantic Conflict: An Argentine Point of View.' *International Defence Review*. Number 2. (1983), 139; C. Parry, *Down South* (London: Penguin, 2012), 41
19. Fursdon, *Falklands Aftermath* (London: Leo Cooper, 1988), 83.
20. In contemporary British military doctrine, the elements which, when combined create military capability, are defined as the Defence Lines of Development and are referred to by the acronym TEPIDOIL that equates to: Training, Equipment, People, Infrastructure, Doctrine, Organisation, Information, and Logistics. Acquisition Operating Framework, 'Defence Lines of Development.' http://www. aof. mod. uk/aofcontent/strategic/guide/sg_dlod. html (accessed 11 February 2015).
21. Including H.D. Train, 'An Analysis of the Falklands/Malvinas Islands Campaign.' *Naval War College Review*. Winter (1988), 49. Also, Parry. *Down South*, xiii.
22. E.A. Cohen et al, *Gulf War Air Power Survey Volume 1 – Planning and Command and Control* (Washington D.C. : US Government Printing Office, 1993), Command and Control, 3.

23. J. Woodward, *One Hundred Days* (London: Harper Collins, 2003), xix.
24. A. Cordesman, A. and Wagner, A. *The Lessons of Modern War Volume 3*. (Oxford: Westview Press, 1991), 319.
25. N. Ward, *Sea Harrier over the Falklands*. (London: Cassell, 2005), 247.
26. Woodward, *One Hundred Days*, 359.
27. United Kingdom. Ministry of Defence. Allied Joint Publication 5-00: Allied Joint Publication for Operational Level Planning. (Shrivenham: The Development, Concepts and Doctrine Centre, 2013); Professor Richard Holmes defined doctrine as, 'an approved set of principles and methods, intended to provide large military organisations with a common outlook and a uniform basis for action.' United Kingdom. British Army. Army Doctrine Publication: Army Doctrine Primer. (Shrivenham: The Development, Concepts and Doctrine Centre, 2011), 1-1.
28. G. Sheffield and J.A. Crang, 'From San Carlos to Stanley: The Falklands Land/Air Operations.' *International Relations*, Volume 20, Issue 3 (2006), 370.
29. United Kingdom. British Army. Army Doctrine Publication: Operations. (Shrivenham: The Development, Concepts and Doctrine Centre, 2010), E-2.
30. P. Gray, *Air Warfare – History, Theory and Practice.* (London: Bloomsbury, 2016), 19.
31. United Kingdom, Army Doctrine Primer, 1-1.
32. United Kingdom, Army Doctrine Publication: Operations, E-18.
33. *Ibid.*
34. J. Thompson, *3 Commando Brigade in the Falklands: No Picnic. (*Barnsley: Pen and Sword, 1985), 31.
35. Defined as a 'logical process of reasoning by which a commander considers all the circumstances affecting the military situation and arrives at a decision as to the course of action to be taken in order to accomplish his mission.' Land Warfare Centre, 'A Guide to the Tactical Appreciation'. https://www. army. gov. au/sites/g/files/net1846/f/a_guide_to_tactical_appreciation_1987_0. pdf (accessed 10 February 2019).
36. J. Strange, *Centers of Gravity and Critical Vulnerabilities: Building on the Clausewitzian Foundation So That We Can All Speak The Same Language.* (Quantico: Marine Corps University Foundation, 1996).
37. C. Von Clausewitz, *On War*. (Princeton: Princeton University Press, 1976), 595-596.
38. J. Warden, *The Air Campaign*. (Washington: Pergamon: Brassey's, 1989).
39. As part of the United States Air Force's Warfighting Concepts Directorate, the Checkmate Division specialised in Soviet and Allied analysis of warfighting

problems and scenarios. R.G. Davis, *On Target* (Washington D. C: Air Force History and Museum Program, 2002), 60; Following refinement, the three centres of gravity used during Operation Desert Storm were: Leadership, Military Forces, and the Nuclear, Chemical and Biological Capability. Cohen, Volume 1, 145.

40. Strange described the centre of gravity as the primary sources of moral or physical strength, power, and resistance. Strange, *Centers of Gravity*, ix.
41. L. Freedman, *Strategy*. (Oxford: Oxford University Press, 2013), 239.
42. Strange, *Centers of Gravity*, 74.
43. Freedman, *Strategy*, 91.
44. Strange, *Centers of Gravity*, 17.
45. As defined in United Kingdom, *Operational-Level Planning*, 3-33 and 3-34.
46. Freedman, *Strategy*, 91.
47. Freedman defined *schwerpunkt* as, 'the central feature of the enemy's power and therefore the point against which all our energies should be directed.' *Ibid*., 91 and 239.
48. A. Galland, *The First and the Last*. (New York: Buccaneer, 1954), 128.
49. Woodward, *One Hundred Days*, 6.
50. *Ibid*., 139.
51. Hobson, *Falklands Air War*, 71-2.
52. Admiral Sir John Woodward, in 'The Falklands War', seminar held 5 June 2002 (Centre for Contemporary British History, 2005, http://www. icbh. ac. uk/witnness/falklands,), 46.
53. Admiral of the Fleet Sir Henry Leach, in 'The Falklands War', seminar held 5 June 2002 (Centre for Contemporary British History, 2005, http://www. icbh. ac. uk/witnness/falklands,), 46.
54. L. Freedman, *The Official History of the Falklands Campaign, Volume 2*. (New York: St Martin's Press, 1992), 212.
55. Admiral of the Fleet Sir Henry Leach, in 'The Falklands War', seminar held 5 June 2002 (Centre for Contemporary British History, 2005, http://www. icbh. ac. uk/witnness/falklands,), 46.
56. TNA, PREM 19/647. Handling of the Falklands Crisis 1982 – Part 5, 5-14 May 1982.
57. Whitmore held the post of Private Secretary to the Prime Minister during the Conflict. C. Moore, *Margaret Thatcher – The Authorized Biography: Volume One* (London: Penguin Books, 2014), 716.
58. Margaret Thatcher Foundation, 'Margaret Thatcher's Falklands Memoir.' http://www. margaretthatcher. org/archive/1982retpap2. asp (accessed 29 June 2015).

59. Cecil Parkinson, in 'The Falklands War', seminar held 5 June 2002 (Centre for Contemporary British History, 2005, http://www. icbh. ac. uk/witnness/ falklands,), 30.
60. Margaret Thatcher Foundation, 'Margaret Thatcher's Falklands Memoir.' http:// www. margaretthatcher. org/archive/1982retpap2. asp (accessed 29 June 2015).
61. *Ibid.*
62. Air Marshal Sir John Curtiss, in 'The Falklands War', seminar held 5 June 2002 (Centre for Contemporary British History, 2005, http://www. icbh. ac. uk/witnness/falklands,), 45.
63. Freedman, *Official History Volume 2*, 307.
64. Margaret Thatcher Foundation, 'Margaret Thatcher's Falklands Memoir.' http://www. margaretthatcher. org/archive/1982retpap2. asp (accessed 29 June 2015).
65. Francis Pym and William Whitelaw, both awarded the Military Cross.
66. United Kingdom, *Operational-Level Planning*, 2-70.
67. *Ibid.*, 2-73.
68. *Ibid.*, 2-72.
69. See Figure 1.1 for further detail; the primary effect that control of the air provides is to secure freedom of action for friendly forces. United Kingdom. Ministry of Defence. Joint Doctrine Publication 0-30: UK Air and Space Doctrine. (Shrivenham: The Development, Concepts and Doctrine Centre, 2013), 3-1.
70. Secondary source evidence suggested that HMS *Hermes* had a crew of 1,700 during the Conflict. 'On This Day.' http://news. bbc. co. uk/onthisday/hi/dates/ stories/july/21/newsid_2515000/2515987. stm. (accessed 3 January 2016); HMS *Invincible* had a crew of 1,066 during the Falklands Conflict. Sourced from P. J Ross, *HMS Invincible – The Falklands Deployment*. (Portsmouth: Eyre & Spottiswoode), 1982.
71. Freedman, *Official History Volume 2*, 179.
72. United Kingdom. Royal Navy. The United Kingdom Approach to Amphibious Operations. (Portsmouth: Maritime Warfare Centre, 1997), 20.
73. Margaret Thatcher Foundation. 'The United Kingdom Defence Programme: The Way Forward.' http://www. margaretthatcher. org/document/121307 (accessed 14 January 2016), 6-8.
74. B. Marston, *Harrier Boys – Volume One*. London: Grub Street, 2015, 59.
75. A. Stephens, 'The Air War in Korea, 1950-1953.' In *A History of Air Warfare*. (Dulles: Potomac Books, 2010), 88.
76. P.D. Grove, 'Falklands Conflict 1982 – The Air War: A New Appraisal.' In *The Falklands Conflict Twenty Years On* edited by S. Badsey et al. (London: Frank Cass, 2005), 266.

77. Air Historical Branch, CTTO/26/2/Ops. CTTO Report on Tactical Lessons Learned from Operation Corporate, 47.
78. A. Stephens, *Air War in Korea*, 105.
79. Hobson, *Falklands Air War*, 17.
80. TNA, DEFE 68/473. Falklands Conflict: Argentine force capabilities.
81. Burden, *The Air War*, 19.
82. Margaret Thatcher Foundation, 'The Franks Report.' http://www. margaretthatcher. org/archive/displaydocument. asp?docid=109481 (accessed 16 October 2016).
83. Freedman, *Official History Volume 2*, 725.
84. *Casa Rosada*, '*Informe Rattenbach*.' http://www. casarosada. gob. ar/ informacion/archivo/25773-informe-rattenbach (accessed 16 October 2016).
85. Gray, *Air Warfare*, 24.
86. J. Grey, *The Last Word? Essays on Official History in the United States and British Commonwealth*. (London: Praeger, 2003), ix.
87. Gray, *Air Warfare*, 21.
88. L. Freedman, *The Official History of the Falklands Campaign, Volumes 1 and 2*. (New York: St Martin's Press, 2005).
89. Sheffield, *From San Carlos to Stanley*, 370; United Kingdom. Ministry of Defence. The Falklands Campaign: The Lessons. (London: Her Majesty's Stationery Office, 1982).
90. Freedman, *Official History Volume 2*, xxi-xxii; Sheffield. *From San Carlos to Stanley*, 370.
91. *Ibid*.
92. Freedman, *Official History, Volume 2*, xxiii.
93. Sheffield, *From San Carlos to Stanley*, 370.
94. *Ibid*., 372.
95. Rivas, *Wings of the Malvinas*, 374.
96. Argentina. *Fuerza Aérea Argentina*. Historia de la *Fuerza Aérea Argentina*. Tomo VI 'La Fuerza Aérea en Malvinas' (Buenos Aires: Dirección de Estudios Históricos, 1998.) and Argentina. Armada Argentina. Historia de la Aviacion Naval Argentina (Conflicto Del Atlantico Sur.) (Buenos Aires: Departamento de Estudios Historicos Navales, 1992.)
97. Grey, *The Last Word?*, ix.
98. J. Ethell and A. Price, *Air War South Atlantic*. (London: Sidgwick and Jackson, 1983), R.A. Burden et al. *Falklands – The Air War*. (London: Arms and Armour Press, 1986).
99. Cordesman, *Volume 3*, Bicheno. *Razor's Edge* and Hobson. *Falklands Air War*. There is some confusion in Cordesman's work between Sea Harriers and Harrier GR3s, but this does not detract from the overall analysis.

100. S. Badsey, 'Introduction.' In *The Falklands Conflict Twenty Years On* edited by S. Badsey et al. (London: Frank Cass, 2005), 1.
101. For example, the then Brigadier Horacio Mir Gonzales provided the Argentine view by delivering an insight into his experiences as a Dagger pilot during the Conflict.
102. Ward, *Sea Harrier*.
103. J. Pook, *RAF Harrier Ground Attack – Falklands*. (Barnsley: Pen and Sword, 2007).
104. D. Morgan, *Hostile Skies*. (London: Weidenfeld and Nicholson, 2006).
105. A. Whitmarsh, 'British Army Manoeuvres and the Development of Military Aviation, 1910-1913.' *War in History*. Volume 14, Number 3 (2007), 327.
106. M. Middlebrook, *The Argentinian Fight for the Falklands*. (Barnsley: Pen and Sword, 2003).
107. R.O. Moro, *The History of the South Atlantic Conflict*. (New York: Praeger, 1989),
108. J.R. Briasco and S.M. Hafes, *Falklands – Witness of Battles*. Valencia: Federico Domenech, 1984; S. Huertas, 'Tabanos at War.' *Air Forces Monthly* (April 1989): 34-38 and J. Cicalesi and S. Rivas, S, 'The Fight for "Las Malvinas."' *Aircraft Illustrated*. (May 2007): 29-34.
109. Rivas, *Wings of the Malvinas*.
110. *Ibid*.
111. http://www. margaretthatcher. org
112. http://www. raf. mod. uk/history/rafhistoricalsocietym. cfm
113. https://www. faa. mil. ar/conflicto/operaciones_aereas. html
114. Gray, *Air Warfare*, 27.
115. Thompson, *No Picnic*; M. Clapp and E. Southby-Tailyour, *Amphibious Assault Falklands* (London: Leo Cooper, 1996).
116. G. Puddlefoot, *No Sea Too Rough*. (London: Chatham Publishing, 2007); J. Johnson-Allen, *They Couldn't Have Done It Without Us*. (Woodbridge: Seafarer Books, 2011).
117. N. Vaux, *March to the South Atlantic*. (Barnsley: Pen and Sword, 2007); I. Gardiner, *The Yompers*. (Barnsley: Pen and Sword, 2016); N. Van der Bijl and D. Aldea, 5th *Infantry Brigade in the Falklands*. (Barnsley: Pen and Sword, 2014) and E. Southby-Tailyour, *Reasons in Writing*. (Barnsley: Pen and Sword, 2003).
118. Gray, *Air Warfare*, 28.
119. *Ibid*., 30.
120. For example, TNA, FCO 7/3271. Annual defence report on Argentina for 1976.
121. Fleet Air Arm Archives, Record Book, 800 Naval Air Squadron; Fleet Air Arm Archives, Fair Flying Log, May – June 1982, 800 Naval Air Squadron; Fleet Air Arm Archives, Flight Authorisation Sheets, May - June 1982, 800 Naval

Air Squadron; Fleet Air Arm Archives, Record Book, 801 Naval Air Squadron; Fleet Air Arm Archives, Flight Authorisation Sheets, May - June 1982, 801 Naval Air Squadron; Fleet Air Arm Archives, Fair Flying Log, May - June 1982, 809 Naval Air Squadron; Fleet Air Arm Archives, Flight Authorisation Sheets, May – June 1982, 809 Naval Air Squadron.

122. TNA, DEFE 69/836.801 Naval Air Squadron flight report.
123. TNA, AIR 20/13126. Operation Corporate (Falklands Conflict): reports and articles; Harrier aircraft operations.
124. TNA, DEFE 19/276. Operation Corporate (Falklands Conflict): weapon systems used in the Falklands Conflict; report of the Scientific Evaluation Team.
125. The author is indebted to the Argentine historians Santiago Rivas and Mariano Sciaroni for their help and support throughout the development of the book.
126. Train, *Falklands/Malvinas Islands Campaign*, 50.

Chapter 2 – Methodology

1. Galland, *The First*, 63.
2. Freedman, *Official History Volume 2*, 7, and 254.
3. British military doctrine defines a campaign fulcrum as, 'the point during a campaign when an approximate, albeit fluctuating, equilibrium between opposing forces is disrupted significantly; one side starts winning and the other losing, potentially irreversibly. In practice, reaching a campaign fulcrum is difficult to predict in advance.' United Kingdom, *Operational-Level Planning*, 2-84.
4. Due to the different time zones in the United Kingdom, Argentina, and the Falkland Islands, the book uses Greenwich Mean Time.
5. Clapp, *Amphibious Assault Falklands*, 132.
6. J. Thompson, 'Force Projection and the Falkland Islands.' In *The Falklands Conflict Twenty Years On* edited by Badsey, S. et al, 94. London: Frank Cass, (2005).
7. *Ibid.*, 84.
8. M. Hastings and S. Jenkins, *The Battle for the Falklands*. (London: Pan, 1997), 273.
9. Clapp, *Amphibious Assault Falklands*, 104.
10. *Ibid.*, 118.
11. Margaret Thatcher Foundation, *The Way Forward*, 3; E. Hampshire, 'The Battle for CVA01.' In *British Naval Aviation – The First 100 Years*. Farnham: Ashgate Publishing Limited (2011), 182.
12. Margaret Thatcher Foundation, *The Way Forward*, 4.
13. D. Healey, *The Time of My Life*. (London: Michael Joseph, 1989), 255.
14. *Ibid.*, 256.

15. Margaret Thatcher Foundation, *The Way Forward*, 5.
16. *Ibid.*, 11.
17. *Ibid.*, 10.
18. *Ibid.*, 11.
19. RAF Historical Society, 'Journal 30 – The Falklands Campaign.' http://www.rafmuseum. org. uk/documents/Research/RAF-Historical-Society-Journals/Journal-30-Seminar-The-Falklands-Campaign. pdf (accessed 20 November 2015).
20. R. Jackson, '*Sea Harrier and the AV-8B*.' (London: Blanford Press, 1989), 14.
21. RAF Historical Society, 'Journal 20 – The RAF Harrier Story.' http://www.rafmuseum. org. uk/documents/Research/RAF-Historical-Society-Journals/Journal-35A-Seminar-the-RAF-Harrier-Story. pdf (accessed 17 January 2016).
22. TNA, CAB 129/124/33. Defence Review: The Statement on the Defence Estimates 1966, Part I.
23. *Ibid.*
24. B. Gunston, *Phantom*. (Runnymede: Ian Allen Limited, 1984), 96 & 10.
25. I. Speller, 'Limited War and Crisis Management.' In *British Naval Aviation – The First 100 Years*. Farnham: Ashgate Publishing Limited (2011), 170; Gunston, *Phantom*, 16.
26. Speller, *Limited War*, 170.
27. Hampshire, *The Battle for CVA01*, 182.
28. TNA, DEFE 69/343. Templer Report on the Rationalisation of Air Power 1965.
29. RAF Historical Society, 'Journal 11 – Air Force Policy in the 1950s and 1960s.' http://www. rafmuseum. org. uk/documents/Research/RAF-Historical-Society-Journals/Journal-11-Sir%20Frank-Cooper-on-Air-Force-Policy-in-the-1950s-1960s. pdf (accessed 17 January 2016).
30. *Ibid.*
31. The Panavia Tornado entered operational service with the RAF in June 1982 when 9 Squadron formed at RAF Honington. RAF Historical Society, 'Journal 27A – Birth of Tornado.' http://www. rafmuseum. org. uk/documents/Research/RAF-Historical-Society-Journals/Journal-27A-Seminar-Birth-of-Tornado. pdf (accessed 17 January 2016).
32. TNA, AIR 8/2629, The Harrier aircraft and the RAF position on maritime VSTOL.
33. TNA, AVIA 18/3473, Harrier GR Mk1: sea trials on HMS *Blake*; Marston, *Harrier Boys Volume One*, 28 and F.K. Mason, *Harrier*. (Wellingborough: Patrick Stevens Limited, 1986), 125.
34. TNA, AIR 8/2629. *Maritime VSTOL*.
35. Consisting of three flights of five aircraft, a single aircraft to support non-embarked training duties, a two-seat training aircraft, and a reserve of eight

aircraft. TNA, DEFE 72/257. Aircraft Specification No 287 D&P: Sea Harrier Fighter, Reconnaissance and Strike.

36. TNA, DEFE 13/1121. Harrier (including Sea Harrier): Discussions on Operational Requirements and Development, 1975.
37. The name Sea Harrier was officially adopted from 16 July 1975. TNA, DEFE 71/233. Sea Harrier training.
38. TNA, DEFE 4/279. Chiefs of Staff Committee Meeting Minutes, 29 November 1973.
39. *Ibid.*
40. *Ibid.*
41. TNA, DEFE 13/1121. Harrier Operational Requirements.
42. *Ibid.*
43. *Ibid.*
44. TNA, AIR 8/2629. Maritime VSTOL.
45. Imperial War Museum, 'Braithwaite, David (Oral History).' https://www. iwm. org. uk/collections/item/object/80032611 (accessed 29 November 2018).
46. TNA, DEFE 13/1121. Harrier Operational Requirements.
47. Fleet Air Arm Archives, *Record Book, 800 Naval Air Squadron*.
48. Fleet Air Arm Archives, *Record Book, 801 Naval Air Squadron*.
49. In 1978, additional funding allowed the purchase of ten further Sea Harriers to maintain an aircraft establishment of sixteen aircraft until 1995. TNA, DEFE 71/126. Correspondence about Sea Harrier and the Advanced STOVL aircraft.
50. Burden, *The Air War*, 230-235.
51. Hobson, *Falklands Air War*, 71-2. The follow-on force of Sea Harriers included five aircraft held in storage at RAF St Athan, two jets from Yeovilton and the remaining aircraft came directly from the production line at Dunsfold. Burden, *The Air War*, 223.
52. R. Westrum, *Sidewinder*. (Annapolis: Naval Institute Press, 1999), 191.
53. TNA, DEFE 13/1228. Sidewinder 9L Procurement.
54. *Ibid.*
55. *Ibid.*
56. *Ibid.*
57. R. Westrum, *Sidewinder*, 195.
58. TNA, DEFE 13/1228. Sidewinder Procurement.
59. *Ibid.*
60. Freedman, *Official History Volume 2*, 54.
61. D. Brown, *The Royal Navy and the Falklands War*. (London: Leo Cooper, 1987), 87.
62. TNA, DEFE 69/1112. Operation Corporate, Falklands Conflict: air matters.

63. TNA, DEFE 69/844. Operation Corporate, Falklands Conflict: HMS *Invincible*; campaign diary.
64. Freedman, *Official History Volume 2*, 386.
65. *Ibid.*, 387.
66. Morgan, *Hostile Skies*, 186.
67. Ward, *Sea Harrier*, 356.
68. D. Wood and D. Dempster, *The Narrow Margin*. (Barnsley: Pen and Sword Aviation, 2010), 84.
69. A. Preston, *Sea Combat off the Falklands*. (London: Willow Books, 1982), 14.
70. Marston, *Harrier Boys Volume One*, 102; TNA, DEFE 71/233. Sea Harrier training. Peter Squire who would later become the Chief of the Air Staff of the RAF during the period 2000-2003.
71. Allied Command Europe; Supreme Allied Commander Europe; Marston, *Harrier Boys Volume One*, 81.
72. As an example of the unit's role, 1 (Fighter) Squadron had recently returned from Exercise Arctic Express – a deployment to Tromso in northern Norway. TNA, AIR 27/3525. No 1 (Fighter) Squadron (Falklands Conflict).
73. Air Vice-Marshal Ken Hayr, the Assistant Chief of Air Staff (Operations), during the Falklands Conflict, was also the squadron commander of 1 (Fighter) Squadron when it deployed on to HMS *Ark Royal* eleven years previously. RAF Historical Society, *Journal 30*; Marston, *Harrier Boys Volume One*, 82.
74. Pook, *RAF Harrier Ground Attack*, viii.
75. TNA, AIR 27/3525.1 Squadron.
76. *Ibid.*
77. Marston, *Harrier Boys Volume One*, 83.
78. *Ibid.*
79. Burden, *The Air War*, 372.
80. Pook, *RAF Harrier Ground Attack*, 3. Pook identified the *Armee de l'Air* aircraft as a Mirage V. *Ibid*., 5. However, it is more probable that the aircraft was a Mirage IIIBE aircraft from ECT2.2 based in Dijon, as Burden stated. Burden, *The Air War*, 372. Hobson also agreed with Burden that the aircraft was a two-seat Mirage III. Hobson, *Falklands Air War*, 31.
81. TNA, AIR 27/3525.1 Squadron.
82. *Ibid*; 'The splash target was a sledge-like device towed behind an RAF launch to throw up a plume of water for us to aim at.' Pook, *RAF Harrier Ground Attack,* 213.
83. Burden, *The Air War*, 372.
84. Marston, *Harrier Boys Volume One*, 83.
85. Burden, *The Air War*, 372.

86. TNA, DEFE 69/1112. Air Matters.
87. TNA, AIR 27/3525.1 Squadron.
88. Marston, *Harrier Boys Volume One*, 89.
89. *Ibid*.
90. A. Brookes, *Vulcan Units of the Cold War*. (Oxford: Osprey, 2009), 66.
91. TNA, AIR 20/13113. Operation Corporate, Falklands Conflict: bombing raids on Port Stanley airfield.
92. TNA, AVIA 54/95. Design Branch Specification B35/46: medium range bomber.
93. The first operational Vulcan squadron was 83 Squadron based at RAF Waddington. http://www. raf. mod. uk/history/83squadron. cfm (accessed 21 February 2016).
94. J. Jefford, 'The View from the Back – The Vulcan Nav/Attack System.' *RAF Historical Society – The Vulcan*. (2014), 57.
95. Brookes, *Vulcan Units of the Cold War*, 25. Jefford. *View from the Back*, 57.
96. N. Baldwin, 'The Post-QRA Era, 1969-1984.' *RAF Historical Society – The Vulcan*. (2014), 65.
97. RAF Historical Society. *Journal 11*.
98. TNA, AIR 27/3577. No 44 (Rhodesia) Squadron (Falklands Conflict).
99. TNA, FCO 7/3730. Arms sales to Argentina: Policy.
100. TNA, FO 371/114053. Supply of Canberra aircraft by UK to Argentine.
101. Rivas, *Wings of the Malvinas*, 32.
102. TNA, FO 371/119893. Air Force of Argentina.
103. TNA, FO 371/155855. Air Force.
104. TNA, FO 371/173756. Air Attaché's annual report.
105. TNA, FO 371/119893. Air Force of Argentina.
106. TNA, FO 371/184660. Air Attaché's Annual Review; aircraft sales.
107. TNA, FO 371/155855. Air Force.
108. TNA, FO 371/184660. Air Attaché's Annual Review.
109. TNA, FCO 7/1100. Defence Attaché's annual report on Argentine armed forces 1968.
110. TNA, FCO 46/3246. UK Defence sales to Argentina.
111. TNA, FCO 7/3730. Arms sales to Argentina.
112. *Ibid*.
113. *Ibid*.
114. *Ibid*.
115. TNA, FCO 7/3874. Arms sales policy to Argentina.
116. TNA, FCO 46/3246. Defence Sales to Argentina.
117. TNA, FCO 7/1492. Sale of military aircraft to Argentina.

118. TNA, FCO 7/4088. Sale of defence equipment to Argentina.
119. *Ibid.*
120. *Ibid.*
121. TNA, FO 371/155855. Air Force.
122. Higham, *Why Air Forces Fail*, 233.
123. *Ibid.*, 236.
124. Rivas, *Wings of the Malvinas*, 32.
125. TNA, FO 371/119893. Air Force of Argentina.
126. TNA, FCO 7/3578. Armed forces of Argentina.
127. TNA, DEFE 58/273. Strike Command Intelligence Branch: Operation Corporate (Falklands Conflict): Results of Actions Against UK forces; Argentinian Air Defences, May 1982 – October 1985.
128. *Ibid.*
129. TNA, FO 371/103202. Report on the Argentine Air Force for 1952.
130. TNA, FO 371/155855. Air Force.
131. TNA, FO 371/184660. Air Attaché's Annual Review.
132. TNA, FCO 7/1886. State of the armed forces in Argentina.
133. TNA, FCO 7/3464. Armed Forces of Argentina.
134. TNA, DEFE 68/473. Argentine force capabilities.
135. Burden, *The Air War*, 116; Rivas. *Wings of the Malvinas*, 28.
136. TNA, FCO 7/1100. Defence Attaché's Report *1968*.
137. Burden, *The Air War*, 39.
138. *Ibid.*, 110.
139. Briasco, *Falklands – Witness of Battles*, 10.
140. Rivas, *Wings of the Malvinas*, 133, 118 and 250.
141. TNA, FCO 7/4566. Falkland Islands conflict: military planning.
142. Rivas, *Wings of the Malvinas*, 133.
143. *Ibid.*, 119.
144. TNA, DEFE 58/273. Actions against UK Forces.
145. S.M. Huertas and J.R. Briasco, *Argentine Air Forces in the Falklands Conflict*. (Poole: Arms and Armour Press, 1987), 29.
146. Burden, *The Air War*, 129.
147. *Ibid.*
148. *Ibid.*
149. J. Godden, *Harrier – Ski-Jump to Victory*. (Oxford: Brassey's Publishers Ltd, 1983), 66.
150. Rivas, *Wings of the Malvinas*, 163.
151. Ethell, *Air War South Atlantic*, 229.
152. Burden, *The Air War*, 34.

153. R. Scheina, 'Super Etendard; Super Squadron.' *US Naval Institute Proceedings*. Volume 109 (1983): 135.
154. R. Braybook, 'Reassessing the Lessons of the Falklands War.' *Asia-Pacific Defence Reporter*. (April/May 1992): 41; R. Scheina, Super *Etendard*, 135.
155. Burden, *The Air War*, 34.
156. R. Scheina, *Super Etendard*, 135. Hobson. *Falklands Air War*, 166.
157. TNA, DEFE 69/1112. Air Matters.
158. J. Corum, 'Argentine Airpower in the Falklands War – An Operational View.' *Air and Space Power Journal*. Volume XVI, Number 3 (2002): 68.
159. TNA, FO 371/103202. Argentine Air Force 1952; TNA. FO 371/114053. Supply of Canberra. Boyle was Air Officer Commanding 1 Group RAF at the time and served as Chief of the Air Staff between 1956 and 1960.
160. *Ibid*.
161. *Ibid*.
162. Burden, *The Air War*, 90.
163. Rivas, *Wings of the Malvinas*, 25.
164. TNA, FO 371/114053. Supply of Canberra.
165. *Ibid*., 29.
166. Burden, *The Air War*, 90.
167. *Ibid*.
168. Rivas, *Wings of the Malvinas*, 27.
169. Burden, *The Air War*, 144.
170. Rivas, *Wings of the Malvinas*, 206.
171. I. Guevara y Moyano, *Latin American Fighters*. (Houston: Harpia Publishing, 2009), 21.
172. Rivas, *Wings of the Malvinas*, 29.
173. TNA, FCO 46/3245. Defence Sales to Argentina.
174. Burden, *The Air War*, 95.
175. Rivas, *Wings of the Malvinas*, 103.
176. Hobson, *Falklands Air War*, 45.
177. A Pucara was responsible for the only Argentine air-to-air kill of the Conflict when it shot down a Scout helicopter on 28 May. Rivas, *Wings of the Malvinas*, 113.
178. Burden, *The Air War*, 29.
179. *Ibid*., 45.
180. Hobson, *Falklands Air War*, 165.
181. Burden, *The Air War*, 31.
182. Rivas, *Wings of the Malvinas*, 233.
183. Burden, *The Air War*, 45.

184. Rivas, *Wings of the Malvinas*, 233.
185. Clapp, *Amphibious Assault Falklands*, 111.
186. For example, Rivas, *Wings of the Malvinas*, 193.
187. On 13 June, a ground launched Exocet struck HMS *Glamorgan*. Although damaged and with the loss of 13 sailors, the ship remained afloat. Freedman, *Official History Volume 2*, 624.

Chapter 3 – Air Power prior to Operation Sutton – *Bautismo de Fuego!*

1. Trans: 'baptism of fire.'
2. TNA, PREM 19/623. Relations with Argentina Position of the Falkland Islands, 1982.
3. TNA, AIR 27/2799. No 83 Squadron: Operations Record Book. With appendices.
4. TNA, AIR 27/2807. No 101 Squadron: Operations Record Book.
5. Clapp, *Amphibious Assault Falklands*, 118. The amphibious force eventually departed from Ascension Island but would not arrive off the Falkland Islands until 18 May. Freedman, *Official History Volume 2*, 466.
6. Control of the air is defined as freedom, over a given period of time, to use a volume of airspace for our own purposes while, if necessary, denying or constraining its use by an opponent. United Kingdom. *UK Air and Space Doctrine*, 3-3. UK doctrine defines sea control as the condition that exists when there is freedom of action to use an area of the sea for one's own purpose for a period of time, and if necessary, deny its use to an opponent. United Kingdom. Ministry of Defence. Joint Doctrine Publication 0-10: British Maritime Doctrine. (Shrivenham: The Development, Concepts and Doctrine Centre, 2011), 2-10.
7. Clapp, *Amphibious Assault Falklands*, 118. Before 12 May, the British military aim was somewhat ambiguous, 'prepare to land with a view to repossessing the Falkland Islands.' Admiral Sir John Woodward, in 'The Falklands War', seminar held 5 June 2002 (Centre for Contemporary British History, 2005, http://www. icbh. ac. uk/witnness/falklands,), 49.
8. Freedman, *Official History Volume 2*, 435.
9. Clausewitz, *On War*, 485-486.
10. TNA, DEFE 58/258. HQ 11 Group: Operation Corporate (Falklands Conflict); operations/training aspects.
11. J. Burns, *The Land That Lost Its Heroes*. (London: Bloomsbury, 2002), 130.
12. TNA, FCO 7/4087. Armed forces of Argentina.
13. Rivas, *Wings of the Malvinas*, 118.
14. *Ibid.*

15. Freedman, *Official History Volume 2*, 286.
16. The figures appear to reflect the total fleet size rather than the deployed force. Ethell, *Air War South Atlantic*, 20.
17. Hobson, *Falklands Air War*.
18. Burden, *The Air War*, 21, 34 and 39.
19. TNA, DEFE 58/262. HQ 18 Group: Operation Corporate (Falklands Conflict); lessons learned.
20. Rivas, *Wings of the Malvinas*, 165 and 206.
21. Hobson, *Falklands Air War*, 40.
22. Rivas, *Wings of the Malvinas,* 132.
23. *Ibid.*, 183.
24. *Ibid.*, 132.
25. Ethell, *Air War South Atlantic*, 28.
26. The A-4Q Skyhawk force disembarked from ARA *Veinticinco de Mayo* to join its *Comando de Aviación Naval* counterparts at Rio Grande on 9 May. Burden, *The Air War*, 20.
27. The contemporary Principles of War are stated in United Kingdom, Ministry of Defence. Joint Defence Publication 0-01: UK Defence Doctrine. (Shrivenham: The Development, Concepts and Doctrine Centre, 2014), 30.
28. M. Bilton and P. Kominsky, *Speaking Out* (London: Andre Deutsch, 1989), 91.
29. Ward, *Sea Harrier*, 179.
30. P. Jacobs, *Staying the Distance.* (London: Frontline Books, 2011), 235.
31. TNA, AIR 27/3525.1 Squadron.
32. *Ibid.*
33. Burden, *The Air War*, 224 and 387.
34. Hobson, *Falklands Air War*, 1.
35. RAF Historical Society, *Journal 30*, 180.
36. However, Operation Corporate did force the cancellation of 1 (Fighter) Squadron participation in Exercise Maple Flag 9, but only after the Squadron's deployment to Canada. TNA, AIR 27/3525.1 Squadron; Although 3 (Fighter) Squadron did partake in Exercise Maple Flag, 4 Squadron only completed the work-up phase and did not deploy. TNA, AIR 27/3527. No 3 (Fighter) Squadron) and TNA, AIR 27/3528. No 4 Squadron; The squadron commander, Wing Commander Holland, was killed in a flying accident during one of these practice field deployments in early June 1982. *Ibid.*
37. Marston, *Harrier Boys Volume One*, 76.
38. TNA, AIR 27/3525.1 Squadron.
39. Both RAF Germany Harrier squadrons provided two pilots each to convert to the Sea Harrier. 3 (Fighter) Squadron pilots, Flight Lieutenants Brown and

Leeming, were selected on 19 April, and both deployed with 809 Naval Air Squadron on board MV *Atlantic Conveyor*. TNA, AIR 27/3527.3 Squadron. In contrast, the 4 Squadron pilots, Squadron Leader Thomas and Flight Lieutenant Gibbons, were selected on 2 June for conversion to the Sea Harrier. TNA, AIR 27/3528.4 Squadron.

40. TNA, AIR 27/3527.3 Squadron.
41. Hobson, *Falklands Air War*, 93.
42. K.L. Privratsky, *Logistics in the Falkland Islands*. (Barnsley: Pen and Sword, 2014), 78.
43. Rivas, *Wings of the Malvinas*, 59.
44. Moro, *South Atlantic Conflict*, 113.
45. Privratsky, *Logistics in Falklands War*, 83; Freedman, *Official History Volume 2*, 564.
46. The six Landing Ship Logistic comprised: RFAs *Sir Geraint*, *Sir Lancelot*, *Sir Percivale*, *Sir Galahad*, *Sir Tristram*, and *Sir Bedivere*; The Landing Platform Docks were HMS *Intrepid* and HMS *Fearless*; Hobson, *Falklands Air War*, 42.
47. Hobson, *Falklands Air War*, 42.
48. D. Hart-Dyke, *Four Weeks in May*. (London: Atlantic Books, 2007), 147.
49. ARA *Hercules* and ARA *Santisima Trinidad*. Moro, *South Atlantic Conflict*, 148.
50. Burden, *The Air War*, 34.
51. The aircraft carrier HMS *Invincible* also employed the Sea Dart surface-to-air missile capability.
52. HMS *Broadsword* and *Brilliant*.
53. Freedman, *Official History Volume 2*, 774.
54. Johnson-Allen, *Without Us*, 214.
55. Parry, *Down South*, 177.
56. Clapp, *Amphibious Assault Falklands*, 133.
57. Rivas, *Wings of the Malvinas*, 135.
58. TNA, PREM 19/647. Handling of the Falklands.
59. Freedman, *Official History Volume 2*, 473 and 57.
60. Hobson, *Falklands Air War*, 56; Ward, *Sea Harrier*, 224.
61. TNA, DEFE 58/273. Actions against UK Forces.
62. Freedman, *Official History Volume 2*, 286; Burden, *The Air War*, 21 and Ethell, *Air War South Atlantic*, 72.
63. Cordesman, *Volume 3*, 253.
64. Argentine Air Force Website, 'Air Operations 1 May 1982.' http://www.fuerzaaerea. mil. ar/conflicto/dias/may01. html (accessed 5 January 2015).
65. Combining the total planned missions within Annexes C and D shows that there were plans for 64 mainland combat air missions on 1 May. However,

analysis of Annex A shows that 60 missions were able to launch successfully. The difference between the two figures reflects the ground aborts by two Daggers, and two cancelled Super Etendard sorties.

66. See Annex J Serials 1 and 2 for further details.
67. Hobson, *Falklands Air War*, 41.
68. Although Rivas agreed with the timing of the move, he suggested that the Daggers flew to their home base at Tandil. Rivas, *Wings of the Malvinas*, 166. In contrast, Burden believed that the event took place on the evening of 30 April but did not specify the destination of the aircraft. Burden, *The Air War*, 146; Hobson, *Falklands Air War*, 42.
69. Rivas, *Wings of the Malvinas*, 166.
70. Data sourced from Annexes A, C to E.
71. Freedman, *Official History Volume 2*, 286.
72. Galland, The *First*, 41.
73. The Harrier Forward Operating Base at Port San Carlos, colloquially known as HMS *Sheathbill* or Sid's Strip, became operational on 5 June. The Forward Operating Base was used to support over 150 Sea Harrier and Harrier GR3 sorties during the remainder of the Conflict. Cordesman, *Volume 3*, 317.
74. A. Ogilvy, '801 Naval Air Squadron.' In *The Navy Review*. Volume 71, Number 2. (April 1983), 123.
75. Ward, *Sea Harrier*, 338.
76. TNA, DEFE 69/836.801 Naval Air Squadron flight report.
77. 1424 sorties flown for a flight time of 1560:30 hours. Ogilvy, *801 Naval Air Squadron*, 123; TNA, DEFE 72/257. *Sea Harrier Specification*.
78. See Annex J Serial 21 for further details.
79. Ward, *Sea Harrier*, 283.
80. TNA, DEFE 69/836.801 Naval Air Squadron flight report.
81. Ratio derived from *Ibid*.
82. S. Edwards, *My Secret Falklands War*. (Sussex: Book Guild Publishing, 2014), 41.
83. TNA, AIR 20/13102. Operation Fingent.
84. E. Southby-Tailyour, *Exocet Falklands*. (Barnsley: Pen and Sword Military, 2014), 88; Freedman, *Official History Volume 2*, 611.
85. TNA, AIR 20/13030. Operation Corporate (Falklands Conflict): Argentine combat reports.
86. Moro, *South Atlantic Conflict*, 112.
87. Freedman, *Official History Volume 2*, 287.
88. Moro, *South Atlantic Conflict*, 106.

89. Freedman, *Official History Volume 2*, 286.
90. Moro, *South Atlantic Conflict*, 116.
91. As demonstrated by comparing the data contained within Annexes C and D.
92. Parry, *Down South*, 41.
93. Burden, *The Air War*, 48.
94. *Ibid.*, 50.
95. Rivas, *Wings of the Malvinas,* 245.
96. B.W. Watson and P.M. Dunn, *Military Lessons of the Falklands War – Views from the United States* (London: Arms and Armour Press), 38.
97. A 'soft kill' occurred when the attack aircraft jettisons its weapons to make it more nimble and evade the fighter aircraft before returning to base without completing its mission.
98. A 'hard kill' occurred when the air defences successfully engaged and shot down the attacking aircraft.
99. Not included in these figures are the three attack aircraft shot down after dropping their weapons. On 12 May, the Argentines lost three A-4B Skyhawks in two separate attacks on HMS *Glasgow*. A Sea Wolf missile fired by HMS *Brilliant* destroyed one aircraft, another flew into the sea in an attempt to evade another missile, and Argentine air defences at Goose Green shot down the last aircraft. Hobson, *Falklands*, 65-66.
100. *Ibid.*, 133.
101. Rivas, *Wings of the Malvinas*, 243.
102. *Fuerza Aérea Argentina, Historia, Tomo VI, Volumen 1*, 182.
103. TNA, AIR 8/3109. Operation Corporate (Falklands Conflict): air intelligence and assessments.
104. Freedman, *Official History Volume 2*, 281.
105. And, arguably, the *Comando de Aviación Naval;* Burden, *The Air War*, 117.
106. Hobson, *Falklands Air War*, 137.
107. Ethell, *Air War South Atlantic*, 208.
108. O'Connell's and Rivas' figures are broadly similar to those stated by Hobson. O'Connell suggested that 435 tonnes of cargo flew into the Islands, with 264 wounded evacuated. J.F. O'Connell, *The Effectiveness of Air Power in the Twentieth Century, Part 3 (1945-2000)* (Lincoln: iUniverse, 2006), 120. In contrast, Rivas suggested that the C-130 Hercules planned 74 sorties, of which 61 launched and 31 landed at Stanley. The missions transported 514 personnel and 416.8 tonnes of cargo to the Islands and recovered 264 passengers back to the mainland. Rivas, *Wings of the Malvinas*, 70.
109. Bicheno, *Razor's Edge*, 126.
110. *Ibid.*

Chapter 4 – Air Power during Operation Sutton: *Muerte Negra* or *Los Moscardones*?

1. Warden, *Air Campaign*, 7.
2. The force also lost the use of a fourth Sea Harrier pilot during the first phase of the campaign. Flight Lieutenant Penfold took no further part in air operations after being deeply affected by the outcome of his Dagger engagement on 1 May. Morgan, *Hostile Skies*, 182.
3. Hobson, *Falklands Air War*, 71-72.
4. Ward, *Sea Harrier*, 255.
5. *Ibid.*
6. Pook, *RAF Harrier Ground Attack*, 34.
7. *Ibid.*, 23.
8. Air Historical Branch, CTTO/26/2/Ops. Tactical Lessons.
9. Clapp, *Amphibious Assault Falklands*, 95.
10. Freedman, *Official History Volume 2*, 466.
11. *Ibid.*, 449.
12. *Ibid.*
13. Following the loss of two aircraft on 1 May, the Canberra force withdrew from combat operations and began to train for low-level night attack missions. Rivas, *Wings of the Malvinas*, 92.
14. Freedman, *Official History Volume 2*, 457.
15. Jacobs, *Stay The Distance*, 242.
16. TNA, PREM 19/647. Handling of the Falklands.
17. Freedman, *Official History Volume 2*, 457.
18. *Ibid.*
19. TNA, PREM 19/647. Handling of the Falklands.
20. Freedman, *Official History Volume 2*, 458.
21. M. Thatcher, *The Downing Street Years* (London: Harper Press, 1993), 194.
22. Radar Malvinas, 'Plan de Operaciones 2/82 – *Mantenimiento de la Soberania*.' http://www. radarmalvinas. com. ar/document_guerra/ABR07%2082%20 plan%20cae. pdf (accessed 20 December 2016).
23. Trans: 'Maintaining Sovereignty.' Moro, *South Atlantic Conflict*, 227.
24. *Ibid.*
25. *Ibid.*
26. Unlike the other aircraft types, Rivas did not state the number of A-4B Skyhawks deployed. However, analysis of the Squadron's activities on 21 May indicated that fifteen different A-4B Skyhawk airframes were used on missions that day. Rivas, *Wings of the Malvinas*, 136-139.
27. Strange, *Centers of Gravity.*

28. The initial assault ships were not the only vessels to attempt to enter San Carlos during the period of Operation Sutton. Follow on forces included RFA *Sir Bedivere* that arrived at San Carlos during the night of 23/24 May. Brown, *Royal Navy*, 210. Also, the MV *Atlantic Conveyor* planned to arrive in San Carlos Water on 26 May. Johnson-Allen, *Without Us*, 87.
29. The seven escorts were HMS *Antrim*, *Argonaut*, *Ardent*, *Plymouth*, *Yarmouth*, *Brilliant*, and *Broadsword*. Freedman, *Official History Volume 2*, 469.
30. Southby-Tailyour, *Reasons in Writing*, 148.
31. Freedman, *Official History Volume 2*, 466.
32. Clapp, *Amphibious Assault Falklands*, 80.
33. Privratsky, *Logistics in Falklands War*, 98.
34. *Ibid.*, 76.
35. The data is from TNA, ADM 202/816/2. Commanders Diary: Headquarters 3 Commando Brigade – Operation Corporate, June 1982 – March 1984.
36. *Ibid.*, 105; Clapp, *Amphibious Assault Falklands*, 81.
37. Privratsky, *Logistics in Falklands War*, 115.
38. *Ibid.,* 109.
39. Thompson, *No Picnic*, 78.
40. For example, Cordesman, *Volume 3*.
41. S. Huertas, 'San Carlos: Insights into an Intense Battle.' *Air Enthusiast*. (September/October 1988): 21. Freedman. *Official History Volume 2*, 471.
42. Higham, *Why Air Forces Fail*, 234.
43. *Ibid.*
44. Burden, *The Air War*, 50.
45. Rivas, *Wings of the Malvinas*, 272.
46. *Ibid.*, 276.
47. Burden, *The Air War*, 48.
48. Clapp, *Amphibious Assault Falklands*, 133.
49. *Ibid.*, 127. In reality, ARA *San Luis* and its sister Type 209 submarine, ARA *Salta*, were operating outside the Total Exclusion Zone during Operation Sutton due to technical defects. Freedman, *Official History Volume 2*, 552.
50. *Ibid.*, 470.
51. Thompson, *No Picnic*, 68.
52. Bicheno, *Razor's Edge*, 147.
53. Clapp, *Amphibious Assault Falklands*, 123.
54. Southby-Tailyour, *Exocet Falklands*, 57.
55. Southby-Tailyour, *Reasons in Writing*, 126.
56. *Ibid.*, 112.

57. TNA, DEFE 67/128. Operation Corporate, Falklands Conflict: Meteorological Records, October 1982.
58. See Annex A for details.
59. Ethell, *Air War South Atlantic*, 130, Burden. *The Air War*, 120 and 135, Rivas, *Wings of the Malvinas*, 138 and 178. Moro, *South Atlantic Conflict*, 229 and Argentine Air Force Website, 'Air Operations 22 May 1982.' http://www. fuerzaaerea. mil. ar/conflicto/dias/may22. html (accessed 9 February 2016).
60. Moro, *South Atlantic Conflict*, 232.
61. Ward, *Sea Harrier*, 318.
62. See Annex B for further details.
63. Woodward, *One Hundred Days*, 372.
64. Ward, *Sea Harrier*, 323.
65. Analysis of Rivas' data showed that, and unlike their British counterparts, many Argentine aircrew flew infrequently during the Conflict. As a result, they were less familiar with procedures and the topography of the Islands. Rivas, *Wings of the Malvinas*.
66. See Annex G for further details.
67. Freedman, *Official History Volume 2*, 483.
68. *Ibid*.
69. L. Freedman and V. Gamba-Stonehouse, *Signals of War*. (London: Faber and Faber Limited, 1990), 361.
70. Freedman, *Official History Volume 2*, 487.
71. Murguizur, *An Argentine Point of View*, 140.
72. Thompson, *No Picnic*, 85.
73. Burden, *The Air War*, 217.
74. Rivas, *Wings of the Malvinas*, 93.
75. R. Schiena, 'Argentine Jointness in the Malvinas.' *Joint Forces Quarterly*. Number 5 (Summer 1994): 99.
76. *Fuerza Aérea Argentina*, *Historia, Tomo VI, Volumen 1,* 224.
77. I. Inskip, *Ordeal by Exocet*. (London: Frontline Books, 2002), 209.
78. V.L. Autiero, 'The Attack on HMS *Argonaut*.' *Aerospacio*. *Numero 468 (1989)*: 36.
79. TNA, AIR 20/13030. Argentine Combat Reports.
80. Radar Malvinas, '*Plan de Operaciones de la Fuerza de Tareas Aeronaval No 02/82*.' http://www. radarmalvinas. com. ar/document_guerra/ABR15%20 82%20plan%20ops%20aeronaval. pdf (accessed 23 December 2016).
81. Armada Argentina, *Conflicto Del Atlantico Sur*, 16.
82. TNA, AIR 20/13030. Argentine Combat Reports.

83. Clapp, *Amphibious Assault Falklands*, 150.
84. Freedman, *Official History Volume 2*, 472.
85. Watson, *Views from United States*, 45.
86. *Ibid*., 190.
87. Burden, *The Air War*, 116.
88. TNA, PREM 19/624. Relations with Argentina Position of the Falkland Islands – Part 13, 3-5 May 1982.
89. Freedman, *Official History Volume 2*, 264.
90. Huertas, *Tabanos at War*, 36.
91. *Ibid*.
92. Freedman, *Official History Volume 2*, 77.
93. F. Fursden, *Falklands Aftermath* (London: Leo Cooper, 1988), 82.
94. Although ten Peruvian Mirage Vs arrived at Tandil, the Dagger's home base, on 4 June, they did not participate in the Conflict. Rivas, *Wings of the Malvinas*, 165.
95. S. Rivas and J.C. Cicalesi, *Latin American Mirages*. (Houston: Harpia Publishing, 2010), 25.
96. TNA, FCO 7/4436. Arms Sales to Argentina by Other Countries.
97. Southby-Tailyour, *Exocet Falklands*, 51.
98. Rivas, *Latin American Mirages*, 51.
99. TNA, FCO 7/4436. Arms Sales by Other Countries.
100. Margaret Thatcher Foundation, 'Margaret Thatcher's Falklands Memoir.' http://www. margaretthatcher. org/archive/1982retpap2. asp (accessed 29 June 2015).
101. See Annex G for further details.
102. Rivas, *Wings of the Malvinas*, 220.
103. *Ibid*., 118.
104. TNA, DEFE 69/836.801 Naval Air Squadron flight report.
105. Clapp, *Amphibious Assault Falklands*, 105.

Chapter 5 – Air Power Post-Operation Sutton – Stanley or Bust!

1. Van Der Bijl, 5th *Infantry Brigade*, 45.
2. Freedman, *Official History Volume 2*, 597.
3. TNA, FCO 7/4565. Falkland Islands conflict: military planning.
4. Clapp, *Amphibious Assault Falklands*, 181.
5. *Ibid*.
6. Thompson, *No Picnic*, 79.
7. *Ibid*., 80.
8. Freedman, *Official History Volume 2*, 586.

9. Van Der Bijl, 5th *Infantry Brigade*, 57.
10. Vaux, *March to the South Atlantic*, 232.
11. Brown, *Royal Navy*, 107.
12. Burden, *The Air War*, 403.
13. *Ibid.*, 268.
14. Brown, *Royal Navy,* 113.
15. Middlebrook, *The Argentinian Fight*, 132.
16. Brown, *Royal Navy,* 122 and 157.
17. HMS *Active, Ambuscade, Avenger*, and *Antelope*, HMS *Minerva, Penelope*, and *Andromeda*.
18. TNA, AIR 27/3525.1 Squadron.
19. Gardiner, *The Yompers*, 98.
20. Vaux, *March to the South Atlantic*, 138.
21. Freedman, *Official History Volume 2*, 584.
22. *Ibid.*, 564,
23. Initial estimates suggested that a company-sized unit occupied the Goose Green Garrison. Thompson, *No Picnic*, 90. However, Freedman reported that the garrison was actually significantly larger and encompassed 150 air force personnel and had a combat strength of 550. Freedman, *Official History Volume 2*, 566 and 584.
24. According to Vaux and based on his first sightings of Argentine prisoners of war, 'press speculation about starvation or widespread exposure amongst them was rubbish. It was all too evident that they were better off than we were for material comforts.' Vaux, *March to the South Atlantic*, 134; Freedman, *Official History Volume 2*, 587.
25. TNA, DEFE 69/868. Operation Corporate, Falklands Conflict: capabilities of Argentinian forces.
26. United States of America, United States Army. Combat History Analysis Study Effort (CHASE): Progress Report (Washington DC: US Army Concepts Analysis Agency, August 1986) 3-20.
27. Freedman, *Official History Volume 2*, 587.
28. Thompson, *No Picnic*, 79.
29. TNA, AIR 27/3525.1 Squadron.
30. Hobson, *Falklands Air War*, 128.
31. Marston, *Harrier Boys Volume One*, 95.
32. TNA, AIR 24/3299. HQ Strike Command (Falklands Conflict).
33. Marston, *Harrier Boys Volume One*, 97; The jammer, known as 'Blue Eric,' was housed within one of the two Harrier under-fuselage gun pods. Ethell, *Air War South Atlantic*, 154.

34. TNA, AIR 24/3299. Strike Command; TNA. AIR 27/3525.1 Squadron; Black Buck 5 and 6, the two Shrike-armed Vulcan missions, were conducted on 31 May and 3 June, respectively. Burden, *The Air War*, 365-7.
35. *Ibid.*, 382-5.
36. TNA, AIR 27/3527.3 Squadron.
37. Burden, *The Air War*, 226.
38. Consisting of ten A-4 Skyhawks and nine Daggers.
39. See Figure 4.1 in Chapter 4 for further details.
40. Wood, *The Narrow Margin*, 212.
41. Morgan, *Hostile Skies*, 276.
42. Hobson, *Falklands Air War*, 90.
43. Rivas, *Wings of the Malvinas*, 160.
44. *Ibid.*
45. *Ibid.*, 29 and 86.
46. See Annex H for further details.
47. Moro indicated that in the early hours of 27 May, two Canberras destroyed 'a brand-new earth satellite station antenna' and damaged a hospital facility at Ajax Bay, Moro, *South Atlantic Conflict*, 252. Likewise, on 31 May, two Canberras damaged the 846 Naval Air Squadron dispersal area. *Ibid.*, 281. However, Burden reported that the first raid 'did not cause any damage or casualties to the British forces. With regard to the second raid at Fern Valley Creek, it also caused no serious injuries or damage, although the bombing created a good deal of alarm.' Burden, *The Air War*, 91.
48. Southby-Tailyour, *Reasons in Writing*, 250.
49. *Ibid.*, 247.
50. *Ibid.*, 262.
51. Transferred to 3 Commando Brigade on 9 June. Thompson, *No Picnic*, 143.
52. Transferred from 3 Commando Brigade to 5 Infantry Brigade, upon their arrival, until 9 June. *Ibid.*, 112 and 143.
53. Moro, *South Atlantic Conflict*, 299.
54. *Ibid.*, 227.
55. The three battalions that encompassed 5 Infantry Brigade had yet to arrive on the Falkland Islands. Clapp, *Amphibious Assault Falklands*, 170.
56. TNA, AIR 20/13054. Operation Corporate (Falklands Conflict): proposed official history of the campaign; Air Historical Branch article on the RAF's roles.
57. Derived from Annex B data, the British flew 654 combat air missions over the period 27 May-14 June, which equates to a daily sortie rate of 34.
58. TNA, AIR 8/3109. Air Intelligence and Assessments.

59. Hobson, *Falklands Air War*, 101.
60. Thompson, *No Picnic*, 91.
61. Ethell, *Air War South Atlantic*, 160.
62. Morgan, *Hostile Skies*, 229.
63. Freedman, *Official History Volume 2*, 563.
64. Thompson, *No Picnic*, 91.
65. Freedman, *Official History Volume 2*, 581.
66. Pook, *RAF Harrier Ground Attack*, 116.
67. Ethell, *Air War South Atlantic*, 165.
68. Freedman, *Official History Volume 2*, 581.
69. There is extensive coverage of the controversy surrounding the last Super Etendard mission of the Falklands Conflict. See Rivas, *Wings of the Malvinas*, 249 for a balanced view on the topic. Moro tells the Argentine viewpoint of the attack. Moro, *South Atlantic Conflict*, 273-279.
70. Southby-Tailyour, *Reasons in Writing*, 304.
71. Bicheno, *Razor's Edge*, 190.
72. Margaret Thatcher Foundation, 'Margaret Thatcher's Falklands Memoir.' http://www. margaretthatcher. org/archive/1982retpap2. asp (accessed 29 June 2015).
73. Initially held in reserve, 40 Commando provided the resilience in case of such an eventuality. In contrast, the Argentine reserve had been committed and captured during the Battle for Goose Green. Gardiner, *The Yompers*, 101.
74. Bicheno, *Razor's Edge*, 283-4.
75. The British allocated the Gurkha battalion to Mount William, but the Argentines retreated from the hilltop prior to the assault. Freedman, *Official History Volume 2*, 647.
76. Specifically, several of the critical vulnerabilities shown in Table 5B; Thompson, *No Picnic*, 253.
77. Privratsky, *Logistics in Falklands War*, 163.
78. See Annex H for further details.
79. Rivas, *Wings of the Malvinas*, 162.
80. Moro, *South Atlantic Conflict*, 313
81. Freedman, *Official History Volume 2*, 637.
82. Depending on the account, the helicopter park was between 100 metres and 500 yards away from the field headquarters. Thompson, *No Picnic*, 174 and Ethell, *Air War South Atlantic*, 206.
83. Gardiner, *The Yompers*, 169.
84. Freedman, *Official History Volume 2*, 638.
85. Rivas, *Wings of the Malvinas,* 209.

86. *Ibid*, 249.
87. *Ibid*.
88. As shown in Annex B, Sea Harrier, and Harrier GR3 sorties over the period 12-13 June stood at 45 and 31 – which when aggregated over the two days is slightly higher than the norm for the phase that stood at 34 missions per day.
89. Vaux, *March to the South Atlantic*, 56.
90. Clapp, *Amphibious Assault Falklands*, 183.
91. Moro, *South Atlantic Conflict*, 332.
92. TNA, DEFE 58/273. Actions against UK Forces.
93. D. Anderson, The Falklands War 1982. (Oxford: Osprey Publishing, 2002), 86.
94. Cohen, *Volume 1*, 186.
95. Rivas, *Wings of the Malvinas*, 131.
96. Some commentators, such as Burden, suggested that *Grupo 4 de Caza*, the A-4C Skyhawk unit, flew its last operational mission on 8 June and ended the Conflict with only four airworthy aircraft. Burden, *The Air War*, 116.
97. Figures encompass most of the Sea Harrier pilots who flew during the Conflict, including those who arrived belatedly with 809 Naval Air Squadron. However, several pilot's details are missing from the primary source document. TNA, AIR 8/3112. Operation Corporate (Falklands Conflict): scientific evaluation team.
98. From the initial cadre of Sea Harrier pilots who survived the Conflict, Lieutenant Mike Watson flew the least with 45 sorties. *Ibid*.
99. T. Clancy, *Every Man a Tiger*. (London: Sidgwick and Jackson, 2000), 130.
100. United Kingdom, *The Lessons*.

Chapter 6 – Defending the British Operational Centres of Gravity – Sea Harrier: The Decisive Factor?

1. Ward, *Sea Harrier*, 269.
2. Thatcher, *The Downing Street Years*, 226.
3. Woodward, *One Hundred Days*, 118.
4. Gardiner, *The Yompers*, 7.
5. B Watson, *Views from United States,* xiii.
6. H.M. Gonzales, 'An Argentine Airman in the South Atlantic.' In *The Falklands Conflict Twenty Years On* edited by Badsey, S. et al, 80. London: Frank Cass, (2005). Gonzales describes himself as a Mirage V pilot in the book, using the original French name for the aircraft, rather than the Israeli-built aircraft, the FAA employed. To avoid confusion, the Argentine name of Dagger is applied here.

7. United Kingdom, *UK Air and Space Doctrine*.
8. Dyndal extensively covers the CVA01 debate in G.L. Dyndal, *Land Based Air Power or Aircraft Carriers?: A Case Study of the British Debate about Maritime Air Power in the 1960s*. (Farnham: Ashgate, 2012).
9. Captain R.D. Lygo, Royal Navy, Deputy Director of the Directorate of Naval Air Warfare, stated in March 1966 that airborne early warning was the most important embarked role. D. Hobbs, *The British Carrier Strike Fleet After 1945* (Barnsley: Seaforth Publishing, 2015), 419.
10. *Ibid*., 464.
11. *Ibid*., 517.
12. There were two documented occasions where Sea Harriers were vulnerable to attack by Argentine aircraft. On 21 May, while attacking a formation of three Daggers, Ward's Sea Harrier was subject to an unsuccessful gun attack by a Dagger, Ward, *Sea Harrier*, 265. On 8 June, Morgan's Sea Harrier flew in front of an unseen A-4B Skyhawk. However, due to a jammed cannon, the Argentine pilot was unable to fire. Morgan, *Hostile Skies*, 267.
13. Diagram derived from R. Shaw, *Fighter Combat*. (Maryland: United States Naval Institute, 1985), 47 and TNA, DEFE 69/1112. Air Matters. The numbers contained within each coloured circle reflect the Annex J serial number of each AIM-9L Sidewinder firing.
14. TNA, DEFE 69/1112. Air Matters.
15. R. Westrum, *Sidewinder*, 192.
16. TNA, DEFE 72/257. Sea Harrier Specification.
17. TNA, DEFE 69/1112. Air Matters.
18. Ward, *Sea Harrier*, 173.
19. Both of the engagements outside of the traditional AIM-9G Sidewinder weapon envelope were due to late target aircraft manoeuvre rather than the Sea Harrier exploiting the tactical advantage of its new weapon system.
20. TNA, DEFE 69/836.801 Naval Air Squadron flight report.
21. TNA, DEFE 67/135. Operational Evaluation Group Report Number 2/83, Operation Corporate: Reconstruction of AAW Conflict, Volume 1 – 1 May 1982.
22. TNA, DEFE 48/1162. Reconstruction and analysis of the air war during Operation Corporate (Falklands Conflict).
23. Ward, *Sea Harrier*, 302.
24. TNA, AIR 8/3112. Scientific Evaluation Team.
25. See Annex J Serials 22 and 23 for further details.
26. TNA, DEFE 72/271. Operation Corporate (Falklands Conflict): includes intelligence summaries.

27. *Ibid.*
28. Imperial War Museum, 'Ward, Nigel David "Sharkey" (Oral History)' https://www. iwm. org. uk/collections/item/object/80012551 (accessed 28 November 2018).
29. Ward, *Sea Harrier*, 93.
30. A. Clarke, 'Sea Control 97'. In *Falklands w/ Sharkey Ward.* Podcast Audio, 12 October 2015. http://cimsec. org/sea-control-97-falklands-w-sharkey-ward/19236.
31. J. Corum, *Argentine Airpower*, 62.
32. TNA, DEFE 58/274. Headquarters Strike Command Intelligence Branch: Operation Corporate Historical Record.
33. R. Westrum, *Sidewinder*, 197 and 218.
34. TNA, DEFE 58/273. Actions against UK Forces.
35. TNA, DEFE 19/276. Scientific Evaluation Team.
36. M.L. Michel, *Clashes: Air Combat over North Vietnam 1965-1972.* (Annapolis: Naval Institute Press, 1997), 287.
37. R. Westrum, *Sidewinder*, 197.
38. E.A. Cohen, *Gulf War Air Power Survey Volume 4 – Weapons, Tactics, and Training and Space Operations.* (Washington D.C. : US Government Printing Office, 1993), 116 and R. Westrum, *Sidewinder*, 219.
39. Some suggest that incorrectly cooled AIM-9L seeker heads and associated false audio tones may have led to confusion before the Canberra engagement on 1 May. TNA, DEFE 67/135. Reconstruction of AAW Conflict. Also, an experienced Harrier GR3 pilot with previous air defence experience on the Lightning, Flight Lieutenant John Leeming, was rapidly converted onto the Sea Harrier at the start of the Conflict. His transition was so rapid that he did not understand how to correctly select weapons on the Sea Harrier. Morgan, *Hostile Skies*, 175.
40. Air Historical Branch, CTTO/26/2/Ops. Tactical Lessons.
41. Freedman, *Official History Volume 2*, 287.
42. TNA, DEFE 19/276. Scientific Evaluation Team.
43. Ward, *Sea Harrier*, 270.
44. TNA, DEFE 69/836.801 Naval Air Squadron flight report.
45. Ogilvy, *801 Naval Air Squadron*, 123; TNA, DEFE 72/257. Sea Harrier Specification.
46. On 21 May, Leeming achieved a guns kill on an egressing A-4Q Skyhawk. Burden, *The Air War*, 41. Additionally, on 23 May, Morgan engaged a formation of 4 helicopters near Shag Cove and achieved a guns kill on an Agusta A-109. Morgan, *Hostile Skies*, 195.

47. On 1 June, and after damaging the enemy aircraft with an AIM-9L Sidewinder, Ward destroyed a C-130 Hercules with a guns kill. Ethell, *Air War South Atlantic*, 175.
48. On 21 May, Ward achieved a guns kill against Tomba's Pucara over Lafonia in East Falkland. M. Middlebrook, *The Falklands War 1982*. (London: Penguin, 2001), 222.
49. Data sourced from Annex J unless otherwise stated.
50. TNA, DEFE 48/1162. Reconstruction of Air War.
51. Clapp, *Amphibious Assault Falklands*, 251.
52. Ward, *Sea Harrier*, 321.
53. See Annex A for further details.
54. The Argentines had an eclectic inventory of air-to-air missiles. All of the Mirage IIIs could carry a single Matra 530F, but only a few aircraft could also carry two Magic 1s; both weapons were French built. The Daggers and A-4C Skyhawks could carry a pair of Israeli-manufactured Shafrirs, whereas the A-4Q Skyhawks carried two AIM-9B Sidewinders.
55. Ward, *Sea Harrier*, 355.
56. TNA, FCO 7/4474. Falkland Islands Conflict: Minutes of Chiefs of Staff Meetings.
57. United Kingdom, *The Lessons*, 45.
58. TNA, DEFE 58/260. HQ 18 Group: Operation Corporate (Falklands Conflict); lessons learned.
59. Ethell, Air *War South Atlantic*, 234-243.
60. TNA, DEFE 67/126. Operation Corporate, Falklands Conflict: Preliminary Overview, July 1982.
61. *Ibid.*
62. United Kingdom, *The Lessons*, 45.
63. Ethell, *Air War South Atlantic*, 234-243.
64. Gonzales, *Argentine Airman in South Atlantic*, 76.
65. *Ibid.*, 78.
66. Freedman, *Official History Volume 2*, 442.
67. TNA, DEFE 19/276. Scientific Evaluation Team.
68. Hobson, *Falklands Air War*, 62.
69. See Annex G for further details. Of note, David Hart-Dyke, the Commanding Officer of HMS *Coventry*, claimed that they had shot down two further Skyhawks during this engagement. Hart-Dyke, *Four Weeks in May*, 145.
70. Hobson, *Falklands Air War*, 110.
71. Burden, *The Air War*, 89.
72. Freedman, *Official History Volume 2*, 638 and Brown, *Royal Navy*, 327
73. Burden, *The Air War*, 93 and Hobson, *Falklands Air War*, 138.

74. TNA, PREM 19/647. Handling of the Falklands.
75. Woodward, *One Hundred Days*, 387.
76. Brown, *Royal Navy*, 221.
77. TNA, T 225/3478. Requirements of surface-to-air guided missiles: development of Seawolf GWS-25 equipment.
78. Hobson, *Falklands Air War*, 79.
79. TNA, DEFE 67/126. Preliminary Overview.
80. United Kingdom, *The Lessons*, 45.
81. Ethell, *Air War South Atlantic*, 234-243.
82. TNA, ADM 202/892. Operation Corporate: Carrier Battle Group (CTG 317.8) (Falklands Conflict), March – May 1982.
83. Hobson, *Falklands Air War*, 95-96.
84. Woodward, *One Hundred Days*, 386.
85. Thompson, *No Picnic*, 69.
86. Hobson, Falklands *Air War*, 78.
87. Thompson, *No Picnic*, 69.
88. *Ibid.*
89. United Kingdom, *The Lessons*, 22; TNA, ADM 201/266. Logistics Situational Reports, 1982.
90. Privratsky, *Logistics in Falklands War*, 118.
91. Freedman, *Official History Volume 2*, 474.
92. *Ibid.*, 478.
93. Thompson, *No Picnic*, 69.
94. Freedman, *Official History Volume 2*, 443. However, and according to Hobson, the second Rapier unit, comprising eight fire units from 63 Squadron, RAF Regiment arrived in San Carlos on board the MV *Atlantic Causeway* on 3 June. Hobson, *Falklands Air War*, 115.
95. Thompson, *No Picnic*, 124.
96. Teal was not attacked by Argentine air power until two days before the end of the Conflict. *Ibid.*
97. From T Battery, 12 Air Defence Regiment, Royal Artillery, and not the RAF Regiment as suggested by Ward. Ward, *Sea Harrier*, 320; Clapp, *Amphibious Assault Falklands*, 246.
98. Freedman, *Official History Volume 2*, 612.
99. Hobson, *Falklands Air War*, 124.
100. Southby-Tailyour, *Reasons in Writing*, 300.
101. Clapp, *Amphibious Assault Falklands*, 251.
102. A. Cordesman and A. Wagner, *The Lessons of Modern War Volume 1*. (Oxford: Westview Press, 1991), 93.

103. Freedman, *Official History Volume 2*, 733.
104. United Kingdom, *The Lessons*, 45. Of note, some analysts give an even more optimistic response suggesting that Rapier achieved 14 kills from 45 firings (giving a probability of kill of 31 per cent). Cordesman, *Volume 3*, 295.
105. Air Historical Branch, CTTO/26/2/Ops. Tactical Lessons.
106. The only Argentine aircraft that links to a Rapier kill is a Dagger on 29 May. Burden, *The Air War*, 137.
107. TNA, WO 305/5600. Royal Artillery: Operation Corporate (Falklands Conflict).
108. Hobson, *Falklands Air War*, 78.
109. TNA, FCO 7/4500. Recapture of the Falkland Islands by British forces: military options and TNA. WO 305/5600. Royal Artillery: Operation Corporate (Falklands Conflict).
110. *Ibid.*
111. United Kingdom, *The Lessons*, 45.
112. TNA, WO 305/5600. Royal Artillery.
113. Burden, *The Air War*, 163.
114. The A-4C Skyhawk mission on 24 May, including Lucero, was one of the few missions aborted due to the weight of ground fire. Rivas, *Wings of the Malvinas*, 123.
115. United Kingdom, *UK Air and Space Doctrine*, 3-30.
116. Freedman, *Official History Volume 2*, 523 and Edwards. *My Secret Falklands War*, 41.
117. Ward, *Sea Harrier*, 259.
118. Brown, *Royal Navy,* 286.
119. Hobson, *Falklands Air War*, 120 and Freedman. *Official History Volume 2*, 604.
120. *Ibid.*, 604.
121. On 28 May, while returning to the aircraft carrier, Ward saw what he believed to be three Argentine bombers. He commenced his attack but lost sight of the aircraft. It later became apparent that the enemy aircraft were, in fact, Harrier GR3s. Ward, *Sea Harrier*, 286. On 3 June, a 3 Commando Brigade unit prepared to shell a Chinook offloading troops nearby. Fortuitously, a brief weather interlude allowed the Royal Marines to identify the interlopers as 5 Infantry Brigade troops disembarking from the sole remaining RAF Chinook. Thompson, *No Picnic*, 125.
122. Air Historical Branch, CTTO/26/2/Ops. Tactical Lessons.
123. TNA, ADM 202/875. Headquarters 3 Commando Brigade, Royal Marines: Operation Corporate; Report of Proceedings, July 1982.

Chapter 7 – Prosecuting the Argentine Operational Centre of Gravity – The British Fascination with Stanley Airport.

1. TNA, FCO 7/4472. Falkland Islands Conflict: Minutes of Chiefs of Staff Meetings.
2. TNA, AIR 20/13113. Bombing Raids.
3. *Ibid.*
4. TNA, FCO 7/4472. Chiefs of Staff Meetings.
5. TNA, AIR 20/13113. Bombing Raids.
6. TNA, DEFE 69/791. Operation Corporate, Falklands Conflict: concept of operations and lessons learned.
7. *Ibid.*
8. Sheffield, *From San Carlos to Stanley*, 373.
9. TNA, FCO 7/4506. The political costs of retaking the Falkland Island.
10. *Ibid.*
11. *Ibid.*
12. TNA, AIR 20/13048. Operation Corporate (Falklands Conflict): Vulcan aircraft operations, including Black Buck operations.
13. *Ibid.*
14. Freedman, *Official History Volume 2*, 281.
15. Jacobs, *Stay The Distance*, 235.
16. TNA, FCO 7/4472. Chiefs of Staff Meetings.
17. TNA, DEFE 69/836.801 Naval Air Squadron flight report.
18. Freedman, *Official History Volume 2*, 282.
19. *Ibid.*, 284.
20. TNA, AIR 20/13046. Operation Corporate (Falklands Conflict): Vulcan aircraft operations, including Black Buck operations. Released on 27 May, the second issue of the Operation Order changed the mission aim to a broader role. The new objective was 'to impede the conduct of Argentine Operations in Falkland Islands Area.' TNA, AIR 20/13049. Operation Corporate (Falklands Conflict): Vulcan aircraft operations, including Black Buck operations.
21. In addition to Leach, Woodward suggested that the Vulcan raid had, 'one specific purpose – to blast a bloody great hole in the middle of the runway of Port Stanley airfield ... prevent the Args [Argentine] fighter/attack aircraft getting off the ground from Port Stanley to bomb my ships has my automatic "unqualified support."' Woodward, *One Hundred Days*, 185-186. Likewise, Beetham's biographer stated that 'it was considered essential to deny the airfield at Stanley to the Argentine Air Force.' Jacobs, *Stay The Distance*, 234.
22. Only one of the chosen Vulcan aircrew had previous air-to-air refuelling experience, but this dated back to 1962, a 20-year sabbatical. R. White, *Vulcan 607*. (London: Bantam Press, 2006), 101.

23. The instructors' experience and knowledge were so beneficial that they would join the 5-man Vulcan crew on the Black Buck missions. M. Withers, 'The Vulcan Bomber in Action – Operation Black Buck.' In *RAF Historical Society – The Vulcan* (2014), 107. See also Air Commodore (Retired) 'Paddy' Teakle's viewpoint in Air Power Review for a personal insight. I. Teakle, 'Viewpoint.' In *Air Power Review*. Volume 20, Number 2 (2018).
24. TNA, AIR 27/3577.44 Squadron.
25. Burden, *The Air War*, 363.
26. Hobson, *Falklands Air War*, 41.
27. Burden, *The Air War*, 363.
28. RAF Historical Society, *Journal 30*.
29. For example, following the Black Buck 2 mission, both Vulcans returned to RAF Waddington on 7 May with two Vulcans returning to Ascension Island on 14 and 15 May in time to meet the Black Buck 3 task. Burden, *The Air War*, 365.
30. Extended range Nimrod missions using Victor air-to-air refuelling commenced on 9 May. *Ibid.*, 395; Long-range Hercules air-drop missions started on 16 May. Hobson, *Falklands Air War*, 70.
31. Ward, *Sea Harrier*, xxiv.
32. See Annex K.
33. Ward, *Sea Harrier*, 108.
34. Hobbs, *The British Carrier Strike Fleet*, 467.
35. *Ibid.*
36. TNA, DEFE 72/257. Sea Harrier Specification.
37. *Ibid.*
38. *Ibid.*
39. *Ibid.*
40. Morgan, *Hostile Skies*, 49.
41. TNA, FCO 7/4472. Chiefs of Staff Meetings.
42. TNA, DEFE 19/276. Scientific Evaluation Team.
43. Ward, *Sea Harrier*, 207.
44. *Ibid.*
45. TNA, DEFE 69/836.801 Naval Air Squadron flight report.
46. Ward, *Sea Harrier*, 297.
47. Pook, *RAF Harrier Ground Attack*, 72.
48. TNA, DEFE 72/257. Aircraft Specification.
49. In his official report, Ward suggested that the four Vulcan bombing missions equated to 665 Sea Harrier missions in a 3-bomb fit dropping 2,000 weapons. TNA, DEFE 69/836.801 Naval Air Squadron flight report. In his book, Ward informed that the Black Buck 1 mission's fuel was the equivalent of 260 Sea

Harrier attack missions, in a maximum 5-bomb fit, resulting in 1,300 weapons. Ward, *Sea Harrier*, 206.

50. T. Blackman, *Vulcan Boys*. (London: Grub Street, 2014), 175.
51. Jurby and Garvie Island were both bombing ranges in the United Kingdom and TNA, AIR 20/13048. Vulcan Aircraft Operations.
52. TNA, DEFE 72/271. Intelligence Summaries.
53. RAF Historical Society, 'Journal 35A – The RAF Harrier Story.' http://www. rafmuseum. org. uk/documents/Research/RAF-Historical-Society-Journals/Journal-35A-Seminar-the-RAF-Harrier-Story. pdf (accessed 17 January 2016).
54. *Ibid.*
55. *Ibid.*
56. TNA, AIR 20/13126. Harrier aircraft operations.
57. *Ibid.*
58. Pook, *RAF Harrier Ground Attack*, 185.
59. *Ibid.*, 190.
60. TNA, DEFE 19/276. Scientific Evaluation Team.
61. Harrier GR3 1000lb weapon employment was 31 free-fall, and 28 retard 1000lb bombs. TNA, AIR 27/3525.1 Squadron; TNA, DEFE 19/276. Scientific Evaluation Team.
62. Pook, *RAF Harrier Ground Attack*, 196.
63. Morgan, *Hostile Skies*, 230.
64. P. Squire, 'Harrier goes to War.' http://www. raf. mod. uk/history/TheHarrier GoestoWar. cfm (accessed 8 January 2016).
65. TNA, AIR 27/3525.1 Squadron.
66. Pook, *RAF Harrier Ground Attack*, 196.
67. TNA, AIR 27/3525.1 Squadron.
68. See Annex K for further details.
69. RAF Historical Society, *Journal 20*; See entry for 31 May 1982 in Annex K for further details.
70. Pook, *RAF Harrier Ground Attack*, 196.
71. TNA, DEFE 58/282. Operation Corporate (Falklands Conflict): Air Commander's Report; Report of Proceedings, October 1982.
72. TNA, DEFE 69/791. Concept of Operations.
73. TNA, AIR 20/13109. Operation Corporate (Falklands Conflict): RAF involvement; TNA. AIR 27/3525.1 Squadron.
74. TNA, DEFE 19/276. Scientific Evaluation Team.
75. Burden, *The Air War*, 372.
76. Pook, *RAF Harrier Ground Attack*, 7.
77. Squire, *Harrier goes to War*.
78. Pook, *RAF Harrier Ground Attack*, 7.

79. *Ibid.*, 148.
80. TNA, DEFE 58/282. Air Commander's Report.
81. TNA, AIR 27/3525.1 Squadron.
82. Burden, *The Air War*, 365.
83. TNA, DEFE 58/282. Air Commander's Report.
84. Hobson, *Falklands Air War*, 101.
85. Blackman, *Vulcan Boys*, 134.
86. *Ibid.*, 179.
87. TNA, DEFE 58/282. Air Commander's Report.
88. Burden, *The Air War*, 365.
89. TNA, DEFE 58/282. Air Commander's Report; some dispute the success of the Shrike missions as 'the damage is not considered to be consistent with the Shrike warhead characteristics.' TNA, DEFE 19/276. Scientific Evaluation Team.
90. TNA, AIR 27/3525.1 Squadron.
91. TNA, AIR 24/3299. Strike Command.
92. *Ibid*; Burden, *The Air War*, 408.
93. TNA, FCO 7/4565. Military Planning.
94. TNA, FCO 7/4566. Military Planning.
95. TNA, DEFE 72/271. Intelligence Summaries.
96. TNA, AIR 20/13126. Harrier aircraft operations; TNA, DEFE 19/276. Scientific Evaluation Team.
97. A. Clarke, 'Sea Control 101 – Falklands 10'. In *21 Days to take a Squadron to War*. Podcast Audio, 16 November 2015. http://cimsec. org/sea-control-101-falklands-10-21-days-to-take-a-squadron-to-war/19976.
98. TNA, DEFE 19/276. Scientific Evaluation Team.
99. TNA, AIR 20/13191. Operation Corporate (Falklands Conflict): report and debriefs.
100. TNA, DEFE 69/844. Campaign Diary.
101. Ward, *Sea Harrier*, 207.
102. *Ibid.*
103. TNA, DEFE 19/276. Scientific Evaluation Team.
104. Neither the Sea Harrier nor the Harrier GR3 incorporated a chaff and flare capability before the Conflict. Consequently, one-shot chaff loads were either fitted in the aircraft's airbrake or between the bomb and its wing pylon, TNA, AIR 24/3299. Strike Command. Despite the rapid introduction of the ALE-40 chaff and flare system, there was no fleet-wide embodiment. Ward, *Sea Harrier*, 245. The 'Blue Eric' I-band jamming system, incorporated into a Harrier GR3 30mm gun pod, was deployed in the latter stages of the Conflict but in limited numbers. Marston, *Harrier Boys Volume One*, 97. Moreover, the jammer was of limited utility. TNA, AIR 24/3299. Strike Command.

105. RAF Historical Society, *Journal 30.*
106. R.P. Hallion, *Control of the Air: The Enduring Requirement*. (Washington DC: Air Force History and Museums Program, 1999), 5.
107. Bicheno, *Razor's Edge*, 351.
108. *Ibid.*
109. TNA, DEFE 69/791. Concept of Operations.
110. TNA, DEFE 69/844. Campaign Diary.
111. TNA, DEFE 69/791. Concept of Operations.
112. *Ibid.*
113. *Ibid.*
114. Due to the incomplete nature of the primary source material not all of the 493 weapons employed can be mapped to specific attacks and target sets. Consequently, 20 weapons remain unaccounted for and shown in Figure 7.3 as 'Unknown.'
115. *Ibid.*
116. *Ibid.*
117. J. Thompson, in '*The Falklands War'*, Seminar held 5 June 2002 (Centre for Contemporary British History, 2005, http://www. icbh. ac. uk/witness/falklands/), p. 51.
118. Unknown author, *The Falklands War – 25th Anniversary* (London: Marshall Cavendish, 2007), 157.
119. B. H Liddell Hart, *Strategy*. (London: Penguin, 1991), xx.
120. TNA, DEFE 58/258. Operations/Training Aspects.
121. *Ibid.*
122. *Ibid.*
123. TNA, DEFE 19/276. Scientific Evaluation Team.
124. TNA, AIR 20/13191. Report and Debriefs.
125. *Ibid.*
126. TNA, AIR 24/3299. Strike Command.
127. TNA, AIR 20/13191. Report and Debriefs.
128. TNA, AIR 24/3299. Strike Command.
129. Squire, *Harrier goes to War.*
130. TNA, AIR 20/13191. Report and Debriefs.
131. TNA, AIR 27/3525. 1 Squadron.
132. TNA, AIR 24/3299. Strike Command.
133. United Kingdom, *UK Air and Space Doctrine*, 3-10.
134. TNA, AIR 20/13126. Harrier aircraft operations.
135. *Ibid.*
136. TNA, DEFE 19/276. Scientific Evaluation Team.
137. TNA, AIR 24/3299. Strike Command.

138. TNA, AIR 20/13126. Harrier aircraft operations.
139. TNA, AIR 27/3525.1 Squadron.
140. TNA, AIR 24/3299. Strike Command.
141. TNA, AIR 20/13126. Harrier aircraft operations.
142. *Ibid.*
143. Pook, *RAF Harrier Ground Attack*, 81.
144. Ward, *Sea Harrier*, 250.
145. Air Historical Branch, CTTO/26/2/Ops. Tactical Lessons.
146. Hobson, *Falklands Air War*, 43.
147. Moro, *South Atlantic Conflict*, 99.
148. Hobson, *Falklands Air War*, 43.
149. *Ibid.*
150. *Ibid.*
151. Moro, *South Atlantic Conflict*, 99.
152. Hobson, *Falklands Air War*, 101.
153. TNA, AIR 20/13046. Vulcan Aircraft Operations.
154. RAF Historical Society, *Journal 20.*
155. Ward, *Sea Harrier*, 310.
156. TNA, AIR 20/13046. Vulcan Aircraft Operations.
157. Moro, *South Atlantic Conflict*, 95.
158. Hobson, *Falklands Air War*, 57.
159. All events sourced from Hobson, *Falklands Air War.*
160. Pook, *RAF Harrier Ground Attack*, 105.
161. Clapp, *Amphibious Assault Falklands*, 143.
162. Pook, *RAF Harrier Ground Attack*, 122.
163. Moro, *South Atlantic Conflict*, 272.
164. TNA, DEFE 69/844. *Campaign Diary*; Ward, *Sea Harrier*, 305.
165. *Ibid.*, 310.
166. Morgan, *Hostile Skies*, 248.
167. Pook, *RAF Harrier Ground Attack*, 136.
168. Blackman, *Vulcan Boys*, 180.
169. See Annex K for details.
170. RAF Historical Society, *Journal 35A.*
171. TNA, AIR 27/3525.1 *Squadron.*
172. Moro, *South Atlantic Conflict*, 99.
173. Woodward, *One Hundred Days*, 190.
174. Middlebrook, *The Argentine Fight*, 90.
175. Moro, *South Atlantic Conflict*, 187.
176. Pook, *RAF Harrier Ground Attack*, 161.

Chapter 8 – The Operational Level Lessons of the Falklands Air Campaign

1. Woodward, *One Hundred Days*, 106.
2. Contemporary NATO doctrine defined the operational level as 'the level at which campaigns and major operations are planned, conducted and sustained to accomplish strategic objectives within theatres or areas of operations.' United Kingdom, *Operational-Level Planning*, 1-19.
3. Cordesman, *Volume 3*, 314.
4. L. Deighton, *Fighter*. (London: William Collins, 2014), xix.
5. UK doctrine defines Joint Action as deliberately using and orchestrating military capabilities and activities to realize specific physical and/or psychological effects. United Kingdom, *UK Defence Doctrine*, 43.
6. Burden, *The Air War*, 158.
7. United Kingdom, Ministry of Defence. Joint Doctrine Publication 3-00: Campaign Execution. (Shrivenham: The Development, Concepts and Doctrine Centre, 2009), 1A-1.
8. Burden, *The Air War*, 19.
9. *Ibid.*
10. R. Schiena, *Argentine Jointness*, 99.
11. Burden, *The Air War*, 161.
12. *Fuerza Aérea Argentina, Historia, Tomo VI, Volumen 1,* 110.
13. Moro, *South Atlantic Conflict*, 78; Burden. *The Air War*, 19.
14. Adapted from *Ibid*., 18 and Moro, *South Atlantic Conflict*, 78.
15. Rivas, *Wings of the Malvinas*, 54.
16. *Fuerza Aérea Argentina, Historia, Tomo VI, Volumen 1,* 177.
17. As described in Ethell, *Air War South Atlantic*, 29, as well as Rivas, *Wings of the Malvinas*, 54.
18. TNA, AIR 20/13054. Proposed Official History.
19. Based on Freedman, *Official History Volume 2*, 32.
20. Imperial War Museum. 'Squire, Peter (Oral History).' https://www. iwm. org. uk/collections/item/object/80025717 (accessed 29 November 2018).
21. *Ibid.*
22. *Ibid.*
23. *Ibid.*
24. TNA, AIR 20/13126. Harrier aircraft operations.
25. United Kingdom, Ministry of Defence. Joint Doctrine Publication 04: Understanding. (Shrivenham: The Development, Concepts and Doctrine Centre, 2010), 2-1.
26. *Fuerza Aérea Argentina, Historia, Tomo VI, Volumen 1,* 108.
27. Brown, *Royal Navy,* 221; Freedman, *Official History Volume 2*, 611.

28. As identified in the report, 'Equipment Lessons from Operation Corporate' contained within TNA, DEFE 58/260. Lessons Learned.
29. TNA, FCO 7/4566. Military Planning.
30. The British assumed that the Argentine force had a 70 per cent availability and that each available aircraft could fly two missions per day. TNA, DEFE 72/271. Intelligence Summaries.
31. Freedman, *Official History Volume 2*, 552.
32. TNA, DEFE 69/855. Operation Corporate, Falklands Conflict: Commander Task Force 317; war diary, 1 May-15 June 1982, section I, synopsis of policy, planning and principal events.
33. R. Hutchings, *Special Forces Pilot*. (Barnsley: Pen and Sword, 2008), 60.
34. Freedman informed that 961 prisoners of war were taken captive with a further 45 killed in action. Freedman, *Official History Volume 2*, 581.
35. Air Historical Branch article on the RAF's roles referred to the involvement of 10, 30, 39, 47 and 51 Squadrons in Operations Folklore and Acme. TNA, AIR 20/13054. Proposed Official History.
36. Deighton, *Fighter*, 275.
37. *Ibid.*, 2-5.
38. United Kingdom, *UK Air and Space Doctrine*, 2-4.
39. *Fuerza Aérea Argentina*, *Historia, Tomo VI, Volumen 1,* 121.
40. *Ibid.*, 120.
41. *Ibid.*, 121.
42. *Armada Argentina*, *Conflicto Del Atlantico Sur*, 79.
43. *Ibid.*
44. *Ibid.*
45. *Ibid.*, 81.
46. *Ibid.*, 82.
47. *Ibid.*, 107 and 331.
48. *Ibid.*, 333.
49. *Fuerza Aérea Argentina*, *Historia, Tomo VI, Volumen 1,* 295.
50. *Armada Argentina*, *Conflicto Del Atlantico Sur*, 377.
51. *Fuerza Aérea Argentina*, *Historia, Tomo VI, Volumen 1,* 121.
52. Imperial War Museum, 'Thomas, Neill (Oral History).' https://www. iwm. org. uk/collections/item/object/80032984 (accessed 29 November 2018).
53. Deighton, *Fighter*, 166.
54. Clausewitz, *On War*, 259.
55. Argentina, *Fuerza Aérea Argentina. Historia de la Fuerza Aérea Argentina. Tomo VI, Volumen 2, 'La Fuerza Aérea en Malvinas'* (Buenos Aires: Dirección de Estudios Históricos, 1998.), 714 and 724.

56. *Ibid.*, 724.
57. Rivas, *Wings of the Malvinas*, 123.
58. Clarin, '*Un aviador en tela de juico.*' https://www. clarin. com/political/aviador-tela-juico_0_HJGj1AgRYg. html (accessed 8 August 2017).
59. Rivas, *Wings of the Malvinas*, 106.
60. *Armada Argentina, Conflicto Del Atlantico Sur,* 371.
61. *Fuerza Aérea Argentina, Historia, Tomo VI, Volumen 1,* 107.
62. Morgan, *Hostile Skies*, 128.
63. Ward, *Sea Harrier*, 226.
64. Pook, *RAF Harrier Ground Attack*, 110-111.
65. Deighton, *Fighter*, 38.
66. *Ibid.*, xxiii.
67. *Armada Argentina, Conflicto Del Atlantico Sur,* 611.
68. *Ibid.*, 614.
69. The *Comando de Aviación Naval* lost 14 aircraft (three A-4Q Skyhawks, five Aermacchi MB-339s, four T-34 Mentors, and two helicopters) for the sinking of the 26,650 tonne MV *Atlantic Conveyor.*
70. *Fuerza Aérea Argentina, Historia, Tomo VI, Volumen 1,* 108.
71. TNA, AIR 27/3525.1 Squadron.
72. United Kingdom, Ministry of Defence. Carrier Enabled Power Projection Concept of Employment, Issue 2. (London: Ministry of Defence, 2014).

Chapter 9 – Conclusion

1. W.S. Churchill, *The Second World War, Volume V: Closing the Ring.* (London: Cassell & Co Ltd, 1952), 316.
2. Deighton, *Fighter*, xvi.
3. J.S. Nye, 'The Information Revolution and Soft Power.' In *Current History*. 113(759). (2014): 20.
4. Freedman, *Official History Volume 2*, 449.
5. TNA, DEFE 13/1121. Harrier Operational Requirements.
6. TNA, FCO 7/4565. Military Planning.
7. For example, Rivas, *Wings of the Malvinas*, 193. See also *Hobson, Falklands Air War*, 84. Additionally, Burden, *The Air War*, 24.
8. TNA, FCO 7/4566. Military Planning.
9. TNA, DEFE 13/1121. Harrier Operational Requirements.
10. Ward, *Sea Harrier*, 129.
11. Imperial War Museum. 'Middleton, Linley Eric (Oral History).' https://www. iwm. org. uk/collections/item/object/80032610 (accessed 29 November 2018).
12. TNA, DEFE 72/271. Intelligence Summaries.

13. *Ibid.*
14. Ward, *Sea Harrier*, xxvi.
15. P. Lee, *Reaper Force*. (London: John Blake, 2018.), 155.
16. United Kingdom, Ministry of Defence. RAF Operations during the Falklands Conflict. (London: Air Historical Branch, 1988), iv
17. TNA, PREM 19/627. Relations with Argentina Position of the Falkland Islands - Part 18, 18-21 May 1982.
18. TNA, AIR 20/13126. Harrier aircraft operations.
19. TNA, DEFE 58/262. Lessons Learned.

Annex A – Argentine Combat Air Sorties Flown During the Falklands Conflict

1. Argentine combat air sortie data has been sourced from Rivas, *Wings of the Malvinas*.
2. The table uses a White, Light Grey and Dark Grey annotation to reflect Good (G), Fair (F) and Poor (P) 12-hourly weather assessments for both the Argentine airfields and the Falkland Islands as articulated in TNA, DEFE 67/128. Meteorological Records.

Annex B – British Combat Air Sorties Flown During the Falklands Conflict

1. Sea Harrier daily flying rates are taken from TNA, DEFE 67/124. Operation Corporate, Falklands Conflict: Harrier Aircraft Operations, April 1983. Although Clapp/Southby-Tailyour's (Clapp, *Amphibious Assault Falklands*), figures correlated with the stipulated archive figures, they do not match the data for 23 May as articulated by Freedman. (Freedman, *Official History Volume 2*, 481.)An independent analysis of Sea Harrier sortie rates using an amalgamation of: Fleet Air Arm Archives. Fair Flying Log, 800 Naval Air Squadron and Fleet Air Arm Archives. 801 Naval Air Squadron Flying Authorisation Sheets, May 1982 failed to clarify the position. Therefore, and despite minor flaws, the Annex uses the Operational Evaluation Group's report to benchmark British combat air sorties.
2. The Harrier GR3 figures promulgated are taken from primary source material. TNA, DEFE 67/124. Harrier Aircraft Operations.
3. Seven Black Buck missions were planned, comprising four airfield attack missions and three suppression of enemy air defence sorties. However, the Vulcans only flew 6 missions; one airfield attack mission (Black Buck 3) was cancelled prior to take off due to a severe weather forecast. One suppression of enemy air defence sortie (Black Buck 4) was aborted 5 hours into the mission due to Victor tanker serviceability issues. Burden, *The Air War*, 367.

4. The table uses a White, Light Grey and Dark Grey annotation to reflect Good (G), Fair (F) and Poor (P) 12-hourly weather assessments for both the Carrier Group and the Falkland Islands as articulated in TNA, DEFE 67/128. Meteorological Records.

Annex C – Argentine Attack Missions on 1 May

1. Topo flight were misidentified as fighter assets by their controlling agency, Malvinas CIC (*Centro de Information y Control*), and vectored to intercept a Sea Harrier combat air patrol. Consequently, Topo flight aborted their intended mission. Rivas, *Wings of the Malvinas*, 133.
2. *Ibid.*, 119
3. Weapon type and number confirmed by Argentine primary sources. *Fuerza Aérea Argentina. Historia, Tomo VI, Volumen 1,* 186. However, Rivas suggested that each aircraft carried three weapons. Rivas, *Wings of the Malvinas.* 168.
4. The ships conducted a naval bombardment of artillery positions near Stanley. *Ibid.*, 172. HMS *Arrow* was attacked by Dimeglio and hit by eleven 30mm rounds, while HMS *Alacrity* received minor damage from near misses by Roman's attack. Faget attacked HMS *Glamorgan* but neither of his weapons struck their target. Rivas, *Wings of the Malvinas*, 174. However, some Argentine commentators suggested that Faget's weapons struck HMS *Glamorgan*. Moro, *South Atlantic Conflict*, 106.
5. During the transit to the Islands, Carmona was forced to return to base due to a technical problem. Burden, *The Air War*, 117.
6. The formation attacked the Argentine cargo ship ELMA *Formosa* during their egress. The ship was strafed and hit by two bombs: one failed to detonate whereas the other bomb ricocheted of the ship's superstructure and fell overboard. Rivas, *Wings of the Malvinas*, 119.
7. The formation leader aborted the mission due to the difficulties in penetrating the target defences. The Argentine aircrew mistook the chaff clouds fired from British ships as missile launches. The only damage to the Argentine aircraft was self-induced; during low-level maneuvering to defeat the perceived missile threat, the leader's wingtip struck the surface of the sea but the damage to the wingtip was superficial. *Ibid.*, 90.
8. Lieutenant Curtis from 801 Naval Air Squadron shot down and killed the crew of a Canberra with an AIM-9L Sidewinder. Despite firing a further three AIM-9L Sidewinders, the two remaining Argentine bombers egressed safely back to Argentina. Hobson, *Falklands Air War*, 49.
9. Foco formation was warned by Malvinas CIC of a Sea Harrier combat air patrol approaching their position. As a result, Foca aborted their mission. Rivas, *Wings of the Malvinas*, 133.

10. Sanchez's aircraft was forced to return with a technical failure. *Ibid.*, 133.
11. The two remaining aircraft were forced to withdraw once over the Islands. In his narrative, Rivas did not allude to the reason for the aborted mission. *Ibid.* However, given the timing and location it is likely that the Sea Harrier combat air patrol that forced Lana formation to abort had the same effect on this formation.
12. Rivas suggested each aircraft carried 3 weapons. *Ibid.*, 119. In contrast, the Official History of the *Fuerza Aérea Argentina* informed that each aircraft carried two bombs. *Fuerza Aérea Argentina, Historia, Tomo VI, Volumen 1,* 192. Nevertheless, the formation aborted due to the presence of a Sea Harrier Combat Air Patrol. Burden, *The Air War*, 111.
13. Columbo and Macheteanz were assigned a target 44 miles south of Stanley. However, the mission was aborted during the transit to the Islands due to a fuel leak onboard one of the Super Etendards while tanking from the KC-130H Hercules aircraft. Rivas, *Wings of the Malvinas*, 243. Of note, no other source mentioned Super Etendard missions planned for 1 May 1982.
14. Bedacarratz and Mayora ground aborted as their tanker aircraft was returning to base. *Ibid.*, 243.

Annex D – Argentine Control of the Air Missions on 1 May

1. Faget in C-412 was unable to take part due to an engine problem. *Ibid.*, 166
2. The mission planned to escort a Lockheed SP-2H Neptune that was due to fly a radar search mission off Stanley in an attempt to locate the British Fleet. *Ibid.*, 46. However, the Neptune failed to make its planned take off time of 0850. Burden, *The Air War*, 130. Nevertheless, the escort mission took off as planned and vectored against two Sea Harriers flown by Lt Cdr Kent and Lt Haigh from 801 Naval Air Squadron. *Ibid.*, 210.
3. Escorted Topo Flight (A-4B Skyhawks) during ingress, Rivas, *Wings of the Malvinas*, 207.
4. Tasked with escorting Topo flight during their egress. *Ibid.*, 184.
5. Although this mission has no Fragmentation Order or callsign, Rivas stated Lopez flew in C-303 and Manzotti in C-310. *Ibid.*, 119.
6. *Ibid.*, 208.
7. Perona was shot down by an AIM-9L Sidewinder fired from Barton's Sea Harrier; Perona ejected and survived. Watson fired an AIM-9L Sidewinder at Cuerva and damaged the Mirage III. With insufficient fuel to return to the mainland, Cuerva elected to divert to Stanley but was shot down and killed by Argentine ground-based air defences. Burden, *The Air War*, 145. See also Annex J, Serial 2 for further details.

8. Provided cover for Torno Flight, Fortin closed to within 2 miles of the Sea Harriers but was unable to achieve missile lock due to the sun. Rivas, *Wings of the Malvinas*, 173.
9. Leader ground aborted, Ardiles continued the mission on his own. Hobson, *Falklands Air War*, 49.
10. Hobson and Burden both suggested that Ardiles launched a missile against Hale's Sea Harrier. However, Rivas informed that Ardiles jettisoned his fuel tanks. *Ibid.*, 49 and Burden, *The Air War*, 131; Rivas, *Wings of the Malvinas*, 184
11. *Ibid.*, 184. Also, see Annex J Serial 3 for further details.

Annex E – Argentine Air Power Prior to Operation Sutton: 2–19 May

1. Although Argentine Official History fails to mention the sorties, Rivas, following interviews with the crews, informed that the mission did indeed take place. Rivas, *Wings of the Malvinas*, 92.
2. Although not specified, the assumed weapon load reflects the standard fit of 3 Expals.
3. Once identified as Argentine ships, the Argentines cancelled the mission. *Ibid.*, 133.
4. Argentine primary source confirmed payload. *Fuerza Aérea Argentina, Historia, Tomo VI, Volumen 1,* 256.
5. The aircraft flown by Garcia and Isaac were unable to conduct air-to-air refuelling, the two remaining aircraft crashed in or around South Jason Island in poor weather conditions. Rivas, *Wings of the Malvinas*, 120.
6. There is a debate regarding the weapon load carried by both formations. The adopted position reflected Freedman's, Moro's and the *Fuerza Aérea Argentina* website's position that both formations carried a single 1000lb weapon. However, Hobson and Burden suggested that the formations carried a pair of 500lb weapons. Bicheno confused the matter further by suggesting the aircraft carried a pair of 1000lb bombs. Freedman, *Official History Volume 2*, 441; Moro, *South Atlantic Conflict*, 186 and *Fuerza Aérea Argentina*, http://www.faa.mil.ar/conflicto/dias/may12.html accessed 22 January 2016); Hobson, *Falklands Air War*, 65 and Burden, *The Air War*, 108; Bicheno, *Razor's Edge*, 130.
7. Nivoli and Iberlucea are both killed when HMS *Brilliant's* Sea Wolf successfully engages them. Iberluca was able to drop his weapon, but it missed HMS *Brilliant*. Hobson, *Falklands Air War*, 65.
8. After dropping his weapon, which missed, Bustos was engaged by a Sea Wolf fired from HMS *Brilliant*. In an attempt to evade the missile, the aircraft crashed into the sea, killing Bustos. Burden, *The Air War*, 118.

9. Gavazzi's bomb passed through HMS *Glasgow* before it exploded in the sea. On his return flight, Gavazzi was shot down and killed by Argentine ground fire at Goose Green. Hobson, *Falklands Air War*, 66.
10. The weapon load carried by the formation is unidentified, the assumed fit reflects the standard Dagger load of 2 x Expal.
11. In addition to the 54 attack missions, Daggers flew 8 escort sorties while A-4Q Skyhawks flew 8 Alert missions. Therefore, over the period 2-19 May the Argentines flew 70 combat air missions.

Annex F – Argentine Air Power During Operation Sutton: 21 May

1. Bean was shot down and killed by a Sea Wolf missile fired from HMS *Broadsword*. Hobson, *Falklands Air War*, 79.
2. The Argentine Air Force website informed that the Perro aircraft are carrying EXPAL not Mk 17 bombs. However, Rivas and the Argentine official history both suggest the latter weapons system. *Fuerza Aérea Argentina*, www.faa.mil.ar/conflicto/dias/May21a.html accessed on 22 December 2014; Rivas, *Wings of the Malvinas*, 187 and *Fuerza Aérea Argentina, Historia, Tomo VI, Volumen 1,* 327
3. The bomb hit HMS *Antrim* but failed to explode. Bicheno, *Razor's Edge*, 153.
4. Senn's aircraft was unserviceable during start up. Rivas, *Wings of the Malvinas*, 175.
5. All bombs failed to release due to an electrical failure. *Ibid.*, 176.
6. Navigation problems generated via the recently installed VLF navigation system forced the cancellation of the mission. Armada Argentina, *Conflicto Del Atlantico Sur,* 377.
7. Castillo was forced to return to base during the air-to-air refuelling phase of the mission. Rivas, *Wings of the Malvinas*, 121.
8. Lopez joined Pato flight, but he was shot down and killed by Sea Harrier/Sidewinder combination during ingress to the target – see Annex J Serial 9 for further details.
9. Martinez was forced to return to base during the ingress phase of the mission. Rivas, *Wings of the Malvinas*, 121.
10. Manzotti was shot down and killed by Sea Harrier/Sidewinder during ingress to the target – See Annex J Serial 10 for further details.
11. Almono was curtailed by a Sea Harrier combat air patrol during the ingress phase and aborted mission. Rivas, *Wings of the Malvinas*, 121.
12. Cachon and Rinke returned to base during the transit due to technical problems. Hobson, *Falklands Air War*, 81.
13. Carmona attacked an abandoned cargo vessel. Middlebrook, *The Argentinean Fight*, 155.

14. Huertas claimed that Carballo hit the rear of HMS *Ardent* with his single bomb, which detonated causing extensive damage. However, most accounts, including Rivas, suggested that Carballo missed his intended target. S.M. Huertas, *San Carlos: Insights into an Intense Battle* (Air Enthusiast, 24.); Rivas, *Wings of the Malvinas*, 137
15. One aircraft returned to base during transit with a technical issue. *Ibid.*, 137.
16. Isaac's aircraft was unserviceable during start-up. *Ibid.*, 121.
17. During the ingress, Garcia joined Pato flight but aborted due to the presence of a Sea Harrier combat air patrol. *Ibid.*
18. Cimatti's aircraft had an oil leak after take-off and he returned to base. Hobson, *Falklands Air War*, 81.
19. The formation leader's aircraft became unserviceable after take-off and he returned to base. Consequently, Filipini, the Leo flight lead, controlled both formations. However, Hobson believed that all six aircraft made it to the target. Rivas, *Wings of the Malvinas*, 137; Hobson. *Falklands Air War*, 80.
20. Luna was shot down by Sea Harrier/Sidewinder combination on ingress, he ejected and survived. See Annex J Serial 11 for further details.
21. The attack left one unexploded bomb on board the ship. Bicheno. *Razor's Edge*, 154.
22. The formation was intercepted by a Sea Harrier combat air patrol prior to reaching the target area. The Sea Harrier/Sidewinder combination shot down all three Daggers, although all three pilots ejected successfully and survived. See Annex J Serials 12-14 for further details.
23. One weapon failed to release from the aircraft. *Fuerza Aérea Argentina, Historia, Tomo VI, Volumen 1*, 341.
24. During egress, a combination of ground fire as well as Sea Harriers using Sidewinders and cannons shot down all 3 aircraft. See Annex J Serials 15 and 16 for further details.
25. One aircraft ground aborted. Rivas, *Wings of the Malvinas*, 121.
26. Neither the Argentine Air Forces web page nor the *Fuerza Aérea Argentina's* Official History include the Canberra missions. Moreover, Hobson, Burden, as well as Ethell and Price fail to mention the Canberra missions on 21 May 1982. However, Rivas suggested that the missions were cancelled during the execution phase forcing three aircraft to return to base. *Fuerza Aérea Argentina*, www.faa.mil.ar/conflicto/dias/May21.html accessed on 22 December 2014; Rivas, *Wings of the Malvinas*, 92.

Annex G – Argentine Air Power during Operation Sutton: 20–26 May

1. Although the various sources are inconsistent in their reporting of Argentine air activities on 20 May, it is clear that activity levels are very light. The table reflects Rivas' position. Rivas, *Wings of the Malvinas*, 137.

2. Although the formation callsign is unknown, the formation comprised: Piuma in C-432, Castillo in C-412 and Dimeglio in C-415. Although not specified, the table assumes that the aircraft carried the usual San Julian weapon load of 2 x EXPAL. *Ibid.*, 175.
3. The formation callsign remains unidentified. Nevertheless, Rivas informed that the formation comprised: Donadille in C-404 and Puga in C-421. Although not specified, the table assumes that the aircraft carried the standard San Julian weapon configuration of 2 x EXPAL. *Ibid.*
4. Assumed payload.
5. Hobson suggested that only two A-4s Skyhawks conducted the bombing raid. In contrast, Rivas informed that two separate formations were involved. Nevertheless, both commentators agreed that the attacks were ineffectual. In the case of Leon formation, they were unable to contact their controller. Hobson, *Falklands Air War*, 85; Rivas, *Wings of the Malvinas*, 121 and 138.
6. Four aircraft returned to base during the air-to-air refuelling phase of the mission. *Ibid.*, 138.
7. The formation dropped their weapons blind from medium level. *Ibid.*, 121.
8. The aircraft dropped their bombs blind onto the pre-planned coordinates and were unable to assess how successful their strike had been. *Ibid.*, 179.
9. Due to poor weather neither Puma nor Potro formations failed to locate the Learjet, which was operating in the pathfinder role. *Ibid.*, 188.
10. This Fragmentation Order is the same as the one used for the Chispa formation of A-4B Skyhawks on the previous day. Rivas and the *Fuerza Aérea Argentina* Official History both repeat the error.
11. Lanza formation leader, Velasco, and the Tejo wingman, Bergamaschi, both returned to base with technical problems. *Ibid.*, 139.
12. Oro and Plata formations fail to rendezvous with the C-130 refuelling aircraft forcing them to return to base. *Ibid.*, 122.
13. Almono, the formation leader, ground aborted. *Ibid.*
14. Palaver ground aborted. Burden, *The Air War*, 120.
15. Hobson and Huertas suggested that Gomez's bomb struck the stern of HMS *Antelope,* but it failed to detonate. In contrast, Rivas informed that Gomez targeted HMS *Broadsword*, which was located nearby, but missed. The table reflects the latter position. Hobson, *Falklands Air War*, 88 and S.M. Huertas, San Carlos: Insights into an Intense Battle (Air Enthusiast, 25); Rivas, *Wings of the Malvinas*, 141
16. The mission was aborted after Cachon fell off his aircraft's ladder. Hobson, *Falklands Air War*, 88.
17. Guadagnini hit HMS *Antelope* with his bomb but it failed to explode. However, the combined effects of air defences brought down the aircraft during the attack.

His wingman failed to drop his bomb due to intense ground fire. Freedman, *Official History Volume 2*, 481.

18. One aircraft was forced to return to base during the air-to-air refuelling phase. Hobson, *Falklands Air War*, 89.
19. Zubizerratta was unable to drop his weapons due to a technical failure. On recovery, as his aircraft slid off the runway, Zubizerratta ejected using a time-expired rocket motor and was killed. Additionally, one other bomb failed to release from another aircraft. Middlebrook, *The Argentinian Fight*, 168; Armada Argentina, *Conflicto Del Atlantico Sur,* 379.
20. HMS *Antelope* was hit by two unexploded bombs. Some accounts suggested that the unexploded bombs were different types. Consequently, it is likely that an A-4Q Skyhawk dropped one of the unexploded weapons. Rivas, *Wings of the Malvinas*, 261
21. After take-off, a technical problem forced Cimatti to return to base. *Ibid.*, 189.
22. Moreno ground aborted. *Ibid.*
23. Unable to find targets, the formation jettisoned their weapons and returned to base. At this point, a Sea Harrier combat air patrol intercepted the formation and Volponi was shot down and killed by Sea Harrier/Sidewinder combination. For further details, see Annex J Serial 17. Hobson, *Falklands Air War*, 89.
24. The Super Etendards failed to detect a target and returned to base. Rivas, *Wings of the Malvinas*, 245.
25. Berrier was forced to return to base post air-to-air refuelling after accidently dropping his sole weapon. Burden identified Bolzan as the most likely culprit whereas Rivas identified Berrier as the individual responsible for the mistake. Moreover, Rivas does not name Bolzan as one of the six pilots who participated in the Chispa and Nene formations. Burden, *The Air War*, 120 and Rivas, *Wings of the Malvinas*, 142.
26. The first attack on the British operational centre of gravity – 1615 on 24 May. Hobson, *Falklands Air War*, 92.
27. The formation aborted prior to being intercepted by combat air patrol. Burden, *The Air War*, 112.
28. Although no formation callsign is stipulated, the formation compromised Lucero in C-319 and Cuello in C-301. The aircraft subsequently aborted their mission due to heavy ground fire in the vicinity of the San Carlos. Rivas, *Wings of the Malvinas*, 123.
29. During recovery to base, Bono crashed and was killed. Burden, *The Air War*, 112.
30. Due to an electrical generator failure, Maffeis was unable to drop his weapon. Hobson, *Falklands Air War*, 91.

31. The bomb failed to detonate, leaving an unexploded bomb on board RFA *Sir Lancelot*. Rivas, *Wings of the Malvinas*, 145.
32. One bomb failed to release from Callejo's aircraft during the attack. *Ibid.*, 179.
33. The formation was intercepted and engaged by a combat air patrol resulting in the loss of all three aircraft and one of the pilots. For further details, see Annex J Serials 18-20.
34. Two aircraft return to base; one with a technical problem and the other was not visual with the other members of the formation. *Ibid.*, 144.
35. The remaining two aircraft suffered from poor navigation and attacked an abandoned Argentine ship, *Monsunen*, near Goose Green. Palaver was shot down during the egress by a Sea Dart missile fired from HMS *Coventry*. *Ibid.*; Burden, *The Air War*, 121.
36. Two aircraft failed to drop their weapons due to technical issues. Lucero was shot down on egress due to ground fire but ejected safely. Garcia was shot down and killed by a Sea Dart missile fired from HMS *Coventry*. Middlebrook, *The Argentinian Fight*, 170.
37. There is contradictory evidence regarding the weapon loads carried by Vulcano and Zeus flights on 25 May. Rivas suggested that Zeus flight were each armed with a pair of EXPALs and the Vulcano formation had three Mk17s each. The Argentine Air Force website was coherent with the Argentine Official History when it informed that Vulcano were armed with a single Mk17 but failed to mention the weapon load of Zeus other than the Zeus wingman registered his leader's three hits on HMS *Coventry*. Although eyewitnesses on board confirmed the three hits, they suggested that the aircraft dropped four weapons. In contrast, Burden confused matters further by signifying both formations carried the three Mk 17 war load. Hobson and Ramsey confirm the stipulated Vulcano weapon load. Consequently, the table reflected the latter solution as the most rationale answer. Rivas, *Wings of the Malvinas*, 145; *Fuerza Aérea Argentina*, www.faa.mil.ar/conlicto/dias/may25c.html accessed 22 December 2014 and *Fuerza Aérea Argentina, Historia, Tomo VI, Volumen 1,* 389; Hart-Dyke, *Four Weeks in May*, 156; Burden, *The Air War*, 121; Hobson, *Falklands Air War*, 96 and G. Ramsey, *The Falklands War Then and Now* (Old Harlow: Battle of Britain International, 2009), 256.
38. Carmona, Vulcano 3, ground aborted. Rivas, *Wings of the Malvinas*, 145.
39. HMS *Broadsword* was hit by a bomb that failed to explode. Freedman, *Official History Volume 2*, 486.
40. Following take-off, Osses' aircraft, Zeus 3, became unserviceable and was forced to recover to base. Rivas, *Wings of the Malvinas*, 145.

41. Velasco dropped three weapons and achieved three effective hits. Barrineuvo had a technical problem and was unable to drop his weapons. Middlebrook, *The Argentinian Fight*, 173.
42. According to Briasco each Super Etendard aircraft had its own callsign rather than the more conventional approach of a formation callsign. Briasco, *Falklands – Witness of Battles*, 227.
43. Rango, Bingo and Pocker formations are Rio Grande-based. Therefore, the table reflects they were carrying their standard weapon load of a single Mk 17 bomb.
44. According to the Official History, the aircraft launched from Rio Grande at 1300 but were recalled by their headquarters. *Fuerza Aérea Argentina, Historia, Tomo VI, Volumen 1,* 392. Of note, Rivas makes no mention of this mission.
45. The weapon fit is confirmed in the *Fuerza Aérea Argentina* Official History of the Conflict. *Ibid.*
46. Due to inclement weather over the Falkland Islands, the three Canberras were forced to abort their mission. Rivas, *Wings of the Malvinas*, 92.
47. The wingman dropped his weapons blind into the San Carlos area from medium level. His commander later criticised the formation leader for not replicating his wingman's act. *Ibid.*, 181.
48. Payload confirmed in the Official History. Armada Argentina, *Conflicto Del Atlantico Sur,* 381.
49. Unable to find suitable targets. *Ibid.*, 261.
50. Mission aborted after one aircraft was unable to refuel from Hercules. *Ibid.*

Annex H – Argentine Air Power Post-Operation Sutton: 27 May – 14 June

1. Although some commentators suggested that the Canberra raid had minimal effect, others informed that they, 'were viewed by the British as having morale-sapping qualities.' Freedman, *Official History Volume 2*, 563; Burden, *The Air War*, 91.
2. The Official History confirmed that the A-4Q Skyhawks carried their normal load of four Mk 82s. Armada Argentina, *Conflicto Del Atlantico Sur,* 381.
3. Rivas failed to mention the weapon load carried by Trueno. However, the *Fuerza Aérea Argentina* website confirmed that both Toro and Trueno formations carried a single Mk 17 bomb. *Fuerza Aérea Argentina*, http://www.faa.mil.ar/conflicto/dias/may27.html accessed 24 January 2016.
4. Toro and Trueno were ordered to recover to base during air-to-air refuelling. Rivas, *Wings of the Malvinas*, 150.
5. Rivas suggested that the Tigre aircraft were each armed with three LAU-61 Rocket pods. In contrast, the *Fuerza Aérea Argentina* website informed that

both Tanque and Tigre carried the more traditional fit of three BRPs. The table adopts the latter position. *Ibid.*, 125 and *Fuerza Aérea Argentina*, http://www.faa.mil.ar/conflicto/dias/may27.htmlaccessed 24 January 2016.

6. One aircraft was forced to return due to problems encountered during air-to-air refuelling. Rivas, *Wings of the Malvinas*, 125.
7. One Skyhawk returned to base due to problems while conducting air-to-air refuelling. *Ibid.*
8. During the transit, Carmona is forced to return to base. *Ibid.*, 151.
9. Burden suggested that the attack caused several casualties and a fire in an ammunition dump, while other bombs failed to detonate. Freedman informs that the attack kills 6 and wounds 30 as well as leaving 2 unexploded bombs located within the Field Hospital. Privratsky identified that 5 of the 16 bombs exploded. Therefore, 9 of the 16 bombs missed their targets. Burden, *The Air War*, 122; Freedman, *Official History Volume 2*, 563; Privratsky, *Logistics in Falklands War,* 134
10. Following his attack, Velasco was hit by small arms fire and was forced to eject. Moro, *South Atlantic Conflict*, 253.
11. Robledo ground aborted. Rivas, *Wings of the Malvinas*, 150.
12. The table assumes that the Dagger formation carried two BRP.
13. The Official History confirmed that Nene and Cuna formations carried three BRPs per aircraft. *Fuerza Aérea Argentina, Historia, Tomo VI, Volumen 2,* 429.
14. One aircraft was forced to return due to technical issues. Rivas, *Wings of the Malvinas*, 153.
15. Nene 3, flown by Cervera, returned to base with a technical problem. *Ibid.*
16. The table assumes that Chispa and Toro carried a single Mk 17 per aircraft.
17. The lead aircraft was forced to return when he inadvertently dropped his weapon when arming his armament panel. *Ibid.*, 125.
18. The A-4Q Skyhawk fit is assumed to be three Mk 82 bombs.
19. The attack caused no serious injuries or damage. Burden, *The Air War*, 91.
20. As stated in the *Fuerza Aérea Argentina* website. *Fuerza Aérea Argentina*, http://www.faa.mil.ar/conflicto/dias/may29.html accessed 24 January 2016.
21. Faget ground aborted due to an oxygen system problem. Rivas, *Wings of the Malvinas*, 181.
22. The mission was cancelled as the Argentine garrison at Goose Green had surrendered. *Ibid.*
23. Bernhardt was shot down and killed by a Rapier during the egress from San Carlos. Hobson, *Falklands Air War*, 107.
24. Both formations aborted due to the presence of a Sea Harrier combat air patrol. Rivas, *Wings of the Malvinas*, 181.

25. Prior to reaching their target, two Skyhawks were shot down by HMS *Exeter*'s Sea Darts, killing both pilots. Hobson, *Falklands Air War*, 110.
26. Although Argentine sources claim that the attack was against HMS *Invincible*, British sources suggested that the Type 21 Frigate, HMS *Avenger,* was attacked.
27. Only one Exocet remained in the inventory. Although two Super Etendards flew the mission, the second aircraft was unarmed and served as a back-up in case the primary aircraft had a radar issue.
28. As shown in the *Fuerza Aérea Argentina* website. *Fuerza Aérea Argentina*, http://www.faa.mil.ar/conflicto/dias/may31.html accessed 24 January 2016.
29. The wingman lost contact with his leader and was forced to return to base. Rivas, *Wings of the Malvinas*, 93.
30. Burden informed that the attack caused no serious injuries or damage. However, Beeny provided evidence that suggested that two members of the 846 Naval Air Squadron forward operating base were injured and required casualty evacuation. Burden, *The Air War*, 91; S. Beeny, The Canberra Experience (United States: edocPublish.com, 2016), 245.
31. In contrast to Rivas' view that each aircraft carried three weapons, Segat, the lead Canberra navigator confirmed that each aircraft carried four weapons. *Ibid.*, 246.
32. One Canberra returned to base due to a technical issue. Rivas, *Wings of the Malvinas*, 93.
33. Neither Rivas nor Burden commented on the success of the raid. Therefore, the table assumes that the military impact of the raid was, at best, minimal. *Ibid.*; Burden, *The Air War*, 91.
34. The *Fuerza Aérea Argentina* Official History suggested that only 2 of the 16 weapons failed to release. In contrast, Rivas reported that the remaining 13 weapons failed to release. The table adopts the former position. *Fuerza Aérea Argentina, Historia, Tomo VI, Volumen 2,* 487; Rivas, *Wings of the Malvinas*, 182.
35. Neither Rivas nor Burden commented on the success of the raid. However, Southby-Tailyour's diary entry for 4 June described the event, 'Canberra bomber attack on the Brigade area in the north but apparently they were off target and bombed down Berkeley Sound which is a delightful waste of their ordnance.' Burden, *The Air War*, 91; Southby-Tailyour, *Reasons in Writing*, 250.
36. Beeny suggested that the formation composition and weapon load was different to that stipulated by Rivas. Beeny informed that Puma formation comprised 3 aircraft; one Canberra carried 5 weapons whereas the other two aircraft carried 8 bombs each. Additionally, Lince formation constituted 2 aircraft each armed with 5 bombs. Beeny, *The Canberra Experience*, 247.
37. Due to the intensity of missile defences, the Canberras were forced to abort their mission. Rivas, *Wings of the Malvinas*, 94.

38. Rivas suggested that only one Canberra participated in this mission. However, the *Fuerza Aérea Argentina*'s Official History confirms the mission involved a second aircraft. *Ibid.*; *Fuerza Aérea Argentina, Historia, Tomo VI, Volumen 2,* 492.
39. Assumed payload. Only Rivas mentioned this sortie. Rivas, *Wings of the Malvinas*, 190.
40. The Official History only confirmed the number of weapons carried by Trueno formation. However, The *Fuerza Aérea Argentina* website suggested that both Trueno and Potro formations were both carrying a bomb load of 3 BRPs. *Fuerza Aérea Argentina, Historia, Tomo VI, Volumen 2,* 505; Fuerza Aérea Argentina, http://www.faa.mil.ar/conflicto/dias/jun7.htmlaccessed 24 January 2016.
41. It is assumed that the Dagger formation was carrying two BRPs.
42. The A-4Q Skyhawk fit is assumed to be four Mk 82 bombs.
43. Rivas informs the attack comprised five Mk 82 bombs. As a result, the table assumes that three bombs failed to release from the aircraft. Rivas, *Wings of the Malvinas*, 262.
44. One bomb hit the Liberian-registered vessel, which had no connection with the Conflict. However, the bomb failed to detonate. Burden, *The Air War*, 92.
45. The *Fuerza Aérea Argentina* website confirmed that both Mastin and Dogo carried the same payload – three BRPs. *Fuerza Aérea Argentina*, http://www.faa.mil.ar/conflicto/dias/jun8.html accessed 24 January 2016.
46. Two aircraft returned to base. Rivas, *Wings of the Malvinas*, 154.
47. Two of Galvez's bombs hit the ship while his wingman missed. RFA *Sir Tristram* is severely damaged and withdrawn from the campaign. Burden, *The Air War*, 124.
48. Carballo in the lead aircraft is forced to recover to base. Rivas, *Wings of the Malvinas*, 154.
49. Carmona's bombs failed to release. *Ibid.*, 155.
50. Rinke's bombs missed but Cachon hit RFA *Sir Galahad* with all three of his bombs. *Sir Galahad* subsequently sank. The raid cost the lives of 49 soldiers and sailors, the largest loss of British life in a single event during the war. Burden, *The Air War*, 124; Freedman, *Official History Volume 2*, 613.
51. One bomb failed to release. Rivas, *Wings of the Malvinas*, 192.
52. None of the four bombs that hit the ship detonated. Burden, *The Air War*, 138.
53. Following a birdstrike, one Dagger is forced to return to base. Rivas, *Wings of the Malvinas*, 192.
54. Dellepaine returned to base with an engine problem. *Ibid.*, 156.
55. LCU F4 is hit by a single bomb drop and sank with the loss of five lives. A Sea Harrier combat air patrol intercepts the A-4 Skyhawks as the attack commences. The net result was three Skyhawks were shot down by AIM-9L

Sidewinders with the loss of all three pilots. Sanchez jettisoned his weapons and recovered to the mainland as the sole survivor from his formation. Freedman, *Official History Volume 2*, 613; Morgan, *Hostile Skies*, 269.

56. The Martillo leader, Berrier, is forced to return with an oxygen problem. Rivas, *Wings of the Malvinas*, 156.
57. Two aircraft had problems attempting to drop their weapons while another had a 'hung' bomb. *Ibid.*, 131.
58. The *Fuerza Aérea Argentina* website confirmed that aircraft in both the Cobra and Piton formations carried 3 BRPs. *Fuerza Aérea Argentina*, http://www.faa.mil.ar/conflicto/dias/jun9.html accessed 24 January 2016.
59. One aircraft returns to base shortly after take-off. During refuelling another Skyhawk also returned. Rivas, *Wings of the Malvinas*, 131.
60. The A-4Q Skyhawk fit is assumed to be four Mk 82 bombs.
61. Due to the presence of Sea Harrier combat air patrols, the mission was aborted. *Ibid.*, 262.
62. The *Fuerza Aérea Argentina* website confirmed that the Daggers were armed with two BRPs. *Fuerza Aérea Argentina*, http://www.faa.mil.ar/conflicto/dias/jun9.html accessed 24 January 2016.
63. Neither Rivas nor the *Fuerza Aérea Argentina* website indicated what the Dagger formation's weapon load was. The table assumes a standard twin BRP fit. *Fuerza Aérea Argentina*, http://www.faa.mil.ar/conflicto/dias/jun10.html accessed 24 January 2016.
64. Both formation wingmen ground aborted. Rivas, *Wings of the Malvinas*, 95.
65. Both Canberras aborted due to the presence of a Sea Harrier combat air patrol. *Ibid.*
66. Beeny suggested that both formations carried five bombs in each aircraft. Beeny, *The Canberra Experience*, 250.
67. One aircraft was unable to jettison its fuel tank. As a result, both aircraft aborted the mission. Rivas, *Wings of the Malvinas*, 95.
68. One aircraft returned to base with a technical problem. *Ibid.*
69. Neither Rivas nor Burden identified the outcome of the strike. Therefore, the table assumes that the attack delivers limited effect. *Ibid.*; Burden, *The Air War*, 92.
70. Post air-to-air refuelling, two aircraft were forced to recover to base. Rivas, *Wings of the Malvinas,* 160.
71. Of the remaining pair of aircraft, one Skyhawk developed an engine problem and both aircraft elected to return to base. *Ibid.*
72. The second aircraft suffered an engine fire on take-off and aborted his take-off. As the aircraft had taken the arrestor cable, the two aircraft behind the

damaged aircraft were unable to take-off. Nevertheless, the leader continued his mission. *Ibid.*

73. The A-4Q Skyhawk fit is assumed to be four Mk 82 bombs.
74. The formation aborted the mission due to the presence of a Sea Harrier combat air patrol in the vicinity of the target – artillery positions to the north of North Basin. *Ibid.*, 262.
75. Both aircraft were forced to return to base due to bad weather and serviceability issues. *Ibid.*, 95.
76. The *Fuerza Aérea Argentina* Official History informed that one aircraft returned to base due to serviceability issues. *Fuerza Aérea Argentina, Historia, Tomo VI, Volumen 2*, 550.
77. Burden suggests British forces report no damage. However, Hobson and Moro both informed that the weapons fell in proximity to General Moore's Field Headquarters on the western side of Mount Kent. Burden, *The Air War*, 92; Hobson, *Falklands Air War*, 134 and Moro, *South Atlantic Conflict*, 309.
78. Neither Rivas nor the *Fuerza Aérea Argentina* website confirmed the formation callsign. However, Rivas informed that the aircraft and pilots are as follows: Maffeis, Valente and Callejo. *Fuerza Aérea Argentina*, http://www.faa.mil.ar/conflicto/dias/jun13.htmlaccessed 24 January 2016; Rivas, *Wings of the Malvinas*, 182.
79. The *Fuerza Aérea Argentina* website confirmed both Dagger formations' bomb load. *Fuerza Aérea Argentina*, http://www.faa.mil.ar/conflicto/dias/jun13.html accessed 24 January 2016.
80. Callejo returned to base with a landing gear problem. Rivas, *Wings of the Malvinas*, 182.
81. Due to the presence of a Sea Harrier combat air patrol, the formation aborted. *Ibid.*, 183.
82. Faget aborted with a brake problem. *Ibid.*
83. Both aircraft aborted due to the proximity of a Sea Harrier combat air patrol. *Ibid.*
84. Although not mentioned by Rivas, the *Fuerza Aérea Argentina* website confirmed the Skyhawk take-off time. *Fuerza Aérea Argentina*, http://www.faa.mil.ar/conflicto/dias/jun13.html accessed 24 January 2016.
85. The Nene flight lead was forced to return to base. Rivas, *Wings of the Malvinas*, 161.
86. The bombs landed in the vicinity of the 3 Commando Brigade Command Post housing General Moore and several other senior officers. Burden, *The Air War*, 125.

87. Rivas suggested that the formation attacked a British helicopter park. However, Burden informed that the formation mistakenly dropped its weapons early and caused no significant damage. In contrast, Freedman identified that the raid damaged three light helicopters. As the damaged helicopters were in the vicinity of the 3 Commando Brigade headquarters, it is likely that Nene's weapons damaged the helicopters whereas the Chispa weapons were ineffective. Rivas, *Wings of the Malvinas*, 162; Burden, *The Air War*, 125; Freedman, *Official History Volume 2*, 637.
88. The Dagger payload is confirmed by the *Fuerza Aérea Argentina* website. *Fuerza Aérea Argentina*, http://www.faa.mil.ar/conflicto/dias/jun13.html accessed 24 January 2016.
89. Moreno ground aborted. Rivas, *Wings of the Malvinas*, 193.
90. Robles aircraft was unserviceable during start up and he failed to participate in the mission. *Ibid.*
91. Antonietti is forced to recover with an engine problem. *Ibid.*
92. A Sea Dart fired from HMS *Cardiff* hits the lead Canberra, killing the navigator. Hobson, Falklands Air War, 138.
93. No damage reported by British forces. Burden, *The Air War*, 92.

Annex I – The Reduction in Argentine Combat Air Capability during the Falklands Conflict

1. All figures taken from S. Rivas, *Wings of the Malvinas*.
2. The figure does not include the 4 aircraft (C-401, C-410, C-415 and C-430) employed at both Dagger bases during the Conflict. The San Julian figures include those 4 aircraft.
3. Although all 4 Super Etendards survived the Conflict, the red scoring reflected the use of their complete Exocet weapon stockpile. The 4 May attack against HMS *Sheffield* expended 2 missiles, a further two on 25 May against MV *Atlantic Conveyor* and the Argentines fired the last missile on 30 May during the alleged HMS *Invincible* attack.

Annex J – Sea Harrier/AIM-9L Sidewinder Employment During Operation Corporate

1. Air Combat Mission Report contained within TNA, DEFE 19/276. Scientific Evaluation Team.
2. *Ibid.*
3. Hobson, *Falklands Air War*, 48; Ethell, *Air War South Atlantic*, 65 and Burden, *The Air War*, 212.
4. Air Combat Mission Report contained within TNA, DEFE 19/276. Scientific Evaluation Team.

5. Hobson, *Falklands Air War*, 48; Rivas, *Wings of the Malvinas*, 209. Archival evidence suggested that the Sea Harrier fired the missile from the 4 o'clock position at 1000 yards. However, the weight of evidence would suggest a missile fired from a stern aspect. TNA, DEFE 67/135. Reconstruction of AAW Conflict.
6. Air Combat Mission Report contained within TNA, DEFE 19/276. Scientific Evaluation Team.
7. Hobson, *Falklands Air War,* 49; Burden, *The Air War*, 95 and TNA, DEFE 67/135. Reconstruction of AAW Conflict.
8. Air Combat Mission Report contained within TNA, DEFE 19/276. Scientific Evaluation Team.
9. Although Ward suggested that the pilot fired the first missile just aft of the beam, primary source material informed that the firing is a stern aspect engagement. Ward, *Sea Harrier*, 203; TNA, DEFE 67/135. Reconstruction of AAW Conflict.
10. Burden, *The Air War*, 214.
11. Air Combat Mission Report contained within TNA, DEFE 19/276. Scientific Evaluation Team.
12. TNA, DEFE 67/135. Reconstruction of AAW Conflict.
13. Burden suggested that the missile detonated under the aircraft, damaging the wing. Hobson inferred that the aircraft made an emergency landing at San Julian. However, Rivas informed that the remaining aircraft were undamaged and recovered to Trelew as planned. Rivas clarified the apparent confusion by reporting that an earlier Canberra formation (Ruta flight) diverted Ruta 1 in airframe B-105 to Puerto Deseado after their wingtip impacted with the sea during low-level manoeuvring against a perceived British attack. Burden, *The Air War*, 212; Hobson, *Falklands Air War*, 49; Rivas, *Wings of the Malvinas*, 90 and 92.
14. *Ibid.*, 187; Ethell, *Air War South Atlantic*, 109 and Burden, *The Air War*, 197.
15. TNA, AIR 8/3112. Scientific Evaluation Team.
16. Ethell, *Air War South Atlantic*, 113.
17. TNA, AIR 8/3112. Scientific Evaluation Team; Burden, *The Air War*, 197 and Hobson, *Falklands Air War*, 81.
18. Ethell, *Air War South Atlantic*, 115; Burden, *The Air War*, 197 and Rivas, *Wings of the Malvinas*, 188.
19. TNA, DEFE 69/1085.801 Naval Air Squadron. Record of Proceedings.
20. Ethell, *Air War South Atlantic*, 119 and Hobson, *Falklands Air War*, 82.
21. TNA, DEFE 69/1085.801 Naval Air Squadron. Record of Proceedings.
22. Burden, *The Air War*, 217.

23. Rivas, *Wings of the Malvinas*, 178.
24. Air Combat Mission Report contained within TNA, DEFE 19/276. Scientific Evaluation Team.
25. Burden, *The Air War*, 199 and Rivas, *Wings of the Malvinas*, 256.
26. Air Combat Mission Report contained within TNA, DEFE 19/276. Scientific Evaluation Team.
27. Ethell, *Air War South Atlantic*, 123 and Rivas, *Wings of the Malvinas*, 255.
28. Ethell, *Air War South Atlantic*, 134 and Burden, *The Air War*, 200.
29. Air Combat Mission Report contained within TNA, DEFE 19/276. Scientific Evaluation Team.
30. Hobson, *Falklands Air War*, 92.
31. Air Combat Mission Report contained within TNA, DEFE 19/276. Scientific Evaluation Team.
32. Rivas, *Wings of the Malvinas*, 180.
33. Air Combat Mission Report contained within TNA, DEFE 19/276. Scientific Evaluation Team.
34. Burden suggested that Puga was in C-419 and Diaz in C-430 both pilots, whom Auld shot down, ejected successfully, whereas Castillo in C-410 died in the engagement with Smith. More recent analysis suggested that the pilots, airframes, and outcomes are incorrect. The table reflects the contemporary viewpoint. Burden, *The Air War*, 200.
35. Morgan, *Hostile Skies*, 236 and Ward, *Sea Harrier*, 288.
36. TNA, DEFE 69/1085.801 Naval Air Squadron. Record of Proceedings.
37. Ethell, *Air War South Atlantic*, 175.
38. TNA, DEFE 69/1085.801 Naval Air Squadron. Record of Proceedings.
39. Briasco, *Falklands – Witness of Battles*, 128.
40. Morgan, *Hostile Skies*, 267.
41. *Ibid.*,
42. Briasco, *Falklands – Witness of Battles*, 128.
43. TNA, AIR 8/3112. Scientific Evaluation Team.
44. Ethell, *Air War South Atlantic*, 196 and Rivas, *Wings of the Malvinas*, 156.
45. Burden, *The Air War*, 204. The range bracket stipulated is significantly outside of the low-level operating envelope for the Sidewinder and is therefore a dubious figure. In the official Air Combat Mission Debrief, Smith fires the missile 'at extreme range 2nm+.' TNA, AIR 8/3112. Scientific Evaluation Team.
46. Morgan, *Hostile Skies*, 270.A Sidewinder missile time of flight of seven seconds equated to a more realistic and credible firing range.

Annex K – Employment of British Attack Weapons during Operation Corporate.

1. 'The next day Woodward reported that photographic reconnaissance now showed that: Vulcan attack made single crater with first bomb halfway down runway just south of centre, remaining bombs landed over to SW [south-west] over 1000m [metres] run without further damage.' Freedman, *Official History Volume 2*, 285
2. The weapons used against the airfield comprised twelve BL755 cluster bombs and three 1000lb bombs. Brown, *Royal Navy*, 120.
3. In addition to attacking the wider airfield infrastructure, two of Penfold's bombs hit the runway. However, Freedman highlighted that Woodward believed that all three of Penfold's bombs had hit the runway. Burden, *The Air War*, 194; Freedman, *Official History Volume 2*, 285.
4. The Sea Harrier force dedicated four aircraft and twelve 1000lb bombs to the suppression of enemy air defences. Hobson, *Falklands Air War*, 45.
5. The Goose Green attack comprised six BL755s and three 1000lb bombs. Brown, *Royal Navy*, 120.
6. The initial British strike assessment was, 'vague but recorded "fires burning but no secondary explosions."' However, subsequent analysis confirmed that the attack destroyed a Pucara, its pilot and eight groundcrew. Two further Pucaras were damaged, a further seven individuals were wounded and the maintenance tent destroyed. Freedman, *Official History Volume 2*, 285; Rivas, *Wings of the Malvinas*, 105.
7. The Lynx HAS2 helicopters came from the embarked flights of the Type 42 destroyers HMS *Coventry* and *Glasgow*. All four missiles hit and damaged the Argentine vessel but failed to sink it. In contrast, Brown suggested, incorrectly, that the helicopters attacked two vessels, sinking one and damaging the other, believed to be the *Alferez Sobral's* sister ship, *Comodoro Somerella*. Additionally, Brown informed that three out of the four missiles fired were successful. Hobson, *Falklands Air War*, 52; Brown, *Royal Navy*, 138.
8. Hobson, *Falklands Air War*, 53.
9. Two aircraft carried three BL755 each whereas the other aircraft carried three 1000lb bombs. Brown, *Royal Navy*, 144.
10. Lieutenant Taylor's aircraft was shot down prior to weapon release, killing the pilot. Hobson, *Falklands Air War*, 56.
11. Burden informed that the results of the raid were not particularly impressive. Although the raid failed to destroy further aircraft it generated further disruption. Burden, *The Air War*, 195.

12. This was the first planned use of Sea Harrier to bomb Stanley Airport during their transit to their Combat Air Patrol area. However, the weather was too poor to drop their bombs against Stanley airport as planned. Nevertheless, the Sea Harrier's detected the *Narwhal* on their radar and following identification and approval, they attacked the ship from low level. One bomb hit but failed to detonate, due to the seven second fusing required for its original task of medium level bombing, the other bomb missed. Ward, *Sea Harrier*, 237; Morgan, *Hostile Skies*, 124.
13. Brown informed that by noon, four 1000lb bombs were dropped by radar aiming during routine combat air patrol. However, Hobson suggested that none of the bombs did any damage. Brown, *Royal Navy,* 159; Hobson, *Falklands Air War*, 65.
14. The attack resulted in no significant damage: one bomb hit the target but there was no explosion. Two bombs missed and the other weapon was unsighted. Burden, *The Air War*, 196.
15. Assumed payload. Mission aborted due to their controlling ship, HMS *Brilliant*, coming under attack by Argentine aircraft. Hobson, *Falklands Air War*, 65.
16. 801 Naval Air Squadron were tasked at short notice to conduct strikes against troop dispositions north-west of Stanley and a radar at Sapper Hill. The aircraft were in combat air patrol configuration with a single bomb. The outcome of the mission is unknown. TNA, DEFE 69/1085.801 Naval Air Squadron. Record of Proceedings.
17. Strong winds forced the cancellation of the mission. Burden, *The Air War*, 365.
18. The four bombs straddled the ship but they failed to hit their target. Morgan, *Hostile Skies*, 140.
19. Although not stipulated, the table assumes that both aircraft were carrying two weapons. Due to the proximity of the nearby settlement, the pilots decided not to drop their bombs but instead strafed the ship. Burden, *The Air War*, 196.
20. Due to poor weather, the weapons were dropped blind from medium level. Burden suggested that despite witnessing explosions there was no damage to the helicopters despite Ward's confirmation that all twelve weapons hit their intended target position. The Squadrons Record of Proceedings, and supported by photographic evidence, show two weapons on each aircraft. Brown, *Royal Navy*, 172; Burden, *The Air War*, 215; Ward, *Sea Harrier*, 253 and TNA, DEFE 69/1085.801 Naval Air Squadron. Record of Proceedings.
21. Ethell suggested that each aircraft carried only two weapons. However, Squire's account in the RAF website informed that the aircraft carried three

weapons each. Squire's account is coherent with the Combat Mission Report. Ethell, *Air War South Atlantic*, 98; Squire, *Harrier goes to War and* TNA, AIR 20/13126. Harrier aircraft operations.

22. The Combat Mission Report only reported on the fall of the leader's weapons. However, Pook confirmed that all three aircraft hit the target. *Ibid.*; Pook, *RAF Harrier Ground Attack*, 52.
23. The Combat Mission Report confirmed the take-off time and payload. Pook dropped his weapons beyond the target and Hare's bombs failed to release from the aircraft. Consequently, Pook strafed the helicopters. Brown confirmed that the attack destroyed a Chinook and a Puma while damaging another Puma. Pook suggested his bombs dropped long rather than short and that the damaged helicopter was a Huey. TNA, AIR 20/13126. Harrier aircraft operations; Hobson, *Falklands Air War*, 78; Brown, *Royal Navy*, 184; Pook, *RAF Harrier Ground Attack*, 60.
24. Assumed payload. The Combat Mission Report only confirmed that the aircraft did not employ weapons on this mission. TNA, AIR 20/13126. Harrier aircraft operations.
25. Due to an aircraft serviceability issue, Squire was forced to return to HMS *Hermes*. Squire, *Harrier goes to War.*
26. A Blowpipe missile at Port Howard shot down Glover during a reattack.TNA, AIR 27/3525.1 Squadron.
27. SCAR or Strike, Coordination and Reconnaissance, is one of the three counter-land attack missions and can be tasked in order to allow aircraft to seek-out and attack enemy targets beyond the battlefield area. SCAR allows air power to focus on areas where potential targets exist.RAF, 'Attack.' http://www.raf.mod.uk/role/attack.cfm (accessed 13 October 2016).
28. Harris and Rochfort were unable to find targets and returned to the aircraft carrier with their weapons. Rochfort had a landing mishap and photographs of the event confirmed that the aircraft were each armed with two BL755s. Burden, *The Air War*, 375 and374.
29. Assumed payload and weapons.
30. There was some debate regarding who was the second pilot in this mission. Burden suggested Hare was the second pilot. In contrast, Pook, the mission leader, informed that Harper was his wingman. Regardless, neither aircraft dropped its weapons during the mission. The Combat Mission Report confirmed that Pook and Harper flew the mission but 'found neither military activity nor evidence of recent use.' *Ibid.*; Pook, *RAF Harrier Ground Attack*, 62; TNA, AIR 20/13126. Harrier aircraft operations.
31. One aircraft's bombs hang. Hobson suggested that the pilot was Harris. The Combat Mission Report concurred with Hobson and also suggested the

carriage of only 8 BL755s. In contrast, Burden believed that Iveson was the pilot. Hobson, *Falklands Air War*, 86; TNA, AIR 20/13126. Harrier aircraft operations; Burden, *The Air War*, 375

32. Assumed payload. Pook suggested that neither Squire nor Harper dropped their weapons. Pook, *RAF Harrier Ground Attack*, 70.
33. The weapon load comprised four BL755s and six 1000lb bombs. Hobson, *Falklands Air War*, 87.
34. Hare dropped his weapons late; the subsequent explosion wounded an Islander. Additionally, one bomb from Hare's aircraft failed to explode. Pook, *RAF Harrier Ground Attack*, 74.
35. Assumed weapons. Rochfort and Pook found suitable targets but were unable to bring their weapons to bear. *Ibid.*, 77.
36. HMS *Argonaut's* Lynx was unable to lock its radar onto the ship. Consequently, HMS *Antelope's* Lynx attacked the ship with two missiles. Both missiles hit their target and detonated, which caused the vessel to sink. Hobson, *Falklands Air War*, 88.
37. The Combat Mission Report informed that the formation comprised three aircraft each carrying two BL755. In contrast, Pook offered that the formation comprised four aircraft with numbers 1 and 3 in the formation carrying BL755s whereas the other aircraft carried three 1000lb bombs each. The Scientific Evaluation Team's Report endorses Pook's position, which shows an updated version of the Combat Mission Report.TNA, AIR 20/13126. Harrier aircraft operations; Pook, *RAF Harrier Ground Attack – Falklands*, 77; TNA, DEFE 19/276. Scientific Evaluation Team.
38. Hare air aborted with an undercarriage problem. Pook, *RAF Harrier Ground Attack*, 77.
39. Due to a persistent weapon systems problem with his aircraft, Rochfort jettisoned his three 1000lb bombs and his fuel tanks during the run-in to the target. *Ibid.*
40. Batt crashed following take-off and was killed. *Ibid.*, 72.
41. Morgan informed that one aircraft returned to the aircraft carrier early with a technical issue and, as a result, was forced to jettison its weapons. Morgan also suggested that the other two aircraft successfully completed their mission. Brown recorded that the weapons were delivered accurately. However, Pook informed that there was no evidence of a bomb impact on the runway. Morgan, *Hostile Skies*, 204; Brown, *Royal Navy*, 211; Pook, *RAF Harrier Ground Attack*, 72.
42. The RAF website suggested that 3/4 of the weapons hit the runway. However, the 1 (Fighter) Squadron F540 informed that the attack struck the runway three times. Nevertheless, although the bombs scarred the runway surface the

attack caused no significant damage. Squire, *Harrier goes to War*; TNA, AIR 27/3525.1 Squadron; Brown, *Royal Navy*, 211.

43. A suppression of enemy air defences mission in support of Harrier GR3 sortie. Thomas landed with a hung bomb on the fuselage centreline weapons pylon. Pook, *RAF Harrier Ground Attack*, 80.
44. Due to a system failure, the bombs dropped into the sea 1.5 miles short of the target. Brown, *Royal Navy*, 216; TNA, AIR20/13126. Harrier aircraft operations.
45. Of note, the 800 Naval Air Squadron weapon analysis contained within the Scientific Evaluation Report failed to mention this mission. The medium level toss attack caused little significant damage. Pook suggested that the first formation's bombs landed beyond the end of the runway. In contrast, the second formation's weapons impacted not far off the side of the runway.TNA, DEFE 19/276. Scientific Evaluation Team; Burden, *The Air War*, 376; Pook, *RAF Harrier Ground Attack*, 84.
46. Assumed weapons and payload. Squire and Rochfort flew an uneventful mission and did not drop their weapons. *Ibid.*, 85.
47. According to Burden, at least three of the six bombs missed the target. Pook was less optimistic and assessed the mission as a particularly useless exercise. The Combat Mission Report informed that the squadron dropped the bombs individually, but the pilots tracked the fall of only three weapons watching them land in York Bay. Burden, *The Air War*, 376; Pook, *RAF Harrier Ground Attack*, 85; TNA, AIR 20/13126. Harrier aircraft operations.
48. The 1(Fighter) Squadron F540 suggested that there were no hits on the runway on 25 May 1982. The Combat Mission Report informed that all three bombs dropped by Harris fell short of their intended target. TNA, AIR 27/3525.1 Squadron; TNA, AIR 20/13126. Harrier aircraft operations.
49. The Sea Harrier bombs were seen to drop short of their target. Burden, *The Air War*, 201.
50. Outcome not stipulated but 'results looked very impressive'. Hobson, *Falklands Air War*, 99; TNA, AIR 20/13126. Harrier aircraft operations.
51. Assumed weapons. The Identification Friend or Foe system was not serviceable on either aircraft. Subsequently, both aircraft aborted their mission after getting airborne. However, Burden suggested that only Pook returned. Pook, *RAF Harrier Ground Attack*, 102; Burden, *The Air War*, 376.
52. Pook informed that the mission was effective. However, Hobson describes the mission as uneventful. The Combat Mission Report confirmed the payload and the effectiveness of the attack. Pook, *RAF Harrier Ground Attack*, 102; Hobson, *Falklands Air War*, 99; TNA, AIR 20/13126. Harrier aircraft operations.

53. One bomb failed to release and the pilots did not see the fall of the weapons. *Ibid.*; TNA, AIR 27/3525.1 Squadron.
54. Only Pook conducted a successful attack with two BL755s on a Puma helicopter at Mount Kent. However, a previous attack damaged the helicopter. Moreover, Morgan and Pook disagreed over the number of weapons carried by each Harrier GR3; Morgan suggested that each aircraft carried three bombs. Pook, *RAF Harrier Ground Attack – Falklands*, 104; Hobson, *Falklands Air War*, 99; Morgan, *Hostile Skies*, 225.
55. Freedman confirmed the take-off time of the Stanley raid. Freedman, *Official History Volume 2*, 491.
56. No direct hits on runway. The Combat Mission Report informed that the pilots saw smoke to the west of the runway and that Harper's bombs landed in the water to the south. TNA, AIR 27/3525.1 Squadron TNA; TNA, AIR 20/13126. Harrier aircraft operations.
57. All weapons were dropped but, due to late detection of the target, the pilots dropped the weapons on multiple passes. Hare dropped on a group of approximately fifteen troops while Iveson dropped on a line of foxholes. Hobson, *Falklands Air War*, 101; TNA, AIR 20/13126. Harrier aircraft operations.
58. Assumed payload. Pook suggested that Squire and Rochfort were unable to find a suitable target to attack. Pook, *RAF Harrier Ground Attack*, 108.
59. According to Middlebrook, the initial cluster bomb attacks caused little or no damage. Small arms fire brought down Iveson's Harrier GR3. Middlebrook, *The Argentinian Fight*, 180; Burden, *The Air War*, 376.
60. Assumed weapons and payload. The mission task was to conduct medium level reconnaissance to locate Iveson, who had ejected earlier that day. TNA, AIR 20/13126. Harrier aircraft operations.
61. Harper did not fire his rockets due to poor weather in the target area. However, the pilots saw secondary explosions during the attack. Pook, *RAF Harrier Ground Attack*, 112.
62. Pook and Rochfort were unable to find suitable targets and returned to their aircraft carrier with their weapons. However, Brown suggested that the other formations performed the attacks: one pair of rocket-armed aircraft conducted reconnaissance of Douglas settlement, whereas the bomb-armed aircraft attack troop positions at Mount Kent. *Ibid.*; Brown, *Royal Navy*, 246.
63. Two aircraft carried two BL755s, while the third carried two Royal Navy 2-Inch rocket pods.TNA, AIR 20/13126. Harrier aircraft operations.
64. The attack was, 'quite decisive.' Brown, *Royal Navy*, 247.
65. A technical problem with one of the Victor air-to-air refuelling aircraft forced an air abort five hours into the mission. Hobson, *Falklands Air War*, 106.

66. The Squadron Record of Proceedings confirmed the payload and that three of the weapons detonated prematurely. TNA, DEFE 69/1085.801 Naval Air Squadron. Record of Proceedings.
67. Brown informed that at least fourteen of the bombs landed in the runway area. Brown, *Royal Navy*, 251.
68. Burden, *The Air War*, 218.
69. Hobson informed that Squire and Hare flew the first mission against Argentine position in the Mount Kent area. Brown added further detail when he suggested that the mission was in support of an SAS patrol. The intervention appeared to have been successful, for the troopers continued their possession of the vital feature. However, at the time, the pilots saw nothing at the target locations. Hobson, *Falklands Air War*, 108; Brown, *Royal Navy*, 251; TNA, AIR 20/13126. Harrier aircraft operations.
70. Brown suggested that the Harrier GR3s only flew one mission on this day. However, Pook disagreed, and although Rochfort ground aborted, Harris continued to look for radar sites but without success. Assumed weapons and payload. *Ibid.;* Pook, *RAF Harrier Ground Attack*, 117.
71. Pook dropped his weapons on target coordinates but did not report the outcome. However, the Combat Mission Report informed that the aircraft attacked two locations but the pilots did not see military targets or activity at either location. Pook, *RAF Harrier Ground Attack*, 119; TNA, AIR 20/13126. Harrier aircraft operations.
72. Pook suggested that Squire and Hare attacked troop positions in the Mount Kent area but he did not report the outcome. However, Freedman informed that enemy positions were successfully engaged. Again, the pilots did not see anything at the target location. Pook, *RAF Harrier Ground Attack,* 118; Freedman, *Official History Volume 2*, 590; TNA, AIR 20/13126. Harrier aircraft operations.
73. The Harrier GR3s had an unusual configuration encompassing one Paveway laser-guided bomb and one 1000lb weapon. Brown, *Royal Navy*, 253.
74. In the first Paveway laser-guided bomb attack, Hare and Harper dropped the weapon from a 60-degree dive with the weapon being laser designated by the wingman. The results of the attack were unseen by the pilots. Pook suggested that the pilots saw no impacts anywhere on the airfield. TNA, AIR 27/3525.1 Squadron; Pook, *RAF Harrier Ground Attack*, 120.
75. An artillery position was attacked at Mount Wall but the combat report fails to mention the outcome. However, after taking ground fire, Pook ran out of fuel forty miles short of the carrier and successfully ejected from the aircraft. However, Pook informed that he was hit prior to the target area. Hobson, *Falklands Air War*, 109; Pook, *RAF Harrier Ground Attack*, 122.

76. Burden suggested that Thomas and Ball's attack led to poor results. Brown mentioned that a second Sea Harrier attack on Stanley airport took place on 30 May 1982. However, Hobson and Burden informed that at 1915, two Sea Harriers took off to conduct an uneventful photographic reconnaissance mission over East Falkland. Burden, *The Air War*, 202; Brown, *Royal Navy*, 257; Hobson, *Falklands Air War*, 110 and Burden, *The Air War*, 202.
77. Squires and Hare were initially tasked to attack the artillery position at Mount Wall but were unable to find the targets. They attacked enemy defensive positions on northern slopes of Mount Kent. Additionally, Brown confirmed that the mission was in support of the SAS. TNA, AIR 20/13126. Harrier aircraft operations; Brown, *Royal Navy*, 257.
78. The Vulcan mission, Black Buck 5, caused a near miss and minor damage to the TPS-43F radar. Hobson, *Falklands Air War*, 111.
79. No specific take-off times are noted other than pre-dawn and one hour later after the first mission. Brown informed that the take-off times were 0320 and 0410 (equating to 0720 and 0810 Greenwich Mean Time). However, Brown suggested that the missions were flown as singletons and not as pairs, as inferred by Hobson. *Ibid.*; Brown, *Royal Navy*, 258.
80. The 801 NAS Sea Harriers were tasked to stimulate the Argentine radars ahead of the Shrike-armed Vulcan mission. *Ibid.*, 259.
81. One aircraft was armed with Paveway laser-guided bombs, one with 1000lb bombs and the other with rockets. Burden, *The Air War*, 379.
82. Burden does not mention the outcome of the attack other than there was no forward air controller available to guide the Paveway laser-guided bombs. Hobson suggested that the mission results were disappointing. Pook informs that the pilots did not observe the weapon impacts. *Ibid.*; Hobson, *Falklands Air War*, 111; Pook, *RAF Harrier Ground Attack*, 127.
83. The mission was flown at short notice following reports of 'Super Etendards' at the eastern end of the Stanley airport. There is no mention of the mission's outcome.
84. Morrell flew a trial mission with a Paveway-armed Sea Harrier. The table reflects an assumed payload for the Sea Harriers. However, the trial failed and not repeated. Burden inferred that the weapons were employed but the results were unconfirmed. Burden, *The Air War*, 379; Hobson, *Falklands Air War*, 112; Burden, *The Air War*, 379.
85. Pook informed that Harris flew a rocket attack against troops in the hills to the west of Stanley. However, there is no mention of the mission success. Pook, *RAF Harrier Ground Attack*, 130.

86. Rockets fired at grid reference but Pook makes no comment on results. The Combat Mission Report suggested that the pilot strafed the target area. *Ibid.*, 131; TNA, AIR 20/13126. Harrier aircraft operations.
87. Assumed payload and weapons. The Sea Harrier attacked a suspected radar site at Mount Usborne. Hobson, *Falklands Air War*, 113.
88. Pook and McLeod were tasked against a suspected radar site. However, due to poor weather the mission was aborted. *Ibid.*, 115; Pook, *RAF Harrier Ground Attack*, 135.
89. The Shrikes successfully homed into an Argentine Army Skyguard anti-aircraft gun-control radar rather than the TPS-43F surveillance radar that the crew aimed at. Hobson, *Falklands Air War*, 116.
90. Mission flown by Harris and Rochfort. Brown confirmed take-off time, weapons and that the mission launched from the forward operating strip at San Carlos. There is no associated Combat Mission Report for this sortie. *Ibid.*, 118; Brown, *Royal Navy,* 283; TNA, AIR 20/13126. Harrier aircraft operations.
91. Squire and Beech attacked the previously damaged Pucaras at Pebble Island. Hobson, *Falklands Air War*, 119.
92. Burden suggested that the aircraft were searching for ground launched Exocet missiles. Burden, *The Air War*, 379.
93. Morrell and Slade joined the Harrier GR3s on the armed recce. However, Burden informed that the Sea Harriers found nothing on their mission. *Ibid.*, 202.
94. Only Squire dropped his BL755s on briefed troop positions south of Stanley, but Beech did not see his battlefield radar target and did not drop his weapons. The combat report fails to mention the mission's results. TNA, AIR 20/13126. Harrier aircraft operations.
95. Brown suggested that two attacks took place against suspected artillery positions. However, Pook explained that due to ground aborts only two of the planned four Harrier GR3s launched. Moreover, once in the target area, the anticipated artillery pieces were not there. Nevertheless, both aircraft fired into the target area but the outcome of the attack is unknown. Brown, *Royal Navy*, 290; Pook, *RAF Harrier Ground Attack*, 142; TNA, AIR 20/13126. Harrier aircraft operations.
96. Again, Brown informed that four pairs attacked artillery with rockets. However, analysis suggested that only two pairs participated. The Combat Mission Report informed that the aircraft fired at the target position without positively identifying a target. Brown, *Royal Navy*, 307; TNA, AIR 20/13126. Harrier aircraft operations.

97. Weapons fired at coordinates but no target present. Pook, *RAF Harrier Ground Attack*, 147
98. Squire and Hare dropped their BL755s in the target area. The Combat Mission Report informed that post-flight film analysis identified heavy artillery and enemy troops in both target areas. *Ibid.*, 152; TNA, AIR 20/13126. Harrier aircraft operations.
99. Due to the carrier rescheduling its flying programme, the Harriers were forced to take off two hours earlier than planned and the ground-based forward air controller was not ready to provide the essential target marking for the aircraft. Consequently, Burden suggested that neither aircraft dropped their weapons. The Combat Mission Report informed that only Harper's aircraft was armed with laser-guided bombs while the wingman's role was for cross cover support only. As a result, Squire informed that the pilot jettisoned the weapons before landing. Hobson, *Falklands Air War*, 130; Burden, *The Air War*, 380; TNA, AIR 20/13126. Harrier aircraft operations and Squire, *Harrier goes to War.*
100. Assumed payload. Special forces support mission at Port Howard but unable to contact the Forward Air Controller. TNA, AIR 20/13126. Harrier aircraft operations.
101. Briefed target area attacked and several secondary explosions seen from Squire's weapons. *Ibid.*
102. Eleven of twelve bombs exploded on the airfield. Hobson, *Falklands Air War*, 131
103. Both AS-12 missiles missed, one by only a few yards while the other missile fell into the sea at Stanley harbour. *Ibid.*
104. An SAS team planned to mark the target but the battery of their laser target marker failed. So, the aircraft dropped their bombs on Wireless Ridge. There is no record of the mission's outcome. *Ibid.*, 132
105. Due to an Identification Friend or Foe failure, Pook and Beech aborted their mission once airborne. Pook, *RAF Harrier Ground Attack*, 155.
106. The original 1(F) Squadron Combat Mission Reports suggested that the aircraft carried BL755. However, the Scientific Evaluation Team's report informed that the aircraft carried rockets. TNA, AIR 20/13126. Harrier aircraft operations; TNA, DEFE 19/276. Scientific Evaluation Team.
107. Rochfort jettisoned his stores post take-off in order to prevent him crashing into the sea. However, he continued on his mission. Hobson, *Falklands Air War*, 132.
108. Pook and Beech could not see their target but dropped their weapons at their allocated grid reference. However, the Combat Mission Report informed that Beech saw a vehicle at his target position. Pook, *RAF Harrier Ground Attack*, 155; TNA, AIR 20/13126. Harrier aircraft operations.
109. Although Burden confirmed that Harris and Gilchrist flew the mission, there is no mention of the outcome. Burden, *The Air War*, 380.

110. The expected targets were not at the target location. Nevertheless, the attack took place. However, the retard tails failed to deploy and the bombs missed. Pook, *RAF Harrier Ground Attack*, 154.
111. The last Vulcan mission, Black Buck 7, caused limited damage due to incorrect weapon fuse settings. The weapon fuses' were set for impact rather than airburst. Freedman, *Official History Volume 2*, 638; Hobson, *Falklands Air War*, 133.
112. Boyens and Beech attacked their allocated target area but without positively identifying a target. TNA, AIR 20/13126. Harrier aircraft operations.
113. Although Hobson does not confirm the outcome of Harris and Mcleod's mission, Argentine sources suggested that a 155mm howitzer was lightly damaged and six soldiers injured. Hobson, *Falklands Air War*, 133; H. Rodríguez Mottino, *La Artillería Argentina en Malvinas*. (Buenos Aires: Clio, 1984), 91.
114. Although Burden confirmed that Harper and Gilchrist dropped their weapons, and the Combat Mission Report informed that an attack against troops in the open took place, there is no record of the attack's results. Burden, *The Air War*, 380; TNA, AIR 20/13126. Harrier aircraft operations.
115. Only one aircraft carried a pair of Paveway bombs, the other aircraft acted as a 'surface-to-air missile lookout.' Pook, *RAF Harrier Ground Attack*, 160.
116. During the first attack, target designation occurred too early and the bomb dropped short, the second bomb scored a direct hit on a company headquarters. The wingman also dropped his BL755s onto the target. TNA, AIR 27/3525.1 Squadron; Hobson, *Falklands Air War*, 136.
117. One weapon fell short whereas the other bomb scored a direct hit on an artillery piece. The Combat Mission Report suggested that Beech, not Rochfort, acted as the wingman for the mission. *Ibid.;* TNA, AIR 20/13126. Harrier aircraft operations.
118. Gun emplacements and troops. No outcome was stipulated. Hobson, *Falklands Air War*, 138.
119. *Ibid.*
120. The Argentine surrender cancelled the mission.TNA, AIR 27/3525.1 Squadron.
121. Not all combat air patrols dropped weapons on Stanley airport. For example, on 28 May only four of the eighteen patrols dropped 1000lb bombs against the target. Hobson, *Falklands Air War*, 106.
122. According to their Record of Proceedings, 801 Naval Air Squadron dropped a total of fifty-four bombs during the Conflict. However, although the data within the document is correct the total is wrong. Burden correctly identified that the figure is fifty-six. HMS *Invincible's* Campaign Diary concurred with Burden's assessment. Analysis informed that 801 Naval Air Squadron dropped thirty-one bombs during combat air patrol missions and a further twenty-five during dedicated attack missions. TNA, DEFE 69/1085.801 Naval Air Squadron. Record of Proceedings; Burden, *The Air War*, 221; TNA, DEFE 69/844. Campaign Diary.

Index

1 (Fighter) Squadron, 56, 77, 107, 174, 294, 299, 346–7
  aircraft availability, 180
  Cold War tasking, 33
  combat reports, 23
  HMS *Ark Royal* trials, 29
  preparations, 34–5
  weapon usage, 161–2, 167, 251–7
  see also Harrier, British Aerospace
2 PARA, 26, 85
  Blowpipe, 146
  breakout from San Carlos, 99
  Goose Green, 113–16
3 Commando Brigade, 21, 81, 84, 103, 110, 202–203, 315
  Air Squadron, 257
  approach to Stanley, 105, 118
  attack on headquarters, 119, 339–40
  commanding officer, 26
    see also Thompson, Brigadier Julian
  Rapier support, 145, 149
3 PARA, 85
  San Carlos Landing, 86
3 (Fighter) Squadron, 56, 107, 300
  pilots seconded to Sea Harrier, 300
  see also Harrier, British Aerospace
4 Squadron, 56
  Ascension Island defence, 57
  pilots seconded to Sea Harrier, 299
  see also Harrier, British Aerospace
5 Infantry Brigade, 101, 104, 110, 188, 203, 308, 315
  approach to Stanley, 105, 117–18
  commanding officer, 22
    see also Wilson, Brigadier Tony
  landing, 26
  Rapier support, 145
12 Air Defence Regiment, Royal Artillery, 84, 143, 314
    see also Rapier missile
29 (Fighter) Squadron, 57
39 Squadron, 24
40 Commando, 84, 110, 115
  bolstering Welsh Guards, 117, 206, 309
  reserve at San Carlos, 105
42 Commando, 85, 110
  commanding officer, 101
    see also Vaux, Lieutenant Colonel Nick
44 Squadron, 250–1, 257
    see also Vulcan, Avro
45 Commando, 84, 110
51 Squadron, 24
    see also Nimrod, British Aerospace
63 Squadron, RAF Regiment, 145, 314
    see also Rapier missile
83 Squadron, 295
101 Squadron, 50, 254–5
    see also Vulcan, Avro
105mm Light Guns, 171–2

530F Matra, 313
see also Mirage III, Dassault
656 Squadron, 257
707 Boeing, 57, 97
800 Naval Air Squadron:
air-to-air performance, 136–7, 246–9
air-to-air tactics, 138
attack missions, 156, 160, 167, 250–6
fatigue, 195
see also Thomas, Lieutenant Commander Neill
formed, 31
Sea Harrier capabilities, 157
801 Naval Air Squadron, 19
air-to-air performance, 136–7, 246–9
attack missions, 160, 166–7, 251, 254–5, 257
command and control challenges, 176
commanding officer, 1, 126
see also Ward, Lieutenant Commander Nigel 'Sharkey'
formed, 31
Invincible, HMS, 32
manning ratio, 66
Mortimer, Flight Lieutenant Ian, 55
post-conflict report, 23
serviceability rate, 137
tactics, 138
809 Naval Air Squadron, 310
Buccaneer squadron, 29
commanding officer, 167
see also Gedge, Lieutenant Commander Tim
RAF pilots, 299-300
transit to Falkland Islands, 55–6, 77
815 Naval Air Squadron, 250, 252
892 Naval Air Squadron, 29
1000lb bomb, 43, 154
aircraft carrier magazine capacity, 156
Argentine use, 43
see also Mk 17 bomb
employment, 160, 250-7
laser-guided bomb conversion, 153, 161
see also Harrier, British Aerospace
Sea Harrier accuracy, 159

A-4 *see* Skyhawk, McDonnell Douglas A-4
A-109, Agusta, 312
AIM-9, *see* Sidewinder
Ajax Bay, 1, 236, 308
Brigade Maintenance Area, 115
Alacrity, HMS, 58, 60
1 May air attack, 68, 326
naval gunfire support, 152, 171
torpedo attack, 102
ALE-40 chaff and flare dispenser, 106
Allied Command Europe, 294
Almono, Capitan Eduardo, 329, 331
AN/ALQ-101D Jamming Pod, 155
AN/TPS-43 Early Warning Radar, 162, 189, 350–1
Antelope, HMS, 17, 346
loss during Operation Sutton, 92, 198, 233, 331-2
Antonietti, Primer Teniente, 340
Antrim, HMS, 304
arrival of General Moore, 101
Operation Sutton damage, 89, 329
ARA *Alferez Sobral*, 250, 343
ARA *Bahia Buen Suceso*, 251
ARA *General Belgrano*, 61, 74, 190
ARA *Hercules*, 300
ARA *Salta*, 102–103, 304
ARA *Sante Fe*, 102
ARA *San Luis*, 86
HMS *Alacrity* attack, 102
reliability issues, 102–103, 304
ARA *Santisima Trinidad*, 300
ARA *Veinticinco de Mayo*, 43
Skyhawks Disembarked, 299
see also Skyhawk
Arca, Teniente de Navio Jose Cesar, 248

Ardent, HMS, 230-1, 304
21 May attacks, 89, 92, 198, 330
Ardiles, Primer Teniente Jose, 227, 328
Argonaut, HMS, 230-1, 304, 36
Operation Sutton damage, 89
Ark Royal, HMS, 28-29
1971 Harrier GR1 deployment, 294
loss of airborne early warning capability, 33
see also Gannet, Fairey
retirement, 31
see also Phantom, McDonnell Douglas F-4
Arraras, Teniente Juan, 249
Arrow, HMS, 58, 60, 234
1 May air attack, 68, 326
naval gunfire support, 152
Artic Express, Exercise, 294
see also Harrier, British Aerospace
AS-12, missile, 257
Ascension Island, 33, 50, 103, 176, 186
air defence of, 35, 57
amphibious force, 56–7, 77, 298
Harrier GR3, 106, 180
Hercules operations, 161
Nimrod operations, 102
Rapier second-line support, 144
Vulcan operations, 155–6, 163–4, 317
Atlantic Causeway, MV, 314
Atlantic Conveyor, MV, 3, 131, 304
loss, 12, 92, 100, 113, 161, 197–8, 205, 324, 340
replacement Harriers, 32, 55–6, 77, 300
Auld, Lieutenant Commander Andy, 249, 342
Avenger, HMS, 307
30 May attack, 117, 238, 336
see also Exocet missile
naval gunfire support, 117

Bader, Douglas, 46
Ball, Flight Lieutenant Ted, 125, 350
Balmaceda, 67
Banderiante, Embraer EMB-111A, 86
Banjul, 35
Barton, Flight Lieutenant Paul, 227, 246, 327
Batt, Lieutenant Commander Gordy, 346
Battle of Britain, 33, 108, 182, 192, 195, 200
Goring's philosophy, 197
Bean, Teniente Pedro, 329
Bear D, Tupolev Tu-95, 30–1, 131, 133
Beech, Flight Lieutenant Mike, 351–3
Beeny, Steven, 336, 338
Beetham, Air Chief Marshal Sir Michael, 316
Sea Harrier advocate, 55
views on Operation Sutton, 78
Vulcan proponent, 154
Bergamaschi, Capitan Jorge, 331
Berkeley Sound, 336
Bernhardt, Teniente Juan Doming, 335
Berrier, Primer Teniente Oscar, 332, 338
Bicheno, Hugh, 18, 171, 328
BL755, Hunting Engineering cluster bomb, 160–2, 251–4, 256–7
Blake, HMS, 29
Blissett, Lieutenant Commander Mike, 247
Blowpipe, surface-to-air-missile, 143
3 Commando Brigade concerns, 149
Argentine usage, 177
British usage, 146
Blue Eric, jammer, 307, 319
Blue Fox radar, 157, 208, 214
based on Sea Spray, 31
training, 133
use in clutter, 131–2
Blue Steel missile, Avro, 36
Bluff Cove, 105, 242, 255
Bolzan, Primer Teniente Danilo, 249, 332
Bono, Teniente Jorge, 332
Boyens, Flight Lieutenant Ross, 353

Boyle, Air Vice-Marshal Dermot, 45, 297
Braithwaite, Lieutenant Commander Dave, 31
Briasco, Jesus Romero, 20, 334
Brilliant, HMS, 229–31, 302, 304, 328, 344
Bristol, HMS, 62, 103, 141
Broadsword, HMS, 58, 230, 233, 304
  21 May Sea Wolf engagement, 329
  25 May attack, 142–3, 235, 331, 333
    see also Coventry, HMS
Broadwater, Lieutenant Commander Mike, 247
Broken Island, 240
Brown, Flight Lieutenant Steve, 77, 299
BRP 250kg bomb, 224–5, 228, 233–4, 236–43
Bruce, Ian, 1
Bryant, Air Commodore Derek, 218
Buccaneer, Blackburn, 29–30, 36, 162
  source of Vulcan jamming pods, 155
Buenos Aires, 44, 46, 52
  British attache, 15, 22, 38–9, 41–2, 189
  protected by fighters, 5, 53, 64, 214–15
  Vulcan fly-past, 50
Burden, 16, 18, 63, 73, 88, 142
Bustos, Primer Teniente Manuel, 328

Cachon, Primer Teniente Carlos, 329, 331
Callejo, Primer Teniente Carlos, 333, 339
Canberra, English Electric, 63, 227
  attacks, 224–5, 228, 231, 235–44
  flying rate, 220–1
  losses, 62, 69, 133, 142, 246–7, 326
  PR9, 24
    see also 39 Squadron
  sales to Argentina, 38, 45
  utility, 94, 109, 118–19, 121, 124, 193, 303, 308
  weapons, 43
    see also Mark 17 bomb
Canberra, SS, 81, 83, 85, 101
Carballo, Capitan Pablo, 330, 337
Cardiff, HMS, 62, 103
  14 June Canberra engagement, 142, 340
  Gazelle fratricide, 148
Carmona Alferez Leonardo, 326, 329, 333, 335, 337
Castillo, Primer Teniente Omar, 329
Castillo, Teniente Carlos, 249, 331, 342
Centre of Gravity, 3, 5, 7, 16, 23, 51, 76, 201–207, 209–10, 216–17
  alternative British Operational, 14, 26
  defending Argentine, 176
  defending British, 126, 136, 150
  definition, 8–10
  different perspectives, 13
  during Operation Sutton, 76–7, 80–2, 89, 92, 94, 98
  excluded Argentine aircraft, 46–8
  post Operation Sutton, 109–12, 115, 118, 122, 125
  prior to Operation Sutton, 57, 60–1, 62, 67, 74
  prosecuting Argentine, 151–2, 164–6, 170–1, 173, 198
  strategic, 10
  traditional view of Falklands Operational, 12
Centro de Information y Control, 189, 326
Cervera, Teniente Luis, 118, 335
Chadwick, Roy, 36
Chalfont, Lord, 38
Chartres, 252
Checkmate Division, 286
Chesworth, Air Vice-Marshal George, 155
Chile:
  support to British campaign, 66–7, 148, 190
  tensions with Argentina, 15, 38

Chinook, Boeing CH-47, 56, 92, 315, 345
Churchill, Winston, 200
Cimatti, Capitan Amilcar, 330, 332
Circular Error of Probability (CEP), 158–9
Clapp, Commodore Mike, 21, 83, 202
  Operation Sutton concerns, 144
  Reattacking Targets, 179
  view on Argentine aircrew, 120
Clausewitz, Carl Von, 51, 195
  centre of gravity explanation, 7
  Freedman critique, 8
    see also Freedman, Lawrence
Columbo, Jorge, Capitan de Fragata, 87, 327
Comando de Aviacion Naval, 63, 74, 86, 119
  command and control, 94, 184–6
  control of the air, 103
  development, 42–44, 47
  doctrine, 71
  inter-service rivalry, 40–1
  jointery, 116, 193–4, 196, 212
  official history, 18, 198
  sanctions, 96–7
  targeting priorities, 79, 95
Comodoro Rivadavia, 46, 67
  attack on, 64, 214
  Fuerza Aerea Argentina headquarters, 54, 94, 184, 194
Comodoro Somerella, 343
Contender Bezant, MV, 107
Control of the air, 9, 12–15, 26, 31, 33–4, 73, 79, 103, 108, 125, 145, 195
  Argentine capability, 46, 119, 210
  Argentine failure to compete, 64–5, 68, 74–5, 138–9, 207, 214, 219
  British capability, 62–3, 128–9, 140, 169–70, 208, 213
  British prerequisite, 51, 55, 58, 78, 126, 152, 201–202
  command and control, 147–50, 184
  definition, 198, 288, 298
  enduring need, 61, 158
  Type 42 destroyer contribution, 59
Cooke, Teniente Juan Carlos, 247
Cooper, Sir Frank, 78
Corum, James, 134
Cordesman and Wagner, 5, 18, 63–4
Coventry, HMS, 3, 58–9, 62, 313, 333, 343
  25 May attack, 92, 142–3, 190, 198, 235
    see also Broadsword, HMS
Crespo, Brigadier Ernesto, 185
Critical Capabilities:
  definition, 8
  during Operation Sutton, 81–2
  Operation Corporate, 165
  post Operation Sutton, 110–12
  Prior to Operation Sutton, 60–1
Critical Requirements, 7
  definition, 8
  during Operation Sutton, 81–2, 93
  Operation Corporate, 165, 170
  post Operation Sutton, 110–12
  prior to Operation Sutton, 60–1
Critical Vulnerabilities, 7, 140, 142, 145, 207, 209, 216
  definition, 8
  during Operation Sutton, 81–2
  Operation Corporate, 164–6, 170, 176, 197
  post Operation Sutton, 110–12, 117–18
  prior to Operation Sutton, 60–1
Cuerva, Capitan Gustavo Garcia, 246, 327
Curtiss, Air Marshal Sir John, 21, 28, 219
  command and control issues, 174–6, 186
  Vulcan success, 170
Curtis, Lieutenant Al, 246, 326

CVA01 aircraft carrier, 129, 199
  cancellation, 28–9

Dagger, IAI, 43–5, 52, 62–3, 67, 97, 119
  attacks, 224, 229–35, 236–43
  co-location, 108
  control of the air missions, 64, 138–9, 226–7
  flying rate, 220–1, 244
  losses, 246–9
  protecting Buenos Aires, 53, 214
  threat perception, 127
  training, 54, 194
Defence Lines of Development, 129, 192, 194, 212
Deighton, Len, 182–3, 192, 200
Dellepaine, Alferez Guillermo, 337
Diaz, Capitan Raul, 249, 342
Dimeglio, Capitan Norberto, 326, 331
Donadille, Capitan Guillermo, 248, 331
Dozo, Brigadier Lami, 51
Dubroca, Primer Teniente Armando, 247
Dunnose Head, 251–2
Dunsfold, 31, 293

Eagle, HMS, 28–30
Electra, Lockheed, 74
Elk, MV, 83
ELMA Formosa, 326
ELMA Rio Carcarana, 252
Escuadron del Grupo 2 de Vigilancia y Control, 189
Ethell & Price, 18, 54, 63, 88, 141, 143
  Exocet missile, 44, 59, 62, 71, 73, 85, 97, 194
    see also Super Etendard, Dassault
  1 May, 225
  4 May HMS *Sheffield*, 228
  23 May, 233
  25 May MV *Atlantic Conveyor*, 92, 235
  30 May HMS *Invincible*, 116–17, 119, 142, 238
Europic Ferry, MV, 85
Exeter, HMS, 62, 103
  30 May attack, 117, 142, 336
    see also Exocet missile
Expal 250kg bomb, 43, 224–5, 228–30, 232, 234–5

F-111, General Dynamics, 29, 36
F-4, *see* Phantom, McDonnell Douglas F-4
Faget, Teniente Aguirre, 326–7, 335, 339
Fearless, HMS, 300
  1981 Defence Review, 27
  arrival of General Moore, 101
  Gazelle fratricide, 148
  Operation Sutton, 81, 84, 86, 202
Fellowship, Fokker F-28, 74
Fieldhouse, Admiral Sir John, 10–11, 78, 83, 101, 135, 142, 201
Filipini, Primer Teniente Alberto, 330
Fisher, Admiral Sir Jackie, 2
Fitzroy, 105
  attack 8 June, 117, 138, 190, 241
  Forward Brigade Maintenance area, 118
  Rapier defence, 145
Fox Bay, 104, 251
France:
  British support:
    air combat training, 34
    Mitterand, Francois, 97
  Dijon, 294
  influence in Argentina, 38, 45–6, 96
  Super Etendard training, 44
Franks, Lord:
  Report, 17, 182
Frederiksen, Lieutenant Commander Rod, 248
Freedman, Sir Lawrence, 153
  centre of gravity critique, 7–8

official history, 11, 17–18, 63–4, 68, 92, 95, 104, 118–19, 141–2
Rapier, 145
Frondisi, Dr Arturo, 50
Fuerza Aerea Argentina, 20, 63, 73, 74, 88, 103, 119–20, 198, 205–206
advisor, 9, 25, 65, 214
see also Galland, Adolf
attack priorities, 79, 96, 111
British Embassy views, 22
command and control, 16, 94, 183–6, 215
control of the air, 139, 214
development, 37–46
ground-based air defence, 177
initial planning, 5
jointery, 116, 193–6, 212
official history, 18, 95, 193
preparations, 51–4, 67
sanctions, 96–7

Galland, Adolf, 8–9, 25, 65, 214
Galtieri, General Leopoldo, 124
Galvez, Teniente Daniel, 337
Gannet, Fairey, 33, 58–9
Garcia, Capitan Jorge, 328, 330, 333
Gardiner, Major Ian, 22, 127
Gavazzi, Primer Teniente Fausto, 329
Gazelle, Aerospatiale, 148
Gedge, Lieutenant Commander Tim, 77, 167
Gibbons, Flight Lieutenant, 300
Gilchrist, Flight Lieutenant Nick, 352–3
Glamorgan, HMS, 58
1 May air attack, 67–8, 326
Exocet attack, 298
naval gunfire support, 152, 171
Glasgow, HMS, 58–9, 343
12 May attack, 62, 142–3, 181, 205, 229, 302, 329
Glover, Flight Lieutenant Jeff, 178–9, 345
Gomez, Alferez Hugo, 331
Gonzales, Primer Teniente Mario, 246
Goose Green, 26, 47, 99, 202
airfield attack, 4, 51, 250, 252–5
air defence, 62, 176–8
battle, 22, 101, 113, 115–16
fractricide, 181
garrison, 104, 191
naval gunfire, 89
Goulter, Christina, 17
Grail, SA-7 missile, 177
Gray, Peter, 17, 22
Grey, Jeffrey, 17
Grupo 1 de Artilleria Antiaerea, 177
Grupo 2 de Bombardero, II Brigada Aérea, 45
Grupo 3 de Ataque, 46
Grupo 4 de Caza, 1, 43, 46, 52
Grupo 5 de Caza, 42
Grupo 6 de Caza, 44
Grupo 8 de Caza, 46
Grupo de Artilleria de Defensa Aerea 101, 177
Grupo de Artilleria de Defensa Aerea 601, 177
Guadagnini, Primer Teniente Luciano, 331
Gulf War Air Power Survey, 5
Gurkha Rifes, 118, 309

Haig, Al, 10, 218
Haigh, Lieutenant Brian, 327
Hale, Lieutenant Martin, 247–8, 328
Hanrahan, Brian, 180
Hare, Flight Lieutenant Mark, 345
Harper, Flight Lieutenant Tony, 345–6, 348–9, 352–3
Harrier, British Aerospace, 3, 12, 15, 19, 22, 28, 55, 89, 108, 127, 153, 157
archives, 23, 166
Argentine Interest, 38–9
GR1, 159

GR3, 310, 315
Ascension Island defence, 57
see also Ascension Island
capability, 159–64, 169, 319
command and control, 176, 191
conversion to Sea Harrier, 77, 312
deployment, 55–6
flying rate, 222–3
ground-based air defences, 177–81
in fighter role, 140
mission tasking, 173–5, 191, 196, 198–9, 348–9, 351–2
NATO Tasking, 33, 159
Operation Sutton losses, 106
RAF Germany support, 57, 299–300
replacements, 106–107, 194–5
see also Operation Bowsprit
San Carlos airstrip, 92, 103, 301
see also Sheathbill, HMS and Sid's Strip
South Atlantic preparations, 34–5, 162
support to 2 PARA, 116
see also Goose Green
weapon employment, 167–8, 209, 251–7
initial naval interest, 28–31
Maritime, 30
Harris, Squadron Leader Peter, 173–4, 345, 347, 349–53
Hart-Dyke, Commander David, 313
see also Coventry, HMS
Hayr, Air Vice-Marshal, Ken, 294
Healey, Denis, 27
1966 Defence White Paper, 28–9
Hercules, Lockheed C-130, 133
Argentine KC-130 tanker, 73, 327, 334
Argentine resupply missions, 74, 302
RAF long-range airdrops, 33, 156, 161, 164, 186, 317
Sea Harrier attack, 132–3, 313
Hercules, MV, 240
Hermes, HMS, 9, 12–13, 26, 32, 35, 58–9, 134, 136, 157, 180, 195, 288
attack missions, 156, 158, 161–2, 164, 167
see also 800 Naval Air Squadron
command and control, 174, 176, 186
see also Middleton, Captain Linley
flying rate, 66
Harrier GR3, 19, 56, 77, 106, 345
see also 1 (Fighter) Squadron
Hispano, HS-831 30mm cannons, 177
Hobson, Chris, 15, 18, 142, 145, 294, 314, 328, 330–1, 333, 339, 341, 344–5, 347, 349–50, 353
Holland, Wing Commander Keith, 299
Holmes, Professor Richard, 6, 286
Howard, Sir Michael, 2
Huertas, Salvador Mafe, 20, 330–1
Hunter, Hawker, 34, 38

Ibanez, Teniente Eduardo de, 246
Iberlucea, Teniente Jorge, 328
Illustrious, HMS, 12
Informe Rattenbach, 17, 182
Inskip, Sir Thomas, 197
Intrepid, HMS, 110, 300
1981 Defence Review, 27
Operation Sutton, 81, 84, 202, 233
Invincible, HMS, 9, 12–13, 19, 26, 58, 157, 167, 179, 288, 300
30 May attack, 117, 336
see also Exocet missile
airborne early warning integration, 129
anti-air warfare, 136, 141, 156
flying rate, 66
Operation Sutton, 61, 86
weapons stockpile, 32–3, 134, 353
Isaac, Alferez Gerardo, 328, 330
Israel, 43, 96–7, 310, 313
Begin, Prime Minister Menachem, 97
Iveson, Squadron Leader Bob, 179, 346, 348

Jaguar, SEPECAT, 15
Joint Action, 178, 183
  definition, 322
Jones, Lieutenant Colonel 'H', 26, 113

Keeble, Major Chris, 116
Kent, Lieutenant Commander Robin, 327
Kfir, IAI, 44
King George Bay, 239

Lafonia, 256
Lancaster, Avro, 36–7, 45
LAU-61 rocket pods, 334
LCU F4, landing craft, 241, 337
Leach, Admiral Sir Henry, 9–10, 78, 152, 201
Leeming, Flight Lieutenant John, 300, 312
Lehman, John, 219
Libya, 97
Liddell Hart, Sir Basil Henry 173
Lightning, English Electric, 312
  air combat training, 34
  radar performance, 31
Lincoln, Avro, 37, 45
Lively Island, 235
Lopez, Teniente Nestor, 247, 327, 329
Los Moscardones, 76, 93
Lozano, Capitan Ernesto, 247
Lucero, Teniente Ricardo, 1, 284, 315, 332
Luna, Primer Teniente, 248, 330
Lygo, Captain Raymond, 311
Lynx, Westland, 31, 92, 250, 252, 343, 346

Macheteanz, Teniente de Fragata Carlos, 327
Maffeis, Capitan Carlos, 332, 339
Magic 1, Matra R.550, 313
Manzotti, Primer Teniente Daniel, 247, 327, 329
Maple Flag, Exercise, 56, 299
Martel, Capitan Ruben, 249
Martel, missile, 162
Martinez, Alferez Guillermo, 247, 329
Matra 1 missile, 32
MB-339, Aermacchi, 47, 116, 146, 324
McLeod, Flight Lieutenant Murdo, 351, 353
Menendez, General de Brigada Mario, 75, 171, 173
Mentor, Beech T-34, 47, 324
Meteor, Gloster, 41
  initial deliveries, 37
Middlebrook, Martin, 20
Middleton, Captain Linley, 106, 207
  command and control, 176, 186–7
Mir Gonzales, Capitan Horacio, 127, 141, 290, 310
Mirage III, Dassault, 63, 119, 138, 210, 226–7
  1 May losses, 62, 64, 131, 180, 246, 327
  air combat training, 34, 294
  defending Buenos Aires, 5, 53, 64, 214, 313
  flying rate, 220–1
  initial deliveries, 46
  logistical challenges, 54
Mirage V, Dassault, 43, 310
  air combat training, 294
  Peruvian Replacements, 97, 306
Mk 17, 1000lb bomb, 224–5, 228–43, 329, 333–5
  Skyhawk clearance, 43
    see also Skyhawk, McDonnell Douglas A-4
Mk 82, 500lb bomb, 43, 193, 230–1, 233, 235–7, 240–2, 337–9
Montgomery, Field Marshal, 2, 6
Moody Brook, 257
Moore, Major General Jeremey, 104–105, 110, 113
  arrival, 101

attack on Field Headquarters, 339
command and control, 176
Gazelle fratricide, 148
lack of memoirs, 21–2
see also Wilson, Brigadier Tony
Rapier concerns, 145
Moreno, Capitan Carlos, 247, 332
Morgan, Flight Lieutenant Dave, 19, 179, 346, 348
8 June intercept, 249, 311
23 May helicopter engagement, 312
Moro, Ruben, 20, 88, 109, 111, 118, 123, 178, 308–309, 326, 339
Argentine morale, 195
operational priorities, 79
Views on 1 May, 57–8, 67–8
Morrell, Lieutenant Clive, 248, 350–1
Mortimer, Flight Lieutenant Ian, 55, 178
shoot down, 179–80
see also Roland 2, Euromissile
Mount Challenger, 105
Mount Harriet, 171, 173, 257
Mount Kent, 105, 172, 179, 238, 251, 254–5, 348–50
3 Commando Brigade headquarters attack, 118, 242–3, 339
Mount Longdon, 173, 256–7
Mount Usborne, 351
Mount Wall, 254, 349–50
Mount William, 118, 309
Muerte Negra, 93, 211, 216
Murchison, Major General Ewen, 304
Murray, Williamson, 2

Narwhal, 250, 344
NATO, 6, 30, 148, 199
Argentine embargo, 44
planning doctrine, 8, 11, 13, 176, 322
UK role, 15, 27–8, 56, 200, 204
Neptune, Lockheed P-2, 71, 86, 327
Nimrod, British Aerospace
air-to-air-refuelling, 156, 317
Ascension Island, 102
maritime radar reconnaissance, 102, 156, 186
R1, 24
see also 51 Squadron
Nivoli, Teniente Mario, 328
Norland, MV, 81, 83, 85, 101
Norway, 294
Nott, John, 3–4
1981 Defence Review, 27
Nye, Joseph, 201

Oerlikon, anti-aircraft guns, 177
Operation Acme, 191
Operation Azul/Rosario, 4, 51, 97, 285
Operation Black Buck, 50, 353
anti-radiation attacks, 107, 350
see also Shrike, AGM-45A missile
Ascension capacity, 317
planning, 73, 316–17, 325
utility, 153, 158, 163, 308, 317–18
see also Ward, Commander Nigel 'Sharkey'
Vulcan Precision, 158
see also Vulcan, Avro
Operation Bowsprit, 106
see also Harrier, British Aerospace
Operation Corporate, 3, 22, 26–7, 33, 54, 96, 144, 153, 155, 173, 190, 201, 204
air commander, 28
Air Operation Order 3/82, 154
see also Operation Black Buck
Argentine performance, 138–9
assault phase, 77, 150, 207
see also Operation Sutton
British weapon usage, 160–2, 164, 167, 209
final phase, 100, 106, 108–11, 115, 122
first phase, 55, 61, 69, 99

Harrier GR3, 34–5, 56, 159, 175
see also 1 (Fighter) Squadron
maritime patrol activity, 102
see also Sea King, Westland and Nimrod, British Aerospace
Sea Harrier, 128–9, 136, 139–40, 150, 208
see also 800 Naval Air Squadron and
801 Naval Air Squadron
see also Curtiss, Air Marshal Sir John
Operation Desert Storm, 5, 7, 124
AIM-9M Sidewinder performance, 134–5, 139
see also Sidewinder, Raytheon AIM-9
Centres of gravity, 7, 13, 287
see also Warden, Colonel John
Operation Fingent, 67
Operation Folklore, 191, 323
Operation Paraquet, 11, 25, 50
see also South Georgia
Operation Plan 2/82, 79, 81, 95
Operation Sutton, 3–4, 61, 63, 69, 73–5, 98, 110, 113, 121–2, 151, 174, 181
Argentine capability, 86–9, 205, 304
Argentine losses, 108, 119, 124, 206
Argentine performance, 89–92, 94, 96, 114, 125, 139, 194, 197–8, 205, 215
Argentine planning, 95, 111, 194–6, 213
British losses, 92, 100, 106, 197–8
see also *Ardent*, HMS, *Antelope*, HMS, *Coventry*, HMS
MV *Atlantic Conveyor*
British preparations, 65, 77–8, 102, 191, 217
British risk appetite, 10–11, 14, 144, 148, 150, 154
British replacement Harriers, 32, 35, 56
centre of gravity, 80–2, 117, 304
see also Centre of Gravity
conclusion, 100
maritime force air defence, 143
see also Sea Wolf missile and Sea Dart missile
Sea Harrier performance, 99, 127, 136, 139, 207, 213
timeframe, 25–6, 85, 99
weather, 88
Operation Tornado, 89
see also *Ardent,* HMS
Operational Level, 6, 182
Argentine views, 94-5, 184, 198, 212, 216, 218
British planning, 14, 117, 148–9, 154, 216, 218
definition, 322
doctrine, 11
lessons, 5, 20, 24, 192–3, 219
Osses, Teniente Carlos, 333

Palaver, Capitan Hugo, 331, 333
Paveway, laser-guided bomb, 161–2, 255–7, 349–50, 353
Pebble Island, 47, 142, 190, 252, 351
SAS raid, 3–4, 47, 116
Penfold, Flight Lieutenant Bertie, 227, 246, 303, 343
Peron, President Juan, 327
Perona, Primer Teniente Carlos, 246, 327
Peru:
Argentine support, 97, 177, 306
see also Mirage V, Dassault and Grail, SA-7 missile
Phantom, McDonnell Douglas F-4
Ascension air defence, 57
RAF flying rates, 32
Royal Navy, 28–9

Sea Harrier comparison, 30–1
USAF support, 163
Philippi, Capitan de Corbeta Hector, 248
Piuma, Mayor Gustavo, 248, 331
Plymouth, HMS, 58, 234, 240, 304
Polaris, nuclear missile, 36, 155
Pook, Squadron Leader Jerry, 19, 196, 294, 345
command and control, 176
Harrier GR3 attacks, 345–53
reattacking targets, 179
Sea Harrier bombing effectiveness, 158
Port Howard, 251–3, 256, 352
air defence, 176–7, 345
Argentine garrison, 104
Port San Carlos, 105
forward operating base, 145, 301
see also Sheathbill, HMS and Sid's Strip
Privratsky, Ken, 335
Pucara, FMA, 152, 351
1 May attack at Goose Green, 343
21 May activities, 116, 146, 313
air-to-air kill, 297
history, 46–7
Puerto Deseado, 341
Puga, Mayor Gustavo Luis, 249, 331, 342
Puma, Aerospatiale SA 330, 142, 345, 348

Queen Elizabeth II, SS, 101

RAF Abingdon, 155
RAF Boscombe Down, 31
RAF Gutersloh, 56
RAF Honington, 292
RAF Marham, 155
RAF St Athan, 293
RAF St Mawgan, 35, 163
RAF Waddington, 35, 155–6, 317
US support, 163
RAF Wittering, 35, 56
Rapier, 4, 314
performance concerns, 18, 149, 315, 335
requirement, 146
San Carlos, 143–6
Red Beard, free-fall nuclear bomb, 36
Red Flag, Exercise, 125, 134
RFA *Fort Austin*, 84, 87, 234
RFA *Olmeda*, 58
RFA *Resource*, 32, 58, 234
RFA *Sir Bedivere*, 234, 300, 304
RFA *Sir Galahad*, 83–4, 300
8 June Fitzroy, 117, 138, 145, 190, 206, 240, 337
San Carlos attack, 92, 234
RFA *Sir Geraint*, 84, 144, 300
RFA *Sir Lancelot*, 84, 300
San Carlos attack, 92, 234, 333
RFA *Sir Percivale*, 83–4, 300
RFA *Sir Tristram*, 84, 300
8 June Fitzroy, 117, 138, 145, 190, 206, 240, 337
RFA *Stromness*, 83–4, 234
transfer of 5 Infantry Brigade, 101
Rinke, Teniente Carlos, 329, 337
Rio Cuarto, 52
Rio Gallegos, 86
Dagger Co-location, 108
Mirage III base, 46
Operation Gelido II, 52
proposed Vulcan target, 154
Rio Grande, 85, 119, 334
A-4Q Skyhawk base, 299
Dagger base, 44
joint training, 194
Naval command and control, 94, 185
proposed Vulcan target, 154
Tracker base, 71
weather, 87
Rivas, Santiago, 20, 52, 55, 63–4, 79, 88, 111, 119, 124, 291, 301–303, 305, 326–34, 336–41

Argentine pilot flying rate, 125
los moscardones, 93
RNAS *Yeovilton*, 107, 293
Harrier GR3 training, 34, 162
Robledo, Teniente Fernando, 335
Robles, Capitan Higinio, 340
Rochfort, Flight Lieutenant John, 345–9, 351–3
Rodino, Capitan Eduardo, 247
Roland 2, Euromissile, 177–80
Roman, Primer Teniente Cesar, 326
Royal Navy 2-Inch Rockets, 160, 162, 254–6, 348
see also Harrier, British Aerospace

Sabre, North American F-86, 46
San Carlos, 1, 3-4, 110, 153, 351, 232, 235, 237–8
approach, 61, 81, 86–7, 203
Argentine response, 85, 94, 109, 115, 118, 121, 197, 251, 334
assault planning, 21, 83, 113, 148, 172
breakout, 14, 26, 93, 99–100, 102–105, 174, 203
British defence, 89, 138, 141, 143–5, 208, 301, 314, 332, 335
reinforcements, 101, 188, 304
San Julian, 64, 214, 340–1
Dagger base, 44
Dagger co-location, 108
morale, 195
proposed Vulcan target, 154
weapon fit, 331
Sanchez, Primer Teniente Hector, 327, 338
Sapper Hill, 118, 256, 344
Schwerpunkt, 8
Sciaroni, Mariano, 291
Scientific Evaluation Team:
Argentine morale, 161, 171
bombing effectiveness, 168–9
British planning, 173, 175
Harrier GR3 inconsistencies, 23, 166, 346, 352
Harrier medium level bombing, 157, 347
Sidewinder, 135
Scots Guards, Second Battalion, 110, 181
Scout, Westland, 297
Sea Cat, missile, 60, 141
Sea Control, 58, 61, 111, 191
Argentine's yield, 74, 103, 190
British assault prerequisite, 26, 51, 57, 78, 189
definition, 298
Sea Dart, missile, 59
25 May Pebble Island, 87, 117
see also Coventry, HMS
Gazelle fratricide, 148
Invincible, HMS, 61, 86, 300
performance, 141–3, 333, 336, 340
Sea Harrier, British Aerospace, 9, 34, 50, 58–9, 73–4, 107, 111, 171, 173, 175, 177, 189–90, 311, 326, 328, 330, 335, 338–9
1 May success, 64, 69, 72, 226–7
8 June Fitzroy, 145
see also RFA *Sir Galahad* and RFA *Sir Tristram*
additional RAF pilots, 57, 77, 299–300
archives, 22–3, 166
Argentine interest, 39
attack, 153, 156, 161–2, 167, 209, 250–7, 351
CAP bombing, 169
capability, 157–9
Stanley airport, 51, 109, 152, 170, 204, 257, 210, 344, 350
command and control, 142
disparity in tactics, 33, 55, 138

expected attrition, 35
flying rate, 65–6, 89, 125, 137, 139, 194, 222–3, 310
history, 28, 32, 293
manning, 33
RAF view, 30
requirement, 30–1
losses, 62, 76, 178, 180, 196, 303
Operation Sutton, 78, 87, 94, 203
losses, 106, 108
operational performance, 122–3, 128–9, 137, 140, 150, 201–202, 208, 211, 213, 215–16, 319, 327, 332, 337
operational readiness, 4
perception, 1–5, 90, 93, 99, 126–7, 198, 207, 213
radar performance, 31, 131–2, 207, 214
replacements, 56, 77, 293
Sheathbill, HMS, 301, *see also* Sid's Strip
Sidewinder, 126–7, 130, 134–6, 141, 207, 214, 246–9, 311, 327, 329–30
training, 44, 133, 148, 312
with US fighters, 133
Ward, Lieutentant Commander Nigel 'Sharkey', 19, 90, 176, 207, 317
Sea King, Westland, 58, 102, 172, 191, 202
airborne early warning, 129, 190
Sea Skua, missile, 250, 252
Sea Slug, missile, 141, 171
Sea Spray, radar, 31
Sea Vixen, De Havilland, 31
Sea Wolf, missile, 22, 87
engagements, 302, 328–9
initial operational assessment, 141
requirement, 142–3
Segat, Teniente Jorge, 336
Segunda Escuadrilla Aeronaval de Caza y Ataque, 44
Senn, Primer Teniente Jorge, 248, 329
Shafrir 1, missile, 43, 313
Shag Cove, 312
Sheathbill, HMS, 301
Sheffield, HMS, 58–9
Exocet attack, 11, 61–2, 205, 228, 340
Sheffield, Gary, 6, 17–18, 153
Shrike, AGM-45A missile, 106, 160, 350
Harrier embodiment, 164
US support, 163
utility, 170, 319, 351
variants, 162–3
Vulcan employment, 164, 254–5, 266, 308
Sid's Strip, 301
Sidewinder, Raytheon AIM-9, 131–2, 141, 208, 329–30, 332, 342
AIM-9G, 311
capability, 32, 43, 130–1
Harrier GR3 firings, 34
stockpile, 32–3
AIM-9L, 66, 69, 126–7, 137, 139
performance, 130–1, 133–4, 204, 207, 214, 313, 326–7, 338
reputation, 5, 214
stockpile, 32–3, 156
AIM-9M, 134–5, *see also* Operation Desert Storm
History, 32
Skybolt, Douglas GAM-87 missile, 36, 155, 163
Skyguard radar, 162, 177, 351
Skyhawk, McDonnell Douglas A-4, 44–5, 54, 62, 64, 95, 119, 308, 313, 331, 335, 338–9
A-4B, 63, 72, 115, 118, 303, 327, 331
8 June Fitzroy, 117, 138, 145, 206, 311, 337
12 May HMS *Glasgow*, 302

25 May HMS *Coventry*, 142–3
attacks, 224–5, 228–37, 239–43
flying rate, 220–1, 244
fratricide, 181
Grupo 5 de Caza, 42–3
losses, 249
maritime training, 54
A-4C, 63–4, 124, 196, 310
30 May Invincible attack, 116–17, 142, 186, 336
air-to-air capability, 139, 313
attacks, 224–6, 228–34, 236–8, 241
command and control, 185
flying rate, 220-1, 244
Grupo 4 de Caza, 1, 43
losses, 247
Lucero, Teniente Ricardo, 1, 315
Operativo Gelido II, 52
A-4Q, 43–4, 64, 94–5, 119, 124–5, 324, 329, 334, 337–9
air-to-air capability, 139, 227, 313
attacks, 230–1, 233, 236–7, 240–2
flying rate, 220–1, 245
losses, 248
Operation Sutton, 194, 312, 332
Tercera Escuadrilla Aeronaval de Caza y Ataque, 42
Argentine procurement, 37–8, 42
co-location, 108
sanctions, 96–7
Smith, Lieutenant Dave, 249, 342
SNEB, 68mm Rocket Pod, 162
South Georgia, 103
ARA *Santa Fe*, 102
invasion, 25
recovery, 11, 25, 50, 57
see also Operation Paraquet
troop transfer, 101
Southby-Tailyour, Major Ewen, 21–2, 110, 325
8 June Fitzroy, 117, 145,
see also RFA *Sir Galahad* and RFA *Sir Tristram*
Canberra air attacks, 109, 336
South Atlantic weather, 87–8
Spangdahlem, 163
Splash target, 35, 294
Spotswood, Air Chief Marshal Sir Denis, 30
Squire, Wing Commander Peter, 56, 175, 180, 294
air operations, 344–52
command and control, 174, 176, 187
preparing squadron, 33–4
see also 1 (Fighter) Squadron
SS-11, missile, 257
Stanley, 26, 86, 166–7, 174, 327, 348, 352
Airfield Attacks, 4, 12, 50–1, 57, 116, 151–3, 159, 170, 204, 213, 250–7
British objective, 154, 316
Sea Harrier, 109, 154, 157–8, 169, 344, 350, 353
Vulcan, 50, 73, 168, 209
Airport, 166, 181, 198, 209
Aermacchi MB-339, 47
Argentine fast jet operations, 54
continued Argentine operations, 155, 209, 302
Argentine defence, 22, 99, 105, 138, 164, 169, 171, 173, 176–7, 179–80, 185, 189, 204–205, 210
British advance, 100–1, 103–105, 109–10, 112–14, 117–19, 125, 145, 188
Harrier GR3 attacks, 175, 351
naval gunfire support, 326
vital ground, 13–14, 50, 78, 201, 203, 206
Stinger, missile, 143, 146
Strange, Joe, 7–8, 81, 287
see also Centre of Gravity
Super Etendard, Dassault, 45, 52, 73, 85, 87, 96, 119, 128, 194, 301, 327, 332, 334, 340, 350

1 May, 225
see also Exocet missile
4 May HMS *Sheffield*, 205, 228
23 May, 233
25 May MV *Atlantic Conveyor*, 235
30 May HMS *Invincible*, 116–17, 142, 186, 238, 309, 336
air combat training, 34
Argentine procurement, 39, 44
flying rate, 220–1, 245
intelligence demands, 71–2
training, 59
use of Stanley airport, 54
Superfledermaus radar, 162, 177
Supreme Allied Commander Europe, 24, 294
Sussex Bay, 232
Sussex Harbour, 232
Sussex Mountains, 26, 99, 115, 146, 202

T Battery (Shah Sujahs's Troop), 143, 145–6, 314
see also 12 Air Defence Regiment, Royal Artillery
Tandil, 44, 301, 306
Task Force 317, 57–8, 61, 67, 71
Task Force 317.1, 110
Teal Inlet, 105–106, 118, 145, 253
Tedder, Baron, 217
Templer, Field Marshal Sir Gerald, 29, 154
Tercera Escuadrilla Aeronaval de Caza y Ataque, 42
Thatcher, Margaret, 78
Foundation, 20
French support, 97
risk appetite, 10–11, 117
Sea Harrier, 126
Thomas, Lieutenant Commander Neill, 195, 247, 347, 350
Thomas, Lieutenant Steve, 227, 246, 248
Thomas, Squadron Leader Richard, 300
Thompson, Brigadier Julian, 21, 172
control of the air, 145
Goose Green, 101, 113
Operation Sutton, 26
Rapier, 143–4
Tigercat, missile, 177
Tornado GR1, Panavia, 15, 29, 36, 219, 292
Total Exclusion Zone, 26, 51, 83, 86, 103, 113, 191, 202–203, 304
Tracker, Grumman S-2E, 71, 86
Train, Admiral Harry, 24
Treacher, Vice Admiral John, 30
Trelew, 45, 341
Trial Athene, 106
Tromso, 294
Trowern, Wing Commander Fred, 175, 188
Tumbledown, 171, 173, 181, 257
Two Sisters, 256
Type 21 frigate, Amazon-class, 60, 103
30 May HMS *Invincible*, 117, 336
see also *Avenger*, HMS
submarine attack, 102
see also *Alacrity,* HMS
Type 22 frigate, 59, 61, 87, 142
Type 42 destroyer, 59, 66–7, 74, 87, 141, 190, 205, 343
4 May HMS *Sheffield*, 61
12 May HMS *Glasgow*, 62
25 May HMS *Coventry*, 3, 143
Argentine procurement, 59
capability, 59
replacements, 142
Type 82 destroyer, 62, 141
Type 95 radar, 67

Valente, Teniente Daniel, 339
Valiant, Vickers, 36
Van der Bijl, Nick, 22
Vaux, Lieutenant Colonel Nick, 22, 101, 120, 307

Vazquez, Alferez Alfredo, 249
VC10, Vickers, 155, 164
Velasco, Primer Teniente Mariano, 331, 334–5
Victor, Handley Page, 36
  tanker aircraft, 50, 106, 155–6, 186, 317, 325, 348
Victorious, HMS, 28
Volponi, Teniente Hector, 247–8, 332
Vulcan, Avro, 28, 204
  Argentine interest, 39
  Buenos Aires, 5, 46, 50, 53, 64, 214
  capability, 155–8, 180, 210
  command and control, 186
  controversy, 209, 219
  flying rate, 222–3
  history, 35–7
  mainland attack, 153
  nuclear role, 29
  Operation Black Buck, 50–1, 73, 152, 154–5, 250–1, 254, 255, 257, 317, 343, 353
  suppression of enemy air defences, 107, 170, 350
  weapon employment, 160–4, 166–8

Walters, General Vernon, 218
Ward, Lieutenant Commander Nigel 'Sharkey', 1, 19, 156, 248–9, 311, 314–15, 341, 344
  Blue Fox performance, 132–3
  CAP bombing, 169
  command and control, 176
  flying rate, 66
  Hercules engagement, 132, 313
  Mirage III withdrawal, 5
  Sea Harrier advocate, 89–90, 93, 99, 123, 126–7, 208
  squadron rivalry, 136, 157
  Vulcan utility, 158, 317
Warden, Colonel John, 7, 13, 76
Watson, Lieutenant Mike, 310, 327
WE177C, free-fall nuclear weapon, 36
Weddell Island, 252
Weinburger, Caspar, 127
Welsh Guards, First Battalion, 117–18, 206
Wessex, Westland, 11, 56, 92, 257
Whitehead, Lt Col Andrew, 100
Whitmore, Clive, 10, 287
Wilson, Brigadier Tony, 22
    see also 5 Infantry Brigade
Wireless Ridge, 171, 173, 257, 352
Woodward, Admiral Sir Sandy, 19, 182, 316, 343
  command and control, 176, 186, 201
  criticality of aircraft carriers, 7, 9–10
  Rapier, 143–4
  Sea Dart, 143
  Sidewinder, 5, 127, 135

Yarmouth, HMS, 58, 304
Yellow Sun, free-fall nuclear bomb, 36
    see also Vulcan, Avro

Zubizerratta, Capitan de Corbeta Carlos, 332